POLICING THE GLOBE

❏ ❏ ❏

POLICING THE GLOBE

Criminalization and Crime Control in International Relations

❏ ❏ ❏

Peter Andreas and Ethan Nadelmann

OXFORD
UNIVERSITY PRESS

2006

OXFORD
UNIVERSITY PRESS

Oxford University Press, Inc., publishes works that further
Oxford University's objective of excellence
in research, scholarship, and education.

Oxford New York
Auckland Cape Town Dar es Salaam Hong Kong Karachi
Kuala Lumpur Madrid Melbourne Mexico City Nairobi
New Delhi Shanghai Taipei Toronto

With offices in
Argentina Austria Brazil Chile Czech Republic France Greece
Guatemala Hungary Italy Japan Poland Portugal Singapore
South Korea Switzerland Thailand Turkey Ukraine Vietnam

Published by Oxford University Press, Inc.
198 Madison Avenue, New York, New York 10016

www.oup.com

Oxford is a registered trademark of Oxford University Press.

Library of Congress Cataloging-in-Publication Data
Andreas, Peter, 1965–
Policing the globe: criminalization and crime control in international relations/
by Peter Andreas and Ethan Nadelmann.
p. cm.

ISBN-13 978-0-19-508948-6

1. Transnational crime—Prevention—International cooperation.
2. Law enforcement—International cooperation. I. Title.
HV6252.A63 2006
363.25'935—dc22   2005029995

3 5 7 9 8 6 4 2

Printed in the United States of America
on acid-free paper

PREFACE

☐ ☐ ☐

"We are compelled by the globalization of crime to globalize law and law enforcement." So declared U.S. Senator John Kerry, who made cross-border crime and crime control one of his signature issues during the 1980s and 1990s. Transnational crime, he exclaimed, is "the new communism, the new monolithic threat," and the United States must "lead an international crusade" to defeat it. Senator Kerry's rhetorical excesses aside, his perspective and concerns are widely shared. More and more crime crosses borders in this era of globalization. Police, prosecutors, and other government agents have no choice but to respond in kind and work together more effectively. And the United States is compelled by the magnitude of the problem to play a global leadership role. Governments push for greater homogeneity in their criminal laws and sign on to bilateral and multilateral agreements and institutions to better collaborate against the spread of transnational crime. Justice ministers and attorneys general are increasingly preoccupied with international matters, as foreign ministers and diplomats are with criminal matters. All this represents a relatively new and important development in both international relations and criminal justice.

This account is very much consistent with what one reads in newspapers, government reports, and scholarly journals and books—and, indeed, in parts of this book. But this standard view, with its portrayal of the growth of international crime control as simply a natural and predictable response to the explosive growth of transnational crime, explains too little and obscures too much. In particular, it lacks a much-needed historical perspective and diminishes the role of politics in determining the very substance of this policy domain. We refer here not only to the domestic politics that compel politicians to blame foreigners for domestic crime problems like illegal drugs, or even to the arm-twisting politics employed to prod foreign governments to cooperate in suppressing crime, but also, more fundamentally, to the politics of defining crime. Thus, while partially agreeing with the conventional wisdom about the internationalization of crime control, we also have two other stories to tell.

The first is historical. It is impossible to explain the origins of any state's criminal laws and policing practices without reference to the influences of other states and transnational forces. States have always relied on criminal laws and law enforcement agents to control interactions between their domestic realms and foreign territories. States have never been immune from the consequences of other states' criminal justice laws and criminal justice actions. And states have never been able to enforce their own criminal laws without devoting at least modest attention to the extraterritorial sources and causes of some domestic criminality. We emphasize the historical perspective for many reasons: because it is so conspicuously absent from contemporary debates about transnational crime and crime control; because it corrects for the hubris of the present and the common tendency to view recent developments as new and unprecedented; because it helps us understand why we are where we are and even where we might be headed; and because it makes clear the extent to which the internationalization of criminal law enforcement is far more than merely a response to the internationalization of crime. Today's wars on drugs and terror are part and parcel of historical processes that date back at least to the nineteenth century, when Britain employed substantial naval and diplomatic resources to suppress the slave trade, European police and intelligence agencies collaborated to keep track of political offenders, and U.S. military, customs, and police agents focused on stemming border smuggling and banditry. Although the depth and extent of contemporary efforts would have been unimaginable to law enforcers a century and more ago, the challenges would not.

This brings us to our other story. Crimes are defined, indeed created, by law. States vary over time, and from one another, in what they choose to criminalize and decriminalize. The trend appears to be toward greater homogenization in defining crime, yet political and religious revolutions as well as evolving moral and security concerns ensure continued heterogeneity among nations. So, too, the impulse to criminalize is rarely sated, particularly in the United States, which has not shied from imposing its own criminal norms on others. The United States is primarily responsible for the pervasive reliance on criminal laws to suppress the production and sale of psychoactive plants and chemicals, and it has led the way in extending criminal sanctions to financial and other activities that are derivative of traditional crimes. Many of the most prominent international crime control efforts today focus on activities that did not exist or were not regarded as criminal in centuries or even decades past. And past international law enforcement efforts were often preoccupied with activities that are no longer prioritized or even criminalized. U.S. law enforcers, for example, once focused on prohibiting the importation of alcohol and on collecting duties on imports of opium and its derivatives; these efforts are now reversed. Prohibitions against money laundering and trafficking in endangered species were nonexistent just a few decades ago.

As we show, the internationalization of crime control is primarily the outcome of ambitious efforts by generations of Western powers to export their domestically derived definitions of crime. Not only political and economic interests but also moralizing impulses have determined these definitions and driven many of the most prominent international policing initiatives. Global prohibitions and international crime control priorities and practices would not be what they are today if different states with different values had dominated international society during the past two centuries. Imagine, for instance, what the world of transnational crime and international crime control would look like if psychoactive substances such as opium and cocaine had not been criminalized early in the twentieth century: a substantial portion of transnational crime would simply be defined away, and much of the infrastructure for international crime control today would likely be absent, given the pivotal historical role of drug control in stimulating international policing agreements, contacts, and capacities. Today's global counterterrorism campaign, we stress, very much builds on and extends policing capacities and initiatives originally developed to suppress drug trafficking and related money laundering.

In the pages that follow, we evaluate the internationalization of crime control from three different vantage points. The first is a global perspective, highlighting the emergence and proliferation of prohibition norms in international society. The second is a more regional perspective, examining the evolution of cross-border crime control in Western Europe, where international policing relations are far more regularized and institutionalized than they are elsewhere. The third is from the perspective of a hegemonic leader—the United States—and its rise to the status of the world's most ambitious and aggressive policing power. Each perspective is treated separately in chapters 1, 2, and 3, and these perspectives then become intertwined in chapters 4, 5, and 6. We believe that these three perspectives capture much of what has been important in the evolution of international criminal law enforcement.

The questions and issues we address in this book are located at the remarkably understudied intersection of two disciplines, international relations and criminology, that traditionally have been strangers but that should be no more. Students of international criminal law will find familiar subjects reinterpreted from the perspectives of political science and criminal justice. Students of criminology and criminal justice may welcome our analysis of the impact of criminalization and decriminalization on crime and crime control. And we hope that students of international relations will derive insights from our examination of this particular realm of transnational and transgovernmental relations, globalization, and international norms and regimes. Given the complexity and diversity of criminalization and crime control in international relations across time, place, and issue area, our account is at once a liberal story about the expansion of international cooperation and institutions built on mutual interest in a context of growing interdependence and transnational flows, a realist story about coercive co-optation and hegemonic leadership, and a constructivist story about transnational moral entrepreneurs and the creation and spread of global norms.

This book is not, of course, comprehensive. Our focus on Western Europe and the United States makes sense given their leading and dominant roles in the internationalization of criminal law enforcement, but much more could certainly be said about Asia, the former Soviet bloc, and other parts of the world. We privilege the international activities of the police more than those of other agents of the state's criminal justice apparatus (such as cross-border judicial cooperation). We say relatively little about the respective roles of intelligence and private investigative agencies and their complex relationships with law enforcement agencies. We say nothing about the International Criminal Court and the prosecution of war crimes, genocide, and other "crimes against humanity" that generally involve enforcement of international, not national, laws (and typically target state rather than nonstate actors). And we offer little in the way of policy prescriptions or recommendations, although readers will certainly be inspired to develop their own.

We joined forces to write this book out of deep concern about the narrowness of the debate on transnational crime and crime control and to help bring policing more centrally into the study of international relations. In researching this book we drew from thousands of historical and contemporary sources and benefited from interviews and discussions with hundreds of law enforcement officials in North America and Europe, including representatives of all the major U.S. federal law enforcement agencies. This book builds on Andreas's earlier work on border controls and transnational crime and Nadelmann's earlier work on global prohibition regimes and the international dimensions of U.S. criminal law enforcement. Chapter 1 substantially expands and updates an article by Nadelmann published in *International Organization* (1990), and chapter 3 draws heavily from his book, *Cops across Borders: The Internationalization of U.S. Criminal Law Enforcement* (1993). Small portions of chapters 4 and 5 draw from articles by Andreas published in *International Studies Review* (2001, with Richard Price) and in *International Security* (2003).

This project has been a collaborative effort far beyond the two of us writing a book together. Many individuals provided much-appreciated feedback and advice at various stages of the process. We are most thankful to those who read all or portions of earlier drafts of the manuscript: Malcolm Anderson, David Bayley, Dave Bewley-Taylor, Tom Biersteker, Corey Brettschneider, Mathieu Deflem, Jorge Domínguez, Cyrille Fijnaut, Cornelius Friesendorf, Aida Hozic, Peter Katzenstein, Gary Marx, Jim Morone, Tom Naylor, Nikos Passas, John Picarelli, Darius Rejali, Peter Romaniuk, Jim Ron, Cathy Schneider, and John Walsh. Peter Katzenstein played a particularly instrumental role as intellectual matchmaker, helping to bring us together and encourage our collaboration. Our editor, Dedi Felman, embraced the project early on, urged us to write for a broad audience, and provided guidance at key stages of the process. We also thank the many U.S. and European law enforcement officials who generously took time from their busy schedules to talk to us over the years about the nature and challenges of international crime control. Edward Ahn, Cornelius Friesendorf, Matthew Lieber, and Peter Romaniuk contributed valuable research and editorial assistance. Brown University generously granted a sabbatical leave to Peter Andreas, and the Department of Political Science and the Watson Institute for International Studies provided funding for research and related travel.

Peter Andreas dedicates the book to the memory of his mother, Carol Andreas (1933–2004), and Ethan Nadelmann dedicates the book to the memory of his former teacher, Maurizio Vannicelli (1952–1992).

P.A. and E.N.
Providence and New York

CONTENTS

❏ ❏ ❏

Contents

POLICING THE GLOBE

❑ ❑ ❑

INTRODUCTION

□ □ □

The Internationalization of Crime Control

There is a memorable scene from the film *Bonnie and Clyde*, set in the 1920s, in which the two fugitives outrun the Oklahoma State Police across the Texas state line, waving good-bye to their frustrated pursuers. This scene, epitomizing the severe limits of municipal policing in the United States prior to the emergence of interstate law enforcement, also very much reflects the basic challenge facing international crime control efforts.[1] In this book, we tell the story of both growing cooperation and enduring conflict in the development of an ever tighter and wider net of criminal justice controls designed by states to detect, deter, and interdict criminalized transnational actors and activities.[2] Policing transnational crime has evolved from a limited and ad hoc assortment of police actions and extradition agreements to a highly intensive and regularized collection of law enforcement mechanisms and institutions.[3]

Criminologists and criminal justice scholars ask how and why states criminalize particular acts and how and why criminal laws are enforced. We extend these inquiries to the realm of international relations. Our story focuses on the United States and Western Europe given their dominant role in the internationalization of crime control. The growth of international crime control is evident in the proliferation of new criminal laws and an aggressive push for cross-national homogenization of such laws; expansion of agency budgets, responsibilities, and enforcement powers; efforts by more proactive states to extend their claims to extraterritorial jurisdiction;[4] deployment of more sophisticated global surveillance and

3

tracking technologies; heightened police cooperation and communication through an increasingly dense set of transgovernmental networks and international institutions at the regional and global levels; and more extensive use of military and intelligence hardware and personnel for law enforcement tasks. The importance of international crime control is also evident in the rising status of policing issues in diplomacy and security discourse. Concerns over transnational law evasions rather than interstate military invasions increasingly drive the security priorities of many states.[5] These shifts predate the terrorist attacks on the World Trade Center and the Pentagon on September 11, 2001, but have been powerfully reinforced and accelerated in their aftermath. The "war on terror," like the "war on drugs," primarily involves policing, not conventional soldiering.

The History and Study of International Crime Control

There has always been an international dimension to crime control and a crime control dimension to international relations. What has changed is the intensity, frequency, and variety of both these dimensions. Unilateral and bilateral efforts against sea piracy, border banditry, and smuggling date back thousands of years. So, too, do governmental efforts to recover and punish fugitives, particularly political offenders, who flee abroad.[6] During the nineteenth century, European police agents, notably those of the tsars and the Habsburg monarchs, kept close tabs on dissidents and other potential threats to their regimes outside their borders. Throughout the same century, Great Britain devoted substantial energies to criminalizing, curtailing, and punishing the transnational commerce in African slaves. These efforts were succeeded by a crusade of sorts directed at the suppression of the "white slave trade." Late in the nineteenth century and during the first decade of the twentieth, terrorist bombings and assassinations of prominent politicians by transnational anarchist groups prompted the first sustained efforts by governments and their police agencies to better coordinate their efforts. Before and after World War I, rising concern over counterfeiting of national currencies provided an impetus for the creation of the International Police Organization (Interpol). During roughly the same period, growing international concern over the opium problem in

4

China and drug consumption in the Philippines, as well as the use and abuse of opiates and cocaine in Europe and North America, prompted the first stirrings of international action to criminalize and control psychoactive drugs.

The modern era of international crime control can be dated to the vigorous law enforcement campaign launched against domestic and international drug trafficking by the United States in the late 1960s and early 1970s. The evolution of international crime control in subsequent decades was powerfully shaped by the drug enforcement efforts of the U.S. government and the internationalization of its general fixation on drug trafficking. There were other significant developments as well during this time. In Western Europe, concerns over terrorist groups beginning in the late 1960s stimulated major efforts to better coordinate law enforcement activities on the continent. So, too, the deepening of European integration has included a proliferation of multilateral European law enforcement treaties and other arrangements as well as increasingly close bilateral cooperation among European law enforcement agencies.

Governments have devoted growing attention to a wide variety of other transnational activities in recent decades, such as the clandestine trade in sophisticated weaponry and technology, endangered species, pornographic materials, counterfeit products, guns, ivory, toxic waste, money, people, stolen property, and art and antiquities. States with strict financial secrecy laws have come under increasing international pressure to relax those laws and cooperate in foreign investigations of drug trafficking, money laundering, terrorist financing, and other criminal activities. And now counterterrorism has reemerged as the principal impetus for breaking new ground in international crime control, driven in part by fears of "catastrophic criminality" involving criminal use of weapons of mass destruction. Although the post–September 11 convergence of law enforcement and security through counterterrorism is in many ways unprecedented, it very much builds on and expands an international crime control infrastructure already in place and also reflects a partial return to the nineteenth-century continental European model of political policing in which a greater share of the state's criminal law enforcement work was devoted to national security concerns. Now, however, international crime control efforts are far more intensive and geographically expansive.

Given the growing importance of the international component of policing and the policing component of international relations, it is perhaps surprising that scholars in all disciplines have been so neglectful of the issues that lie at the intersection of international relations and criminal justice. One can read hundreds of books and articles on criminology and criminal law (including a burgeoning comparative literature)[7] without stumbling across much discussion of international relations and foreign policy.[8] Criminologists and criminal justice experts remain overwhelmingly preoccupied with domestic crime and crime control, notwithstanding efforts by a relatively small band of (mostly European) scholars to provoke greater attention to policing across national borders.[9] Similarly, one can read a like number of publications by scholars who study international relations and foreign policy and find scant reference to police and crime.[10] Interest in cross-border policing has grown in recent years (especially after the shock of September 11 and its aftermath),[11] but far too little attention has been devoted to examining the international dynamics of criminalization and crime control across time, place, and issue area.

Even the upsurge in attention to global governance, transgovernmental networks,[12] and law in world politics has yet to invite substantial attention to processes of criminalization and criminal law enforcement. When international relations scholars speak of the heightened importance of law, they still mostly mean legal advisors, trade negotiators, and the International Criminal Court, not cops, customs agents, and prosecutors.[13] Equally curious is that the sizable literatures on globalization and transnational relations largely overlook the criminalized side of the transnational world and state efforts to police it.[14] Much is written about the shrinking of the regulatory state through market liberalization and deregulation, but much less noticed and studied is reregulation and state expansion through criminalization and crime control. Consider the realm of global finance, where financial deregulation has been paralleled by reregulation via efforts to curtail money laundering and terrorist financing.[15] Similarly, the loosening of state controls through trade liberalization has been accompanied by efforts to tighten controls on illegal trade. In short, even as economic barriers have fallen, police barriers have risen, and increasingly extend outward through regional and global law enforcement initiatives. The policing function of the state, we argue, is ever more integral to the study of international relations.

Narratives of International Crime Control

What is driving the growth of international criminal law enforcement? The most common answer is seductively simple: it is a response to the growth of transnational crime in an era of globalization. This explanation tends to be uncritically embraced, and indeed has long been the mantra of law enforcement practitioners across the globe. It is the master narrative in official policy debates, providing a powerful political rallying cry for greater international police cooperation. The story line has commonsensical appeal. After all, modern police forces developed with urbanization, national police bureaucracies developed with nationalization, and thus one might understandably expect that more internationalized policing would emerge with globalization. As crime problems become more global, so the logic of this functionalist narrative goes, so do the responses to these problems. As we show in this book, this conventional account captures an important aspect of the expansion of international crime control but also misses much. It is at best incomplete and at worst misleading.

In the chapters that follow, we develop a more nuanced and historically grounded narrative that places greater emphasis on political forces that have evolved and changed over time.[16] International relations scholars typically ask what theoretical perspective—such as liberalism, realism, or constructivism—best explains a particular phenomenon. The answer in our case is that only an analytically eclectic approach, selectively combining elements of different perspectives, can effectively make sense of the internationalization of crime control.[17] Thus, we tell a liberal story emphasizing the growth of international police cooperation propelled by mutual interests between increasingly interdependent states in a context of more intensive and expansive transnational interactions; we tell a realist story stressing the enduring importance of power, conflict, and the priorities and influences of dominant states in shaping the agenda, reach, and intensity of international crime control; and we tell a constructivist story highlighting how and why certain cross-border activities once considered "normal" are redefined and condemned as "deviant"—often through the proselytizing activities of transnational moral entrepreneurs—and become the subject of prohibition norms possessed of powerful symbolic appeal regardless of their effectiveness. Weaving together these story lines gives us greater analytical leverage in understanding the interaction among power, interests, and norms.[18] Our account would be deficient if we relied on only one story line, as each captures an essential aspect of the internationalization of crime control.

The liberal tradition in international relations inevitably emphasizes the mutual interests that motivate states to cooperate and the international institutions that facilitate such cooperation, especially in a world of growing interdependence and ever more intensive and expansive transnational flows. It also unpacks the notion of the state as a unitary actor, emphasizing instead domestic politics,[19] bureaucratic competition,[20] transgovernmental relationships, and the interaction between competing and contradictory policy objectives.[21]

Viewed from a traditional liberal perspective, the evolution of international crime control in recent decades looks a lot like the evolution in law enforcement cooperation among state and local law enforcement in the United States between roughly 1890 and 1970. Indeed, many of the challenges and advances of international criminal law enforcement can be accurately described by copying verbatim the proceedings of police conferences in the United States during those years, excising references to the federal government and simply substituting the word "international" for "interstate" in the remaining text. Just as uniform acts and interstate compacts have homogenized state laws and procedures in the United States, so model laws, international conventions, and multilateral law enforcement treaties have contributed to the homogenization of criminal laws and procedures among nations. Just as state and municipal police agencies have sent their agents to other jurisdictions to cooperate on investigations, so federal (and occasionally state and municipal) police agencies have sent their agents abroad to perform investigative tasks and collaborate with foreign police agencies. Just as municipal and state police agencies have developed more efficient means of communicating and sharing information both on their own and with the assistance of federal agencies, so Interpol has provided an increasingly efficient means of communicating across national borders and centralizing intelligence gathered around the world.[22]

The rising tide of international collaboration on crime control has involved both the *homogenization* of criminal justice systems (and particularly criminal laws) toward a common norm and the *regularization* of criminal justice relationships across borders. Criminal laws around the world are far more homogeneous today than ever before. Some, especially those that prohibit undesirable transnational activities, are even institutionalized in global prohibition regimes (the focus of chapter 1). But common laws are not enough. International crime control is mostly the work of police and prosecutors, not diplomats, yet they retain no power to interrogate or arrest anyone beyond their nation's borders. Nor do they tend to be well versed in either diplomatic niceties or the intricacies of foreign laws and cultures. The remedy involves regularizing relations, both formally, through extradition and other law enforcement agreements, and informally, through the personal and professional relationships developed in international training programs, bilateral working groups, joint investigations, liaison postings abroad, and Interpol and other international meetings. As a consequence, a transnational criminal law enforcement community[23] based on expanding cross-border governmental networks[24] with shared technical and investigative expertise has become an increasingly important—though often overlooked and poorly understood—dimension of global governance and transgovernmental relations.

Attempts to overcome frictions and facilitate greater cooperation in international crime control increasingly involve not only bilateral but also multilateral arrangements at the regional and even global level. These enhance efficiency insofar as they negate the need to negotiate individual bilateral arrangements with large numbers of foreign governments. All multilateral policing arrangements—whether regional police conferences, international organizations such as Interpol and the World Customs Organization, extradition and legal assistance treaties, or treaties directed at suppressing particular types of transnational activity—are created to reduce, transcend, or circumvent the basic obstacles presented by conflicting sovereignties, political tensions, and differences among law enforcement systems. They seek consensus on the substance of each nation's criminal laws, promote greater predictability and communication, create commitments to cooperate, and establish guidelines and frameworks to regularize and facilitate international police and prosecutorial cooperation.

All of what we've said in the preceding paragraphs conforms to a liberal perspective on international relations. But on its own it masks the enduring importance of power and conflict.[25] We need a strong dose of realism in our story to remind us that international crime control efforts ultimately reflect the interests and agendas of those states best able to coerce and coopt others.[26] Throughout history, imperial and colonial states have introduced, often by imposition, their own criminal justice norms to whatever peoples fell under their rule.[27] This was true of the European colonial empires that dominated much of the globe from the eighteenth century to the twentieth, just as it was true of the Ottoman Empire before and the Soviet Empire thereafter. And, to the extent that the United States today behaves as an imperial power, albeit with the objective of territorial access rather than direct territorial rule,[28] it very much follows the historical pattern of exporting criminal justice norms, law enforcement priorities, and policing practices. Indeed, international crime control is one of the most important—and one of the most overlooked—dimensions of U.S. hegemony in world politics. This hegemony is exercised through a mixture of "hard" and "soft" power,[29] utilizing the full range of unilateral, bilateral, and multilateral law enforcement mechanisms and transgovernmental networks.[30] Globalization and Americanization increasingly mean the same thing in this domain.

Less powerful and especially less developed countries have typically played a more secondary and reactive role in the internationalization of crime control: they host the police attachés of Europe and the United States, harmonize their criminal laws and procedures to foreign tunes, and ratify international conventions drafted at the initiative of others. Consider, for instance, the profound impact of U.S.-promoted antidrug efforts on many Latin American and Caribbean countries.[31] And contrast this to the largely futile calls from Mexico and other countries for the United States to tighten its gun control laws and curb the illegal outflow of arms to criminal groups throughout the region.[32] This is not to suggest that developing countries do not have their own cross-border law enforcement interests and relationships[33] and sometimes latch on to international policing efforts to further their own domestic agendas, but rather that the models, methods, and priorities of international crime control are substantially determined and exported by the most powerful states in the international system.[34]

A realist perspective also helps to explain why, in the absence of a central global law enforcement authority, law enforcement conflicts between states persist unabated, notwithstanding the rising tide of international collaboration. Because they involve the most sovereign of a state's tasks, policing practices are more constrained than most other dimensions of a state's international relations by the sovereign concerns of other states.

Frictions and tensions endure partly because the universe of international crime control is ever changing and expanding, principally at the initiative of the United States and other assertive powers but also as a consequence of legal and technological developments affecting transnational crime. Priorities shift, demands change, capabilities improve, and expectations grow. To take just one example, U.S. pressures on offshore financial havens and other jurisdictions to cooperate in drug trafficking investigations during the 1980s and 1990s induced governments to carve out exceptions to their strict financial secrecy laws. Now those exceptions are becoming the rule as the U.S. government demands assistance in all sorts of criminal investigations that have nothing to do with drugs. The option of taking unilateral punitive action is never entirely off the table.

The realist emphasis on the state as the most important actor in the international system also provides a necessary reminder that states monopolize the power to criminalize—and that criminalization is a prerequisite for all international crime control endeavors. Laws, simply stated, precede and define criminality.[35] Through their lawmaking and law-enforcing authority, states set the rules of the game even if they cannot entirely control the play and the outcome. States monopolize the power to determine who and what has legitimate territorial access and define the terms of such access.[36] For example, changes in tax, tariff, and duty laws and in the intensity with which those laws are enforced have profound effects, for better and worse, on the incidence and profitability of smuggling ventures.[37] Of particular importance, criminalization can be self-reinforcing, as the difficulty of enforcing new laws prompts calls for tougher laws and more vigorous law enforcement efforts.

The variability of criminalization across states provides an invitation for transnational opportunists to make the most of the legal asymmetry.[38] The same is also true where states agree on the criminality of an activity but apply disparate sanctions and allocations of criminal justice resources. But those same asymmetries also provide the incentive for more powerful states to insist on greater symmetry. The internationalization of crime control, particularly the homogenization of criminal norms throughout international society, can thus be understood in part as a historical process driven primarily by the criminalizations of dominant states (notably, those of Europe and the United States) and their efforts to export their own criminal justice preferences to other states.

The centrality of the state, rather than crime, in determining international crime control is, at the most basic level, evident in the making and unmaking of national borders. Creations and dissolutions of borders have transformed crime and crime control throughout modern history. The splintering of the Austro-Hungarian Empire during World War I, for example, internationalized what had previously been intra-imperial criminal and law enforcement activities; indeed, the need for law enforcement officials in the newly independent states to collaborate and to ensure continued access to the extensive police files collected in Vienna before the war played no small role in the creation of Interpol in 1923.[39] Similarly, the dissolution of the Ottoman Empire during roughly the same period, and of the British, French, and other Western European empires following World War II, transformed what had been intra-imperial and intercolonial police activities into international interactions. Much the same happened with the splintering of the Soviet Union and of Yugoslavia in the early 1990s. Border shifts can also turn transnational crime into domestic crime: consider the respective consolidations of Italy, Germany, and the United States during the nineteenth century and the absorption of the Baltic states by the Soviet Union during the early 1940s. Each transformed what had been transnational criminal activity and law enforcement relationships among sovereign states into domestic criminality and criminal justice activities. To the extent that nonstate activities predating the imposition of borders continue, they are often subjected to new controls and redefined as criminal. Previous trading relations and population flows may be recategorized as smuggling and illegal migration. Enduring examples are the ancient trade routes and migrations throughout much of Asia and Africa that persist despite the imposition of borders, first by European colonialists and later by the states left in their wake. Finally, the imposition of borders can stimulate transnational crime that previously had not existed in the region as either criminal or legitimate activity. The impetus has often come from the inducements to smuggling that are generated by tariffs, duties, and differences in criminal laws and enforcement on either side of the border.

Ultimately, however, the combined insights of liberalism and realism fail to fully account for why some activities but not others become the subject of international crime control efforts in the first place. They provide an inadequate understanding and appreciation of the normative context and symbolic dimension of policing practices. Adding social constructivist insights to our story reveals that there is nothing natural, permanent, or inevitable about what states choose to criminalize or decriminalize.[40] It provides an important corrective to the common tendency to bracket and take for granted the prior process of delegitimizing and criminalizing particular transnational activities and to view state policing behavior as determined exclusively by narrow economic and political interests. As we emphasize in chapter 1, the internationalization of crime control has historically been driven not just by the political and economic interests of the most powerful states in international society but also by moral and emotional factors involving religious beliefs, humanitarian sentiments, faith in universalism, paternalism, fear, prejudice, and the compulsion to proselytize.[41] E. H. Carr long ago recognized that realism was deficient in failing to take into account the role of emotional appeal and moral judgment in world politics. "Political action," he observed, "must be based on a co-ordination of morality and power."[42] As discussed in chapter 1, transnational moral entrepreneurs have often played an influential role, such that many international crime control campaigns, including the nineteenth-century campaign against the slave trade, the twentieth-century campaign against drug trafficking, and the past and present campaigns against the trafficking of women, cannot be explained without considering their moralizing impulses and motivations.

From this perspective, states internationalize policing efforts not only to better control transnational interactions but also to promote their own ethical and social norms. Similarly, international institutions and transgovernmental networks not only serve to solve collective action problems and enhance efficiency by facilitating information sharing and other forms of law enforcement cooperation but also play an important socializing, legitimizing, and norm-promoting role. Indeed, some of the most prominent international policing campaigns continue to grow, notwithstanding persistent failure and even counterproductive consequences, in part because they prop up prohibition norms and reaffirm collective moral condemnation of the activities targeted by the campaigns.[43]

The Plan of the Book

In chapter 1, we examine how and why certain prohibited cross-border activities became criminalized around the world, not just in the municipal laws of states but in international conventions signed by virtually all states. This homogenization process has included the creation of global prohibition regimes targeting piracy, slavery and the slave trade, the production and sale of cannabis, cocaine, heroin, and other psychoactive substances, and the killing of endangered species. Not just states but individuals and nongovernmental organizations, including some that can best be described as "transnational moral entrepreneurs," can and do play important roles in stimulating and shaping such regimes.

In chapters 2 and 3 we examine the historical roots and evolution of international crime control from the perspective of the regularization of police relations across borders. Given the European origins of the modern state and interstate system, our story necessarily begins there. "Political policing" motivated many of the most important early cross-border law enforcement collaborations in Europe, but it was not until international policing was sufficiently depoliticized and came to target more "common" crimes that such collaborations could become much more institutionalized. After exploring the European origins of cross-border policing, we examine the belated emergence of the United States in the forefront of international crime control in the twentieth century. No other government has pursued its international criminal law enforcement agenda more aggressively. No other government has dealt with the frictions between its own criminal justice norms and those of other states principally by inducing other states to change their norms and accommodate their systems to its own requirements. No other government has stationed so many police agents abroad, signed so many bilateral law enforcement treaties, trained so many police and regulators in other countries, and given such high priority to policing issues in its foreign policy. The U.S. commitment to and aggressiveness in international policing initiatives has profoundly shaped criminal law enforcement institutions and policies across the world.

In chapters 4 and 5 we evaluate the contemporary period, focusing on the sharp acceleration and intensification of U.S.- and European-promoted international policing efforts in the post–cold war and post–September 11 eras. For the United States, this has included a militarization of policing, a hardening and outward extension of increasingly high-tech border controls, and a selective outsourcing of policing tasks to other countries and private actors. For the European Union, this has included building an increasingly institutionalized system for policing a shared EU border-free

14

space with a fortified outer perimeter that co-opts immediate neighbors as law enforcement buffer zones. On both sides of the Atlantic, more intensive and expansive policing of criminalized transnational activities has continued to blur traditional distinctions between internal and external security and brought law enforcement and national security missions and institutions closer together. Thus, there has been a pattern of transatlantic convergence amid enduring political tension and regional variation.

We conclude the book by integrating the story lines in our account of the origins and transformation of international crime control. We speculate what past and present developments may tell us about the future, examine what all this means for assessing popular arguments regarding the growing transnational crime challenge to state power in an age of globalization, and underscore some of the most important lessons and implications.

CHAPTER ONE

□ □ □

Criminalization through Global Prohibitions

Most accounts of transnational crime and international crime control simply take for granted the prior process of criminalization, leaving unexplained how certain transnational activities came to be prohibited and targeted by international crime control efforts in the first place. Thus, this is where our story begins. In this chapter, we examine how and why prohibition norms and the criminalization of particular cross-border activities have become internationalized in the form of global prohibition regimes.[1] Transnational activities such as piracy, slavery, trafficking in slaves as well as in women and children for prostitution, and trafficking in controlled psychoactive substances are all prohibited by powerful global norms. Other acts, including the killing of endangered species, the laundering of dirty money, and the financing of terrorism are becoming the subject of increasingly powerful norms.[2] These norms strictly circumscribe the conditions under which states can participate in and authorize these activities. Those who refuse or fail to conform are labeled as deviants and condemned. The substance of these norms and the processes by which they are enforced are institutionalized in global prohibition regimes.

The Nature and Evolution of Global Prohibition Regimes

International regimes tend to reflect the economic and political interests of dominant members of international society. At the same time, how-

ever, moral and emotional factors—religious beliefs, humanitarian sentiments, faith in universalism, compassion, conscience, paternalism, fear,
prejudice, and the compulsion to proselytize—play important roles in the
creation and evolution of international regimes. This role is particularly
pronounced in global prohibition regimes (especially those that involve
not just interstate relations but intersocietal interactions). The actions of
states must be understood as the culmination of both external pressures and
domestic political struggles in which national and transnational organizations and movements shape the actions and opinions of diverse societies.
Indeed, many of the norms of dominant societies, notably those of Europe
and the United States, are not just internationalized but also internalized
to varying degrees by diverse societies across the world.

International prohibition regimes resort to force in the form of criminal justice (and, in some cases, military) measures in part because the violators—whether pirates, slave traders, or elephant poachers—are themselves
armed and reliant on violence to perform their illicit deeds; in part because
efforts to prohibit anything that many people desire are bound to require
some degree of coercion; and in part because criminal justice measures are
the principal, and typically most punitive, means of dealing with those
who defy the norms of developed societies.

The criminal laws that evolve into international prohibition regimes
are few in number; those that attain truly global dimensions are even fewer.
Although human sacrifice and cannibalism are not just illegal but virtually
unknown in every nation today, neither is the subject of an international
prohibition regime. Rape and incest, both of which are criminalized in all
states, are not the targets of international prohibition regimes. The same
is true of murder and theft, except when committed under certain conditions. Only those crimes that evidence a strong transnational dimension
are likely to become the subject of international prohibition regimes: larceny on the high seas, cross-border commerce in slaves, counterfeit money
and psychoactive substances, and so forth.

A central inducement to the creation of international prohibition regimes is the inadequacy of unilateral and bilateral law enforcement measures in the face of criminalized activities that transcend national borders.
No government possesses sufficient resources to police effectively all of the
high seas or to investigate and punish the array of illicit activities committed abroad that harm its interests or citizens. Furthermore, no government

is willing, except on rare occasions, to unilaterally pursue a criminal when doing so involves a blatant affront to another state's sovereignty. International prohibition regimes are intended to minimize and even eliminate the potential havens from which certain crimes can be committed and to which criminals can flee to escape prosecution and punishment. They provide an element of standardization to cooperation among governments with few other law enforcement concerns in common. And they create an expectation of cooperation that governments challenge only at the cost of some international embarrassment.

The existence of international prohibition regimes directed at the suppression of a number of these activities also owes much to the proselytizing efforts of governments and nongovernmental transnational organizations, what might be called "transnational moral entrepreneurs."[3] Often organized and linked through transnational advocacy networks,[4] they mobilize popular opinion and political support both within their host country and abroad, they stimulate and assist in the creation of like-minded organizations in other countries, and they play a significant role in elevating their objective beyond its identification with the national interests of their government; indeed, their transnational efforts are often directed toward persuading foreign audiences (especially foreign elites) that a particular prohibition regime reflects not merely the peculiar moral code of one society but a more widely shared, even universal, moral sense. Although the activities that they condemn do not always transcend national borders, those that do provide the proselytizers with the transnational hook typically required to provoke and justify international intervention in the internal affairs of other states.

Why do certain prohibition regimes attain global proportions? Certainly not all of them are destined, or even intended, to do so. Some reflect little more than the peculiar collective security concerns of a multinational region or an alliance of states confronting a common transnational challenge. Other regimes are concerned not with particular criminal activities but with the mechanisms of international cooperation against crime: extradition, mutual legal assistance, transfer of prisoners, and so on. Such "procedural" regimes (which are not the focus of this chapter but are discussed in later chapters) often prove essential to the effective functioning of the "substantive" prohibition regimes as well as to international cooperation against crimes—such as murder, rape, and assault as well as white-collar crimes such as tax fraud and insider trading—that are not the subject of international regimes. These procedural regimes are limited in scope, however, by the fact that consensus on procedure in criminal justice matters often proves more elusive than consensus on substance. Sufficient differences over the nature and process of the extradition obligation make the construction of a formal global extradition regime a formidable challenge. Nonetheless, all states today acknowledge the norm of extradition as well as the principles that underlie it.[5]

Underlying the emergence of most global prohibition regimes, as well as the emergence of much international cooperation in criminal matters, has been the evolution of what some scholars have termed "a universal international society" grounded in the gradual homogenization and globalization of norms developed initially among the European states.[6] In the evolution of global society, the centrality of Western Europe initially and of the United States during the past century cannot be overemphasized. Virtually all of the norms that are now identified as essential ingredients of international law and global society have their roots in the jurisprudence of European scholars of international law and in the notions and patterns of acceptable behavior established by the more powerful Western European states. This relationship is particularly true of many of the norms reflected in global prohibition regimes. Their emergence in Europe reflected the needs and impositions of the most powerful states as well as the influence of the Enlightenment and contemporaneous religious and moral beliefs. The globalization of these norms, manifested by the emergence of global prohibition regimes, reflected the dominance of Europe over much of the world from approximately the seventeenth century to recent decades. To an extent virtually unprecedented in world history, a few European states and the United States proved successful in proselytizing to diverse societies around the world, in shaping the moral views of substantial sectors of elite opinion outside their borders, and in imposing their norms on foreign governments.

Most global prohibition regimes, including those directed at the suppression of piracy, slavery, and drug trafficking, evidence a common evolutionary pattern, one roughly divisible into four, and in some cases five, stages. During the first stage, most societies regard the activity to be proscribed as entirely legitimate under certain conditions and with respect to certain groups of people; states often are the principal protagonists and abettors of the activity; and the central constraints on involvement in the activity have far more to do with political prudence and bilateral treaties than with moral notions or evolving international norms. The second stage involves the redefinition of the activity as a problem and as an evil—often by international legal scholars or religious groups and other moral entrepreneurs—and the gradual delegitimation of explicit government involvement in the activity, even as many individual governments continue to tolerate and even sponsor the involvement of private groups and individuals in the activity. During the third stage, regime proponents begin to agitate actively for the suppression and criminalization of the activity by all states and the formation of international conventions. The regime proponents include both governments, typically those able to exert hegemonic influence in a particular issue area, as well as transnational moral entrepreneurs. Their agitation takes many forms, ranging from diplomatic pressures and economic inducements to military interventions and propaganda campaigns.

If the efforts of the regime's proponents prove successful, a fourth stage is attained in which the activity becomes the subject of criminal laws and police action throughout much of the world, and in which international institutions and conventions emerge to play a coordinating role. It is only at this point that one can speak of a global prohibition regime having fully come into existence. During this stage, social pressures on all states to acknowledge and enforce the norm are quite powerful. Nonetheless, regime proponents must contend with a variety of challenges: dissident or deviant states that refuse to conform to the regime's mandate, states that accede to the regime formally but that are unable or unwilling to crack down on violators within their territory, and dissident or deviant individuals and criminal organizations that elude regime enforcers and continue to engage in the forbidden activity.

In some cases, a fifth stage is attained, in which the incidence of the deviant activity is greatly reduced, persisting only on a small scale and in isolated areas. No international prohibition regime could attain this stage until the nineteenth century for the simple reason that states had not yet eliminated or neutralized the effective vacuums of sovereign authority, both on land and sea, on which regime dissenters depended for their freedom and sanctuary.[7] As the power of states vis-à-vis criminals both within and without their borders grew over the past two centuries, so too did the potential of states to cooperate in suppressing undesirable activities.

Success in attaining the fifth stage of regime development has thus come to depend primarily on the nature of the criminal activity and its susceptibility to criminal justice measures, both of which can be strongly influenced over time by technological developments. Criminal laws and international prohibition regimes are particularly ineffective in suppressing criminal activities that require limited and readily available resources and no particular expertise to commit, those that are easily concealed, those that are unlikely to be reported to the authorities, and those for which the consumer demand is substantial, resilient, and not readily substituted for by alternative activities or products.[8] That is why, as we argue in the following pages, the global drug prohibition regime is destined never to achieve the success attained by regimes directed at the suppression of piracy and slave trading, or even those against currency counterfeiting and hijacking.

Piracy and Privateering

Prior to the seventeenth century, international norms proscribing banditry on the high seas were limited in scope and effect. Indeed, piracy was widely sanctioned in much of the world.[9] Kings, princes, sultans, and assorted other political magnates accordingly viewed piracy as a valued source of wealth and political power, useful both for building up their own possessions and undermining the strength of competitors. With the broad expansion of European maritime commerce in the sixteenth century, the rewards and the incidence of piracy jumped dramatically.[10] Much of it was officially or unofficially sponsored by European governments.[11]

In wartime, the practice of privateering was in effect an officially sanctioned version of piracy directed at a state's enemies and anyone engaged in trading with its enemies.[12] In peacetime, the same private shippers were granted letters of reprisal by their governments. These authorized them to recoup any losses due to piracy by pirating from other ships bearing the same nationality as the pirates.[13] When professional privateers lost their official sanction as a consequence of a peace treaty between their sponsor and the enemy, they either sought employment by another monarch or else became unsanctioned pirates. Even in the latter situation, it was often possible to find sponsors and protectors among high-ranking officials in the monarch's retinue.

Early in the seventeenth century, Turkish corsairs began expanding their piratical activities from the Mediterranean to the Atlantic. "To the seventeenth-century [European] mind," C. M. Senior wrote, "the prospect of infidels carrying Christians into bestial captivity in North Africa gave efforts to eradicate piracy an urgency and crusading zeal which they had previously lacked. In a Europe strongly divided by political and religious difference, the one objective on which all Christian nations were agreed was the desirability of crushing the Turkish pirates."[14] Accordingly, French, Spanish, Dutch, and English fleets sailed against the pirate bases in North Africa between 1609 and 1620, transcending their own powerful disputes to unite against a more feared common enemy.

As the seventeenth century drew to a close, the rules and structures of Europe's international relations were beginning to change. The volume of trade and diplomacy was increasing rapidly, both among European states and with far-flung colonies and countries outside Christendom. The advantage to be derived from stealing from one another was giving way to the greater advantage of stable commercial relations. Governments wanted and needed to monopolize the forces of violence, both within their borders and on the high seas. Accordingly, private fiefdoms and armies were co-opted or eliminated, and pirates were warned to abandon their ways or risk the wrath of increasingly powerful navies.

The dramatic expansion of the British Royal Navy in the 1690s, which greatly improved England's power to police the high seas and its growing empire, gave particular force to the new injunction against pirating.[15] Pirates and their collaborators were hunted down, colonial administrators admonished to enforce the new antipiracy laws ardently, and foreign leaders warned to cease sponsoring pirate expeditions and to crack down on unauthorized pirates operating within and from their territories. Those who failed to comply often found British and other European naval forces crowding local harbors to lend force to their demands. Piracy "was in fact undergoing a transformation from being a national industry to becoming an international threat."[16] Although wars were becoming fiercer, peacetime relations between governments were becoming more orderly. Where peacetime had previously been associated with anarchy, it increasingly promised a degree of security from both publicly and privately sponsored violence.

The civilizing of international society did not progress smoothly, but in fits and starts. Even as European states regularized their relations in and around the European continent, Adam Watson has noted, "both states and privateers continued to operate against one another in the Americas and Asia in ways that were no longer permissible in Europe between states not formally at war."[17] Also, the European powers did not apply the same standards of behavior to their dealings with most countries beyond their continent as they did to one another. At the same time, non–European states and even some of the colonies regarded the European efforts against piracy and privateering as unwarranted and unwelcome incursions into local struggles over power and wealth.[18] In the American colonies, for example, where imperial law and order was less easily enforced, businessmen and public officials alike continued to provide havens and markets for pirate ships for decades after London ordered a halt to such activities; by the mid-eighteenth century, however, most had acceded to the ban on piracy.

Elsewhere, government-sanctioned piracy persisted until well into the nineteenth century, when it was largely eradicated by military force. The Barbary tradition of exacting tribute by piracy was stunned first by U.S. naval intervention, then by a combined British and Dutch naval attack on Algiers, and finally ended with the French conquest of Algiers in 1830.[19] Pirate bases on Crete and Borneo were effectively destroyed by British naval interventions in, respectively, 1828 and 1849, after local rulers had failed to take satisfactory action.[20] In Oman and China, British forces combined with local forces to destroy pirate bases and fleets. And in the West Indies, piracy declined dramatically during the 1820s as a result of U.S. naval interventions, which succeeded in seizing dozens of pirate ships and destroying their bases.[21]

Privateering, or government-sanctioned piracy during wartime, was not effectively delegitimized until well into the nineteenth century. The U.S. government relied on privateers for most of its naval representation during both the Revolutionary War and the War of 1812.[22] The same was true of South American governments in their wars of independence against Spain.[23] Attacks on American maritime commerce by French privateers at the turn of the century almost brought the two countries to outright conflict. So long as governments legitimized the pirating of private vessels at sea during wartime, their efforts to delegitimize unsanctioned piracy were bound to meet with both skepticism and frustration.[24] Calls for the abolition of privateering began in earnest during the nineteenth century.

In 1856, Great Britain, France, Russia, Prussia, Austria, Sardinia, and the Porte signed the Declaration of Paris, formally abolishing privateering. The United States, however, refused to accede, insisting that the small size of its navy required that it retain the option of privateering during wartime.[25] Only with the growth of the U.S. Navy toward the end of the century and the growing sentiment that privateering no longer represented an acceptable mode of warfare did the U.S. government formally outlaw the practice.[26] By the end of the nineteenth century, a once customary form of waging war had been all but eliminated from the face of the earth.

The eventual globalization of the norms against piracy and privateering involved more, however, than merely the economic and security interests of the most powerful states in monopolizing the forces of violence on the high seas. As international society became more orderly and international relations more regularized, and as the high seas ceased to be perceived as a no-man's-land, larceny at sea became less justifiable. As with larceny on land, the fact that the victim was a stranger and a foreigner no longer exempted piracy from moral condemnation. Piracy increasingly was seen as an evil in its own right. The maxim *Pirata est hostice humani generis* (a pirate is an enemy of the human race) had seeped from the treatises on international law into the political psyches of governments.

An international criminal law is most potent—indeed, some would say it exists only—when it reflects not just self-interest but a broadly acknowledged obligation as well. The law against piracy was the first to attain such a consensus. And the international regime dedicated to the enforcement of this law was the first to attain global proportions. That the regime was not codified in an international convention until the 1958 Convention on the High Seas may well be explained by the fact that global norms condemning piracy were so universally acknowledged by the middle of the nineteenth century that a convention would have been perceived as superfluous. Indeed, many states explicitly condemned other transnational activities, such as slave trading, by linking them with, and even labeling them as, piracy.[27]

The delegitimation of government-sanctioned piracy was not, however, sufficient to ensure the virtual elimination of piratical activities from the high seas. Unlike privateering, piracy could subsist without the active support of governments. Yet pirates found even informal and discreet government sponsorship more elusive by the late 1700s. By the mid-1800s, island havens such as Madagascar and the Bahamas were no longer available as increasingly powerful states eliminated, one by one, the vacuums of de jure and de facto sovereignty on which unauthorized pirates had depended. Pirates also were acutely vulnerable to government action. The same sea vessels that allowed them access to the high seas also made them dependent on harbors and ports for rest and supplies. Their vessels could not be easily hidden; once captured, they afforded few opportunities for pirates to flee.

Yet by all accounts, the fatal blow to piracy was delivered by the development of steam vessels.[28] Pirates generally lacked the substantially greater resources needed to operate and build steam vessels. Legitimate steam cargo and passenger carriers thus became more elusive at the same time that naval steam vessels were increasingly available to pursue pirate ships. An early example of this occurred in 1837, "when a paddle wheeler, the *Diana*, of the East India Company, steamed toward six Malay pirate vessels against the wind and sank them all."[29] By the late nineteenth century, piracy had been all but eliminated from the high seas.

The fact that piracy persists today in particular geographic hot spots (most evident in Southeast Asia) reflects the inevitably limited capabilities of governments to eliminate entirely anything that lies wholly outside their control.[30] Of course, unlike their predecessors, today's pirates have access to speedboats to facilitate their attacks and getaways, meaning that law enforcers in this case have lost the decisive technological edge that steamships once provided them. Piracy has made something of a comeback during the past decade,[31] and is also becoming a more prominent international law enforcement concern due to growing worries over the potential nexus between piracy and terrorism. Of particular concern is terrorist targeting of maritime transportation (for example, hijacking an oil tanker for use as an explosive device, or use of a cargo container to smuggle a weapon of mass destruction). A range of ambitious maritime security initiatives have consequently been launched in recent years, conceived and backed by the United States and other major powers and institutionalized through multilateral organizations such as the International Maritime Organization and the World Customs Organization.[32] Such a convergence of security and economic concerns (discussed in more detail in chapter 5) may also, as in the past, generate a more militarized international law enforcement response.[33]

Slavery and the Slave Trade

No international prohibition regime so powerfully confirms the potential of humanitarian and similar moral concerns to shape global norms and the creation of a global regime as that directed against slavery and the slave trade. Until just a few centuries ago, slavery and slave trading were legal and commonplace features of society and commerce throughout the world. Sophisticated slave trading systems existed throughout much of Africa, Asia, and the Ottoman Empire. During the seventeenth and eighteenth centuries, European governments acquired a strong interest in developing the transatlantic slave traffic as black Africa came to be seen as a limitless source of labor for the plantations and mines of the Americas.[34] Following the Peace of Utrecht in 1712, British slavers quickly assumed a dominant role in the highly profitable trade, transporting a substantial portion of the estimated 10 million black Africans ultimately imported into the Americas.[35]

By the beginning of the nineteenth century, however, the British government had reversed stride and become the leading opponent of both slavery and the traffic in slaves. Parliament banned the slave trade in 1807 and abolished the institution of slavery throughout its colonies in 1833, thereby freeing more than three-quarters of a million slaves throughout the empire. Throughout the nineteenth century and into the twentieth, the British government consistently devoted naval, diplomatic, and economic resources to the antislavery campaign, often pursuing it in areas where Britain had little else to gain and often much to lose.[36] During the 1840s, the Royal Navy devoted between a sixth and a quarter of its warships to suppressing the slave traffic;[37] it thus assumed many of the qualities of an international criminal police force, one that has had few successors since.

Britain supplemented its naval efforts by negotiating a series of bilateral diplomatic agreements in which African rulers and fellow governments in Europe agreed to prohibit the slave trade and authorized the Royal Navy to use force if the treaty were violated, and in which other states, albeit not the United States, agreed to Britain's proposal for the reciprocal right to search and seize slave trading vessels sailing under their flags.[38] When foreign governments proved overly reluctant either to enter into such agreements or to enforce the anti–slave trading agreements that they had signed, the British Navy provided whatever additional inducements were deemed necessary.

Britain promoted its antislavery campaign not just unilaterally and bilaterally but also multilaterally, targeting first the international traffic in slaves and thereafter the institution of slavery itself. Its delegates to the Paris Peace Conference of 1814–1815, the Congress of Vienna in 1815, and the Congress of Verona in 1822 emphasized Britain's wish for multilateral condemnation of the slave trade. Among the notable results of the conventions, Harold Nicholson has observed, were the invention of two new diplomatic devices: the imposition of economic sanctions in peacetime—in this case, to punish those countries that refused to abolish the slave trade—and the creation of a multinational oversight committee to monitor compliance with the international agreements signed by member governments.[39]

Britain's reasons for undertaking its global campaign against slavery and the slave trade are no longer in doubt. Economic considerations, in particular the argument of Adam Smith that slavery was a highly inefficient economic system, played a role.[40] Thomas Clarkson, one of the first and most influential advocates of abolition, integrated such arguments into his broader condemnations of slavery.[41] Yet powerful economic arguments were also available to support slavery and the slave trade.[42] Most historians on the subject have concluded that the fundamental impetus behind Britain's reversal on slavery and its subsequent efforts to suppress the slave trade was a moral one derived in good part from religious and humanitarian impulses and the principles of the Enlightenment.[43]

Antislavery opinion gained ground slowly during the 1700s, stimulated by sympathetic literary accounts of Africa, the pamphlets of abolitionist religious leaders, the exhortations of the Quakers, and the antislavery legal activities of Granville Sharp.[44] During the early 1800s, a new generation of moral entrepreneurs emerged, among whom William Wilberforce was the acknowledged leader and the Anti-Slavery Society the driving organizational force. Their efforts played a crucial role in turning both popular and elite opinion in Britain, as well as Parliament, strongly against the slave trade.[45] When domestic enthusiasm for Britain's global campaign began to wane at midcentury, David Livingstone's reports on the brutality of the slave trade in Central Africa[46] and Joseph Cooper's books in the

1870s on African slavery reinvigorated public interest.[47] As the end of the century approached, popular concern was increasingly driven by notions of "the white man's burden"—notions that spurred and justified, in European eyes, the imperialistic race to lay claim to African territory as well as the imposition of paternalistic measures such as liquor and gun control regimes, but that nonetheless were rooted in humanitarian sentiments.[48]

The impact of Britain's abolitionists on the fate of slavery and the slave trade outside the empire was twofold. First, they played a central role in instigating the British government's international campaign, both by applying domestic political pressures on legislators and other government officials and by influencing the personal moral views of Britain's leaders and high officials. But as influential as the British government was, it could do little to shape the moral views of foreign societies and regimes. The governments that acquiesced to Britain's demands did so for a variety of reasons, including monetary and territorial compensation, trade advantages, a desire for some political advantage, fear of incurring British wrath, and only occasionally a common moral sentiment regarding the slave trade. So long as the behavior of foreign governments conformed to acceptable standards, British officials did not concern themselves with determining the underlying belief systems.

There were, moreover, limits to the British government's ability to influence foreign governments. Some, such as the governments of the Ottoman Empire, France, and the United States, were less susceptible to British coercion than were the Brazilian and black African rulers, either because they possessed significant military power in their own right, or because Britain's other interests restrained it from undertaking such actions. The Ottoman Empire gradually proved susceptible to British pressures during the late 1800s to withdraw from the African slave trade, but strongly resisted any efforts to restrict the traffic in white Circassian and Georgian slaves, who played an important role in Ottoman society not readily analogous to Western notions of slavery.[49] British pressures on France over the right of search in the early 1840s actually backfired, arousing popular French resentment and temporarily undermining the French abolitionist movement.[50] And despite pro forma efforts by the U.S. government to suppress the slave trade, its de facto policy all but condoned the trade.[51]

The second and, in some respects, more significant impact of the British abolitionists was their powerful influence on foreign opinion, particularly among elites, regarding the immorality of slavery. Once the struggle within Britain had been won, British religious and antislavery organizations directed their energies abroad. The most prominent among these was the British and Foreign Anti-Slavery Society, founded principally by radical Quakers in 1839. Assuming as its ultimate objective the abolition of slavery throughout the world, it "kept close watch on British policy, freely tendering the government both criticism and advice." It also "called several international conventions, thus gaining for itself the image of leading a world-wide crusade against slavery, and it kept in close touch with abolitionists abroad, made appeals to foreign rulers, and sometimes sent out its own fact-finding missions."[52]

Where the motives of the British government's antislavery campaign were often suspect in foreign eyes, those of the Anti-Slavery Society were much less so. It played a role in prompting the creation of similar societies in France, the United States, Brazil, and elsewhere,[53] and it ensured continuing British opposition to slavery in Africa and the Middle East following the demise of slavery across the Atlantic. Toward the end of the century, its efforts were supplanted by non-British abolitionists, notably Cardinal Lavigerie, archbishop of Algiers, who in 1888 "began preaching a new crusade against the Islamic infidel, a crusade that would send out Christian knights to destroy the internal African slave trade."[54] The British and Foreign Anti-Slavery Society thus represented perhaps the first "transnational moral entrepreneur"—religious movements aside—to play a significant role in world politics generally and in the evolution of a global prohibition regime specifically.

The powerful diffusion of religious and liberal abolitionist sentiments throughout much of the world[55] was also a reflection of the great regard in which Britain and France, which abolished slavery in 1833 and 1848, respectively, were held by intellectuals and other elites elsewhere in Europe and beyond. Abolitionism in both Britain and America had originated with the Quakers' critiques of slavery in the late 1600s.[56] American abolitionists during the following centuries were deeply influenced by the British antislavery movement.[57] The spread of abolitionist principles throughout the European continent during the late eighteenth century, and throughout Latin America during the nineteenth century, derived from the same evolving Christian and Enlightenment notions regarding the rights and obligations of man.[58] During the last decades of the nineteenth century, these ideas strongly influenced elite opinion in the countries that had developed the strongest dependencies on African slavery.[59] Both Spain, which continued to defend the institution of slavery in Cuba until its ultimate abolition in 1886, and Brazil, which did not emancipate the last of its slaves until 1888, were strongly influenced by the violent fate of slavery in the United States and by the growing sense of moral isolation that followed.[60]

Still, abolitionist sentiment in those countries also drew strong sustenance from the liberal (and, to a certain extent, anticlerical) principles that had gained dominance throughout much of Europe.[61] Brazilians were eager, the abolitionist Joaquim Nabuco wrote to the British, "to imitate every European progress, and possess each new material, moral, intellectual, or social improvement of civilization."[62] Only in the Ottoman Empire and in Africa did such considerations play a relatively minor role in gradually turning opinion against slavery in the late 1800s.[63]

The processes by which legal slavery was abolished involved far more than the influences of Britain and the Enlightenment. In many countries, the waning political and economic power of slaveholders proved crucial to the success of local abolitionist efforts. In the United States, a civil war was required to resolve the issue. In parts of Asia, Africa, and the Middle East, the institution of slavery was not abolished until well into the twentieth century. But even among the laggards, indeed especially among the laggards, the consciousness of being perceived as deviant surely weighed heavily in the decisions of local rulers to abolish slavery. It is, in short, impossible to explain the abolition of slavery throughout the world without emphasizing the powerful role of shared moral notions derived primarily from the religious and secular principles of the Enlightenment.

Although the regime against piracy represented the first global prohibition regime, the regimes against slavery and the slave trade added new dimensions that have since been replicated in more recent global prohibition regimes. The initial regime to ban the slave trade was the first to be institutionalized in a series of international conventions signed by the vast majority of governments; it was the first in which blatantly moral impulses as well as transnational moral entrepreneurs played leading roles; it was the first to criminalize international commerce in a particular "commodity"; and it was the first to evolve into a far more ambitious regime aimed at the criminalization of all activity involving the production, sale, and use of that "commodity" in every country.

Caution, though, is necessary in equating Britain's efforts against slavery, and the emergence of a transnational antislavery consensus, with the eradication of slavery. Often taken for granted is the fact that slavery could be eradicated (or at least relegated to a few obscure corners of the earth) because it was particularly susceptible to efforts directed at its suppression. Illegal slave traders, unlike smugglers of most other contraband, could hardly hide their cargo from naval inspections and customs inspectors. And slave owners could not readily hide or disguise their illegally acquired slaves from government authorities determined to prohibit the acquisition of imported slaves. Also important to the eradication of slavery was the possibility of other forms of labor, including the employment of former slaves under conditions not much different from their former status, the importation of wage laborers from abroad, penal servitude, and other types of forced labor.[64] In some cases, these alternatives actually proved more profitable than slavery had been. Slavery was, in short, largely replaceable by other legal and social institutions.

The most important vulnerability of slavery, however, involves its substantial dependence on legal institutions. Unlike piracy, murder, rape, drug dealing, and prostitution, which usually tend to be episodic in nature, slavery typically involves an ongoing, highly coercive relationship between private individuals. It thus requires social institutions that are sufficiently powerful and encompassing to sustain that relationship by deterring slaves from challenging their owners and returning runaway slaves to their masters. Absent the support of a legal institution, slavery can persist only where nonlegal social norms in support of slavery are strong, where the state is sufficiently uninterested in eradicating slavery that it ignores the efforts of slave owners to retain their slaves, or where slaves acquiesce, in one way or another, to their enslavement. Each of these conditions is increasingly absent since the early nineteenth century. At the same time, few states now lack the effective jurisdiction over their territories required to suppress slavery. That the antislavery regime has succeeded in virtually eradicating institutionalized slavery is largely a result of the peculiar vulnerability of the activity to criminalization and enforcement. Other forms of slavery have persisted, but not in the formal sense of legally owning people. Contemporary slavery, explains Kevin Bales, is about slave holding rather than slave owning.[65] As Neta Crawford points out, "What is significant beyond the continued existence of unfree labor is that those who practice slavery

32

and forced labor seek to conceal it, whereas in previous eras, concealment was not considered necessary."[66]

Prostitution ("White Slavery")

During the second half of the nineteenth century, reformers in Europe and the United States focused substantial energies on eliminating "white slavery."[67] Originally, this term referred to the entire system of licensed prostitution in existence throughout much of Europe and parts of the United States. Arguing that government-licensed prostitution institutionalized the oppression and corruption of women and was not successful in stemming the spread of venereal disease, growing numbers of activists sought its abolition. After the 1870s, the term "white slavery" developed two additional meanings. To some, it was synonymous not just with licensed prostitution but with all prostitution; the abolitionist movement thus split between those who favored nonpunitive measures designed to reduce the incidence of prostitution and those "purity crusaders" who desired the immediate criminalization of all prostitution.[68] The more popular definition of white slavery and, more specifically, the white slave trade, was the recruitment to prostitution by force or fraud.[69]

The international movement to abolish white slavery was led primarily by nongovernmental transnational moral entrepreneurs. Initially, these entrepreneurs looked beyond their own borders for two reasons: to oppose the efforts of the International Medical Congress to internationalize the licensing of prostitution to better regulate venereal disease,[70] and to lend moral and organizational support to one another. The dominant figure in this movement in the early years was a British woman, Josephine Butler, who played a central role in persuading Parliament to repeal the Contagious Diseases Prevention Acts regulating prostitution in Britain, and who traveled widely throughout Europe proselytizing against licensed prostitution.[71] The British, Continental, and General Abolitionist Federation that she established in 1875 provided an effective means for organizing and mobilizing abolitionist sentiment in both England and continental Europe.[72]

The true internationalization of the movement, however, was largely a result of the perceived internationalization of prostitution. Beginning about 1880, Butler and other reformers, journalists, and novelists began to focus their attention and rhetoric on the international traffic in women and children for purposes of prostitution. Convinced of the immorality of prostitution and firmly believing that no woman could ever freely and rationally choose such a career, they crusaded for the worldwide elimination of this traffic, which eventually proved to be far smaller and more insignificant than popularly depicted.

Like the contemporaneous antidrug and antialcohol movements, moreover, the antiprostitution movement was motivated in no small part by the perceived links between prostitution and disfavored minorities.[73] In the United States, charges that an international criminal syndicate was running the white slave trade obliged the U.S. Immigration Service to send hundreds of agents into cities as underground investigators and induced Congress to pass the Mann-Elkins Act prohibiting any interstate or international traffic in women for purposes of prostitution.[74] At the international level, the campaign against the white slave trade secured the cooperation of governments and led to international conferences and agreements condemning the practice, notably the Agreement for the Suppression of the White Slave Trade, signed in Paris in 1904 and ultimately ratified by about one hundred governments.[75]

The internationalization of the movement was driven in part by the popular image, successfully propagated by the moral crusaders and sensationalistic media accounts, of young women driven by poverty, lured by trickery, and compelled by force to prostitution in foreign lands. But it also derived from a tactical lesson that crusaders against the white slave trade had learned from their predecessors in the struggle against the black slave trade: that focusing on prostitution's cross-border dimension provided the essential transnational hook needed to pursue the abolition of licensed prostitution and more vigorous efforts against all prostitution around the world. By the start of the Second World War, opponents of the white slave trade had succeeded in abolishing state regulation of prostitution in a number of countries, replacing them in most cases with prohibition measures. The moral crusade instigated by Josephine Butler and others to end the state's control and exploitation of prostitutes had, Gail Pheterson concluded, "dissolved into a social purity crusade to abolish prostitution."[76]

The creation of a global regime directed at the suppression of the white slave trade early in the twentieth century accomplished relatively little toward its objectives. Regime proponents who sought primarily to improve the conditions of prostitutes met largely with failure.[77] Those who were concerned primarily with outlawing prostitution proved somewhat more successful, but unlike the prohibition regimes directed at the suppression of the slave and drug trades, the creation of a regime directed at the international traffic in women was not followed by the virtually universal enactment of legislation prohibiting prostitution. And although the formation of a global regime coincided with an apparent reduction in the transnational movement of women and children for purposes of prostitution, the regime itself played a relatively minor role. Pressures from the League of Nations combined with tougher law enforcement measures directed at prostitution and the international traffic had some impact. Far more important were changes in the social, economic, and demographic conditions that had stimulated the transnational movement of prostitutes during the late 1800s, in particular the presence of millions of male immigrants in North and South America with scant chance of female companionship apart from prostitutes. As most countries imposed far more restrictive immigration controls, as population migrations declined markedly, and as the unbalanced sex ratios were corrected, the international market for prostitutes declined.[78]

The immediate post-WWII traffic in women was largely at the local and regional level, with the main international response being the 1949 UN Convention for the Suppression of the Traffic in Persons and of the Exploitation of the Prostitution of Others. The self-reporting requirements and nonbinding provisions made it possible for countries to "gain the moral high ground by loudly proclaiming that they had signed a document condemning the buying and selling of women's bodies, when in reality prostitution continues unchecked in their own countries."[79]

In more recent decades, there has been enormous growth in both the transnational movement of women for purposes of prostitution (most notably in parts of East Asia and Eastern Europe and the former Soviet Union) and in global attention devoted to it.[80] As in the earlier burst of activity and moral outrage over the issue of white slavery, this recent development has been linked to the more general upsurge in mass migration across the world, with some women going voluntarily, some by trickery, and some in between—and then being kept in prostitution by exploitive economic relationships backed by ignorance, fear, force, and other threats of violence and humiliation. The fall of the Iron Curtain, the crumbling of the Soviet

Empire, and conditions of economic dislocation and relatively open borders have helped facilitate the movement of people, including the movement of women for purposes of prostitution, from the former Soviet bloc into Western Europe, the Balkans, and elsewhere.[81] Much of the growth of prostitution in East Asia has been tied to a boom in "sex tourism," facilitated by declining costs of travel and customer access to information through new technologies such as the Internet.[82] In Thailand, which has served as a regional hub for sex tourism, women and children are trafficked from neighboring countries such as Myanmar (Burma) to work in urban brothels that are a major component of the country's tourism industry.[83]

Intense media coverage and activism by governmental and nongovernmental organizations have drawn enormous attention to sex trafficking in recent years, leading to a flurry of new international criminalization initiatives that very much echo the earlier debates and moralizing rhetoric about white slavery.[84] Now, as then, the United States and nongovernmental transnational moral entrepreneurs have taken the lead in drawing attention to the issue, wrapping it in moralistic discourse and elevating it on the international agenda.[85] Now, as then, critics charge that the dominant focus of antitrafficking efforts has been more on criminalizing acts of trafficking and prostitution than on protecting the rights of those who are trafficked.[86] And now, as then, the international antitrafficking movement remains deeply divided due to the sharply opposing views of abolitionist feminists and sex worker rights feminists concerning the appropriate legal status of prostitution.[87] For example, the international NGO Global Alliance Against Trafficking in Women argues that legalizing prostitution would help reduce trafficking, whereas another leading international NGO, the Coalition Against Trafficking Women, takes a more prohibitionist approach.[88] These bitter definitional divisions and battles, Eileen Scully has argued, are even greater than they were in the pre-WWII period and promise a repetition of the failures of the earlier antitrafficking movement.[89]

Supporting the prohibitionist model, the United States has enthusiastically promoted the construction of a global antitrafficking prohibition regime and embraced an aggressive monitoring and reporting role.[90] A growing number of countries have agreed to criminalize the trafficking of persons for the sex industry and adopt a common set of legal definitions, standards, and procedures, formalized in the 2000 UN Convention

Against Transnational Organized Crime, and its "Protocol to Prevent, Suppress, and Punish Trafficking in Persons, Especially Women and Children."[91] The U.S.-initiated[92] Protocol was the source of intense and bitter battles among competing antitrafficking NGOs and state actors.[93] Richard Friman suggests that although earlier international antitrafficking initiatives failed, this latest effort represents "a significant step toward the establishment of a global prohibition regime."[94]

As in the earlier prohibitionist crusade against white slavery, an underlying agenda for some of the most influential state and nonstate actors today is the targeting of prostitution via the transnational angle of targeting trafficking. Prostitution nevertheless persists in all countries, even in those that have applied the most repressive measures in an attempt to eradicate it. Although "the police and the law have played a role in changing the form and scope of prostitution," Vern and Bonnie Bullough conclude, "they have never had much effect in lessening prostitution."[95] Like drug dealing and other vice activities, prostitution has proven peculiarly resistant to criminal justice measures. Unlike slavery, it does not require legal institutions or even strong social institutions to perpetuate itself. Prostitution tends to be criminalized in those societies that most prize the symbolic value of the law (even while often tolerating the criminalized activity in practice) and in those that prefer to keep their vices underground.[96] We see little prospect that the existence of a nearly universal moral notion that prostitution is wrong will translate into a robust global prohibition regime directed not just against trafficking but toward the suppression of prostitution itself.

International Drug Trafficking

The desire of people to alter their state of consciousness is a constant in history; so, too, is the use of psychoactive substances to accomplish this task.[97] Alcohol, tobacco, opium, cannabis, coffee, and coca have each been consumed in different societies, and in various forms, for many hundreds, in some cases many thousands, of years, as have a variety of other psychoactive substances.[98] Each has been used for medicinal, ritual, and recreational purposes and perceived as both a great evil and a great good. Each has been subject to government controls and sanctions ranging from the death penalty to taxation, zoning, and other regulatory measures. And each has been widely available in entirely unregulated markets. Prior to the twentieth century, no global patterns were discernible in the norms and legal sanctions governing the trade and use of any of these substances.

Today the vast majority of states count themselves members of the global drug prohibition regime. Almost all are parties to the 1961 Single Convention on Narcotic Drugs (or are parties to that convention as amended by the 1972 protocol), the 1971 Convention on Psychotropic Substances, and the 1988 Convention Against Illicit Traffic in Narcotic Drugs and Psychotropic Substances (the Vienna Convention).[99] The production, sale, and even possession of cannabis, cocaine, and most opiates, hallucinogens, barbiturates, amphetamine, and tranquilizers outside strictly regulated medical and scientific channels are now punished with criminal sanctions in virtually every nation; criminal justice agencies in most countries are deeply involved in investigating and prosecuting drug law violations; and even the rhetoric of the "war on drugs" has been globalized. The processes by which this regime has evolved must be understood as a confluence of the perceptions, interests, and moral notions among dominant sectors of the more powerful states, along with the exceptional influence of American protagonists in shaping the regime according to their preferred norms.

Until well into the nineteenth century, the British government was the principal sponsor of the opium trade. So great was its financial interest that efforts by the Imperial Government of China to ban the flow of opium from British India in the late 1830s were suppressed with military force.[100] Within Britain, however, opposition to the opium trade emerged during the Opium Wars and gained force as the century wore on. As with the antislavery movement, British Quakers quickly emerged as the leading moral entrepreneurs of the antiopium campaign;[101] indeed, a number of leading Quakers were actively involved in both movements.[102] In 1874, they formed the Anglo-Oriental Society for the Suppression of the Opium Trade, which played a major role during the next four decades in organizing sentiment against the opium trade, proselytizing to the public, and lobbying the government.[103] They were abetted in their efforts by missionaries (who blamed opium for their notable lack of success in China),[104] other antiopium societies, and politicians predominantly from the Liberal Party.

The Liberal Party's victory in the elections of 1906 ensured the antiopium forces their principal objective: a commitment by the British government to phase out all opium exports from British India to China. Although the declining significance of opium revenues to the government of British India certainly helped persuade those less committed to the antiopium cause, the reversal of British government policy was almost entirely a reflection of the triumph of moral, religious, and humanitarian impulses over political and economic interests.

Unlike Britain's role in the antislavery campaign, however, its role in the antiopium campaign did not extend to support for an aggressive global campaign against the trade. The principal impetus for a more multilateral approach was provided instead by Americans, notably missionaries returned from the Far East. "So great was their role," Arnold Taylor has written, in "evoking the inauguration of the movement, and in promoting the early work once the movement had been started, that in its early stages the international campaign might quite appropriately be referred to as a missionary movement—or better still, as missionary diplomacy."[105] The missionaries were soon joined, however, by a great variety of economic and political interests as well as an eclectic assortment of moral entrepreneurs. Their combined efforts were to prove largely successful in stimulating both state and federal drug prohibition legislation within the United States, as well as the creation of a global drug prohibition regime institutionalized in international conventions and the drug control agencies of international organizations.[106]

The emergence of drug control legislation in a great variety of states during the last decades of the nineteenth century and the first decades of the twentieth was in part a consequence of revolutionary developments in the technology of drug production: the isolation of morphine from opium early in the nineteenth century and the invention of heroin toward the end of the century, as well as the isolation of cocaine from the coca plant and the perfection of the hypodermic injection during the middle of the century.[107] These developments were initially greeted with great enthusiasm by the medical profession, pharmaceutical companies, patent medicine manufacturers, and recreational drug users. Morphine and heroin were hailed as tremendous advances in the medical treatment of pain; both are still used for such purposes today.[108] Cocaine, too, was hailed as a miracle drug, one that doctors could—and still do—use as a local and regional anesthetic.[109] Both of the opiates as well as cocaine were also popularized as tonics for a great variety of ills; Vin Mariani and Coca Cola were among the most famous of these.[110] But as appreciation of the value of these drugs came to be tempered by greater awareness of their harmful potential, government controls over their distribution came to be perceived as important components of emerging public health policies.[111]

In the United States, fears of unregulated drug sales combined with the reform movement's anger at unscrupulous manufacturers of patent medicines and popular drinks, whose concoctions often contained large amounts of cocaine, opiate derivatives, and other potentially addictive and dangerous substances.[112] Also influential were the increasingly powerful associations of doctors and pharmacists, whose altruistic motives were closely intertwined with their financial and professional interests in better controlling and even monopolizing the public's access to medicinal advice and substances.[113]

The emergence of drug prohibition both in the United States and internationally cannot be explained, however, solely by the legitimate concerns over the harmful potential of drug use. Consumption of opium was quite common in the United States, Britain, and elsewhere during the nineteenth century; much of it was properly viewed as benign. The introduction of prohibition laws, moreover, often followed rather than preceded significant decreases in consumption—decreases that resulted from a decline in the incidence of iatrogenic addiction as the medical profession recognized the dangers of these drugs and as new therapeutic drugs were devised, an increase in public awareness of the potential dangers posed by these substances, and the institution of nonprohibitive governmental measures such as labeling requirements on patent medicines. Furthermore, the vigorousness with which the U.S. government has pursued the creation of a global drug prohibition regime cannot be explained solely by the desire to better restrict the export of drugs to the United States.

Between the missionaries and the public health reformers stood a varied assortment of moral entrepreneurs. Many of these were concerned not just with the opiates and cocaine but with a whole array of vices, including alcohol and tobacco use and prostitution. In the U.S.-occupied Philippines, for instance, a pragmatic plan favored by Governor Taft to reinstitute the legal opium control system devised by the displaced Spaniards was derailed when a leading antivice moral entrepreneur, Reverend Wilbur Crafts, head of the International Reform Bureau in the United

States, mobilized vigorous opposition to it.[114] Within the United States, moral entrepreneurs played a central role in inspiring the passage of federal and state legislation prohibiting not just opiates and cocaine but alcohol, cigarettes, prostitution, and much more. Their moral conviction that any form of inebriation was abhorrent struck a responsive chord with millions of Americans. And their advocacy of sobriety appealed to sectors of the American elite, whose paternalistic concerns regarding the vulnerability of the lower classes to alcohol and other drug abuse combined with fears that their economic productivity might suffer.

Both the alcohol and drug prohibition movements drew great sustenance as well from the popular association of drugs with feared and despised minorities. Many Protestant Americans identified alcohol and its ills with the fearsome flow of millions of Catholic and Jewish immigrants into the United States in the decades before and after the turn of the century.[115] Although opium consumption in the form of laudanum and other opiate liquids was widespread in the late 1800s and early 1900s, particularly among native-born, older white women in the South,[116] the first antiopium laws, beginning with city ordinances in San Francisco in 1875 and Virginia City, Nevada, in 1876, were directed at the smoking of opium, which was associated with Chinese immigrants and deviant whites.[117] Their use of the drug was perceived as symbolic of the immigrants' decadence and as a potential weapon that could be used to undermine American society.[118] In the South, the white majority feared that cocaine use among African Americans might cause them to forget their assigned status in the social order.[119] In the West and Southwest, the association of marijuana with Mexicans provided a powerful impetus to legislation effectively outlawing the substance.[120] In each case, law enforcement officials, journalists, and political leaders provided sensationalist, albeit largely unsubstantiated, reports of the horrid crimes ostensibly committed under the influence of the respective drugs. Much of the public and their legislators accepted unquestioningly the truth of these reports.

Particularly influential in promoting both federal drug control legislation and a leading role for the United States in international drug control activities were Charles Brent, the Episcopal bishop in the Philippine Islands, and Dr. Hamilton Wright, a politically connected physician specializing in tropical diseases. They played a major role, David Musto has written, in persuading President Theodore Roosevelt that "a humanitarian movement to ease the burden of opium in China would help his long-range goals: to mollify Chinese resentment against America, put the British in a less favorable light, and support Chinese antagonism against European entrenchment."[121]

Their principal successor during the 1920s and 1930s was the charismatic Richmond Hobson, a Spanish-American War hero and former congressman who had been the Anti-Saloon League's highest paid "special speaker."[122] Hobson agitated widely, speaking on radio programs, lobbying his former colleagues in Congress, and founding a variety of drug prohibition organizations, including the International Narcotic Education Association. He played an important role in propagating popular misconceptions regarding the extent of drug addiction in the United States and the relationship between narcotic use and violent crime.[123] The dominant figure in the antidrug crusade during the second third of the century was Harry Anslinger, the ambitious first director of the Federal Bureau of Narcotics (FBN) from 1930 to 1962.[124] He played an important role in popularizing tales of drug-induced crime, in opposing most efforts to treat drug addiction primarily as a medical problem, and in designing and instigating increasingly repressive drug control legislation at both the state and federal levels. Drawing on his previous experience as head of the Foreign Control Section of the Prohibition Unit during the late 1920s, Anslinger also assumed the dominant role of advocate for the American interest in international drug control and the evolution of the global drug prohibition regime.[125]

The U.S. role in promoting the drug control regime bears important resemblances to Britain's earlier role as advocate of the antislavery regime. Just as British proponents of the regime argued, when it served their domestic interests, that the antislavery campaign was in Britain's economic and political interests, so American promoters of the drug prohibition regime have argued that their international efforts are necessary to reduce the extent and costs of drug abuse in the United States. And just as Britain's vigorous antislavery campaign was motivated primarily by humanitarian sentiments, Christian moralism, a strong sense of righteousness, and the compulsion to proselytize, so U.S. efforts at home and abroad have been driven by fears of deviant drug use, moralistic abhorrence of recreational use of psychoactive substances other than alcohol and tobacco, a similar sense of righteousness, and, again, the compulsion to proselytize. The principal difference, however, between the roles of Britain and the United States is that whereas the former sought to abolish repressive laws throughout the world, the United States has advocated for the imposition of punitive control systems in all countries.

The evidence for these assertions lies not just in the rhetoric employed by U.S. officials in support of a global war against drugs but also in the exceptional scale and scope of Washington's international effort and the fashion in which it has been pursued. The United States has played a leading role, from the first opium conference held in Shanghai in 1909 to the antidrug convention adopted by the United Nations in 1988, in drafting and lobbying for increasingly far-reaching antidrug conventions, designed first to restrict and then to criminalize most aspects of drug trafficking both internationally and in the domestic legislation of all member countries.[126]

The United States has lobbied since the 1930s for the global criminalization of cannabis and its treatment on a par with heroin and cocaine, despite abundant scientific evidence questioning the need for such a punitive approach.[127] U.S. drug enforcement officials have persistently criticized foreign governments, first Britain, then the Netherlands, and more recently Canada, for their emphasis on public health approaches to the drug problem, and pressured them to change, despite substantial evidence that these countries have proven far more successful than the United States in dealing with illicit drug addiction.[128] Moreover, the U.S. Drug Enforcement Administration now plays a role as global enforcer and advocate of U.S. drug policies and the global conventions not unlike that performed by the Royal Navy on behalf of Britain's campaign against piracy and the slave trade in previous centuries.

The U.S. success in globalizing its drug prohibition policy was dependent, however, on both the absence of powerful and widespread opposition elsewhere and the existence of common perspectives on drug control, moral and otherwise, in many other states. The same could not be said of the efforts by the United States and a few other governments during the early decades of the twentieth century to establish an international regime to criminalize and control the international traffic in alcohol.[129] Despite the vigorous international efforts of American prohibitionists, the emergence of transnational moral entrepreneurs,[130] and the existence of alcohol prohibition laws in some countries[131] and antialcohol sentiment in most,[132] efforts to create an antialcohol regime were stillborn.

By contrast, the U.S. demand for an international drug prohibition regime directed first at the opiates and cocaine, then at cannabis, and ultimately at a wide array of psychoactive drugs, struck a sympathetic chord in a great variety of societies. Laws prohibiting one or another drug have existed in most societies for millennia. The fear that morphine, heroin, and cocaine, as well as the great variety of synthetic psychoactive substances created during the past century, could not be controlled without resorting to criminal justice measures was and is omnipresent. So, too, the very newness of the drugs stimulated the urge to prohibit, just as the introduction of tobacco and coffee in earlier centuries had prompted laws banning their sale and use. In the United States and many other societies as well, the association of opiate, cocaine, and cannabis use with the lower classes, disfavored minorities, and deviant groups also favored punitive approaches.

Perhaps even more important was the fact that drug prohibition laws did not threaten or antagonize powerful constituencies in any but a few countries. Although products such as Vin Mariani, the Bordeaux wine containing a coca extract, could claim kings, presidents, and popes among its avid consumers, few were so committed to it as to protest its unwilling demise.[133] Also, the major pharmaceutical companies in Europe and the United States were not so threatened by any one component of the regime as to mount a vigorous opposition; rather, they focused their efforts on ensuring that new regulatory schemes reflected their broader interests. In those Asian, African, and Caribbean countries where opium or cannabis use was prevalent, members of the elite tended not to partake; indeed, their moral views regarding drug use more often resembled those of Western elites.

In those countries in which use of a drug was limited to relatively powerless minorities or the poorer sectors of society, few governments objected strongly to signing an international convention and implementing the necessary domestic legislation to fulfill their international obligation, particularly when pressured to do so by the United States and the United Nations.[134] Indeed, in many countries, early drug prohibition legislation was powerfully shaped by the example set by the United States, the rhetoric of Harry Anslinger and other transnational moral entrepreneurs, and propaganda officially sanctioned by the U.S. government and the drug control agencies of first the League of Nations and then the United Nations.

That alcohol and tobacco have retained their legal status in international society while opium, coca, and cannabis were delegitimated, stigmatized, and prohibited did not, it should be stressed, reflect any objective calculation of their potential harms, as in many respects the former present greater health and societal risks than the latter substances. The near universality with which human beings early on figured out how to make and enjoy alcohol afforded this drug a unique status in human civilization. Tobacco and coffee, like alcohol, gained legitimacy because their use was successfully integrated into key social functions in diverse societies, notably including Europe, before global society had advanced to the point of being able to construct an international prohibition regime. Cannabis, coca, and cocaine, and to some extent the opiates, by contrast, did not have time to be integrated into many societies, especially in Europe and America, before those opposed to their use were able to mobilize an international regime to restrict and prohibit their distribution and use.

Most important, the nature of the global drug prohibition regime reflected the dominance of the United States and Europe in establishing global norms concerning the selection and appropriate uses of psychoactive substances. Some Asian states, for instance, might have opted for a different global regime that legitimized the use of opium, some African and Asian states for a regime legitimizing cannabis, many Muslim states for a regime prohibiting alcohol, and some Latin American states for a regime that sanctioned coca. Just as the global prohibition regimes against piracy and the slave trade reflected the desire and capacity of Britain and other European powers to impose their norms on the rest of the world, so the global drug prohibition regime reflected the desire and capacity of the United States to impose its drug-related norms on the rest of the world.

Unlike the antipiracy and antislavery regimes, however, the emergence of a fully developed drug prohibition regime coincided with a blossoming, in some respects unprecedented, of the activity that the regime had been created to eradicate. Indeed, there may be no greater example of the capacity of a transnational activity to resist the combined efforts of governments than the persistence of illicit drug trafficking. Unlike currency counterfeiting, no substantial expertise or resources are required to produce, smuggle, or sell many of the illicit drugs. Unlike slaves, illicit drugs are easily concealed by producers, smugglers, dealers, and consumers. And unlike piracy, slavery, and counterfeiting, drug trafficking produces few victims who have an interest in notifying criminal justice authorities. Drug prohibition laws, like prohibition laws directed at prostitution, gambling, and other vices, can powerfully affect the nature of the activity and the market, but they cannot effectively deter or suppress most of those determined to participate in the activity.

Endangered Species

An emerging antiwhaling regime in recent decades offers valuable insights into the future of global prohibition regimes. International efforts to limit the killing of whales began in the 1930s and 1940s, motivated largely by industry concerns that the overharvesting of whales was proving detrimental to the long-term economic interests of the whaling industry.[135] During the following decades, environmental and ecological concerns began to play important roles. Whales were coming to be seen, as former U.S. Secretary of State Dean Acheson stated in his 1970 address to the plenary session of the International Whaling Commission, as a "truly international resource . . . the wards of the entire world."[136] During the 1960s, popular perceptions of not just whales but all cetaceans, including whales, dolphins, and porpoises, began to develop in an unexpected but not entirely unprecedented direction; these sea mammals increasingly were seen as not merely another endangered species in need of international conservation measures but as unique and unusually intelligent forms of animal life that should not be killed at all. At the 1972 United Nations Conference on the Human Environment, delegates from all fifty-two countries present voted unanimously in favor of the immediate halt to commercial whaling.

The evolution in human perceptions of whales, and of the immorality of whale hunting, was a consequence of many factors. The economic significance of the whaling industry to many countries had declined significantly as the number of whales dwindled and alternative products became available; hence, economic imperatives no longer required most people to shut their eyes to whales' unique characteristics. But equally important, opponents of whale killing were increasing in number and influence. Some were scientists struck by the growing evidence of cetacean intelligence.[137] Far more numerous were the people exposed to the "humanity" of whales and other cetaceans at aquariums and through the media, such as the television program *Flipper* and the theme of the mid-1980s film

Star Trek IV: The Voyage Home.[138] Behind many of the efforts to generate sympathy for whales could be found members of Greenpeace, a vigorous transnational entrepreneur founded in 1970, and allied environmental activist groups.[139]

Today, the antiwhaling regime is poised between the third and fourth stages of regime development. An international convention to regulate whale killing is in force, but it does not ban the killing of all whales. Most governments currently ban whaling, but some countries, most notably Japan, Norway, and Iceland, continue to lobby for greater whaling quotas and to tolerate violations of the international whaling convention by their whalers. The U.S. government has played a major role in enforcing the antiwhaling regime, enacting strong domestic legislation, lobbying with the International Whaling Commission, and employing diplomatic pressures on foreign governments to crack down on pirate whaling.[140] Others have done likewise, including the Australian government, which switched dramatically from being a regime dissenter to being a leading regime advocate in 1978.[141] But the most vigorous role, one unique in the history of transnational moral entrepreneurship, has continued to be played by Greenpeace. Its members have engaged in direct confrontations at sea with whalers, disrupting their hunting operations, filming violations of the convention, and generally harassing whaling operations. Sympathizers have gone even further, sinking pirate whaling ships at port.[142]

It is now possible to speak of an emerging global consensus that the killing of whales is wrong, notwithstanding the dissenting—and often highly vocal—views of many Japanese, Icelanders, Norwegians, Eskimos, and others for whom whaling represents a traditional custom and whale meat a dietary staple or delicacy (not unlike the coca-chewing tradition of many Bolivians and Peruvians). As scientific understanding of cetacean intelligence progresses, and as new generations of children grow up with firm views regarding the immorality of whale killing, this transnational moral consensus is likely to strengthen. In a growing number of countries, moreover, whale watching and other nonconsumptive uses of whales are rapidly proving more lucrative than whale killing, thereby lending a powerful economic reinforcement to the moral arguments.[143] At the same time, as whale conservation efforts have proven increasingly successful, pressures have been building from states such as Japan to allow the controlled harvesting of whales for commercial purposes.

Whether the regime ultimately succeeds in virtually eliminating the killing of whales will depend not only on the resources that governments devote to enforcement of regime regulations and on the substitutability of whale products, but also on the capacity of whalers and consumers of whale products to elude suppression efforts. The position of the Japanese government, and its willingness to conform to the regime in both law and fact, will prove an important determinant of the regime's success, especially as a black market in whale meat would probably prove vulnerable to vigorous Japanese enforcement efforts.[144] The skills and resources required to engage in whaling are scarcer than those needed to engage in most transnational vice activities, but not nearly so scarce as those required by currency counterfeiters. Because whaling occurs on the high seas, it is not easily detected; nonetheless, whaling ships are readily identifiable, far more so than ships and planes smuggling drugs, alcohol, and most other illicit cargoes apart from slaves. The victims of whaling, moreover, lack the capacity to complain to the authorities at the same time that all humans directly implicated in the whaling industry possess no greater incentive to inform on one another than do those involved in vice activities. Efforts to protect whales and other cetaceans are also hampered by the fact that much whale killing is an unintended byproduct of economical fishing methods, notably purse-seining for tuna, and other human exploitations of the seas ranging from overfishing to pollution. Although the antiwhaling regime has the potential to succeed in virtually eradicating the intentional killing of whales, its prospects for changing the conditions that unintentionally abet the killing of whales are far less promising.

Elephants, like whales, are large, intelligent, and endangered, and unusually able to arouse the interests and sympathies of humans. The population of elephants in East and Central Africa has declined dramatically under pressures from drought, growing human population, dwindling amounts of open land, and poaching by Africans who sell the tusks and skins of elephants on the international market. Government officials in this region, having ignored the trend for many years and even profited both legally and illegally from the trade in ivory, are now eager to protect the elephant. Their principal concern is the increasing economic value of nonconsumptive uses of elephants, principally tourism. They have been joined by legions of conservationists, many of whom are motivated not just by the moral obligation to preserve endangered species, but also by their moral sense that the killing of elephants for either fun or profit is wrong. Backed strongly by the U.S. government, the conservationists and the African governments succeeded in October 1989 in mandating a ban on the global trade in ivory at a meeting of the Convention on International Trade in Endangered Species (CITES).[145] Only a global prohibitionist policy, they argued, could succeed in substantially curtailing poaching.

Proponents of the emerging regime have been opposed by other conservationists, as well as park managers and governments, notably in South Africa, Zimbabwe, and Botswana, where elephant populations have stabilized and even grown. Those charged with safeguarding and culling the herds have claimed that effective management of the national parks accounts for their success and that the lack of such management is the central explanation for the plight of elephants elsewhere. They have insisted that the southern Africans should not be obliged to forgo the revenue earned each year from the sale of ivory—revenue that is channeled back to the national parks—merely because other Africans have mismanaged their elephant resources.

The entire debate over the future of the elephant has been characterized by differences over morals, tactics, and the feasibility of significantly diminishing the international market for ivory.[146] The principal moral struggle has revolved not so much around the necessity of preserving a sustainable number of elephants as around the issue of killing elephants per se. Those who oppose elephant killing on moral grounds have employed many of the same tactics that have proven effective in arousing popular opinion against whaling and the killing of other animals, both endangered and nonendangered; a 1978 movie, for instance, entitled *Bloody Ivory*, portrayed the slaughter of elephants by poachers in graphic detail;[147] it helped build support for the CITES ban. Relatively few black Africans, however, have been moved by this effort to condemn on moral grounds the killing of elephants; indeed, some, as well as many white African conservationists, have argued that the prohibitionist approach to elephant killing reflects the imposition of the white man's morality on those in Africa who must coexist with the elephants.[148] The more important question for the future of the regime, however, is whether the moral condemnation of elephant killing and of the sale and purchase of new ivory will spread throughout the world and be internalized in diverse societies, notably those in Japan and other parts of East Asia that represent the principal markets for ivory.

The tactical dispute between those who favor a prohibition policy and those who prefer a conservationist policy that permits culling is important principally because those who favor the former believe that their own efforts to save the elephant require global uniformity.[149] East and Central Africans, together with Americans, have argued that the southern Africans cannot prevent ivory poached in other countries from being sold through their marketing system. They also have argued that international demand and the international ivory distribution system cannot be effectively curbed so long as some countries legitimize the sale of new ivory. The southern Africans have responded to the first point by insisting that they will be able to prevent leakage through their ivory marketing system, in part by utilizing spectrographic and dating processes to identify when the tusks were taken; as for the second point, they have made it clear that they have no desire to undermine the global market for their lucrative product.

The question of whether or not the international market for ivory can be significantly diminished hinges in good part on questions of substitutability. Various synthetic ivory substitutes have been developed; nevertheless, many consumers of ivory still insist on the real thing, just as many consumers of diamonds insist on the real thing. Piano makers and concert pianists, who prefer the touch of ivory keys to that of other materials, may grudgingly accept the synthetic substitutes, but collectors of ivory artwork and jewelry are not so amenable. The viability of the ban will be greatly influenced by how demand is dealt with in Japan, which has been the world's single largest consumer of ivory (primarily used for signature seals and fine carvings).[150]

The efforts to construct regimes prohibiting the killing of whales and elephants have been complemented by efforts to protect an expanding list of other endangered species. When the UN's CITES was first signed, it focused on protecting a few well-known species, but hundreds of endangered plant and animal life species are now banned from being traded.[151] Entirely new and lucrative transnational black markets have consequently been created, ranging from the smuggling of rare wild orchids to the trafficking of Russian caviar.[152] The transnational moral entrepreneurs in the case of orchids have primarily been European botanists, plant growers, and lawyers. Through their aggressive lobbying efforts, almost every orchid species has been placed on the CITES Appendix I list prohibiting their trade.[153]

Some prohibitions on trade in endangered species have clearly been more successful than others. The inclusion of leopards and crocodiles on the CITES endangered species list in the early 1980s, for example, combined with an international media campaign to sway public opinion, succeeded in reducing international demand for leopard coats and crocodile leather handbags enough to protect the animals at risk. By contrast, the CITES listing of the rhinoceros proved much less effective, in good part because the demand for the rhinoceros horn, which is used to make dagger handles in the Middle East and a purportedly aphrodisiac powder in the Far East, could not be substantially curbed.[154] The varied experience of international regimes designed to protect endangered species suggests that notions of morality regarding both the human obligation to preserve endangered species and the sense that any killing of particular animals is wrong have played a central role in instigating such regimes, that success in globalizing these regimes has hinged to a large degree on the success of moral entrepreneurs and other regime proponents in internationalizing their moral notions, and that the ultimate success or failure of such regimes hinges on the susceptibility of antiregime activities to enforcement efforts.

New and Emerging Global Prohibitions

A variety of other prohibition regimes have emerged in recent years, some more successful than others in reaching the global aspirations of their proponents. A particularly striking case has been the U.S.-led push to criminalize money laundering, which builds on and is very much derivative of the global drug prohibition regime.[155] The U.S.-inspired inclusion of provisions against money laundering in the 1988 Vienna drug prohibition convention provided an avenue for promoting a global anti–money laundering regime that has expanded and matured in an astonishingly short period of time. Since the 1980s, money laundering has gone from being largely tolerated and accepted to criminalized and condemned across the globe. As Michael Levi has described it, "What was formerly a genteel sovereign right of any nation to ensure 'customer confidentiality' has become redefined pejoratively as unacceptable 'bank secrecy' that facilitates the drug trade."[156]

The rules, norms, principles, and decision-making procedures that constitute the global anti–money laundering regime are most clearly articulated in the Financial Action Task Force (FATF) and its list of "40 Recommendations" that states are expected and pressured to implement.[157] The FATF was created in 1989 by the Group of Seven (G-7), with the mandate to analyze existing efforts to counter money laundering and to promote new statutory and regulatory standards. Although the FATF has a limited membership (thirty-one states and two international organizations), its influence is far broader by virtue of five FATF-style regional bodies across the world. A distinguishing characteristic of the FATF is that it operates on the basis of informal agreements and mutual evaluation of members rather than binding multilateral treaties. In 1996, the FATF formalized a policy of sanctioning members that failed to adopt the "40 Recommendations," and in 2000 it developed more teeth by initiating a high-profile campaign of "naming and shaming" noncooperative states.[158] The stigma of being blacklisted not only brought embarrassment but could also have serious material repercussions. As one offshore financial regulator put it, countries "would do anything to make sure we are not on that list" because being on the list would prompt a flight of business.[159] Levi has noted that the global anti–money laundering movement has an "evangelical tone," reflected in the title of the 2000 FATF annual report, "Spreading the Anti–Money Laundering Message Around the World."[160]

The objective of this newly emerging prohibition regime has been the global homogenization of domestic anti–money laundering laws and procedures. The regime also encourages information sharing and greater law enforcement cooperation in investigations, prosecutions, and asset seizures unencumbered by financial secrecy laws.[161] The dominant U.S. position in the international financial system has been a prerequisite for mobilizing international action and conformity.[162] On the occasion of the fiftieth anniversary of the United Nations, President Clinton told the General Assembly, "We will help nations bring their banks and financial systems in conformity with international anti–money laundering standards, and, if they refuse, apply the appropriate sanctions."[163] But whereas the United States provided much of the initial impetus for the money laundering prohibition regime, it has very much taken on a life of its own, as evident in the metamorphosis of the FATF guidelines into regulations that are far more ambitious than its creators initially intended and the proliferation of regional-level FATF-style bodies across the globe.

Even as the money laundering prohibition regime has grown at a rapid pace, like the drug trafficking prohibition regime, the prospects of reaching the fifth stage of development appear slim due to the nature of the activity itself.[164] The days of walking into a major bank with duffel bags of cash without causing suspicion and attracting the attention of the authorities are long gone in most countries, but money laundering remains difficult to detect. Money launderers continue to have many methods and mechanisms for hiding and moving "dirty money" at their disposal and are willing to accept certain occupational risks due to the highly inflated profits of the activity.

Just as efforts to globally criminalize money laundering emerged out of the international drug prohibition campaign, the more recent efforts to globally criminalize terrorist financing have drawn on, been integrated into, and further expanded the anti–money laundering regime. Soon after the events of September 11, for example, the FATF's mandate was extended to formally include terrorist financing. This added "8 Special Recommendations" (subsequently nine) on terrorist financing and a revision of the initial "40 Recommendations," including the criminalization of terrorist financing and the freezing and confiscation of assets. The World Bank and the International Monetary Fund also began to include anti–money laundering and terrorist financing evaluations in their country assessments. September 11 clearly provided a catalyst: before then, only four countries were signatories to the 1999 International Convention for the Suppression of Terrorist Financing; after the attacks, the number jumped to 105. There was also unanimous passage of UN Security Council Resolution 1373 in the fall of 2001, much of which deals with ambitious requirements of all states to criminalize and tackle terrorist financing. Cooperation on combating terrorist financing also became a permanent part of the agendas of regional organizations such as the Association of Southeast Asian Nations and the Asia Pacific Economic Cooperation, the European Union, and the Organization of American States.[165]

Just as the U.S. government was able to use the drug issue to mobilize international support in criminalizing money laundering, so too has the unprecedented concern over the issue of terrorism in recent years been used by policy entrepreneurs to push governments across the globe to more intensively track and crack down on the financing of terrorism, including previously unregulated Islamic charities and informal financial systems. Yet, even as a global architecture has been quickly set up to combat terrorist financing—very much building on the preexisting anti–money laundering regulatory infrastructure and technical expertise—measuring its effectiveness has proven extremely difficult, and the overall amount of seized funds has been fairly modest. Beyond questions of effectiveness, however, the global mobilization against terrorist financing has proven symbolically popular as a political mechanism to signal collective disapproval and condemnation of transnational terrorism.[166]

Other international campaigns to prohibit the funding of violent non-state actors include initiatives to restrict the export of so-called "conflict diamonds" (also labeled "blood diamonds").[167] Since the late 1990s, international NGOs (most notably Global Witness), in collaboration with sympathetic Western governments, have taken the lead in drawing attention to, delegitimizing, and mobilizing international action to curb the clandestine export of alluvial diamonds used to fund armed conflicts in sub-Saharan Africa.[168] Transnational moral entrepreneurs have drawn further international attention to the issue by pointing to an alleged link between such smuggled diamonds and the financing of terrorism.[169] The targeting of conflict diamonds in recent years is the beginning of a potentially much larger effort to curb the production, trade, and sale of "conflict commodities" more generally, and the various regulatory models being promoted include the possibility of broadening and adapting existing and emerging tracking and enforcement mechanisms aimed at illicit financial and trade flows. Such ambitious proposals reflect the potential for integrating enforcement mechanisms across a wide range of global prohibition regimes.[170]

The United States has also taken the lead in pushing for a new global prohibition regime targeting intellectual property theft, formally institutionalized in the Trade-Related Aspects of Intellectual Property Rights (TRIPS) regime, which took effect in 1995. This newly emerging regime, which came out of the Uruguay Round Negotiations, outlines rules of enforcement and standards of protection and applies World Trade Organization (WTO) dispute settlement mechanisms to handle intellectual property rights disagreements between member states. Inclusion of intellectual property rights enforcement within the WTO gives it far more teeth than it would have had under the auspices of the UN's World Intellectual Property Organization. The fact that this is instead part of the

WTO is explained in large part by the hegemonic position of the United States and the inclusion of property rights protections as part of a larger package of issues agreed on during the Uruguay Round negotiation process.[171] Among its many requirements, TRIPS signatories are obligated to provide for criminal prosecution procedures against counterfeiting and piracy.[172] The regime's effectiveness so far appears rather limited, however, as evident in particularly egregious cases such as China, the world's top producer of a wide range of pirated goods. An emerging international prohibition regime and pressures from other governments (particularly the United States) has influenced China's copyright and patent laws but has yet to translate into more than minimal enforcement.[173]

Recent years have also witnessed the rapid rise of an international campaign to establish new global prohibition norms against corruption, focusing especially on the criminalization of bribery.[174] The 1997 Organization for Economic Cooperation and Development Convention on Combating Bribery of Foreign Public Officials in International Business Transactions represented widespread criminalization of an activity that at one time many countries considered to be a normal business practice.[175] Indeed, many countries had previously even classified bribes as a legitimate tax deduction. What began as a unilateral U.S. initiative to criminalize bribery through the U.S. Foreign Corrupt Practices Act of 1977 eventually turned into a much broader multilateral effort institutionalized through the OECD Convention, which required signatories to prohibit their corporations from paying bribes to foreign officials.[176] U.S. government policy entrepreneurs played an aggressive advocacy role. Patrick Glynn, Stephen Kobrin, and Moises Naim describe the process through which State Department officials in the 1990s pushed their ambitious agenda for policing bribery, both behind the scenes in negotiations with the OECD and in public through strategic use of the media. They note that European powers such as France and Germany initially resisted U.S. initiatives, protesting that Washington was trying to create and impose a standardized global criminal code, but eventually relented.[177] Pointing to the dominant position of the United States on this issue, Ivan Krastev has called the emerging global anticorruption norm "the Washington consensus on corruption."[178]

But whereas U.S. hegemonic leadership was an essential precondition for these changes, it was not a sufficient condition. Nonstate transnational moral entrepreneurs played a key role in mobilizing action to condemn and criminalize bribery practices. Particularly influential in this regard was Transparency International, founded in 1993 by former World Bank officials who quickly established local chapters in a growing number of countries across the globe.[179] As part of its international campaign to raise awareness of and draw attention to the bribery issue, in 1994 Transparency International began to publish an annual "Corruption Perceptions Index," providing a ranking of countries from most to least corrupt, and in 1999 also began to publish the "Bribe Payers Index." Even if based on impressionistic evidence, these annual rituals were an effective public shaming tactic that generated widespread media attention, and in turn made governments much more self-conscious of their international image. The World Bank and the IMF also joined the global anticorruption bandwagon, announcing that they would make corruption concerns a priority in the allocation of international loans and contracts.[180] The implementation of antibribery initiatives included using anti–money laundering rules as a mechanism to freeze and return bribe payments and embezzled and defrauded public funds related to international business transactions.

"By the beginning of 2000," write Jennifer McCoy and Heather Heckel, "the anti-corruption norm was globally recognized."[181] Indeed, in an effort to further expand and institutionalize this global norm, a United Nations Convention against Corruption was adopted in 2003.[182] The global anticorruption prohibition regime, especially in regard to prohibiting bribery, can be characterized as having reached the third stage of regime development.[183] In his 1984 book, *Bribes*, John Noonan provocatively predicted that "as slavery was once a way of life and now . . . has become obsolete and incomprehensible, so the practice of bribery in the central form of exchange of payment for official actions will [one day] become obsolete."[184] It is still too early to determine whether this bold prediction will become true or whether the international anticorruption campaign will someday be remembered as simply a passing global fad.[185]

Another area in which global prohibition regimes may play an increasingly prominent role is in efforts to protect the environment.[186] For instance, there are nascent global prohibitions to curtail cross-border hazardous waste dumping and the manufacture, use, and trade in ozone-depleting chlorofluorocarbons (CFCs), as evident in the Basel Convention[187] and the Montreal Protocol.[188] Transnational moral entrepreneurs, ranging from Greenpeace (in the case of the waste trade) to a global epistemic community of scientists (in the case of CFCs), have played leading roles in re-labeling these activities as environmental "bads."[189] Many governments are increasingly inclined to police cross-border violations of environmental laws not merely with civil regulatory agencies but also with criminal sanctions and agencies. As global prohibition regimes in these areas develop, sanctions against violators are likely to become increasingly punitive; the nature of the violators, moreover, will likely evolve from the legitimate corporations of today, who are willing and able to contend with civil fines and white-collar criminal charges, to entirely criminal individuals and organizations willing to assume greater risks in return for greater profits.

Finally, a particularly challenging and intriguing new frontier of global prohibitions is the criminalization of undesirable conduct in cyberspace. This nascent regime targets so-called cybercrimes, a rather vague umbrella term used to categorize a broad range of computer-related crimes, including the spread of computer viruses, child pornography, and pirated software, music, and films via the Internet. As summarized by P. N. Grabosky, this usually involves information systems as either vehicles or targets of crime, including dissemination of offensive materials, theft of information services, electronic money laundering, information piracy, counterfeiting and forgery, electronic vandalism and terrorism, illegal interception of information, and various types of fraud involving sales and investment and electronic funds transfers.[190] Some aspects of these transnational activities are novel, but for the most part they are simply old and familiar crimes using a new medium. As noted by the director of the U.S. Customs Service's Cybersmuggling Center, "We have not found any new crimes as a result of the internet." Criminals "are just finding new ways to commit old crimes."[191] Vandalism, for example, is an old practice and persistent police problem, but in the era of the Internet it has also become a transnational and electronically based concern. Whereas vandalism has historically been largely a local law enforcement matter, the emergence of cyberspace has given it the necessary transnational dimension to attract international policing attention. As with past regimes, the backing of major powers has been essential. The United States has played a key role in both defining cybercrimes and in promoting laws and law enforcement initiatives targeting such crimes. David Speer notes that at the 1997 and 1998 G-8 summits, "the United States was the country arguing most strongly for a prohibition regime targeting cybercrimes."[192] European backing has also played a prominent role, most evident in the 2001 completion of a Convention on Cybercrime, a "world cybercrime treaty," by the Council of Europe's Committee of Experts on Crime in Cyber-Space.[193] This document and its revisions and amendments (which entered into force in July 2004) have been a major focus of subsequent debates and initiatives to deter and detain so-called cybercriminals.[194] What some legal scholars have called an "emerging consensus on criminal conduct in cyberspace"[195] reflects a nascent global prohibition regime at the third stage of development.[196] The growing homogenization of laws in this policing realm has, in turn, facilitated globally coordinated sweeps against online crimes.[197] International criminal law enforcement has also required more active cooperation with nonstate actors in this area, given that most of the critical information infrastructure is owned or maintained by the private sector.

Having examined the cross-border homogenization of particular criminal law norms and their institutionalization at the global level, we now turn to the regularization of cross-border relations between different criminal justice systems. Our story begins in nineteenth-century Europe and then examines the late but rapid rise of the United States to a global leadership position in international crime control matters in the twentieth century.

CHAPTER TWO

☐ ☐ ☐

European Origins of International Crime Control

We now examine the historical roots and evolution of cross-border police relations. As in the preceding chapter, the theme of states weaving an ever tighter and more inclusive net of criminal justice controls is developed. But whereas the preceding chapter focused on the homogenization of criminal justice norms, this chapter analyzes the regularization of law enforcement across borders: the increasing frequency and intensity of international law enforcement interactions, the progression from unilateral to bilateral and multilateral initiatives, the creation and development of the infrastructures required to facilitate international interactions, and the emergence and consolidation of a transnational police subculture. Unlike the following chapter, which focuses on the internationalization of U.S. criminal law enforcement, this chapter is Eurocentric and regional in its orientation, given that so many of the important transnational developments in policing were initiated from and within Europe.[1]

Most recent developments in international criminal law enforcement represent a dramatic evolution from a century ago, when criminal investigators rarely pursued leads overseas and prosecutors rarely attempted to collect evidence from abroad. Extraditions were relatively infrequent in comparison with today. No international police organization existed, and international police contacts (apart from interactions between police officials working near national borders) were relatively rare. Few multilateral conventions addressed criminal activities of mutual concern to most states. The paucity of international law enforcement interactions until well into the nineteenth century should not, however, be confused with their absence. Most governments paid some attention to transnational criminality, even if their principal responses were confined to law enforcement actions along and within their borders. There were perennial concerns with smuggling, cross-border banditry, and itinerant vagabonds and brigands, although these were rarely met with extraterritorial law enforcement efforts. Focused principally on the transnational mobility of professional criminals and anarchists (and other political agitators), the rudiments of a transnational police community began to take shape during the second half of the nineteenth century.

The internationalization of policing cannot be comprehended without reference to the broader political, moral, and technological developments of which it has been a part. The consolidation of both the notion and the reality of nation-states during the past two centuries was a precondition to the internationalization of law enforcement. The nature of international criminal law enforcement was drastically transformed, moreover, by the destruction of empires, realignments of borders, and political reorientations of regimes that accompanied each of the world wars (just as it has been transformed by the realignments that swept Europe in the early 1990s). The international criminalizations described in the previous chapter, most notably of the international markets in psychoactive substances, have profoundly shaped the international law enforcement agenda. Technological developments in transportation, telecommunications, and information processing have dramatically enhanced the capacity of both transnational law evaders and law enforcers to operate across national borders.

In the pages that follow, we focus on the police over and above other criminal justice actors involved in the process of internationalization. Most international criminal law enforcement matters are handled by police, and have been ever since the role of navies in suppressing piracy and the slave trade and of armies in suppressing border banditry diminished during the nineteenth century. Police agents constitute most of the manpower and conduct most of the legwork. They have traditionally played the lead role in collecting and disseminating intelligence on transnational criminal activity. Also, they have been primarily responsible for finding, collecting, and delivering the information, evidence, and criminals to judicial authorities. Others may negotiate the agreements that provide the authorization and context for transnational police work; prosecutors and magistrates occasionally will coordinate and direct transnational criminal investigations. But international law enforcement has traditionally been largely the preserve of police.

The "High Police" and the "Low Police"

The roots of contemporary international criminal law enforcement can be traced in two directions. First, an essential precondition for the internationalization of law enforcement was the development, during the nineteenth century, of domestic criminal justice agencies, particularly criminal investigative, or detective, divisions within those agencies. This development arose as governments, confronting ever more populous and urbanized societies, sought the more efficient mechanisms of law enforcement associated with professional police agencies. The emergence of criminal investigative branches improved the capacity of governments to apprehend criminals at the same time that it provided elements of substance and continuity to international relations pertaining to crime. Also, it was a condition precedent to the emergence of a transnational police community, with its own value system and professional understandings, that would become the lifeblood of contemporary international law enforcement.

Second, the principal impetus for most of the early international law enforcement initiatives derived from concerns with criminal activities motivated not by passion or profit, but by politics—particularly the revolutionary activities of political émigrés. Some of these initiatives were undertaken by the "political police," otherwise known as the "high police" or the "secret service," but more often than not, and especially in cases involving violent acts, criminal investigative agencies were also involved. Indeed, many police agencies were routinely called on to conduct internal security, counterintelligence, and espionage tasks having little to do with enforcement of domestic criminal laws. States varied greatly in the degree to which they criminalized political activities and in the extent to which they separated the jurisdiction and functions of the criminal, or "low," police from those of the high police.[2] But given the penchant of most autocratic nineteenth-century European regimes to criminalize any activities that challenged their grip on power, a wide array of political offenders were readily targeted as criminal offenders. Governments reluctant to devote resources to immobilizing common criminals abroad did not hesitate to allocate resources to immobilizing democratic activists, violent anarchists, conspiring Bolsheviks, terrorists of various political stripes, and assassins of the rich and powerful (and indeed, quite a number of major international law enforcement initiatives were stimulated by the assassination of leading political figures).

Governments acted not just on their own but bilaterally and multilaterally, motivated by self-interest, mutual interest, and the pressures applied by other states. The ultimate consolidation and institutionalization of most multilateral law enforcement initiatives depended, however, on two developments: a convergence in perceptions as to which politically motivated acts merited criminalization and international law enforcement cooperation, and a mutual recognition among leading police officials that transnational criminality of an essentially apolitical character had become sufficiently common and noxious that more systemic means of cooperation were necessary. Neither of these developments really occurred on a substantial multinational level within Europe or anywhere else until the beginning of the twentieth century.

The distinction between the political policing functions of the high police and the more mundane crime control functions of the low police has not always been evident in practice. The functions that the police perform are all, to one degree or another, chores assumed by the state to serve its interests. The laws that they enforce, moreover, typically reflect the interests and prejudices of those who possess the greatest political power within the state.[3] Yet, despite the inevitable disagreements over the boundaries between high and low policing, or between political and common crime, certain distinctions are apparent. Political policing is generally directed at those individuals who challenge (or are perceived to challenge) the legitimacy and rules of a regime in ways not acceptable to the regime.[4]

The modus operandi of political police agencies typically differs in at least three respects from those of other police agencies (although all three distinctions are more a matter of degree than of absolute contrast). First, and most significant, whereas the low police generally seek to bring criminals within the clutches of the criminal justice system, the high police are rarely concerned with criminal prosecution; their principal objectives are the collection of political intelligence and the disruption of disapproved political activities. The high police regard themselves as primarily involved in a political process and struggle, in which resort to arrest and prosecution is no more than one option among many. They may be keen to avoid any entanglement with judicial processes, both because the courts, even in many relatively autocratic states, may circumscribe their operations and because judges may look less kindly upon their extrajudicial activities. Criminal investigators are not entirely immune to such considerations, as they, too, exercise all sorts of discretion in selecting their investigative priorities and targets and in juggling their relationships with informants and other collaborators. But by and large, the low police are primarily motivated to apprehend criminals by resort to the criminal justice system.

Second, high police are more likely than low police to act extralegally. The extent to which their activities lie outside the law is a function of regime type. The high police in many states tend to become more involved, for instance, in "black bag" operations, ranging from illegal break-ins, letter openings, and electronic surveillance, to physical threats, reliance on agents provocateurs, interrogations by torture, and murder—although none of these activities is unique to the high police. In quite a number of countries, for example, the police still rely on extrajudicial killings and torture, not just of political activists but of common criminals, as a convenient alternative to the often cumbersome and unreliable process of the criminal justice system.[5] Nonetheless, it is the political police, with their greater independence from legal oversight and laws and their association with the higher security interests of the state, that are most likely to engage in extralegal activities.

Third, the investigative methods of the political police tend to be far more invasive and often more aggressive and manipulative than those of the criminal investigators, although this distinction has faded quite dramatically within Europe in the past century and especially in the past few decades. Throughout the nineteenth and early twentieth century, for example, the use of undercover operations and the notorious role of the agent provocateur were far more intimately associated with political policing than with routine criminal investigation.[6] The same was true of the practice of pressuring those apprehended to inform on their fellow accomplices in return for compensation.

Many of the aggressive measures of the high police, in particular the employment of undercover agents, were greatly curtailed in democratic Europe as part of the popular reactions against authoritarian regimes that followed the world wars. But they now have returned to favor in most

European countries, reintroduced first by internal security agencies in reaction to the renewal of terrorist activity during the 1960s and then, far more widely, by criminal investigative agencies as a response to illicit drug trafficking. And again, especially in the poorer countries of the world, the aggressive measures of the high police continue to be common.

Most states draw some jurisdictional and bureaucratic distinctions between their political police and other police agencies. Some maintain political branches within their criminal investigative divisions; many others maintain entirely separate internal security services; and some possess both, reserving to the former, for instance, powers of arrest and permitting the latter far broader powers of investigation and detention. From the perspective of international policing, two issues are particularly important. The first is whether responsibility for extraterritorial counterespionage tasks and surveillance of expatriates and other perceived threats from nonstate actors abroad is delegated to political police agents connected to a criminal investigative agency or to a nonpolice intelligence agency charged either with internal security or foreign espionage. Insofar as the latter is the case, the issues that arise have relatively little to do with the processes of criminal law enforcement (or, for that matter, the substance of this book).

The second issue emerges from the unpleasant—and rarely admitted—fact that, in practice, many of the extraterritorial dimensions of political policing fall within the provinces of both criminal investigative and security/intelligence agencies, regardless of which is the formally delegated authority. The consequence is that much of international law enforcement is complicated not just by the sorts of frictions between different criminal justice systems that hamper ordinary transnational policing efforts, but also by fierce turf squabbles, divergent policy objectives, and fundamentally distinct investigative philosophies among agencies of the same government. Although not discussed much in the pages that follow, this issue has played a prominent role in shaping international action and inaction against transnational political criminality.[7]

The Emergence of International Criminal Law Enforcement in Europe

Dating the origins of a nation's police and detective agencies is a most haphazard enterprise.[8] There is the challenge of defining what is meant by the term "police."[9] There is the problem of distinguishing military and paramilitary enforcement of the law from police enforcement. There is the waxing and waning of police agencies as regimes fall to revolts and conquests. And there is the problem, in dating the origins of criminal investigative agencies, of assuming that there was ever a period in history when those charged with enforcement of the law did not use their deductive powers, investigative skills, informants, and "secret" agents to solve crimes.

At the least, one can date the origins of police in something resembling their contemporary form to 27 B.C., when the Roman emperor Augustus Caesar created a public police force to deal with political and other violence in Rome.[10] For our purposes, however, the appropriate date is the emergence of Europe's nation-states in the late Middle Ages.[11] In France, the origins of modern policing are most often traced to Louis XIV's appointment of Nicolas-Gabriel de La Reynie to the newly created post of lieutenant of police in 1667. Yet even this "pioneer in the art and science of policing the big city," as the police historian Philip John Stead has called him, cannot be credited either with establishing France's earliest detective force or with initiating its first international law enforcement actions. Cardinal Mazarin, in the years before Louis XIV took power, had created an organization of special agents called *exempts* to undertake secret police work. La Reynie maintained this force and was known to have sent his agents abroad when the need arose.[12]

The principal impact of the Parisian police beyond its borders was the example it provided to foreign regimes in constructing their own police forces. "It served as a model," Alan Williams has written, "to many of France's neighbors."[13] The Parisian police system was admired in part for its success in maintaining public order and dealing with the ills of urban society, but its most striking feature, one that both enticed and intimidated foreign regimes, was its pervasive intelligence system.[14] To European regimes deeply fearful of the contagious spread of new political ideas, the French system was attractive.

Police officials in Europe occasionally concerned themselves with keeping track of criminal fugitives who had fled abroad, but their primary concern beyond their borders was with political activists. In 1801, Napoleon I and Alexander I agreed in the Treaty of Paris to punish those within their jurisdiction engaged in activities against the regime of the other.[15]

Clemens von Metternich, who served as the Habsburg foreign minister from 1809 to 1848, acted as a powerful advocate of rigorous internal security systems and close international cooperation. Working closely with the Police Ministry, he emphasized the importance of maintaining tight surveillance of dissidents both within and without the empire. Informants and police agents were employed, mails intercepted, and strict controls placed on the entry of foreigners into the empire. Secret agents were sent abroad to spy on those suspected of subversive activities. Foreign monarchs and police chiefs were repeatedly urged to exchange information, keep track of subversives, arrest and extradite them if necessary, and impose common restrictions on the press as well as the movement of both citizens and foreigners across state borders.

Levels of cooperation varied depending on changes in regime, political interests, and police personnel. But by and large, the experience of Metternich during the 1820s—when his international law enforcement efforts generally met with favorable responses from fellow autocratic governments in Russia, Prussia, and Bavaria as well as the restored Bourbon government in France, but substantial resistance from the more liberal regimes in Switzerland and England[16]—set the stage for the next hundred years.

Police officials in Prussia were similarly active in promoting ties across jurisdictional borders both within and without the German Confederation. Between 1848 and 1856, the director of the Berlin Schutzmannschaft, Police President Carl Ludwig von Hinckeldey, fostered links with fellow police presidents elsewhere in Prussia and other German states; weekly police reports containing information on the movements and activities of social democrats and other purported agents of revolution were circulated among them.[17] Hinckeldey also established the formal Police Union of German States, which operated from 1851 to 1866. During the 1870s and 1880s, German police officials and leaders stepped up their efforts to suppress social democratic and anarchist activities. In 1871, Bismarck and the Austrian chancellor Beust met to discuss the international repercussions of the Paris Commune; in 1872, they met again to consider joint measures against socialist activists.[18] During the late 1870s and early 1880s, the Berlin police chief Guido von Madai maintained close contacts with top police officials throughout much of Europe.[19] The police director in Metz, France, sent photographs of social democrats and anarchists who had been deported from Switzerland in 1884–1885; direct ties with the tsar's political police were established via the Russian consulate in Koudriawtzew as well as between German and Russian police agencies at five border points, and informants recruited to spy on anarchists, social democrats, and Poles in Switzerland, Belgium, and elsewhere in Europe were shared; an active correspondence was maintained with police directors in Vienna, Paris, and other European capitals; and assistance was obtained, not always entirely willingly, from police in Denmark and Switzerland. In January 1885, Prussia and Russia signed an extradition treaty containing no exception for political offenders. All these efforts, Dieter Fricke wrote in his history of Bismarck's political police, were designed to create a "Police International" committed to the suppression of social democrats, anarchists, and all other revolutionaries.[20]

The "Third Department," created by Tsar Nicholas I in 1826 shortly after his accession to the throne the previous year, paralleled and complemented the efforts of the Habsburg higher police.[21] Under the direction of one of Nicholas's most trusted aides, General Benckendorff, it focused its efforts not just on subjects and foreigners within the borders of the empire but also on external activities. Much of the impetus arose in the aftermath of the Polish uprising of 1830–1831, when groups of Polish émigrés in France, England, and Belgium formed Polish Committees to agitate against the tsar.[22] Agents were sent abroad by the Third Department to investigate the Committees, to build up networks of informants, and to establish closer relations with local police organizations. In 1834, the governments of Russia, Austria, and Prussia agreed on a system of extradition. The following year, at the suggestion of Metternich, Benckendorff sent an aide to Vienna to work closely with the Austrian higher police.[23] During the 1840s, the Third Department's agents began to focus their surveillance efforts more closely on Russian émigrés, notably the Russian anarchist Mikhail Bakunin and the early socialist Aleksandr Herzen. In early 1849, Bakunin was arrested by police in Saxony following the suppression of the short-lived revolution in Dresden, handed over to the Austrians, and then in turn delivered to Russia, where he was imprisoned until 1857.[24] Although the actual extent of the Third Department's operations outside Russian borders has remained obscure, the memoirs of numerous Russian émigrés reveal the common perception that the tsar's agents were omnipresent throughout Europe.[25]

Even more active than the Third Department was its successor, the

Zagranichnaia Agentura, or Foreign Agency, of the tsarist political police agency known as the Okhrana, created shortly after the assassination of Tsar Alexander II in 1881 to deal with the antigovernment activism of its émigrés.[26] Based in the Russian embassy in Paris, the chief of the Foreign Agency and his two or three case agents relied on a network of informants drawn from among the émigré groups and on investigative and surveillance detectives recruited from among the local population. Their total numbers never amounted to more than thirty of the former and forty of the latter, with the plurality located in Paris and the remainder distributed around the continent. In 1901, a branch office was established in Berlin to keep track of the Russian revolutionaries and students in Germany.[27]

The Foreign Agency's effectiveness depended heavily on the willingness of local police to offer assistance. Bereft of any police powers, the tsarist agents in Europe had little choice but to cultivate good relations with local authorities in the hope that they would lend their powers and resources to controlling the émigré population. Contacts ranged from personal and professional relationships between the chief of the Foreign Agency and top officials at Scotland Yard, the Belgian Sureté, and other police agencies in Europe to informal relationships with low-level police officials and post office workers paid by the Russian agency without the knowledge of their superiors. These arrangements, Richard Johnson observed in his history of the Zagranichnaia Agentura, "were the outcome of a shared concern with radical activities, a developing sense of professional esprit de corps, various kinds of material and honorific rewards, and even . . . personal friendships among police officials."[28] The Foreign Agency also benefited greatly from the wave of antianarchist sentiment that spread throughout Europe toward the end of the century. Even the Swiss, British, and American authorities proved cooperative where violent activists threatened local security.[29]

The Foreign Agency confronted obstacles of two sorts. Representing the interests of a powerful and reactionary regime, the Russian agents were not formally welcomed throughout much of the continent. Liberal and socialist politicians objected to their governments' willingness to extend assistance, and regimes that maintained relatively distant relations with the tsar's government were not inclined to offer broad cooperation. Whereas the German police generally offered extensive cooperation to the Foreign Agency, for instance, police authorities in Vienna never warmed to its overtures.[30] Their mutual interests were generally limited to preventing acts of violence by the more radical émigrés. In Britain, France, Switzerland, and elsewhere, moreover, too ready acquiescence by a government to Russian demands could generate public outcries by the media and opposition politicians. Despite these political obstacles, the Foreign Agency was often able to secure extensive cooperation from local police who demonstrated, if not a common distaste for the radical Russian émigrés, a resentment at political interference with what they perceived as their professional concerns and prerogatives.

In Western Europe, French police performed much the same function during the Second Empire of Louis Napoleon Bonaparte as their Austrian and Russian counterparts.[31] Customs and postal officials tried to identify all people and correspondence crossing French borders. Secret agents were posted throughout Europe to keep track of the political activities of émigrés. Foreign police agencies were pressured to provide information on French agitators, to restrict their movement and propagandizing, to coordinate joint surveillance with French police, and occasionally to extradite or deport some of the émigrés to France. Particularly vigorous efforts were mounted in the years immediately following the 1848 Revolution, when many French police officials feared an "invasion" by political refugees from Great Britain, Italy, or Switzerland.[32] During the 1850s and for decades thereafter, French police found the Belgian police most cooperative, whereas the Swiss and especially the British governments both proved, not surprisingly, far more resistant to French police overtures.

Belgium's willingness to assist the French police was somewhat at odds with the liberal principles on which the nation had been founded following its revolutionary break from Dutch rule in 1830. But throughout the remainder of the century, Belgian authorities regarded "the surveillance of refugees . . . [as] synonymous with preserving the working classes from utopian and egalitarian theories."[33] Following the 1848 Revolution, Belgian police willingly assisted the French in surveilling the frontier region, tolerated the presence of French secret agents, conducted joint surveillance of refugees in Brussels with French police and prefects, and suppressed publications attacking the French regime.[34] French police thereafter worked quite closely with the Belgian Sureté, the Brussels police, and the Gendarmerie, all of which kept a hand in political policing.

The Brussels police began collecting information on suspects in 1848, when they "filled out and sent to the Sureté forms containing the civil status, occupation, means of support, past record, and morality of each foreigner seeking to reside either temporarily or permanently in Brussels."[35] Four years later, the Sureté created its own office to keep track of refugees. Thereafter, the two police agencies interchangeably cooperated and competed in their surveillance of foreigners and cooperation with foreign authorities, sending agents to attend meetings and rallies of foreign refugees, maintaining contact with French prosecutors and police, and extending substantial cooperation to police officials from France, Britain, Germany, and elsewhere.[36]

Quite a different response, however, generally awaited French, German, Russian, and Austrian police who sought assistance from Switzerland and Great Britain, "the mavericks in the history of European police cooperation since the days of the Metternich system."[37] Throughout much of the century, political refugees from autocratic regimes in Europe flocked to Great Britain and Switzerland, where they generally remained safe so long as they refrained from violence within those countries. In both countries, popular sentiment powerfully supported the right of asylum, and citizens expected their governments to act accordingly. The relative immunity did not, however, include immunity from the pressures exerted by more autocratic neighbors anxious to get their hands on expatriate troublemakers. Governments in both countries found themselves squeezed between the demands of foreign governments and popular domestic pressures to the contrary. Switzerland in particular was subjected to frequent and intense pressures, to which it occasionally succumbed. In 1822, the Congress of Verona authorized Metternich to demand, on behalf of the French, Austrian, Russian, and Prussian governments, that the Swiss take strong action against the refugees; fearful of Metternich's threats, and of the potential for military intervention, the Swiss Federal Diet passed the Press and Aliens Conclusum of 1823, which restricted the ability of political refugees to enter and remain in the country.[38]

In response to strong pressures from Napoleon III, many French refugees were removed from border regions or expelled.[39] From 1870 to 1890, a continuing flow of anarchist and socialist refugees into Switzerland added to diplomatic problems for the Swiss. When the pressures became too great, the government responded with expulsions of those refugees who refused to forgo their political activism, as well as suppression of their newspapers. Under intense pressure from both Berlin and Vienna in 1884–1885 following a series of anarchist assassinations, the Swiss government assented to a request that they open their police files on resident anarchists to a top German police official.[40] In 1889, tensions between Switzerland and Germany rose to threatening heights when Swiss police arrested and expelled a Prussian police official named Wohlgemuth who had been trying to hire Swiss informants.[41] Yet, despite the series of accommodations to foreign pressures, the persistent migration of political refugees into Switzerland throughout the century provided continuing evidence that its reputation for political asylum remained intact.

Although far less susceptible to foreign threats than Switzerland, Great Britain was not entirely averse to accommodating foreign requests when other interests were at stake.[42] Perhaps the most notorious case of British acquiescence to a foreign request for assistance was revealed in 1844, when a Radical member of Parliament announced that the post office, at the request of the Austrian ambassador, had been opening the mail of Giuseppe Mazzini, then exiled in London, and informing the ambassador of its contents.[43] The practice of opening mail, in fact, dated back centuries to the Tudor period; it had played a central role in the detection of antigovernment conspiracies during the seventeenth century, when both King Charles II and King James II relied on the surveillance practice extensively.[44] The revelations regarding Mazzini's letters, and the provision of confidential information to the despised Austrians, infuriated the British public and Parliament. What so incensed the British public about the Mazzini incident was not just the sense, well articulated by the Irish orator Richard Sheil in his speech before Parliament, "that the British nation [had been] degraded by playing eavesdropper for the Austrian and Russian despotisms,"[45] but disgust at the thought that British officials should be involved in so invasive an activity on anyone's behalf. A persistent theme in British public opinion throughout the century, both in reaction to the gradual development of a uniformed police force and thereafter a plainclothes detective division, was a common revulsion at the police systems and spy networks created by the French and imitated elsewhere.

Confronted with such a powerful popular prejudice against spying and police surveillance in general—one shared by many British leaders—foreign governments were often frustrated in their efforts to obtain information and other satisfaction regarding those who had sought asylum on the British Isles. Britain's policy was not, it should be stressed, one of consistent refusal to extend any sort of cooperation to foreign authorities. Instead, it combined public refusals intended primarily for domestic consumption with discreet efforts at international police cooperation, intended primarily to appease foreign authorities. Information was provided, some of it useful, but never any people. During the 1850s, some fifteen hundred refugees were induced with financial incentives to emigrate to North America. This policy both alleviated Britain's refugee burden and pleased the police authorities on the continent, who regarded the other side of the Atlantic as a much less worrisome haven for their exiles.[46] Unlike the Belgian government, however, British leaders expressed relatively little fear of the assorted revolutionaries in their midst. They focused their efforts on deterring any acts of violence on British territory and, to a lesser extent, on investigating refugee conspiracies to commit violent acts on the continent. But by and large, they regarded the British public, including the working classes, as not particularly susceptible to the accented oratory of the continental radicals.

The most serious incident during this period occurred in 1858, following a bomb attack in Paris by an Italian refugee, Felice Orsini, that failed to kill the intended target, Napoleon III, but that did kill eight bystanders.[47] The disclosure that Orsini had planned his attack while in England led to intense diplomatic pressures on the British government, including a threat by Napoleon III to break off diplomatic relations. Efforts by the prime minister, Palmerston, to appease the French emperor by proposing in Parliament a law directed at conspiracies to assassinate foreign leaders failed, however, when the bill was rejected amidst a popular backlash against the foreign pressure.[48] Britain's efforts on behalf of foreign authorities were even more meager thereafter.

The one great exception to Britain's distaste for spying involved Ireland and the Fenian nationalist movement—a threat that, as Gladstone put it, had its roots in Ireland but its branches in America.[49] From the 1860s onward, the British government relied on its police and other official representatives, as well as a collection of informants and undercover agents, in Britain, Ireland, Canada, and the United States to collect information on Fenian plots and activities. Scotland Yard's detectives, as well as an occasional uniformed policeman from the London police department, kept tabs on Fenian movements throughout England and pursued their investigations to Ireland and the continent. Assistance was sought, and often obtained, from the U.S. State Department, from federal, state, and local police (in particular those in New York City), and from the Pinkerton Detective Agency.[50]

It was during these years that a Special Irish Branch was created within Scotland Yard and charged with surveillance of Fenian activities in London. Its agents, however, constituted only a small portion of the total anti-Fenian effort mounted during the 1880s, which included sending agents to Le Havre, Rotterdam, Antwerp, Bremerhaven, and Hamburg, and placing a contingent of up to six agents in Paris.[51]

Cooperation from foreign authorities was, not surprisingly, relatively restrained given Britain's long-standing reluctance to reciprocate in kind. On one occasion, the agents in Paris even found themselves placed under arrest by local police.[52] But following Fenian bomb attacks on Westminster Palace and the Tower of London in early 1885, the French police obliged the British government by arresting and deporting a few leading Fenians from France.[53] By 1887, the Fenian threat had receded and the anti-Fenian network was accordingly reduced in size and reorganized. In the administrative reorganization that followed, a separate Special Branch created within Scotland Yard was eventually merged with the Special Irish Branch; the result was the Special Branch that has survived into the early twenty-first century.[54]

In 1881, just as British police officials were beginning to focus more seriously on the Fenian threat, the assassination of Tsar Alexander II in St. Petersburg prompted renewed pressures on all European regimes, including Britain, to cooperate against the anarchists and other activists within its borders. Among Britain's first actions was the prosecution and subsequent imprisonment of a resident German anarchist, Johann Most, for publishing in his newspaper, *Freiheit*, an article that lauded the assassination and called for more.[55] The prosecution, British officials readily observed, served Britain's interests in a variety of ways, notably in appeasing the demands on the continent for more vigorous action against the anarchists and in strengthening its requests to the Americans to clamp down on a Fenian newspaper in New York, the *Ulster Irishman*.[56]

With the waning of the Fenian threat, the British turned more of their attention to the European anarchists and other revolutionaries found in Britain, including that bane of the tsarist Foreign Agency, Vladimir Burtsev.[57] The chief inspector of the Special Branch from 1893 to 1903,

William Melville, is believed to have spent a number of years thereafter as Britain's special antianarchist agent on the continent.[58] By 1909, the Special Branch included thirty-eight officers, up from twenty-five in 1895 but still small in comparison with the political police agencies to be found on the continent.[59]

With the turn of the century, British police officials turned their attention to a series of other perceived political threats: German spies, Russian nihilists, English suffragettes, and Egyptian and Indian nationalists resident in London.[60] The assassination in London of Sir William Curzon Wyllie, the political aide de camp to the secretary of state for India, by an Indian student in July 1909 was the event that catalyzed police action against Indian nationalists.[61] The Special Branch had kept track of Indian activists in London as part of its overall surveillance of Fenians, anarchists, and other potentially violent political groups. Following the assassination, a small section was created within the Special Branch to focus on the Indians.[62] The British Home Office's New York branch, which focused most of its energies on Fenian activities, had also begun collecting information on Indian activists and their contacts with the Fenians, as had the Canadian police. But the task of keeping track of the worldwide activities of the Indian revolutionaries quite naturally fell to the government of India's Department of Criminal Intelligence (DCI). Scotland Yard's preoccupation was with the security of London, not India. Although willing to send agents to the continent on Indian matters, Police Commissioner Sir Edward Henry was not keen on stationing anyone there. And the French police were far from receptive to British requests for assistance. The Indian DCI accordingly took matters into its own hands. Early in 1909, a secret agent, "C," was placed in London without the knowledge of Scotland Yard to collect intelligence on nationalist activities there. When his reports began providing information that Scotland Yard had failed to collect, two additional agents were sent and a decision was made to create a new Indian Secret Service for Europe.

In January 1910, John Arnold Wallinger, the police superintendent in Bombay, was chosen as the "itinerant officer" charged with setting up the intelligence network. Seconded to the India Office in London, he quickly applied his diplomatic and detective skills to the recruitment of informants and the establishment of close personal ties with police officials in London, Paris, and elsewhere throughout the continent. Central to Wallinger's success, Richard Thurlow observed, "was his ability by *personal* contacts in Great Britain and in France to overcome the *official* difficulties brought by each country's tradition of political asylum."[63] As Wallinger himself observed in a report to his superiors:

> You can put proposals and carry on work through [me] which it would be impossible to do officially—either direct with the India Office or Scotland Yard, as both in most cases are unwilling to act owing to political considerations. [I] can visit any of the Government officials and do what is necessary, without it being interpreted as an official act. . . . The continental Police dare not correspond officially on matters political, except through the recognized channels; which would really mean a waste of everyone's time.[64]

By contrast with Wallinger's efforts in Europe, surveillance of Indian nationalists in North America was left primarily to the Canadians and the British.[65] On the West Coast, the principal agent charged with surveillance of Indian nationalists in both Canada and the United States from 1909 to 1914 was an Englishman, William Hopkinson, who had served in the Indian Police prior to leaving for Canada. Based in Vancouver, his employer was not the DCI but the Canadian Department of the Interior, which had become concerned over the Indian presence in British Columbia following a serious race riot in 1907. Hopkinson's relationship with the DCI remained relatively distant until 1913, when he traveled to London and was put on retainer by the DCI. Even thereafter, the DCI preferred to keep its relationship with Hopkinson on an unofficial basis, recognizing that his effectiveness in the United States would be enhanced by his not being associated with a "repressive colonial regime." The Canadian agent proved effective at his task, establishing a substantial network of informants among West Coast Sikhs as well as fairly close but discreet relations with U.S. immigration officials, operating (according to some reports) undercover and in disguise and providing his superiors with highly regarded reports on the activities of the Sikh Ghadr Party and other Indian nationalists up and down the Pacific coast.[66] In February 1914, U.S. immigration authorities obliged Hopkinson by arresting the Indian nationalist and anarchist Har Dayal.[67] As with Wallinger's initiatives in Europe, the success of Hopkinson's American activities was primarily a function of his ability to recruit reliable informants and establish close personal relationships with foreign officials of a government that might well have repudiated his efforts had they been pursued more openly or exposed publicly.

The Development of Criminal Investigative Bodies

The relationship between the development of political police agencies and of criminal investigative branches varied from one state to another. In virtually all states, governments relied on domestic spy networks of one sort or another long before any consideration was ever given to the creation of relatively apolitical criminal investigative agencies. But in many states, the creation of political police agencies with some connection to criminal law enforcement awaited the establishment of detective branches in low police agencies. Such was the case in Britain, and in many other states in which detective branches emerged from the uniformed civilian police agencies. On the continent, high police agencies often developed independently of criminal investigative branches, which often were associated with urban police departments rather than directly subordinate, as the high police generally were, to the central government. In some countries, such as France, the pervasive police state apparatus construed the interests of the state as well as its own mandate so broadly that its political functions and its less politicized criminal investigative functions often seemed as one.

Prior to the creation of criminal investigative divisions in most countries, uniformed police officials occasionally conducted criminal investigations and relied on intelligence garnered from both ordinary citizens and informants. Often such investigative tasks were initiated and directed by magistrates and prosecutors. The credit for establishing the first plainclothes bureau to investigate crimes has traditionally been bestowed on François Eugene Vidocq, an ex-convict and police informer who in 1812 set up the investigative agency that became known as the Brigade de la Sureté. Vidocq developed and routinized many of the detective methods that have become so central to American criminal investigations, in particular the use of informants cultivated from the criminal milieu to provide information. These informants were cultivated then as they are today, by being given the choice when apprehended of working for the police or going to jail. The most unusual feature of Vidocq's agency was that both he and all those he recruited as detectives were ex-convicts; one advantage of this recruitment requirement was that most of his agents excelled at undercover investigations. Vidocq also was among the first to use both ballistics tests and blood tests to solve crimes.[68]

In England, the first detectives were all too close descendents of the "thief-takers" of the seventeenth and eighteenth centuries. These self-appointed detectives were rewarded by communities or the government for apprehending fugitives. With few compunctions about handing in both guilty and innocent parties for the reward, the thief-takers were often little different from the worst criminals. The most notorious of their lot was Jonathan Wild,

> who grew up as a confidence man and highwayman and secretly organized the London underworld—an ancestor of the American gangster boss. Wild dubbed himself "thief-taker general of Great Britain and Ireland." He always carried a gold-headed cane, and he maintained an office in London and owned a country estate with a large corps of servants. He delivered some hundred highwaymen to the courts and the gallows—always those who refused to submit to his organization. In 1725 he himself, convicted of robbery, went to the gallows at Tyburn.[69]

In the middle of the eighteenth century, a justice of the peace who doubled as a novelist, Henry Fielding, persuaded the home secretary to allocate some of the Secret Service's funds for what became a primitive predecessor of Vidocq's Sureté. Known as the Bow Street Runners, Fielding's small group of detectives employed many of the same methods later associated with Vidocq and received compensation from both the public purse and private employers of their services. Within a few years of their creation, they had become, Leon Radzinowicz wrote, "something of a national institution."[70] But they, too, proved highly susceptible to the sorts of illicit tactics and inducements that had discredited the thief-takers before them.[71]

Britain acquired its closest equivalent to Vidocq's creation in 1842, following a series of heinous crimes that pointed to the need for more effective criminal investigation. The home secretary, Robert Peel, had already created a uniformed police force of one thousand men in 1829, overcoming popular opinion to do so. During the 1830s, a few of the more talented of these policemen, some of them from the Bow Street Runners, were drawn by need and curiosity to investigate certain crimes that required that they employ detective skills. By the end of the decade, this select group had come to be known as "active officers." In 1842 their status was formalized when the Home Office agreed to the creation of a Detective Department within the Metropolitan Police.[72] Based out of a few offices in Scotland Yard, these were the first police officers to become known as "detectives."[73]

The creation of detective divisions elsewhere normally followed a pattern similar to that in London and Paris. In some cases, notably the principal cities in British and French colonies, they were deliberately imitated and even implemented by police officials imported from the metropolis.[74] Typically, a particularly resourceful individual or group within the police force would be asked, or would volunteer, to undertake a criminal investigation of greater difficulty than the norm, and within a few years or decades, their functions would be institutionalized within the department. Not long after the creation of the detective units in each city, the new agents found themselves called on to look beyond their jurisdictions. Detectives in Glasgow investigating stolen goods transported from Ireland, for instance, were obliged to contact the master of police in Greenock.[75] In 1835, Dublin detectives traveled to Birmingham to collect an embezzler who had fled across the Irish channel.[76] In 1864, the notion of police detectives chasing down fugitives who had fled abroad seized British attention. Investigating the first railroad murder in British history, a Scotland Yard detective, Dick Tanner, learned that the suspect, a German tailor named Franz Mueller, had sailed for the United States aboard the sailing ship *Victoria*. According to Jürgen Thorwald's account of the investigation:

> On July 20, a warrant in his pocket and a few important witnesses accompanying him, Dick Tanner boarded the steamship *City of Manchester*. The swift steamer arrived in New York two weeks before the *Victoria*. When the sailing vessel at last arrived, a number of busybodies rowed out to it in a boat and shouted up to the deck: "How are you, Murderer Mueller?" Tanner made his arrest on the dock, and reached England again on September 16. Two months later, Mueller was hanged.[77]

Less than a decade later, the search for a few sophisticated swindlers who had perpetrated a sizable fraud on the Bank of England found one of them in Havana and another in New York. A cablegram from Inspector Bailey of the City of London Police to Superintendent Kelso of the New York City Police assured the arrest of one, George McDonald, upon his arrival in the United States. Following an extradition proceeding instituted by the British consul and American agents of the Bank of England, three British detectives were delegated to return the fugitive to British justice.[78] Two of the detectives then proceeded to Havana, where the Spanish colonial authorities had agreed to hand over the (American) fugitive, Austin Bidwell, despite the absence of an extradition treaty between Britain and Spain.

In all of these matters, the American Pinkerton Detective Agency played a substantial role, having been hired by the Bank of England to catch the globe-trotting defrauders.[79] In 1877, Scotland Yard once again became involved in a transnational investigation of a major fraud in France. Although the perpetrators were caught and convicted, revelations that they had bribed a number of British police officers, including a "Detective Druscovitch, who was specially charged with the Continental business at Scotland Yard," led to a major scandal, the appointment of a committee of inquiry, and the wholesale reorganization of Scotland Yard.[80]

Multilateralism in European Policing

The decades prior to the First World War were marked by significant advances in the internationalization of both crime and law enforcement. Greater ease of travel and communication as a result of both technological and political developments were largely responsible, but criminals, in the eyes of most observers, proved both quicker and more adept than criminal justice authorities in responding to the new opportunities. In 1893, Franz von Liszt, a professor of criminology at Berlin University, pointed out the growing gap between criminals' multinational activities and the provincial focus of national police agencies.[81] It was a time, he wrote, "when the professional thief or swindler feels equally at home in Paris, Vienna or London, when counterfeit rubles are produced in France or England and passed in Germany, when gangs of criminals operate continuously over several countries."[82] The same considerations and consequences of national sovereignty that hindered international police efforts provided abundant opportunities for criminals to commit crimes and avoid detection or apprehension. Police were limited not just by sovereign restrictions on their police powers beyond their borders, but by political conflicts, diplomatic formalities, different systems of identification, and varying methods of investigation. Criminals, by contrast, suffered few comparable limitations.

The principal legal strategy of governments throughout much of the nineteenth century was to negotiate extradition treaties authorizing and committing one another to deliver fugitives from justice. According to one count, upwards of ninety extradition treaties were concluded between 1718 and 1830, almost all between contiguous, or nearly contiguous, states. Twenty-eight of these treaties dealt exclusively with military deserters, who tended to take to the roads as brigands and vagabonds; seventeen concerned frontier offenses, especially those committed in boundary forests, and recognized a right of hot pursuit; and the remainder alluded to criminals generally or a listing of various types of offenders.[83] Toward the middle of the nineteenth century, the number of extradition treaties began to proliferate rapidly, a consequence of both the increase in the number of fugitives seeking refuge abroad and of the increasingly widespread incorporation of Cesare Beccaria's humanitarian principles of criminal justice by diverse legal systems. (The publication in 1764 of Beccaria's influential *Essay on Crime and Punishments*, with its advocacy of more enlightened and humane criminal justice measures, provided the first significant application of Enlightenment thinking to criminal justice issues.) At the forefront of the extradition field in Europe was France, which claimed twenty-eight extradition treaties in force by 1870. "The important substantive treaty provisions commonly contained in modern extradition treaties," I. A. Shearer wrote in his treatise on extradition, "were initiated by France: the non-extradition of nationals, the exception of political offenders, the concept of speciality, the exception of prescriptive offenses and the inclusion of convicted as well as accused offenders."[84] By the end of the nineteenth century, all of the major European states were parties to extradition treaties with states beyond their neighbors.

A second series of developments favoring the internationalization of law enforcement were the efforts of scholars in the areas of comparative criminal law, criminology, and criminal policy. The International Penal and Penitentiary Commission, founded at Bern in 1874, took the lead in organizing conferences at which scholars and officials compared and exchanged approaches for dealing with "new forms of criminality, the problem of persistent offenders, the prison system and what later came to be called the treatment of offenders."[85] The efforts of both scholars and practitioners to apply the various insights of the evolving social sciences to the study of crime yielded the discipline of criminology.[86] The desire to integrate the new criminological insights into the study and formation of criminal justice policy inspired von Liszt, G. A. van Hamel, and Adolphe Prins to found the International Association of Penal Law in 1888.[87] "One might assert, as a general principle," Marc Ancel theorized, "that the moment a criminal problem is no longer viewed solely from the angle of pure legal technique, it is immediately internationalized."[88] The search for scientific insights into questions of crime and crime control required comparative analysis, and the search for more effective means of investigating and controlling criminal activity inevitably led reformers to examine what other states were doing.

Proliferating in tandem with the extradition treaties and criminological conferences were the international activities of Europe's police agencies. As the Sureté, Scotland Yard, and other criminal investigative departments around Europe gained in sophistication and resources, their international activities gained in frequency. Acting both unilaterally and cooperatively, police agencies began to collect and share information on criminals who had crossed borders with foreign counterparts. Counterfeiting by both common criminals and political activists was of particular concern. In 1865, the Russian Finance Ministry stationed an agent, Gabriel Kamensky, in Paris for the specific purpose of investigating counterfeiting. Working closely with French and Swiss police, he successfully uncovered a number of counterfeiting ventures before being arrested in 1871 by Swiss police for abetting those he was supposed to be investigating.[89]

Opportunities to establish contacts were also created by the growing professionalism of criminal investigation. Aspiring criminal investigators from around the world flocked to study with the leading criminologists; the treatises of some, such as Hans Gross, were translated and circulated widely.[90] Journals on police science were founded that contributed to the dissemination of new investigative techniques around the world. In the 1870s, a successful candidate for the position of chief of Scotland Yard, Sir

Howard Vincent, bolstered his campaign by visiting the Sureté and drafting a report on the organization of its detective system.[91] Police officials from Asia, Latin America, and elsewhere toured European cities in search of lessons for organizing and modernizing their own agencies. A yearlong investigation of European police systems in 1872 by Kawaji Toshiyoshi, the founder of the modern Japanese police, resulted in Japan's adoption of the French model, although that was rejected a decade later in favor of the German model.[92] In the 1890s, police experts from around Europe converged on Paris to learn the new anthropometric method of criminal identification created by, and named after, Alphonse Bertillon.[93] Within a decade, similar contacts were resulting in the substitution or addition of fingerprinting for the less efficient *bertillonage* system.[94]

As the collection and analysis of criminal intelligence improved around the world, police simultaneously found it more useful to communicate with and assist their foreign counterparts. Some, such as those in Paris and Brussels, exchanged photo albums containing mug shots of local criminals and established direct and continual telephone contact.[95] But the more they attempted to extend their investigations internationally and to work with foreign counterparts, the more they encountered political, bureaucratic, and legal obstacles to efficient cooperation. One response was to convene international conferences at which the challenges of transnational crime and the frustrations of international law enforcement could be addressed.

Perhaps the first multinational gathering of police officials was the Central Investigation Commission created by the Bundestag of the German Confederation at the initiative of Metternich in September 1819. "Its charge," the historian Hsi-Huey Liang wrote,

> was to investigate the origin and the ramifications of the current revolutionary agitation in Germany against the constitution and the domestic peace of the Bund and of its separate states. Seven federal states were elected to appoint the members of the commission whose seat was to be at Mainz: they were Austria, Prussia, Hannover, Bavaria, Baden, the Grand Duchy of Hesse, and Nassau. Its field of activity was limited to the territory of the Deutscher Bund, though discreet investigations were also made in Alsace through covert agents, and the Commissioners' sources of information included Swiss and French newspapers.[96]

Its final report, issued in 1828, concluded that the future of Germany depended less on what government and revolutionaries did inside the confederation than on outside forces.

When revolutions swept through Europe in 1848, most governments responded not with police force but with massive military power. Following the restoration of order, military-style police forces were introduced in Prussia, Austria, and other nations most affected by the revolutions. "International police solidarity," Liang observed, "was for a moment a very persuasive doctrine as each country faced the possibility of renewed internal outbreaks and with the exception of France eschewed ambitious foreign political activities."[97]

The revolutions of 1848, though more national than transnational in character, were the first in which the news passed from town to town by telegraph. In their wake could be seen the first real glimmerings of international police consciousness. Obliged to keep track of the unprecedented flood of political refugees unleashed by the revolutions and increasingly aware of the transnational capabilities of common criminals, top police officials throughout Europe began to take a few tentative steps toward communicating with one another.

By the 1870s, the agitations of anarchists, socialists, nihilists, and other opponents of the conservative regimes were increasingly transnational in character, or at least so they appeared to European law enforcement authorities, who tried to respond in kind.[98] The assassination of Tsar Alexander II in 1881 produced a flurry of contacts among police officials in Berlin, Vienna, and St. Petersburg as well as a diplomatic initiative to convene an international conference.[99] Similar developments followed the assassination of French president Sadi Carnot by an Italian terrorist in 1894. But in both cases, efforts to generate multilateral action faltered, in good part because of British resistance.

The murder of the popular Empress Elizabeth of Austria by a young Italian anarchist in September 1898, however, provided the necessary stimulus for action.[100] The Italian government, under pressure from Berlin and Vienna, called for a pan-European conference to coordinate the suppression of anarchist violence and propaganda.[101] With England no longer so resistant to the notion, in part because growing numbers of anarchist fugitives had sought haven in Britain, the conference convened in Rome. Fifty-four delegates representing twenty-one countries attended; ambassadors and other diplomats were joined by the national police chiefs of Russia, France, and Belgium as well as the municipal police chiefs of Berlin, Vienna, and Stockholm.

The results of the conference were by no means extraordinary. Proposals that the members adopt similar antianarchist legislation were voted on favorably in Rome but had little consequence thereafter. The attendees agreed that all of the states should adopt a refinement of the bertillonage system known as *portrait parle* for both anarchists and common criminals; most of the members did, in fact, do so during the following decade, although all eventually switched to the fingerprint system. The attendees also responded favorably to a Russian proposal that all states include a clause in their extradition treaties providing that attacks on heads of state or their families be made grounds for extradition. Known as the "Belgian" or *attentat* clause, it was rapidly adopted by governments eager to respond to the rash of anarchist attacks on heads of state during the 1890s.

The most significant impact of the conference, however, was the increase in international police cooperation that followed. The attendees approved a German proposal requiring each state to establish a central agency to keep a close watch on anarchists and to facilitate direct communications with other central agencies. The central offices were authorized to bypass diplomatic channels, to expedite their communications by means of telephone and telegraph, and to drop all formal addresses and salutations in their written correspondence. Many of the governments took steps to implement this proposal thereafter. Equally important, the conference provided a valuable opportunity for the police officials present in Rome to establish closer professional and personal relations.[102] The "international system" created in Rome, Sir Howard Vincent later claimed, had effectively prevented serious anarchist incidents during the following year and a half.[103]

The assassination of the U.S. president William McKinley in September 1901 by a Hungarian-born anarchist, Leon Czolgocz, triggered calls for a second meeting to reinvigorate and strengthen the outcomes of the Rome conference—although once again, the U.S. government declined to become involved.[104] During the two years of negotiation that followed, most European governments refused to accede to the more far-reaching legislative and extradition proposals put forward by the tsar's representatives; most also refused to support a proposal requiring governments to surrender all foreign anarchists on demand. But in a secret protocol signed by ten European states (albeit not England, France, or Switzerland) in St. Petersburg in March 1904, the governments did agree to regularize the co-operative arrangements agreed on in Rome. The significance of the St. Petersburg conference, and of the Rome conference that preceded it, Richard Bach Jensen has argued, was their success in transforming the European response to anarchist violence from one that was essentially political to one in which the bureaucratic and technical challenges confronting European police agencies could be addressed in their own right.[105]

By the end of the century, not just anarchists but growing numbers of smugglers, swindlers, counterfeiters, and other sorts of fraud artists and common criminals were crossing national borders with increasing frequency. The white slave trade was high on the agenda of international police concerns, a consequence less of the magnitude of the problem than of the vigorous efforts by moral entrepreneurs in Europe and the United States. The results were the convocation in London in 1899 of the First International Congress for the Suppression of the White Slave Traffic, attended by delegates from eleven countries;[106] a police conference on the subject in Paris in July 1902 attended by representatives of sixteen states; a May 1904 conference in Paris at which more than a dozen European states and Brazil signed a convention on white slavery; and a follow-up conference in Paris in 1910 addressed to the traffic in pornography.[107] Among the more significant consequences of the 1902 conference was the creation of white slavery offices in most European police departments, charged in part with facilitating international cooperation against the trade. (According to one report, all these efforts resulted in yet another conference, in Warsaw in 1913, which was attended not by the police but by the traffickers themselves. Their plans to concoct a counterstrategy, however, were disrupted by a police raid.)[108]

More general police matters were discussed at international police conferences in Madrid in 1909, São Paulo in 1912, and Washington in 1913, as well as at meetings of the International Criminological Association and federal police conferences in Germany.[109] Comparable regional efforts were also under way in Latin America, where European military and police advisors had trained many of the national police and constabulary forces.[110] But despite the proliferation of conferences and cross-border interactions between police agencies, meaningful international cooperation against criminals remained relatively sporadic. In an otherwise flattering survey of European police systems shortly before the outbreak of World War I, the American scholar Raymond Fosdick concluded:

> There has been no consistent international action [against crime] worthy the name. To be sure, criminal records are often exchanged between nations on the basis of special treaties and a few cities co-operate in reference to certain cases or classes of cases. . . . But of broad cooperation on a systematic basis there is none. Indeed, the difficulties in the way of such actions are not to be minimized. Diplomatic usage and the prescribed formalities of official communication between nations have greatly complicated the task. If a thief operating in Berlin is thought to have made his escape to England, the Berlin police may not communicate directly with Scotland Yard. The information must first be sent to the Prussian Minister of the Interior, by him to the German Ambassador in London, by him to the British Secretary for Foreign Affairs, by him to the Home Secretary, and by him to Scotland Yard. . . . [Such] is the common practice among civilized nations everywhere. To be sure, some of the police departments, particularly Paris and London, occasionally communicate directly with each other, leaving the diplomatic formalities to follow in their own good time, but this practice is irregular and is generally frowned upon in high places.[111]

Fosdick went on to fault the lack of a uniform system of identification, criticizing harshly those who clung to the Bertillon system, and stressed the need for an international bureau of identification, a universal extradition treaty, common police codes or ciphers to facilitate international police communication, and a uniform method of distributing information on international criminals.[112]

Many of the criticisms and proposals discussed by Fosdick were debated at another international criminal justice conference in Monte Carlo in April 1914, shortly before the outbreak of World War I.[113] The impetus for the meeting was provided by Monaco's police chief, Henri Smart, whose reliance on international cooperation to effectively police his jurisdiction was accentuated by Monaco's size.[114] Sponsored by Prince Albert I of Monaco, the First International Congress of Judicial Police drew more than three hundred law enforcement and other public officials, lawyers, and scholars from most of Europe as well as Persia and four Latin American countries: Brazil, Cuba, Guatemala, and El Salvador. The vast majority of the delegates, however, were French. With nationalist sentiments running rampant and the majority demanding that all opinions be expressed in their native tongue, the potential for concrete accomplishments was limited at best.[115] The participants discussed ways of improving international efforts to track down fugitives; among the suggestions was a proposal that international reports be circulated in Esperanto. The resolutions adopted included proposals for the establishment of centralized international criminal records and standardized extradition procedures.[116] Plans to move forward with the proposals were set awry by the onset of world war.

The Origins of Interpol

In 1919, as old and new governments alike sought order in the aftermath of World War I, the prewar proposals were promoted once again. The first was advanced by Captain M. C. van Houten of the Dutch Royal Marechaussee, who sent a circular letter to several European police chiefs suggesting the creation of an international police bureau under the auspices of the League of Nations and the creation of central police offices modeled after the white slavery offices established before the war.[117] Nothing came of his proposal, although police efforts to consolidate and formalize bilateral links quickly got under way.[118] Four years later, with pressures rising for greater police cooperation, an International Criminal Police Congress was convened at the initiative of the police commissioner of Vienna (and past and future chancellor of Austria) Dr. Johann Schober. Although most of the 131 participants again were European, the majority of these were from Central Europe and most were police officials; largely absent were the diplomats, scholars, magistrates, and lawyers who had attended the Monaco congress.[119] Present, however, was the first American delegate to a European police convention, Richard Enright, chief of the New York City Police Department.

Among the proposals considered, but not implemented, were the creation of an international police bureau attached to the League of Nations Secretariat and the assignation of police attachés to embassies. It was eventually decided to create an International Criminal Police Commission (ICPC), headquartered in Vienna—although the fingerprint department was located in Copenhagen—and presided over by that city's police commissioner. The choice of the Austrian capital was prompted, Malcolm Anderson has written, by factors other than the Austrian government's willingness to provide the initial resources. The breakup of the Austro-Hungarian Empire made the police forces of the successor states particularly dependent on Vienna's excellent records on international criminals; the "intermingling of the peoples of the former Hapsburg territories and the social dislocation resulting from the First World War facilitated the migration of criminals and encouraged the development of transfrontier crime; [and] the strong *Polizeistaat* tradition in Austria and the successor states encouraged the belief that police co-operation had a role in maintaining political stability in central Europe."[120]

High on the agenda of the Vienna meeting was the problem of counterfeiting, principally of currency but also of bonds, securities, checks, and passports, which was increasingly seen as an international crime in need of a systematic international response. Counterfeiters had numerous incentives to forge and pass their banknotes outside the country whose currency they were counterfeiting: legislation in many states treated forgery of foreign currency more lightly than forgery of domestic currency,[121] police tended to give lower priority to cases involving counterfeiting of foreign currency, and foreign populations were less likely to be able to identify counterfeit bills. The chief inspector of the Amsterdam police, M. Broekhoff, for instance, noted that most forgeries of Dutch currency were "being circulated not in Holland but in Germany, Austria, Switzerland, France, Belgium, and Denmark" and were produced "in Germany and Belgium."[122] International cooperation, involving personal travel to all of the countries involved, had been essential, Broekhoff insisted, in finding and suppressing the illicit printing presses. But cooperative efforts were severely hindered, he observed, by the absence of central offices in each country to handle all domestic and international counterfeiting matters.

The challenges presented by the rash of counterfeiting were perfectly suited to the emerging capabilities of the police and their international endeavors. All governments were quick to acknowledge their mutual interest in suppressing counterfeiting of both their own and foreign currencies. Although some counterfeiters claimed that their activities were politically motivated and directed at undermining illegitimate regimes, no governments were willing to acknowledge the legitimacy of their methods.

In the famous 1861 case of *The Emperor of Austria v. Day and Kossuth*, the British High Court of Chancery enjoined the exiled Hungarian patriot, Louis Kossuth, from producing Hungarian currency in England in order to continue his fight against the emperor. The power to issue money, the court declared, belonged solely to the "supreme power in every state."[123] Unlike the illicit international trafficking in drugs and women, counterfeiting involved more than the internationalization of domestic vice markets. It posed a fundamental threat to the common interests of all states in monopolizing the production of currency, and it challenged the rapidly advancing technical and investigative capabilities of police agencies.

At the same time, counterfeiters themselves tended to be the types of professional criminals with whom the more clever police investigators particularly enjoyed tangling. As a result, the internationalization of policing proceeded more rapidly and effectively with respect to counterfeiting than against any other type of criminal activity. The ICPC quickly assumed a leading role, setting up a central office on counterfeiting and counterfeiters, publishing a periodical devoted to the dissemination of information on counterfeiting, and hiring specialists in the detection of counterfeit currency. Police agencies in dozens of countries established central offices dedicated to the investigation and suppression of counterfeiting;[124] some of these would evolve into the national central bureaus of Interpol that today handle most international police communications. Specialists in the detection and investigation of counterfeiting emerged in many police departments.

During the late 1920s, the anticounterfeiting efforts of the police were bolstered by the negotiation of a multilateral convention, under the auspices of the League of Nations, for the suppression of counterfeit currency. The initiative was provided in 1926 by the French government in reaction to the counterfeiting of substantial sums of French francs in Hungary in 1925 and the Hungarian government's subsequent leniency in prosecuting and punishing those responsible.[125] The international negotiations that followed provided one of the first opportunities to address the varied difficulties that had arisen in trying to facilitate cooperation among heterogeneous law enforcement systems. The challenge was not specific to counterfeiting, although the negotiators were obliged to reconcile widely varying notions of the crime itself as well as debate over whether the convention should be extended to include checks, securities, and other documents. But the negotiations inevitably entered into consideration of broader issues, such as whether their ultimate objective should be the unification of national laws to as great an extent as possible or merely the reconciliation of diverse systems to the extent necessary.[126] The substantial differences between civil law and common law systems were addressed, as were various national views on criminal jurisdiction. Preliminary efforts to harmonize extradition and judicial assistance arrangements were also attempted. The negotiators drew on both the input of Interpol and national police officials and the more academic perspectives provided by scholars associated with the Association Internationale de Droit Penal and the International Institute for the Unification of Criminal Law. The completed treaty was signed in Paris on April 20, 1929, and entered into force on February 22, 1931. The substance of the negotiations would be reproduced with increasing sophistication and success in decades to follow.

Unlike the prewar efforts to institutionalize some manner of international police cooperation, Schober's creation blossomed, eventually evolving into the organization known as Interpol.[127] Austrians dominated the ICPC during its first fifteen years of operation, providing much of its funding and manpower. Following the Anschluss in 1938, the organization came under Nazi control and soon ceased to function in anything resembling its previous form.[128] In 1946, with Europe confronting many of the same problems it had faced after World War I, with displaced people, thriving black markets, and breakdowns in law and order, a Belgian police inspector general, Florent Louwage, duplicated Schober's initiative. Although the first post-WWII meeting convened in Brussels, French police officials soon stepped into the Austrians' shoes, providing a headquarters for the organization and most of the manpower. During the 1950s and 1960s, the membership expanded dramatically to include the vast majority of states, with the notable exceptions of China and most of the Soviet bloc countries. The French dominance of Interpol continued until the early 1980s, when growing frustration with the French leadership and a more activist involvement by U.S. and other national police agencies more effectively "internationalized" the organization.

As its founders intended, the ICPC developed as a criminal information exchange service, composed primarily of an international headquarters and police liaison bureaus in each member country, through which police agencies around the world could readily communicate with one another, bypassing the diplomatic formalities that had hindered earlier attempts to cooperate across borders. The Vienna-based office supplemented its prewar file on criminals with additional information and fingerprint and photograph files on transnational criminals. It also circulated "wanted" notices, generally facilitated the extradition process, played a role in the creation of an international police radio network, and devoted efforts to impressing on police departments throughout the world the need for closer collaboration against transnational crime. Although currency counterfeiting remained a top priority, efforts were also directed at curtailing passport forgeries, the white slave trade, the illicit drug trade, criminal activities by gypsies, and a variety of other economic and violent crimes.

The organization's annual conventions, moreover, provided valuable occasions for forging international police links. Harry Soderman, a Swedish police expert with extensive international experience, wrote about the significance of the annual ICPC conferences during the 1930s:

> [These gatherings] served a more important purpose than to furnish opportunity for talk and eating at banquets. They fostered personal relationships between the police chiefs, and this is all-important. If Herr Banziger, chief of the Federal Police of Switzerland in Berne, received a telegram from Police Chief Mustapha Pasha in Cairo asking him to arrest a certain Spaniard called Ramon Gonzales for having committed a fraud in Egypt, Herr Banziger would know that Mustapha Pasha was a thoroughly reliable person, that he need not worry about whether Gonzales was being accused of some special sort of crime for which he could not also be arrested in Switzerland, and that he could be certain the Egyptian authorities would eventually ask for his extradition.[129]

Even as the ICPC network and conferences proved increasingly valuable to police agencies during the 1930s, it was accompanied by the proliferation of direct working relationships among police agencies. Many of these relationships developed among police officials stationed in towns and cities near national borders, who found direct communication with their foreign counterparts far more efficient than relaying requests through officials in the capital cities. Others arose among the criminal investigators associated with the police departments of Europe's major cities.

Most high-level police officials in Europe's major cities also developed close contacts. Jean Belin, commissioner of the Sureté during the 1930s, later wrote of his abundant international contacts:

> In my capacity as Commissioner of the national police-force I came into frequent contact with the chiefs of police of other countries. . . . I was frequently on the move, traveling on investigations to foreign capitals, and at my headquarters in the Rue des Saussaies I was host to all the leading international police-officers at various times, including prominent members of the Nazi Gestapo. With the exception of the latter, it was always a matter of co-operation, or alternatively, friendly rivalry.[130]

As was the case before World War I, the agents and informants of Europe's political police agencies teamed throughout the continent, keeping tabs on opponents of their respective regimes, maintaining ties with local police officials and occasionally assuming the guise of agents provocateurs. Particularly active was the foreign branch of Mussolini's secret police agency, known as OVRA, which pursued opponents of the regime beyond Italy's borders, trying to trick them either into returning to Italy or committing the sorts of acts that would have them arrested and/or deported from their havens.[131] Hitler's police did much the same after 1933, as did the political police agencies of most other governments troubled by expatriate agitators. The most concerted international police efforts were reserved, however, for the Bolsheviks, who provided much the same spark for international police collaboration that the anarchists had before the war. The Gestapo was particularly active in initiating such efforts, which extended not just throughout Europe, but also Brazil and Argentina.[132] At the same time, the Soviet secret police had stepped eagerly into the shoes of the tsar's Zagranichnaia Agentura, conducting its own operations against anti-Bolshevik émigré groups in Europe.[133]

Politically motivated crimes and investigations continued to influence the evolution of police cooperation in Europe during the 1930s. Interpol's channels were generally closed to communications in this area, so police and other security officials charged with surveillance of Bolsheviks and other political adversaries maintained direct contacts with one another. One of the more celebrated convergences of international politics and criminal investigation followed the 1934 assassination in Marseilles of King Alexander I of Yugoslavia and the French foreign minister, M. Louis Barthou, by a member of the Croatian nationalist organization, the Ustashi.

As with the international law enforcement efforts against anarchists a few decades earlier, politics proved both an inducement and an impediment to police cooperation. On the one hand, politically motivated murders, especially those that targeted politically significant personages, instantly received the top priority of police investigators. The need to travel abroad and to devote the greater resources necessary to international investigations did not present an obstacle as it did in less notorious crimes. On the other hand, because politics played such a significant role in the crime and its investigation, cooperation between police tended to hinge on the political interests of their governments. Both Jean Belin and Vladeta Milićević, the Yugoslav delegate to Interpol who coordinated his government's investigation of the murders, wrote of the obstacles that Hitler's and Mussolini's police placed in the way of their investigation. The French detective recalled, "As soon as I was given my orders I called on some Croatian exiles in Paris, and, by exerting pressure on them, was given some very useful information. This I passed on to my Yugoslav colleagues, who were able to draw their own conclusions. Apart from this, many of the clues that I followed up seemed to lead to the Italian or German consulates and embassies, and there, of course, my investigations had perforce to come to an abrupt end."[134] Milićević, who ultimately received limited cooperation from the German police and the Gestapo, described his initial reception at police headquarters in Berlin:

> I remembered that I had met Police President, Count Helldorf, before, and I visited him on the day following my arrival. I was received cordially, but he was obviously not over enthusiastic about giving me his assistance. He explained that it had been easy for him to help me in [an earlier] forgery affair, since, in that instance, it had been a matter of mutual assistance between two police authorities in a criminal affair; this time, however, it was a matter of a political crime, which made things very much more difficult for him.[135]

It is interesting to note that Milićević, in his capacity as the Yugoslav Ministry of the Interior's representative in Europe, wore three hats: one as his government's delegate to Interpol, a second as a roaming police liaison to other European police agencies, and a third as director of an intelligence network, similar to the tsarist Foreign Agency, designed to keep track of Ustashi émigrés plotting against the Yugoslav regime.[136] Milićević's combination of high and low policing functions was not entirely unique. Jean Belin, as head of the Sureté, supervised both a criminal section and a political bureau; the chief of Scotland Yard also supervised the Special Branch; and among U.S. law enforcement agencies, both the Secret Service in its earlier days and the FBI thereafter performed both high and low police tasks.

The interwar years also witnessed the extensive drafting of international conventions directed at the suppression of crime, many of them at the behest of the League of Nations. Its influence was particularly notable in the case of the 1926 Convention to Suppress the Slave Trade and Slavery, which sough to eliminate the isolated havens in which slavery and the slave trade remained legal. The continuing crusade against white slavery was reflected in the 1933 International Convention for the Suppression of the Traffic in Women of Full Age, which substituted a more prohibitionist model for the regulatory approaches of the previous conventions.[137] International traffic in pornography was the target of a 1923 convention. The first international convention directed at the destruction and/or theft of national treasures was signed in 1935. The assassination of King Alexander I of Yugoslavia provided the impetus for two potentially significant conventions signed in 1937, the Convention for the Prevention and Repression of Terrorism and the Convention for the Creation of an International Criminal Court, but neither achieved the requisite number of signatures to enter into force before the onset of the Second World War interrupted all such endeavors.[138] The problem of international drug trafficking was the subject of three conventions, in 1925, 1931, and 1936; the last, which was drafted by Interpol and put forward by the League of Nations, focused on the enhancement of municipal and international law enforcement measures.

None of these conventions, it should be noted, significantly affected the nature of international law enforcement during the interwar period, and only the last anti–drug trafficking convention, the Convention for the

Suppression of the Illicit Traffic in Dangerous Drugs (which entered into force in 1939), was to play a significant role in postwar international law enforcement matters. But the fact that they were negotiated at all reflected both the rising sense of international consciousness vis-à-vis transnational crime and the broadly optimistic faith, epitomized by the treaties directed at the elimination of war, in the power of international legal documents to transform international society.

The rise of fascism and Nazism within Europe during the same period, however, revealed another side of the processes associated with the internationalization of crime and law enforcement. As the memoirs of Belin and Milicevic reveal, police officials in many of Europe's democratic states were often called on to assist, or to seek assistance from, police agencies in Nazi Germany, fascist Italy, and other nondemocratic states. Political investigations were not always easily distinguished from ordinary criminal investigations, and more often than not, police officials in the fascist states found cooperation forthcoming. The common alliance against Bolshevism was partially responsible, as was the heightened sense of a transnational police community that had become stronger and more developed since World War I, but it no doubt also reflected the common tendency of police authorities to favor the interests of governments and established authorities over challengers. Hannah Arendt, in *The Origins of Totalitarianism*, claimed:

> Even before the outbreak of the war, under the pretext of "national security," the police of a number of democratic countries had embarked on so close a cooperation with the Gestapo and the G.P.U. [the political police] that one could well speak of an independent police initiative in matters of foreign politics. The cooperation, for instance, between the French police and the Gestapo was never closer and never functioned better than [when the French police were] under the anti-Nazi government of the Popular Front.[139]

We lack the evidence to fully prove or disprove Arendt's contention, but there can be no question that German law enforcement authorities continued to play a prominent and even leading role in continental policing until the end of the 1930s. In 1937, German police skipped the annual Interpol convention, held in London, and organized their own police conference in Berlin to discuss police cooperation against Bolshevism.[140] Sponsored by the Gestapo, the conference drew delegates, including chiefs of political police, from fourteen countries.

Following the German-Austrian Anschluss of March 1938, Interpol came under the domination of Nazi police officials, who presumably took advantage of the organization's files to advance both low and high police interests.[141] The annual Interpol conference convened shortly thereafter in Bucharest, where a French proposal to move the organization's headquarters to a neutral country, Switzerland, was voted down by the predominantly pro-fascist attendees.[142] Plans to meet the following year in Berlin did not come to fruition as Germany embarked on its conquest of continental Europe, one consequence of which was the creation of a far-reaching police force in the form of the Gestapo.[143] Throughout Nazi-occupied Europe, police were obliged to choose between accommodating themselves to the new regime or departing. Many chose the former.

The Modern Era of European Police Cooperation

Following the close of the Second World War, the pace and scope of international law enforcement evolved gradually and modestly until the 1970s. After that, however, the evolution proceeded at a dramatic pace, stimulated by a variety of developments. The growth in the scale of illicit drug trafficking played a major role; rising concern over organized criminal activity, drug-related and otherwise, also generated pressures for closer international police cooperation; periodic outbursts of terrorist activity provided a catalyst for some important international law enforcement initiatives; and the overall expansion in the amount and scope of transnational criminal activity attendant to the rapid growth in legitimate transnational interactions occasioned a great variety of law enforcement efforts. The movement toward broader integration in Europe, rather than simply the proliferation of cross-border crime, heightened the need for closer cooperation in law enforcement matters, even as the revolutions in Central and Eastern Europe promised to increase dramatically the scale of interactions, criminal justice and otherwise, between the formerly divided European blocs.

Interpol developed rapidly, especially in the 1980s, dramatically upgrading its headquarters operations, the participation of its national central bureaus, and its regional activities.[144] A growing array of other international law enforcement organizations, treaties, and conventions emerged, some under the auspices of the United Nations, others at the initiative of national police agencies. Of particular significance was the United Nations Convention Against Illicit Traffic in Narcotic Drugs and Psychotropic Substances, adopted in December 1988, which committed signatory states to extensive cooperation in drug enforcement matters; it promised to broaden and strengthen international cooperation in a wide array of law enforcement matters, ranging from extradition and mutual legal assistance to the more operational aspects of international drug enforcement.[145] The United Nations Convention also addressed the issues of identification, seizure, and forfeiture of criminally derived financial assets, which were widely perceived as playing increasingly important roles in future international efforts against transnational crime.

The United States was a dominant player in many of these organizations and agreements; Western Europeans had progressed much further than the United States, however, in developing integrated multilateral law enforcement measures. The rising significance of criminal justice concerns and approaches was highlighted after the late 1980s by the attention devoted to terrorism, drug trafficking, money laundering, and environmental crimes at the annual summits of the G-7 countries.

It should be emphasized that the internationalization of policing in postwar Europe was as much a part of the broader movement toward European integration as it was a response to the internationalization of crime. As early as the 1950s, the Council of Europe began to provide a framework for the sorts of multilateral extradition and other law enforcement treaties called for in the police conventions of previous decades.[146] Treaties providing for mutual assistance in criminal matters, recognition of foreign penal judgments, transfer of criminal proceedings, and transfer of prisoners reduced the frictions of international law enforcement and narrowed the jurisdictional loopholes through which transnational criminals could evade prosecution.[147] Other treaties addressed the issues of terrorism, traffic offenses, gun control, repatriation of minors, compensation of victims of violent crimes, and other mutual criminal justice concerns.

Although the treaty negotiators could neither ignore nor overcome the fact of conflicting national sovereignties, they were successful in minimizing the procedural obstacles that hampered cooperative efforts and in achieving some degree of homogenization among the criminal justice laws and policies of the treaty members. Also important was the creation of central offices in most Western European ministries of justice responsible for handling all international law enforcement matters that did not fall entirely within the jurisdiction of the police: the processing of extradition and other legal assistance requests, the negotiation of treaties, the drafting of legislation concerning international law enforcement matters, and so forth. The officials in these offices evolved into a sort of cross-border prosecutorial subculture linked by both their highly developed expertise in the domain of international criminal law and by the personal ties that develop over years of collaboration.

A similar sort of transnational police subculture, albeit substantially more multidimensional, evolved among the police agencies of Western Europe as direct contacts among them proliferated. Interpol channels were clogged with transmissions among European police agencies; these contacts were supplemented by direct interactions, joint operations, police liaison officers stationed abroad, bilateral and multilateral working groups, and membership in a variety of European and global law enforcement organizations. Relations between police officials on either side of national borders were often closer than between them and the officials based at police headquarters in their capital. Barriers of language, culture, and historical animosity remained, of course, and were unlikely to evaporate despite the movement toward broader European integration. But there can be no doubting the existence of a powerful transnational police subculture within Europe bound by the basic notion that a cop is a cop no matter what state's badge is worn, and a criminal is a criminal regardless of citizenship or language.

No one country or police agency can fairly be described as the pioneer of international criminal law enforcement within Europe. Certainly the German Bundeskriminalamt (BKA) played an important role in initiating closer law enforcement ties with its neighbors, and in advocating U.S.-style approaches to law enforcement on the continent.[148] But the role models for future cooperative efforts, such as those envisaged in post-1992 Europe, were provided by the Nordic and Benelux countries. The Netherlands, Belgium, and Luxembourg were parties to a multilateral extradition and mutual legal assistance treaty, signed in 1962, that provided for greater judicial cooperation than the Council of Europe treaties as well as more

extensive police cooperation, such as the right of hot pursuit across national borders. The Nordic states reached similar agreements that provided
for even greater levels of cooperation, particularly between Norway and
Sweden. Local police authorities routinely cooperated with one another
without notifying central authorities; the national police agencies collaborated in stationing liaison officers abroad and performing law enforcement intelligence tasks that benefited all of the Nordic states equally; and
extradition and mutual legal assistance relations were far more extensive
than the Council of Europe's arrangements, authorizing the extradition of
nationals as well as international summons for residents to appear as witnesses in foreign prosecutions.[149]

European law enforcement officials also devised (often at the initiative
of German officials) somewhat less intensive cooperative arrangements.
West Germany and France, for instance, agreed in 1978 to cooperate more
closely in policing their frontier regions. Belgian, Dutch, and German
police had cooperated informally since 1969 in policing the borderland of
Aachen.[150] Since the mid-1970s, the BKA had sponsored police working
groups with its neighbors to better coordinate investigations of drug trafficking, criminal activity in frontier regions, and other types of transnational crime.[151] And most of Europe's drug enforcement units combined
both bilaterally and multilaterally to work out more efficient methods of
coordinating "controlled deliveries" of illicit drugs across borders. The
permanent Cross Channel Conference provided an annual forum in which
British, French, Dutch, Belgian, and German police could address mutual
concerns along their coastlines.[152] The European Capital Chiefs of Police
Conference offered a similar annual forum for its members. There was
even an emerging European effort among police officials to share their
expertise in dealing with traffic concerns.[153] The Pompidou Group, created
by the French president in 1971 to better coordinate European anti–drug
trafficking efforts, provided a forum in which European officials could
focus their energies on just one form of criminal activity.

Late in the 1980s, rising concern over crimes involving fraud led to the
creation of a central antifraud unit within the Secretariat General of the
European Community. The Europeans also played a leading role in two
international organizations: the International Association of Airport and
Seaport Police, which focused on the problem of marine fraud,[154] and the
Customs Cooperation Council (later renamed the World Customs Or-

ganization), which slowly made progress in its efforts to develop closer cooperation among the world's customs agencies.[155] As for Interpol, the European Technical Co-operation Committee provided both a link between the international organization and the European police agencies and a forum in which issues not adequately addressed elsewhere could be handled.

Growing frustration among Europeans during the 1970s with Interpol's antiquated technology and cautious conservatism in police matters sparked some of the movement toward greater internationalization within the confines of the European community.[156] Some European police officials wanted Interpol to undertake a significant modernization of its intelligence and communications operations and to play a role in creating multinational teams of police experts to assist in major investigations. Still others called for the creation of a "Europol" organization capable not just of coordinating international investigations and facilitating information exchange but operating on a supranational level in initiating investigations. At Interpol headquarters, the French police authorities that dominated the organization viewed all such proposals disdainfully.

Whereas the bilateral and limited multilateral undertakings of the 1970s and 1980s were motivated primarily by concern with customary criminal activity and drug trafficking, the most significant international law enforcement endeavor of those decades, as in previous decades, was prompted by concerns over terrorism and other extremist activity.[157] With attacks by the Italian Red Brigade, the German Baader-Meinhof, and a host of other groups on the rise during the mid-1970s,[158] and abundant evidence that the terrorists were thinking and acting transnationally, the rationale for a more multilateral European response was becoming increasingly apparent. The Council of Europe took the initiative with the drafting of a European Convention on the Suppression of Terrorism, which was signed in January 1977 and implemented fifteen months later. By 1990 it had been ratified by eighteen of the Council of Europe's twenty-one member states. Designed to complement and reinforce the existing extradition and mutual assistance arrangements within Europe, its actual impact in alleviating the legal obstacles to improved cooperation, in particular the "political offense" exception to extradition, was relatively slight.[159] Far more important, especially as the number of ratifiers increased, was its symbolic and political impact in a continent that had never proved singularly successful in coordinating state actions against transnational terrorism.[160]

Of greater consequence than the legal convention was the favorable response by the newly created European Council of the European Community to a British-German initiative in late 1975 calling for the interior ministers of the member states to meet periodically to discuss problems of internal security. In June 1976, the ministers agreed to set up a number of working groups and entitled their new arrangement TREVI (after the famous fountain in Rome, according to one account; as a French acronym for the subject of its mandate—terrorism, radicalism, extremism, and international violence—according to another).[161] Although the ministers agreed that they would exchange information about their respective police organizations and work closely with respect to air traffic, the safety of nuclear installations and transport, and contingency measures for responding to emergencies, the central initial focus of TREVI was the desire to more effectively combat and suppress terrorist activities.

The secretive nature of much of TREVI's work made it difficult to evaluate its successes and failures. The fact that it persisted and retained the support and participation of high-level interior and justice officials is perhaps an indication of its importance. As Peter Katzenstein has noted, "TREVI and its various working groups provided not only for regular high-level contacts but also for institutionalized cooperation in practical police work. The institutionalization of European police cooperation under TREVI's auspices surpassed all previous efforts: operating out of the limelight, TREVI's study groups added an important international dimension to what may be the most national of policy domains in all governments, interior affairs and justice."[162]

TREVI may have played a role during the 1980s in encouraging French authorities to cooperate more closely with Spanish police in suppressing Basque terrorism and other violence and in inspiring Ireland and Britain to work more cooperatively against the Irish Republican Army. Success in coordinating policy against Middle East terrorism in Europe was, however, somewhat more elusive. Quite vigorous and often high-level disagreements over the prosecution, extradition, deportation, and release of both European and non-European terrorists persisted. Nonetheless, as Cyrille Fijnaut has argued, the creation and operation of TREVI represented an important development in the internationalization of policing:

Important, because the co-operation between the police services of Western Europe was taken up on a level and in a manner which surpassed anything that had been accomplished or pleaded for during the past hundred years in this part of the world. Important also because with TREVI the political cooperation between the member states of the European Community was extended to the domain of interior politics. . . . And important lastly, because in principle TREVI offered possibilities for further internationalization of investigation—although provisionally limited to matters of anti-terrorism only—in nearly all fronts.[163]

Perhaps the ultimate indicators of TREVI's significance were the decisions of the member interior and justice ministers in 1985 and 1986 to create additional working groups to improve coordination in dealing with organized crime (especially drug trafficking)[164] and problems associated with immigration, respectively.[165] This would also provide an important foundation for more formalized and institutionalized cooperation in later years.[166] Their initiative no doubt reflected both the decline in concerns over terrorism on the continent and rising anxieties over more conventional cross-border crimes. But it may also have reflected the heightened awareness of the need for a coordinating body at a level higher than the criminal investigators but not so elevated that important procedural questions and details could not be competently addressed. Interpol, with its global membership and mechanisms for facilitating and routinizing international police communications, represented one fulfillment of the aspirations of the early police conferences; TREVI, with its provisions for high-level political consultation and coordination, represented another. In March 1989, TREVI's role in European internal security was consolidated when the European Council member interior ministers agreed, in response to a proposal by the Spanish government, to establish a Permanent Secretariat of TREVI to better coordinate cooperation among the police agencies of the Community.

Toward the end of the 1980s, European law enforcement authorities also began devoting increasing attention to the possibilities of better immobilizing transnational criminals by identifying, tracing, seizing, and forfeiting their assets. Much of the impetus for this development emanated from the United States, which vigorously promoted its own model legislation and legal assistance treaties through Interpol channels, in the negotiations leading up to the 1988 drug enforcement convention, and in its bilateral relations with European law enforcement and other officials.[167]

The Europeans responded through various channels, with the European Parliament, the European Economic Community's Council of Ministers, the Council of Europe, and the Bank of International Settlements each issuing resolutions and directives supportive of greater unilateral and international efforts in this area. By the end of the 1980s, most EEC states had passed legislation providing for the forfeitures of drug trafficking assets, and four states—Britain, France, Spain, and Luxembourg—had followed in the footsteps of the United States and criminalized the act of laundering criminally derived funds.[168] More could be expected to follow as the European states signed the 1988 drug enforcement convention obligating them to cooperate in this area.

Unlike the movement within Europe during the 1970s and 1980s to improve cooperation against drug trafficking per se, efforts to focus on the financial dimensions of criminal activity faced more substantial obstacles. Criminal investigators accustomed to following the drugs instead had to follow paper trails, a task generally involving a very different sort of skills than those developed by the typical drug enforcement agent. Great obstacles were also presented by the powerful traditions of financial secrecy, and the interests that had developed around those traditions, not just in EEC states, but also in Switzerland, Austria, Luxembourg, and Liechtenstein.

Under persistent pressure from the United States and others beginning in the early 1970s, the Swiss took the lead in designing legislation and other measures to reconcile the interests of its domestic banking industry in financial confidentiality with the needs of foreign law enforcers for information and evidence. All of the financial secrecy havens in Europe were wary, however, lest too vigorous cooperation in international criminal investigations scare away substantial funds involving foreign tax evasion, capital flight, and political upheaval to safer havens outside Europe less amenable to U.S. and other international law enforcement pressures. Within the European Economic Community, moreover, those involved in planning for a unified market in banking and securities were wary of seeing their efforts bogged down by the sorts of measures required to better identify the tiny percentage of overall financial transactions involving criminal activity.

The greatest challenge looming over European police during the 1980s was the proposed elimination of border controls in 1992, in effect extending the Nordic and Benelux arrangements to all members of the EEC. In anticipation of 1992, the governments of France, Germany, and the Benelux states agreed—in a treaty signed in Schengen, Luxembourg, on June 14, 1985—to move toward the elimination of border controls for both persons and goods along their mutual borders by 1990.[169] The implementation convention was postponed, however, in late 1989. The political upheavals in Central and Eastern Europe, in particular the opening of the borders between East and West Germany, were partially responsible. But many also saw in the postponement the failure to resolve long-standing fears and antagonisms among the parties to the Schengen agreement, including concerns that the treaty did not sufficiently protect citizens' rights and the right to political asylum.[170] Many key issues had yet to be adequately resolved, such as refugee policy, hot pursuit, data protection, and the management of border controls between East and West Germany.[171] In June 1990, the five states reached agreement on a plan to eliminate border checks within the Schengen space by late 1992—only months before the scheduled removal of all internal border controls within the twelve-nation European Community on January 1, 1993.

The success of the earlier Benelux and Nordic law enforcement alliances was part and parcel of the broader willingness of these relatively small states to relax their sovereign prerogatives vis-à-vis nonthreatening neighboring states and collaborate closely on a great variety of mutual concerns. The challenge of the new Schengen arrangement, which was both broader and more ambitious than these predecessors, was to reproduce these relaxations of sovereignty among states of drastically unequal size, some of which retained bitter memories of past offenses against their national sovereignties. We look at these issues in greater depth in chapter 4. But first we turn to examine the historical evolution of the United States from being a laggard in the internationalization of crime control to its most enthusiastic and aggressive advocate.

CHAPTER THREE

□ □ □

U.S. Origins of International Crime Control

Where the previous chapter presented an opportunity to evaluate the origins of international crime control from a more comparative, regional, and multilateral perspective, in this chapter we examine the internationalization of crime control from the perspective of a single state. On the one hand, it is the story of one country's evolution in the realm of international crime control, pursuing objectives and confronting challenges that are in many ways similar to those explored in the previous chapter. On the other hand, it is a story of American exceptionalism insofar as it examines how an empowered and emboldened United States internationalized its criminal justice efforts to an unrivaled and unprecedented degree, with profound consequences for countries across the globe.

Both stories reinforce a central point made in previous chapters: that the internationalization of crime control is substantially a function of domestic politics producing new criminal statutes, rather than simply a response to proliferating transnational criminal activities. Most contemporary U.S. international policing efforts involve the enforcement of criminal laws that did not exist a century or even a few decades ago—not just drug prohibition laws but criminal laws directed at insider trading, money laundering, computer fraud, and the smuggling of sophisticated weaponry and other technology to blacklisted countries. Immigration controls imposed on Chinese migrants in the late nineteenth century and on most other foreigners in the early twentieth century created a new domain of international law enforcement. The proliferation of federal statutes during the

1980s explicitly extending U.S. jurisdiction to terrorist and other violent acts against U.S. citizens abroad provided the legal basis for significantly internationalizing the FBI's investigations. Conversely, U.S. international law enforcement efforts prior to the Civil War focused heavily on the rendition of fugitive slaves, and Prohibition-era law enforcers struggled to suppress the illicit traffic in alcoholic beverages. Both preoccupations ended suddenly with the abolition of the offended laws.

The modern era of U.S. international law enforcement emerged in the late 1960s with the dramatic increase in illicit drug use in the United States, much of it involving imported heroin and marijuana, and President Nixon's declaration of a "war on drugs." International drug enforcement efforts expanded rapidly in the 1980s when presidents Reagan and Bush declared their own wars on drugs. Federal law enforcement agencies persuaded Congress to criminalize financial activities connected to drug trafficking, thereby creating the relatively new crime of money laundering. The dramatic internationalization of the securities markets during the 1980s was accompanied, inevitably, by increases in transnational violations as well as calls by the Justice Department and the Securities and Exchange Commission for more resources and new criminal statutes. More personnel and resources translated into more criminal investigations and prosecutions. In many cases, an important motivator for developing a law enforcement agency's international capabilities could be traced to interagency rivalries and the desires of agency chiefs to claim more jurisdiction and responsibilities.

What makes the U.S. case unique is the extent to which the U.S. government has successfully internationalized its own criminal laws, procedures, and enforcement efforts. No other government has acted so ambitiously in collecting evidence from foreign jurisdictions, apprehending fugitives from abroad, targeting foreign government corruption, and persuading foreign governments to change their criminal justice norms to better accord with its own. No other has devoted comparable diplomatic and financial resources to pursuing its international law enforcement agenda. And no other has proved so willing to intrude on the prerogatives of foreign sovereigns, challenge foreign political sensibilities, and circumvent and override foreign legal norms. Only Great Britain's global campaign against the slave trade during the nineteenth century provides something of a precedent.

This aggressive course of action has yielded substantial results. Foreign governments have changed their own laws and enforcement methods and signed extradition, mutual legal assistance, and other law enforcement treaties demanded by U.S. authorities. Beginning with the adoption of the U.S. prohibitionist approach to drug control during the first decades of the twentieth century, foreign governments have followed in the footsteps of the United States, adopting U.S.-style investigative techniques, creating specialized drug enforcement agencies, stationing law enforcement representatives abroad, and enacting conspiracy statutes, asset forfeiture laws, and checks and bans on drug-related money laundering. Pressures to cooperate in U.S. drug trafficking investigations were largely responsible for instigating changes, beginning in the 1970s, in financial secrecy laws to authorize greater assistance to U.S. (and other foreign) law enforcement authorities. Even apart from the area of drug enforcement, the influence of the United States was readily apparent during the first decades of the century in shaping foreign and international approaches to white slavery, during the cold war era with respect to export controls on weapons and sophisticated technology, and starting in the mid-1980s with respect to the regulation of securities markets (in particular the criminalization of insider trading). The end result has been something of an "Americanization" of criminal justice systems throughout much of the world.

The Beginnings of U.S. Involvement in International Crime Control

The internationalization of U.S. crime control during the first 150 years of the nation's existence was quite modest compared to either the European experience at that time or the American experience to follow. Police and prosecutors paid relatively little heed to international law enforcement matters. Criminal fugitives tended to flee across a state border or disappear into the nation's frontier regions. The few that fled abroad were often wished good riddance and forgotten. Federal police agencies were slow to evolve, their funding and jurisdiction strictly limited by Congress and a citizenry wary of centralized police power. Most municipal police agencies lacked the professionalism of many European police departments,[1] and their scant resources hardly allowed for foreign jaunts and international criminal investigations. It was difficult enough to coordinate with counterparts in other U.S. states. The void was partly filled, from the mid-nineteenth century to the beginning of the twentieth, by private detective agencies. They often provided the only effective option for those in need of competent criminal investigators capable of operating across and beyond state and national borders.

The principal exceptions to this insular disposition could be found along the borders of the United States. Even today, with the globalization of transnational crime and international law enforcement, U.S. borders remain the focus of most international law enforcement concerns and activities.[2] There, one encounters almost all the types of transnational crime found elsewhere, as well as many that are unique to border regions. The frontier region is the only place where international law enforcement is often synonymous with local law enforcement. Nowhere else must local officials be so concerned about the state of law and order in a foreign country; nowhere else do state and local law enforcement officials play such a prominent role in international law enforcement matters, routinely liaising with foreign officials and crossing national boundaries; and nowhere else does one find such a diversity and concentration of federal law enforcement agencies.

Early U.S. law enforcement authorities were drawn into international policing endeavors by concerns not unlike those of the Europeans. Transnational banditry, particularly in less populated and developed frontier regions, was endemic. U.S. authorities were obliged to contend with outlaws first along the borders with Canada and Spanish Florida and then with Mexico, as well as a problem unfamiliar to Europeans: marauding Indian warriors. Occasional efforts were made to recover criminal fugitives and military deserters who had fled abroad, but most rendition efforts focused—unlike in Europe—on the recovery of fugitive slaves. There were the two problems posed at sea by piracy and the illicit slave trade, both of which receded as the nineteenth century passed its midpoint. Whenever the United States was at war, or otherwise troubled by foreign political intrigues and agitators, there were the calls on police agents to undertake the sorts of tasks that professional intelligence agencies and secret services would perform in later decades. And there was the need to respond to foreign requests to extradite fugitives from foreign justice, to keep tabs on political dissidents and agitators havened in the United States, and to enforce the U.S. neutrality laws by suppressing gun running and the plots of filibusters.

Finally, there was the very substantial concern with smuggling, not so much of forbidden goods as of goods on which customs duties were supposed to be paid. Because customs duties provided the majority of the federal government's revenues until the institution of the income tax in 1913 (excepting the years during and immediately following the Civil War, when an income tax was imposed to pay for war expenses), high priority was given to ensuring their payment. Customs agents, unlike other law enforcement agents, were primarily interested not in apprehending felons but in maximizing the collection of revenue. They therefore represented a sound economic investment in the eyes of legislators charged with appropriating funds. Not surprisingly, the first significant U.S. involvement in international law enforcement arose with the delegation of Treasury agents and informants to investigate smuggling and other efforts to circumvent the revenue laws.

The historical analysis that follows demonstrates the porous boundaries of what may be defined as international crime control. On the one hand, U.S. law enforcement agents were occasionally called on to perform chores that had little or nothing to do with the enforcement of U.S. criminal laws; their peculiar talents and skills rendered them particularly well suited for conducting espionage and counterespionage tasks for a government that had yet to develop specialized agencies for such purposes. On the other hand, police agents were neither the only nor even the principal agents of U.S. international crime control activities until well into the twentieth century. The U.S. army and navy performed law enforcement functions ranging from the suppression of piracy and slave trading to the tracking down of transnational bandits and revolutionaries and the suppression of Indian raids and revolts. The enactment of the Posse Comitatus Act in 1878 severely restricted but did not entirely end the military's involvement in domestic and international law enforcement matters. Much of the work of international law enforcement in foreign countries, including the collection of information, evidence, and people, was performed by consular officials operating out of U.S. embassies. Government agencies often hired special agents to carry out the sorts of tasks that today would be performed by federal law enforcement agents. The most challenging transnational criminal investigations were routinely undertaken by private detective agencies. Fugitives in foreign lands were as likely to be pursued and apprehended by the employees of such agencies, or by freelance bounty hunters, as by officials of the U.S. government. Law enforcement raids across the Mexican border were as likely to include vigilante parties and undeputized posses as U.S. military units and officially sanctioned posses. And both government and private police agencies routinely relied on the services of informants, including U.S. civilians, foreign nationals, and even Indian scouts, to facilitate their international activities.

Policing Slavery

The federal prohibition on importing slaves was signed by President Thomas Jefferson in 1807, entered into force in 1808, and was subsequently amended by an 1820 act equating the illicit slave trade with piracy and authorizing the death penalty for violators. Few federal prohibitions were ever so poorly enforced. During the early 1820s, and again from 1842 until the Civil War, a few U.S. naval vessels were sent to patrol the west coast of Africa and the waters around Cuba. They developed joint cruising arrangements with the British Royal Navy's African squadron, but were generally handicapped by the lack of political, logistical, and moral support from home.[3] U.S. naval officers, marshals, and others who attempted to enforce the laws risked condemnation by superior officials as well as the likelihood that those they arrested would be set free by sympathetic judges and juries.[4]

The institution of slavery depended on the capacity of slave owners to deter their slaves from escaping and to recover and punish them when they did. Slave owners who lived in close proximity to Free states and to foreign jurisdictions in which slavery was prohibited clearly had the greatest cause for concern. When their slaves escaped, they sought to recover them through both formal and informal procedures. Congress enacted a series of Fugitive Slave Acts to help slave owners recover escapees from Free states, and the federal government attempted to negotiate treaties with neighboring countries to require the rendition of fugitive slaves. This issue dominated international law enforcement activities by U.S. citizens and officials prior to the Civil War.

The principal foreign havens for slaves seeking their freedom were Florida (prior to its annexation in 1819),[5] Mexico, and Canada. Rendition efforts were similar in each location: frequent diplomatic overtures as well as repeated attempts to negotiate extradition treaties; private and state-sponsored expeditions across the border to recover runaway slaves; efforts by foreign citizens and officials to lure slaves across the border; steadfast refusal by the foreign government to return escaped slaves; discreet complicity by foreign officials near the border in the U.S. initiatives to recover slaves; and differences of opinion within the refuge nation over how to handle the issue.

Most slaves who made it to Canada and Mexico won their freedom. By 1842, an estimated twelve thousand former slaves had found freedom north of the border.[6] British and Canadian authorities were reluctant to hand over fugitive slaves.[7] Disagreements over the issue remained a sore point in U.S.-British relations until the Civil War and were largely responsible for the inability of the two governments to conclude an extradition treaty during the 1820s and 1830s. Slaveholders and their agents often took matters into their own hands, attempting to abduct their former property from foreign territories (which was legal under U.S. law but illegal under Canadian law)[8] and initiating extradition requests alleging that the fugitive slaves had committed criminal offenses before or pursuant to their flight.

Mexico was no more cooperative than Canada, especially after it declared independence in 1821, prohibited the slave trade in 1824, and abolished slavery in 1829. Repeated efforts by the U.S. government to negotiate a treaty for the extradition of fugitive slaves were consistently rejected by the Mexican government,[9] ensuring that the flight of fugitive slaves into Mexico would continue to generate bilateral tensions so long as slavery persisted in the United States.[10]

The Emergence of Federal Law Enforcement

From the country's origins until the Civil War, federal law enforcement was monopolized by three law enforcement agencies: the Customs Service, the Postal Inspection Service, and the U.S. Marshals. The first was charged with the most common and essential of all international law enforcement responsibilities: detecting and suppressing smuggling. Its first priority was to collect duties on legal imports; its second priority, which looms larger now than in earlier eras, was to keep out prohibited goods. The Customs Service focused most of its energies along the border, supervising crossing points, patrolling the shores in revenue cutters, and employing inspectors to police the borders. But some secretaries of the treasury and their collectors of customs were also quick to recognize the advantages of securing cooperation and information from abroad, where most smuggling ventures were planned. They thus were responsible for initiating and developing most of the tactics and approaches that are commonly associated with international law enforcement: bilateral agreements, both formal and informal, with foreign customs and police authorities; employment of informers in foreign locales; offers of rewards for information resulting in seizures; reliance on U.S. consular officials abroad to provide intelligence; stationing of agents in foreign cities; and delegation of undercover agents and other employees to penetrate smuggling rings and collect intelligence.

The extraterritorial employment of U.S. law enforcement agents dates back at least to the 1820s, when special agents were employed by customs collectors in New York to discreetly collect information on smuggling ventures from Canada. In the 1850s, with the development of trade between the west and east coasts of the United States via the Isthmus of Panama, Customs agents were assigned to special duty in the foreign transit point. By the turn of the century, Treasury agents were stationed in five European cities: Paris, London, Berlin, Cologne, and St. Gall, Switzerland.[11] By the late 1930s, forty-six Treasury agents could be found throughout Europe.[12] These agents, as well as others sent abroad on particular cases, performed a variety of tasks. They investigated plots to smuggle both licit and illicit goods into the United States; they found ways to determine the actual value of imported goods that were undervalued by those declaring them;[13] they investigated corruption among the Customs inspectors; and they generally sought to uncover all other varieties of fraud on the U.S. Treasury.

Most of the work of Customs agents, however, focused inevitably on the borders with Canada and Mexico. In 1886, "mounted inspectors," later known as customs patrol inspectors, were posted along the Mexican border to deter and intercept smuggling ventures. The size of the force remained relatively modest for forty years, until Prohibition prompted both the creation of a second inspector force along the northern border and an overall increase in the number of inspectors from 111 in 1925 to 723 in 1930.[14] Most of the inspectors' efforts focused on interdicting the smuggling of goods and animals—particularly cattle around the turn of the century, on which a stiff protective tariff had been imposed—into the United States, but they were also obliged to keep an eye on the outward flow of particular items, notably guns being exported to Mexican revolutionaries and government forces. Following the enactment of the Chinese Exclusion Act in 1882, they were also charged with curtailing the smuggling of Chinese into the United States via Mexico and Canada, a responsibility that overlapped substantially with the morally charged campaign to suppress the "white slave trade" in Chinese women and girls to American houses of prostitution.[15] This duty was partly taken over in 1904 by the Immigration Service, which hired a renowned customs inspector, Jefferson Milton, as its first "Chinese Inspector."[16] Following the enactment of far broader and more restrictive immigration legislation in the early 1920s, the U.S. Border Patrol was formed in 1924 with a $1 million budget and a total force of some 450 officers to stem the cross-border flow of unauthorized migrants (as well as alcohol smugglers during the Prohibition years).[17]

Many of the successes of the Treasury and border control agents depended on their abilities to cultivate good relations with local officials, operate covertly, and develop effective informant networks. Although they frequently obtained assistance from foreign police agencies, they did not always restrict their activities to those countenanced by the formal rules of international diplomacy. Nowhere was this more true than along the border with Mexico, which U.S. agents often crossed with impunity. In many ways, these agents were the forefathers of the activist approach to international law enforcement employed by the Drug Enforcement Administration in recent decades.

The two other federal police agencies focused relatively little energy abroad. The Postal Inspection Service concentrated on investigating thefts of the mails, although its agents were occasionally called on to perform investigative and other law enforcement tasks having little to do with the mails: tracking down safecrackers, transporting gold bullion for the federal government, protecting foreign dignitaries, and so on.[18] The U.S. Marshals, authorized by the Judiciary Act of 1789 to support the federal courts, were the closest thing to a general law enforcement agency prior to the development of the FBI. They served as the "handymen" of a number of government agencies in the first part of the nineteenth century.[19] Among their international chores was the collection and delivery of fugitives between the United States and other countries.

The Secret Service was established in 1865 with the sole purpose of preventing and investigating cases of counterfeiting. The agency quickly established a good reputation for criminal investigation and soon found itself called on to perform similar services for other branches of the government both within the United States and abroad.[20] Its agents established connections with European and other foreign law enforcement agencies. They investigated smuggling cases, including some in which U.S. Customs officials had been corrupted. Their most extensive efforts abroad, however, involved not counterfeiting but political intelligence operations. During the 1880s, the Secret Service cooperated with the newly created Special Branch of Scotland Yard's Criminal Investigation Division against Irish terrorists seeking independence for their country.[21] Before and during the 1898 war with Spain, Secret Service agents were called on to undertake espionage and counterespionage operations within the United States, as well as in Canada and Spain.[22] Until 1908, when Congress forbade the Justice Department to borrow any Secret Service operatives from Treasury—reportedly because the agents' investigations had led to the indictment and conviction of some of their members[23]—the Secret Service reigned as the leading federal law enforcement agency.

The Justice Department, established in 1870, was not authorized to create its own specialized law enforcement agency until 1908. Federal prosecutors relied on Secret Service agents and other investigators borrowed from other agencies, private detectives, an assorted array of special agents whose status remained ambiguous, and their own investigative skills and resources. The congressional ban on Justice Department employment of Secret Service agents, however, met with strong pressures from President Theodore Roosevelt and Attorney General Bonaparte to allow the creation of a federal detective service. Congress relented and voted in 1908 to specifically appropriate funds for special agents in the Justice Department. The following year, Bonaparte's successor, Attorney General George C. Wickersham, christened the now officially sanctioned department of detectives, composed initially of former Secret Service agents, the Bureau of Investigation.[24] (The word "Federal" was added in 1935.) Its jurisdiction included a hodgepodge of crimes, including bribery; antitrust and banking violations; customs, post office, and internal revenue frauds; violations of the neutrality, peonage, and bucket-shop laws; white slave cases; crimes on the high seas; and murders on government reservations. Within a few years, the demands of reporting on Mexican revolutionary activity and enforcing the neutrality laws along the southwest frontier would provide the bureau with both a rationale for substantial growth and an opportunity to prove its worth. Yet, despite the wide variety of criminals whom they were expected to encounter, the Justice Department agents were not authorized to carry arms, serve warrants and subpoenas, or make seizures and arrests until 1934.[25] Their role during that first generation was considered purely investigative.

The most effective law enforcement organization in the United States between the Civil War and the First World War—and the first that could be characterized as a transnational police organization—was the Pinkerton Detective Agency. Founded during the 1850s by a Scottish immigrant and former special agent of the Post Office, Allan Pinkerton, the agency expanded throughout the United States and around the world following the Civil War.[26] It made the most of its ability to liaise with and among federal, state, local, and foreign law enforcement agencies unable or unwilling to communicate with one another.[27] Pinkerton's sons, particularly William Pinkerton, also assumed leading roles in U.S. police circles. They spoke out forcefully in favor of more professional police forces, the adoption of modern investigative techniques, and more efficient interstate cooperation. They also were elected to high positions in U.S. police associations, notably the International Association of Chiefs of Police.[28]

The rising demand for private detective agencies' services arose from many corners. Most prominent among these were America's industrialists, who hired the detective agencies to spy on labor organizers, compile blacklists of suspected agitators, disrupt efforts at unionization, and otherwise police their factories and other properties—all of which eventually proved harmful to the popular reputations so carefully cultivated by the leading agencies. The agencies' clients, however, were far more diverse, sharing only in their capacity to pay the fees required. Major banks and other commercial institutions turned to the detective agencies to investigate significant frauds and thefts; foreign governments paid them to collect information on political émigrés and other perceived threats; and federal, state, and local governments in the United States turned to them wherever the services of police agents were either lacking or under suspicion.

The Pinkertons and other private detectives did not shy from traveling virtually anywhere in the world on behalf of an investigation or in pursuit of a fugitive. Hired by the Bank of England during the 1870s to investigate a major fraud, Pinkerton agents coordinated one of the first major transnational criminal investigations.[29] They tracked down fugitives across the globe, including in Bolivia the famous duo of Butch Cassidy and the Sundance Kid. It was a Pinkerton agent, Henry Julian, working on a case commissioned by the Justice Department, whose successful abduction of a larcenist named Frederick Ker led to the 1886 Supreme Court decision, *Ker v. Illinois*, affirming the legality of extraterritorial abductions.

By the 1890s, Pinkerton's sons had opened branches in Europe.[30] So well-known had the name Pinkerton become by then that many Europeans thought it was the title of the U.S. criminal police.[31] In extending their operations overseas, the private detectives possessed two advantages that the federal agents lacked: they were already experienced in undertaking criminal investigations without the benefit of state authority, as even in their domestic investigations they were not entitled to carry any police badge; and, as private rather than government investigators, they were far less likely than U.S. federal agents to be perceived as challenges to a foreign government's sovereign powers. Police around the world offered them their cooperation not out of any sense of international comity but because the Pinkerton agents were seen as fellow professionals pursuing the same ends. In the nascent transnational police subculture of the late nineteenth and early twentieth century, the Pinkertons provided the initial transatlantic link.

Policing Borders

In the United States, as in Europe, most transnational law enforcement relationships involve one's neighbors. Police along the U.S.-Canadian border tended to work out cooperative relationships, particularly after the tensions of the late 1700s and early 1800s had passed, with local officials often eager to avoid complicating matters by involving the central government. Some formalities might be required in extradition proceedings, but typically both sides maintained a strong interest in keeping their relations informal. The same was true to some extent along the U.S.-Mexican border, where local officials cultivated informal links that often ignored considerations of sovereignty and international law,[32] but political and cultural differences presented significant obstacles. Mexican resentment over the seizure of their territory by U.S. forces in the 1840s ebbed slowly and bitterly. Political relations between the two central governments often soured, with concomitant disruptions in the law enforcement arena. And the ineffectiveness and corruption of Mexican law enforcement agencies frustrated U.S. police officials, occasionally stirring them to take unilateral action.

The border represents the point across which ordinary domestic law enforcement activities—recovery of fugitive criminals and escaped slaves, suppression of outlaw gangs and Indian marauders, pursuit of cattle rustlers and train robbers, and even ordinary policing—becomes internationalized. It also represents the dividing line between sovereign jurisdictions with distinct regulations, law enforcement systems and political interests, constituencies and upheavals. Criminals who cross these lines sometimes do so with indifference to its jurisdictional consequences; more often, however, they regard the easily crossed borders as an advantage, one that offers lucrative profits to smugglers, safe havens to bandits, fugitives, and filibusters, and economic opportunities to illegal migrants. Law enforcement officials, by contrast, typically perceive borders as a serious impediment. Borders symbolize the limits of their police powers, lines across which they have no control and are typically dependent on foreign authorities, and which they cross only at the risk of offending foreign authorities and being arrested by them.

U.S. Customs officials alongside the northern and southwestern borders focused their efforts both on nonsmuggling customs frauds and the smuggling of licit and illicit goods: diamonds, watches, textiles, opium, booze, Chinese "coolies," garlic, and just about anything else that could be profitably transported. Some of these smuggling activities, particularly across the Mexican border in the decades after the U.S.-Mexican War of 1846–1848, involved no more than the continuation of commercial relations that had been established before the relocation of the border; most, however, were stimulated by the desire to earn the higher profits associated with illicit commerce.

The border during this time was also a place where the entire array of law enforcement and investigative authorities could be found: the U.S. military (including the cavalry, the intelligence divisions, National Guard units under federal control, and the special agents of the War Department); the State Department's consular officials in Mexican cities near the border as well as the department's special agents; the assorted federal law enforcement agencies (including the Customs officials, U.S. Marshals, Secret Service, Bureau of Investigation, Postal Inspection Service, U.S. attorneys, and immigration officials); the Ranger units and National Guards of the border states; the local sheriffs and police officials of counties, cities, and towns alongside the border; and the nongovernmental private detective agencies, posses and vigilante bands, and unorganized private citizens. This multitude of law enforcers combined, competed, and struggled with one another as well as with the array of federal, state, local, and private Mexican law enforcement authorities who operated across the border.

High among the concerns of law enforcement officials along the border throughout the nineteenth century was cross-border raiding by Indians—some of them native to the region, others recently transplanted to government reservations—as well as assorted outlaw gangs, vigilantes, military soldiers and deserters, and hopeful filibusters and revolutionaries.[33] Law enforcement activities directed at the suppression of the Indians fell largely to the cavalry. Suppression of non–Indian outlawry, however, was largely in the hands of nonmilitary state and federal agents, in part because the 1877 Posse Comitatus Act prohibited the military from playing a domestic police role absent a declared state of emergency. In Texas, the Rangers, created at the outbreak of the Texas Revolution in 1835, and in particular its Frontier Battalion, which operated from 1874 to 1881, assumed many of the responsibilities for tracking down Indians and assorted outlaws.[34] The marshals, like the cavalry, occasionally crossed the border in pursuit of their antagonists, both with and without permission from Mexican authorities, but their freedom of action was constrained to some extent by directives from Washington.[35] The Rangers, by contrast, possessed the freedom of a relatively single-minded unit with neither distant overseers nor broader foreign policy considerations to hamper them; they crossed the border often in pursuit of Indians and outlaws and acquired a reputation for shooting first and asking questions second.

Political upheavals within Mexico inevitably affected those living across the border. Refugees, revolutionaries, filibusters, and assorted other insurrectionists viewed the United States, particularly Texas, as a natural refuge for those fleeing oppression, disorder, and armed forces and as an ideal base of operations for those plotting an insurgency, revolution, or coup d'état. For all these Mexicans, the territory north of the border represented not just a relatively safe haven into which Mexican troops and agents were leery of entering but also a source of weapons, intelligence, manpower, and the political and financial support of sympathizers. At the same time, not a few Mexicans viewed the United States with great hostility; they sought both revenge and reparations for the territorial seizures, capitalist exploitations, and general arrogance of the gringos to the north.

The political turbulence generated between 1910 and 1920 by the Mexican Revolution presented law enforcement authorities north of the border with a disparate set of challenges: ensuring both the territorial integrity of the United States and the security of Americans and others north of the border; enforcing the neutrality laws of the United States, which involved surveillance of Mexican activists, suppression of armed expeditions into Mexico, and curtailment of gun running; and protecting American lives and interests south of the border. During the course of the decade, virtually every federal, state, and local agency present at the border played a role in responding to these challenges. Conflicts among them were often severe, reflecting not just ordinary turf squabbles but intense differences of opinion regarding which Mexican groups should be supported or suppressed, what U.S. interests in Mexico were, what restrictions should be placed on U.S. law enforcement operations south of the border, and how to interpret and apply the neutrality and other laws of the United States. The sharpest disagreements were typically between federal authorities in Washington and state and local officials along the border, with the latter generally dismissive of Washington's broader foreign policy concerns and perceived detachment from the particular problems of the border. Relations with Mexican authorities accordingly varied depending on the particular interests and perspectives of the assorted U.S. agencies involved in the fray, all of which were further complicated between 1911 and 1915 by the recurring question of which Mexican forces were actually in control of Mexico City and Mexico's northern states and cities.

Following the outbreak of the Mexican Revolution in 1910, U.S. officials sought to prevent the violence and armed combatants from spilling over into U.S. territory.[36] U.S. authorities responded by mobilizing federal troops, the Rangers and National Guard units of the border states, and local police and civilian posses under the command of border sheriffs. Throughout much of the Mexican Revolution, presidents Taft and Wilson refrained from sending U.S. forces across the border. The principal exception occurred in March 1916, when Pancho Villa's forces attacked Columbus, New Mexico, killing seventeen Americans and burning and looting the town before being chased out by U.S. army troops. Wilson responded by ordering General John "Black Jack" Pershing to lead a "punitive expedition" into Mexico in pursuit of the Mexican revolutionary and his forces.[37] Pershing's punitive expedition represented one of the largest, as well as one of the last, employments of U.S. military force to find and apprehend criminal fugitives who had fled abroad.

During this time, the Mexican border region was also the focus of efforts to investigate violations of U.S. neutrality laws. The network of agents that developed thereafter to enforce the neutrality laws outlasted the Mexican Revolution and ultimately included agents representing every federal law enforcement agency.[38] The process of enforcing the neutrality laws was both complex and laden with intrigue.[39] State and federal officials often clashed with one another and among themselves over differing interpretations of the neutrality laws and varying perceptions of which side to support in the Mexican Revolution. Mexican agents were afforded wide latitude in investigating the various revolutionary groups, often conducting the principal investigations and only calling on the local U.S. authorities to make the necessary arrests. Hundreds of Mexican agents and informants could be found in El Paso, Texas, and other centers of revolutionary intrigue, monitoring and infiltrating the antigovernment plotters and gun smuggling rings.[40] Their substantial presence and frequent indiscretions angered some U.S. authorities, but the Americans' dependence on the Mexican agents for intelligence and manpower ensured their continued presence.[41]

The Early International Law Enforcement Activities of City Police

So long as the federal police agencies remained underdeveloped, most overseas investigations of noncustoms criminal matters fell to municipal police agencies. Most murderers, thieves, rapists, and other common criminals violated not federal but state and municipal laws. From the middle of the nineteenth century until the first decades of the twentieth, the detective divisions of municipal police departments were likely to be as large and sophisticated as anything the federal government had to offer. Its principal competitors and collaborators were the private detective agencies, which themselves were often composed of former police officials. Even as early as the first half of the nineteenth century, a number of chief constables in leading U.S. cities had acquired impressive reputations based on their knowledge of the criminal world and their detecting skills. For example, for much of the first half of the nineteenth century, Jacob Hays, the high constable of New York City, was consulted frequently by European police officials.[42] The first public detective branches were created in Boston in 1846, then New York in 1857, Philadelphia in 1859, and Chicago in 1861.[43] Thomas Byrnes, appointed police chief in New York City, desired his detective force to be regarded as the equal of the Sureté and Scotland Yard.[44] His department assembled an extensive rogues' gallery, including pictures of European as well as U.S. criminals, and exchanged information on criminals and fugitives with European police departments.[45]

By the beginning of the twentieth century, municipal police departments, not just in New York but throughout much of the United States, were undergoing the same process of professionalization that had occurred decades earlier in Europe. Motivated partly by European influences, but even more so by a wave of police corruption investigations around the country, police reform movements were contributing to an increasing sophistication in U.S. criminal investigations.[46] One aspect of these developments was the increasing police consciousness of the need to interact with foreign counterparts. First, however, police departments needed to resolve the problems of domestic cooperation across state lines and develop some sense of a national police community. In 1893, the National—later International—Association of Chiefs of Police (IACP) was created, and shortly thereafter it began holding annual conferences. Three years later, a group of law enforcement officials from around the country met in Chicago to discuss ways of improving interstate coordination in criminal investigations.[47] As U.S. policemen gradually grew accustomed to looking beyond their municipal and state borders, the notion of dealing with foreign counterparts began to seem more realistic.

One of the principal factors contributing to U.S. participation in the developing international police community was the dissemination of European developments in police science. The Bertillon method of identification, for instance, had gradually taken hold among U.S. police departments following the translation of the Frenchman's book into English in

1896.[48] Likewise, the fingerprint method was gradually gaining notice.[49] In 1903, the IACP appointed a committee of three to examine the new methodology. One of the members, W. G. Baldwin of the Baldwin Railroad Detectives, toured European police departments in 1904 and returned with favorable reports.[50] At the 1905 World's Fair in St. Louis, the IACP sponsored a display of the various systems of criminal identification in use around the world. Scotland Yard was persuaded to send a representative to demonstrate the Henry Finger Print Method, which had been published five years earlier.[51] The IACP had also established a National Bureau of Criminal Identification to serve as a central repository of Bertillon cards of major criminals from around the country.[52] In the 1920s, this bureau was given over to the Justice Department. Eventually, its files and those from the federal penitentiary in Leavenworth were combined under the supervision of the FBI.

As with many techniques, fingerprinting took time to be accepted and used by U.S. police, who were accustomed to more familiar methods and who had already gone through the laborious process of being converted to the Bertillon method. In New York shortly after the turn of the century, the newly appointed police commissioner, William McAdoo, was eager that his department keep up with developments in Europe. Accordingly, in 1904 he sent a detective sergeant, Joseph A. Faurot, to London to learn what Scotland Yard was doing in the area of fingerprinting. Two years later, Faurot was able to prove the merits of the new identification technique to American skeptics. Back on foot patrol, he happened to arrest an Englishman who was lurking suspiciously in the Waldorf Astoria Hotel. Uncertain of his true identity, Faurot sent the suspect's fingerprints to Scotland Yard. The reply two weeks later confirmed that the Englishman was a professional hotel thief and fugitive from British justice.[53] Given prominent play in the New York newspapers, the incident gave some impetus to persuading U.S. police departments to develop fingerprint files on criminals. It also suggested the potential of greater cooperation with foreign police departments.

At the 1905 annual convention of the IACP, Major Richard Sylvester, chief of the Washington, D.C., police and president of the association, delivered his annual report and address. The portion addressing international aspects of law enforcement, although excessively optimistic, reflected the sense of growing international cooperation among police agencies:

The International Association continues to grow in numbers and influence. . . . Police co-operation is more prompt and thorough throughout the world than ever before. There was a time when responses from authorities abroad were only obtained after the aid of the State Department had been invoked and procured, but such confidence has been established within a short time between the police authorities of our own and other lands that the delays, interferences and suspicions which once prevailed have generally disappeared.[54]

The Early Years of U.S. Drug Enforcement Abroad

The use of federal law enforcement agents to enforce federal narcotics laws dates back to 1890, when Congress first levied heavy duties and restrictions on imported opium.[55] These were enforced primarily by Treasury agents assisting the Customs Service. Following the enactment of the Harrison Narcotic Act in 1914, a small drug enforcement section was created in the Treasury Department. It was incorporated into the Prohibition Unit during the 1920s. In 1930, enforcement of the narcotics and alcohol laws was separated, and a Federal Bureau of Narcotics (FBN) was created within the Treasury Department. There the latter remained until a major reorganization of the drug enforcement bureaucracy in 1968.

For the first thirty-two years of the FBN's existence, the agency was presided over by Commissioner Harry J. Anslinger. As a Foreign Service officer during the 1920s, Anslinger had been assigned to the Bahamas, where he targeted the smuggling of liquor into the United States. After he persuaded the British to establish landing certificates that would keep a record of all ship movements, the Treasury Department asked that he be detailed temporarily to its Prohibition Unit.[56] There he soon was appointed chief of the unit's Foreign Control Section, which had agents stationed in about ten foreign countries, before being elevated to assistant commissioner of prohibition in 1929.[57] His successful investigation of liquor smuggling cases, and his lead role in negotiating a smuggling information agreement among eighteen nations, contributed to his next promotion as head of the Prohibition Bureau's Narcotics Division.[58] When that division was legislated into a separate agency a few months later, Anslinger was appointed commissioner of narcotics. Not surprisingly, given his background and perception of the problem, Anslinger began his tenure by stressing the international dimension of the narcotics traffic. He became a leading figure in the international conferences and agencies concerned with narcotics, as well as the leading U.S. diplomat on drug control issues.[59] He also played a pioneering role in coordinating the collection and dissemination of intelligence on international drug production and trafficking and had few inhibitions about sending his agents abroad.

Customs agents also continued to devote some of their time and resources to curbing the drug traffic. U.S. agents stationed along the border routinely supervised undercover antidrug operations in Mexican territory. Throughout the 1930s, a combination of drug enforcement agents, Treasury agents, Customs officials from border stations, and U.S. consular officials collected information on drug smuggling. In Shanghai, a Treasury agent kept tabs on drug and other smuggling from China, the source of much of the illegal opiates in the United States. Narcotics matters in Europe were mostly handled by Treasury agents until 1936, when three FBN agents were stationed in Rome and Paris. They departed three years later, when war broke out in Europe.

U.S. International Crime Control during the Cold War

The expanding scope of U.S. international law enforcement activities since the close of the Second World War was part of two broader developments: the U.S. government's decision not to return to a policy of relative isolationism, as it had following the First World War, but rather to assume leading roles in the struggle against communism and the invigoration of the capitalist world; and the proliferation of transnational nongovernmental activities—financial, industrial, legal, environmental, and otherwise—in which the U.S. government perceived a political or regulatory interest.

Even absent this new internationalist perspective, however, two other developments would have obliged U.S. law enforcement officials to expand their international efforts. The more readily anticipated was the increase in transnational criminal activity that inevitably accompanied the dramatic growth in the volume of legitimate transnational exchange. As transnational securities transactions, banking exchanges, commercial ventures, and credit card charges all increased dramatically, so did the number of frauds associated with them. One need only assume that the criminal proportion of overall transnational economic activity was constant to conclude that the overall magnitude of transnational criminal activity must have increased dramatically. Less readily anticipated, from the perspectives of the 1940s and 1950s, was the explosive growth in the illicit traffic in cannabis, cocaine, and heroin, which had been criminalized earlier in the century. Related to all these developments was a persistent expansion in the reach of both the substantive criminal law and the claims of extraterritorial jurisdiction to cover an ever broader array of undesirable activities. Much of this was driven, as before, by domestic politics. But much of it was also initiated and driven—to a far greater extent than ever before—by the advocacy efforts of federal law enforcement officials.

The leadership of the United States in the anticommunist struggle resulted in a number of significant developments in the domain of international law enforcement. U.S. law enforcement agencies were charged with investigating violations of new laws prohibiting the export of weapons and sophisticated technology to pro-Soviet and other unfriendly governments. And espionage activities directed against the United States needed to be investigated, not just by the intelligence agencies but, because criminal prosecution of spies is a key counterespionage weapon employed by democratic governments, by law enforcement agents as well.

Apart from the national security incentives, the most important factor contributing to the internationalization of both crime and law enforcement was the growing ease of transnational interactions as a consequence of developments in technology. Increasingly rapid and accessible jet travel permitted both criminals and police to travel easily and quickly almost anywhere in the world. Advances in telecommunications allowed criminals to conspire and commit crimes transnationally, even as the same advances facilitated transnational exchange of information and coordination of joint investigations among law enforcement agents. Internationally linked computers presented new opportunities for criminals, both in defrauding legitimate actors and in setting up their own operations, but they also provided police with more efficient means of keeping track of transnational criminals, exchanging intelligence with foreign counterparts, and creating databases on criminals and criminal activities. In all these respects, crime and law enforcement were internationalized by technological developments in much the same way as other types of international commerce and governmental regulation.

Equally significant was the enactment of new laws that created new types of transnational crime. Some did so by criminalizing conduct that had not previously been criminalized. The Export Control Act of 1949 and subsequent legislation enhancing that act, for instance, extended the reach of the criminal law to transnational activities that previously had been legal.[60] The crime of transnational money laundering did not exist until 1970 at the earliest, when Congress made it illegal to take $5,000 or more in or out of the country without reporting that fact, and it attained independent standing only in 1986, when Congress criminalized the act of money laundering. By 1990, enforcement of criminal laws directed at money laundering would become a major preoccupation of U.S. international law enforcement efforts.[61] Other laws extended the reach of U.S. criminal jurisdiction abroad, such as by criminalizing terrorist and other offenses and conspiracies against U.S. citizens and interests that previously had fallen outside the purview of U.S. courts.

Many of these developments followed from the nationalization of crime and crime control within the United States.[62] The emergence of crime as a national issue, and of crime control as a federal responsibility, is best dated to 1964, when Senator Barry Goldwater focused attention on rising crime rates during his presidential campaign and President Lyndon Johnson reluctantly responded by placing crime control on the federal agenda. Both the nationalization of the crime issue and the federalization of crime control had received their first substantial impetus during the 1930s, when the administration of Franklin Delano Roosevelt included crime control among the array of issues on his New Deal agenda.[63] Congressional interest in racketeering provided additional impetus in the following decades.[64] By the 1960s, the inhibitions on federal intrusions into what had traditionally been perceived as domains of state jurisdiction had faded substantially. The Johnson administration laid the initial groundwork, after which the Nixon administration entered office committed to an aggressive federal involvement in crime control and a dramatic escalation in the "war on drugs."[65] The Ford and Carter administrations brought both a diminution in the rhetoric as well as revelations of legal and illegal excesses by federal police agencies. But the Reagan and Bush administrations revived the crime issue in the 1980s and sponsored dramatic increases in both the reach of federal criminal laws and the resources of federal criminal justice agencies.

The internationalization of crime control represented extensions of these domestic developments. Having declared a war on drugs, the Nixon administration focused substantial attention and resources on the foreign sources of the heroin, cocaine, and most of the marijuana consumed in the United States. Indeed, the international dimension was attractive because it offered a rare domain of criminal justice activity where the federal government could proceed unencumbered by state and local agencies and because it provided an inviting political target for those who preferred not to focus too much attention on domestic causes for increasing illicit drug use. The rapid growth of the federal law enforcement agencies also provided the institutional bases required to sustain a substantial international presence. As these agencies expanded their activities but found their investigations frustrated by both criminal ingenuity and restrictions on their investigative powers and capacities, they proposed and lobbied for new criminal legislation to improve their powers of detection and to increase the variety of legal stumbling blocks on which criminals and their accomplices might trip up. The results were laws requiring the divulgence of information about financial transactions, criminalizing involvement in the laundering of illicitly derived revenues, authorizing the forfeiture of assets associated with criminal activity, and otherwise seeking to complicate and uncover criminal endeavors.

These developments meant increases in interactions with foreign police, international travel, international investigations, and, for many of the U.S. law enforcement agencies, foreign offices. Some U.S. police agents became intimately involved in the more operational aspects of criminal investigation, typically in collaboration with foreign police officials. They recruited and ran informants, conducted physical and electronic surveillances, employed undercover operations, supervised controlled deliveries of illicit drugs and other illegal commodities, and so on. Although the internationalization of law enforcement was a two-way street, most of the traffic carried U.S. badges.

The Expansion of U.S. Drug Enforcement Abroad

From the end of the Second World War until its demise in 1968, the over-seas presence of the Federal Bureau of Narcotics remained quite modest, numbering no more than a dozen or so agents even in its last year. U.S. Customs retained substantial jurisdiction over international drug traffick-ing investigations and employed a greater number of agents abroad than the FBN. Nonetheless, both the international orientation of the longtime director of the FBN, Harry Anslinger, and the international nature of the drug traffic ensured that the agency would continue to place special em-phasis on foreign drug trafficking.

Immediately following the end of the war, five FBN agents were at-tached to General Douglas MacArthur's staff in Japan and assigned to assist in dismantling the opium monopolies in Japan, Korea, and other Asian na-tions.[66] Another FBN agent was sent to Germany to assist in reestablishing its drug enforcement system.[67] As international drug traffickers resumed their activities in Europe and the Middle East, Anslinger sent a number of his top agents to the continent to pursue their investigations. In late 1951, the FBN opened a permanent office in Rome, and a second was opened in Beirut the following year. During the early 1960s, additional offices were established in Paris, Istanbul, Bangkok, Mexico City, and Monterrey, Mexico. The men stationed abroad maintained contact with high-level police officials, developed informants, pressured local police and other officials to do more against drug trafficking, conducted operations both unilaterally and in league with local police, pursued leads from U.S.-based investigations, and generally performed whatever services they were called on to do.[68]

Rarely welcomed by State Department officials abroad and operating with relatively few legal or organizational guidelines, the FBN agents re-lied on their own discretion and adapted as the various circumstances and environments required. Like private detectives, their success substantially depended on their ability to cultivate informants, conduct investigations, and develop effective working relationships with local police and other con-tacts. Interpol proved especially valuable in this regard.[69] Indeed, in a few countries, the FBN and hospitable local police found it useful to designate the U.S. agents officially as Interpol representatives, thereby deflecting un-desired attention from the fact that police agents of a foreign sovereign were active on local soil. According to Myles Ambrose, a U.S. official periodically involved in international law enforcement matters from the 1950s to the 1970s, "Operational agents from the Bureau of Narcotics abroad could claim and did claim to be Interpol agents to give their work a veneer of legitimacy. We didn't give a goddamn about Interpol early on. We wanted Interpol to legitimize our police operations overseas as we were the only country in the world that sends cops abroad operationally."[70]

Much was to change in the late 1960s and early 1970s. In 1968, the FBN was transferred from the Treasury to the Justice Department. There it was merged with the Bureau of Drug Abuse Control (BDAC), which had been created in 1966 to regulate barbiturates, amphetamine, hallucinogens, and counterfeit drugs. Housed in the Food and Drug Administration within the Department of Health, Education and Welfare, BDAC had often come into conflict with the Treasury Department's drug enforcement agency. With the consolidation of the two agencies under the Justice Department roof, the Bureau of Narcotics and Dangerous Drugs (BNDD) came into being. Five years later, a second reorganization sought to resolve the increasingly fierce turf battles among BNDD, Customs' drug enforcement section, and two other drug enforcement agencies that had been formed in the interim: the Office of National Narcotics Intelligence and the Office of Drug Abuse Law Enforcement. The proposed solution was the merger of all federal drug enforcement personnel and operations into one organization within the Justice Department: the Drug Enforcement Administration (DEA).[71]

In 1967, the last full year of the FBN's existence, the budget of the Treasury Department's drug enforcement agency was approximately $3 million. Roughly a dozen of its three hundred agents were stationed in eight locations outside the United States. Six years and two bureaucratic reorganizations later, in the last full year of BNDD operations, the drug enforcement agency boasted a budget of $74 million and 1,446 agents, of whom 124 were abroad in forty-seven offices in thirty-three countries. By 1976, the DEA's budget was just short of $200 million; 228 of its 2,141 agents were stationed overseas in sixty-eight offices in forty-three countries. In less than a decade, a small overseas complement of U.S. drug enforcement agents had grown into the first global law enforcement agency with operational capabilities. About three hundred agents would be stationed in over seventy foreign locations by the early 1990s.[72]

The dramatic expansion of the U.S. drug enforcement presence abroad was motivated in large part by the Nixon administration's declaration of a war on drugs and its desire to involve foreign governments in its campaign. The campaign to internationalize the drug war combined an expansion of the global presence of U.S. agents with efforts to develop the vicarious drug enforcement capabilities of foreign police agencies. The U.S. agents stationed abroad also played a symbolic role, providing a visible manifestation of the U.S. commitment to supply-side drug enforcement and its willingness to assist foreign police. Their presence in U.S. embassies served as a constant reminder both to foreign governments and to U.S. ambassadors that drug enforcement was now a high-level foreign policy objective in Washington.

More practically, the proliferation of overseas agents contributed to the central objective of the agency: immobilizing drug traffickers. This meant obtaining the information necessary to identify, locate, and convict them. Because most illicit drugs originated from abroad, most of the information, evidence, and international traffickers could be found there as well. The drug enforcement agents sent abroad also were expected to devote substantial efforts to building up and training foreign drug enforcement units. This was true not just in Latin America and Asia, where many criminal investigative units were neither specialized nor particularly concerned with illicit drugs, but also in Europe, where illicit drugs represented a relatively minor concern of the police, the public, and the politicians. The overseas drug enforcement agent was tasked to carve out drug enforcement units from local police forces and to train them in the investigative techniques employed by the agency in the United States. They were expected to push for structural changes in drug enforcement wherever they were stationed, to lobby for tougher laws, to train local police in drug enforcement techniques, and to sensitize local officials to U.S. concerns. By the late 1980s, both foreign police and U.S. embassies had become accustomed to the presence of DEA agents in their midst.

The internationalization of the U.S. war on drugs brought about three sorts of changes in the criminal justice environments of many foreign countries. One was institutional. Until well into the 1960s, relatively few foreign police agencies possessed specialized drug enforcement squads and virtually no prosecutors specialized in drug trafficking cases. By the late 1980s, many foreign police agencies claimed such units and quite a few worked closely with specialized prosecutors. This was especially true in Europe, where drug enforcement units had proliferated at all levels of government. A second change was operational. When U.S. drug enforcement agents set foot in foreign countries, they brought with them a variety of investigative techniques, including "buy and bust" tactics and more extensive undercover operations, "controlled delivery" of illicit drug consignments, various forms of nontelephonic electronic surveillance, and offers of reduced charges or immunity from prosecution to known drug dealers to "flip" them into becoming informants. These tactics had been practiced in the United States for decades and approved by U.S. courts during Prohibition, if not before.[73] In most countries, however, and particularly in the civil law nations of Europe and Latin America, most of these techniques were viewed as unnecessary, unacceptable, and often illegal. Nonetheless, during the following two decades, most of these investigative tactics were adopted, to varying degrees, by foreign drug enforcement units. A third change was legal. Even as foreign drug enforcement agents adopted DEA-style techniques during the 1970s and 1980s, their legality remained highly questionable. By the late 1980s, however, many of the DEA-style methods had not only been adopted by the local police but had been authorized, and hence legalized, by local courts and legislatures.

It is therefore quite accurate to speak of the "Americanization" of international drug enforcement during this period.[74] Where once most foreign police and prosecutors shunned undercover operations, were skeptical of controlled deliveries, and shied away from efforts to flip drug dealers into becoming informants, by the late 1980s police and prosecutors in most European countries openly acknowledged their involvement in such practices. What began as a discreet police tactic employed first by DEA agents and informants working closely with local agents, and then by local agents and informants operating without the clear sanction of either prosecutors or the law, had evolved into a relatively common law enforcement practice explicitly authorized by prosecutors, courts, and legislatures in most countries. In some European nations, the initial impulses in this direction were motivated by the need to extract information from arrested members of terrorist groups. But in quite a number of countries, the evolution was one in which the hand of the DEA—as proponent, example, tutor, and lobbyist—was also readily apparent.

The FBI Abroad

Throughout much of the world, the law enforcement agency most identified with the U.S. government was the Federal Bureau of Investigation. On the one hand, the FBI's overseas presence paled beside that of the drug enforcement agencies after the early 1970s. In 1990, its overseas agents, known as LEGATs (short for legal attachés), numbered only forty in seventeen countries. It remained among the least operational of all U.S. law enforcement agencies overseas. On the other hand, starting in the 1980s, its international presence expanded significantly. FBI agents traveled abroad with increasing frequency to conduct international investigations, lead training programs, lend their expertise in forensic and other investigative techniques, and attend international law enforcement conferences.

The heyday of the FBI's international program paralleled the history of the CIA's predecessor, the Office of Strategic Services (OSS). In June 1940, President Roosevelt assigned all intelligence responsibilities for the Western Hemisphere to the FBI. Shortly thereafter, FBI Director J. Edgar Hoover created a Special Intelligence Service (SIS) to undertake the major task of countering Axis activities in South and Central America. Within a few years, 360 agents were stationed throughout the region, particularly in Mexico, Argentina, and Brazil. South American officials working covertly for the Nazis were exposed, as were the pro-Nazi activities of the large German communities throughout the continent. Local police were cultivated with money and invitations to the National Police Academy in Washington. Throughout the war, a network of FBI-trained police was built up that would continue to aid the FBI's more mundane law enforcement efforts in peacetime.[75]

Toward the end of the war, Hoover vied with the OSS to have the SIS serve as the nucleus of the postwar intelligence system. When he failed, many of the SIS agents based in Latin America went to work for the new CIA. A few remained where they had been stationed, becoming the first of what would soon develop into a modest international network of LEGATs. Unlike the SIS agents, the LEGATs were charged not just with counter-espionage responsibilities but with investigating criminal matters as well. They also were ordered to refrain from engaging in the types of operational activities undertaken by the SIS during the war and by U.S. drug enforcement agents thereafter. Within a few years, the LEGATs became widely recognized as the official U.S. police liaisons to foreign governments and police agencies. LEGATs were expected to handle all international matters that fell within the FBI's jurisdiction. This included counterintelligence, criminal investigation (much of it involving white-collar crime and organized crime), and counterterrorism (which could involve both counterintelligence and criminal investigative tasks and contacts). LEGATs typically refrained from investigating criminal matters personally, confining their involvement to that of liaison between U.S. and local law enforcement agencies and prosecutors. They facilitated requests to and from the United States for information, evidence, interrogations, searches, arrests, and extraditions. Requests were transmitted in a variety of ways: informally by phone, wire, letter or personal visit, or formally via Interpol, letters rogatory, or the procedures laid out in mutual legal assistance treaties. Where information was required in the form of evidence admissible in U.S. courts, U.S. prosecutors could request by letter rogatory or pursuant to a treaty that the resident LEGAT be permitted to conduct an interview, attend an interrogation, or collect documents.

Throughout the 1950s and 1960s, the LEGAT program was limited to approximately ten foreign offices, with each responsible for liaison with many other countries as well. The program grew during the Nixon administration when J. Edgar Hoover persuaded the president of the advantages of expanding the LEGAT network, primarily for intelligence purposes. During the 1980s, the international activities of the FBI increased dramatically. Agency policies that had prevented U.S.-based agents from pursuing their investigations abroad were eased. In 1982, the FBI was made the parent agency of the DEA and given joint jurisdiction over drug cases involving organized crime.

Even more important to the internationalization of the FBI's investigations was congressional legislation in 1984 and 1986 that greatly broadened U.S. extraterritorial jurisdiction over terrorist acts.[76] Coordinating their efforts with the CIA and the State Department's Counterterrorism Office as well as foreign police agencies, FBI agents played a role in investigations of more than fifty terrorist incidents outside U.S. borders between 1985 and mid-1989, including a number of abductions of U.S. citizens in Lebanon.[77] FBI agents were later sent to assist in the investigation of the hijacking of the Italian cruise ship *Achille Lauro*, in particular to gather forensic information on board the ship.[78] Agents also were sent to investigate the June 1985 hijackings of a TWA flight while en route from Athens to Rome and of a Royal Jordanian Airlines flight in Beirut, the November 1985 hijacking of an Egypt Air flight, the April 1986 bombing of a TWA flight, and the September 1986 bombing of a Pan Am flight in Karachi.[79]

During the late 1980s, FBI agents joined with agents of the military's law enforcement agencies in investigating bombings at U.S. military bases in Spain, Italy, Greece, and the Philippines as well as the assassinations of U.S. military personnel in Athens in June 1988 and Manila in April 1989 by the 17 November organization and the Philippine New People's Army, respectively; they combined with Italian police in investigating the Japanese Red Army's attack on the U.S. embassy in Rome in June 1987; and they participated in the investigation of the August 1988 airplane crash in Pakistan that killed President Mohammad Zia ul-Haq, many top Pakistani military officials, and the U.S. ambassador, Arnold Raphel—although only after congressional criticism of the initial State Department decision to bar the FBI agents from Pakistan cleared the way ten months later.[80] The most intensive international investigation by the FBI during the decade involved the terrorist explosion of Pan Am Flight 103 over Lockerbie, Scotland, in December 1988. Dozens of FBI agents, including LEGATs as well as forensic experts and other U.S.-based agents, combined with English, Scottish, and German police in tracking down leads in over forty countries from Sweden and Malta to the Far East.[81]

By late 1986, the need to provide some coordination over the FBI's growing number of international activities prompted the creation of an Office of Liaison and International Affairs (OLIA) at FBI headquarters. OLIA also was charged with supervising the growing number of foreign police representatives based in the United States as well as most visits by foreign police officials, including the growing number of foreign students participating in the eleven-week command-level training program at the FBI's National Academy in Quantico.

The Activities of Other U.S. Law Enforcement Agencies Abroad

The one agency whose jurisdiction most naturally encompassed transnational crime was the U.S. Customs Service. For much of the twentieth century, its overseas presence exceeded that of any other civilian law enforcement agency, until the BNDD surpassed it during the late 1960s. From 1930 to 1973, Customs vied with first the FBN and thereafter the BNDD for greater jurisdiction over international drug trafficking cases, until it lost the turf struggle in a major bureaucratic reorganization in 1973. By 1979, its presence abroad had been reduced to eight foreign offices focused almost entirely on enforcement of antidumping statutes and non-drug-related smuggling. During the 1980s, it reasserted its role in international matters, assuming the lead in investigating high-tech smuggling and money laundering, both of which required Customs to focus on illicit exports rather than imports.

Customs had investigated high-tech smuggling since the beginning of the cold war, but new opportunities emerged with Congress's passage of the 1979 Export Administration Act, the Carter administration's growing interest in this issue following the Soviet invasion of Afghanistan, and the high priority subsequently given the issue by the Reagan administration. In late 1981, Customs launched Operation Exodus, a more systematic effort to investigate and curtail high-tech smuggling. Its initial efforts were somewhat haphazard and plagued by turf conflicts with the FBI, the Bureau of Alcohol, Tobacco and Firearms (ATF), the intelligence agencies, and especially the Commerce Department's Export Enforcement Office, which opened offices in Vienna, Bern, and Stockholm during the 1980s.[82] Customs retained its lead role, however, and its agents gained in expertise. By the late 1980s, high-tech smuggling had emerged as the top priority of virtually all Customs attachés overseas.

The second development, the potential of which Customs was initially slow to recognize, was the enactment of the Bank Secrecy Act in 1970. The legislation was prompted by growing concern over the use of foreign financial secrecy jurisdictions to launder illegally earned money and the emerging realization that tracing the paper trail of laundered money could implicate high-level drug traffickers and other criminals. One provision of the Act, which required that individuals taking more than $5,000 in or out of the country file a Currency Transaction Report, provided Customs with a reentry into the area of drug enforcement as well as other areas of criminal investigation. In the first interagency task force to focus on money laundering, Operation Greenback in Miami, Customs agents once again began to travel overseas in drug-related cases, although their focus was now on the movement of money rather than drugs.

Apart from high-tech smuggling and money laundering, Customs attachés continued to investigate violations of antidumping laws, commercial fraud, arms and pornography smuggling, and other contraband activities. These attachés tended to be slightly more "operational" than the LEGATs, in that they became directly involved in investigations, but with one or two exceptions they exercised greater restraint in their activities than did most overseas DEA agents. Only toward the late 1980s did Customs start shedding its inhibitions against acting more operationally overseas. But Customs attachés still interacted primarily with foreign customs agencies.

Customs' principal obstacle overseas, one that it shared with the Immigration and Naturalization Service (INS), was that many of the violations of U.S. laws that concerned them were not violations of local laws, or were violations only in egregious cases. Only toward the end of the 1980s, for instance, did a number of governments begin to criminalize money laundering. Similarly, most non-NATO countries demonstrated relatively little interest in regulating high-tech exports. With regard to many other forms of contraband, relatively few states prohibited the export of goods the import of which into the United States was illegal. All of this contrasted with the laws that DEA and the Secret Service were charged with enforcing, which were in effect throughout the world and backed by global conventions. Customs tried to compensate for this disadvantage by vigorously developing bilateral relationships with dozens of foreign customs agencies—not least by offering a broad array of training and other assistance programs—and by playing a leading role in the Customs Cooperation Council and the assorted regional customs conferences.

With more than half of all counterfeit U.S. dollars produced and circulated overseas, the Secret Service had operated internationally since its origins. The emergence of the U.S. dollar as a sort of international currency following World War II increased this need. The most common task required of Secret Service agents abroad was to assist in the identification of counterfeit dollars, a process that generally involved checking a suspected note against the "circularized note" files at headquarters. Like DEA agents abroad, Secret Service agents cooperated closely in foreign investigations, providing intelligence on suspected counterfeiters and their techniques, assisting in the recruitment, evaluation, and payment of informants, performing undercover roles, testifying in court, providing affidavits, keeping tabs on retail paper producers, and offering technical and professional advice to foreign police agencies.

The federal agency that underwent the most dramatic expansion in overseas activities in the 1980s was the U.S. Marshals Service. In November 1979, the U.S. attorney general transferred some of the responsibility for apprehending federal fugitives from the FBI to the Marshals Service; this authority was augmented in August 1988.[83] The agency responded by setting up an international branch to coordinate the apprehension and recovery of fugitives who had fled abroad. Much of the marshals' international work involved no more than escorting fugitives who already had been captured by foreign police agencies back to the United States. But during the 1980s, the marshals began to play a more direct role in locating fugitives abroad, assisting foreign police in their apprehension, and devising sting operations to lure fugitives to the United States or into the hands of cooperative authorities overseas.

Apart from their involvement in collecting and delivering fugitives, the Marshals Service shared its expertise in other matters with foreign law enforcement agencies. During the 1980s, police officials in a number of countries confronting threats by organized crime and terrorist groups became aware of the Marshal Service's Witness Protection Program; representatives from Canada, Britain, Australia, Italy, and Germany came to the United States to learn about the program, and in a few cases the U.S. program was even used to assist foreign criminal justice authorities in protecting vulnerable witnesses. In the area of court security, the Marshals Service studied the court security systems of foreign countries, notably France and Italy, which had been obliged to protect their judicial officials and courtrooms from Arab terrorists and powerful organized crime gangs.[84] The Marshals Service's Special Operations Group, created in 1971 to respond to emergency situations such as civil disturbances, terrorist incidents, and the more difficult courtroom security and fugitive apprehension tasks, trained foreign police in counterterrorist methods and helped to coordinate the transport of particularly notorious fugitives to the United States; the most prominent example during the 1980s was the Panamanian dictator General Manuel Noriega, following the U.S. invasion of Panama in late 1989.

The Bureau of Alcohol, Tobacco and Firearms was lured into international law enforcement matters during the early 1970s primarily by foreign demands to crack down on the smuggling of firearms and explosives out of the United States.[85] Although this issue fell primarily within the jurisdiction of Customs and the FBI, ATF was called on by both foreign police agencies and Congress because of its greater expertise in regulating domestic sales of weapons. The first to request its assistance was the Mexican government, which had enacted a tough gun control law in 1968 that generated a lucrative black market for imported firearms and which was concerned about the flow of weapons into the hands of domestic insurgents. Additional requests followed from the British government, whose concerns focused—as they had for more than a century—on weapons acquisitions in the United States by and for the Irish Republican Army. ATF played a similar role in curtailing the illicit traffic in explosives. At the request of the State Department and various foreign governments, ATF agents trained foreign law enforcement personnel in explosives detection and handling. In 1987, ATF established liaisons with bomb data centers in Canada, Germany, Australia, and Israel to exchange information on explosives incidents in those countries.

Despite the expanding array of contacts with foreign law enforcement officials, as well as closer collaboration on international terrorism investigations with the FBI, CIA, and the State Department's Anti-Terrorism Office, ATF had yet to assume a strong international presence by the end of the 1980s. Like most other federal U.S. law enforcement agencies, ATF's most frequent foreign contacts were with law enforcement authorities in Canada and Mexico; like the U.S. Marshals Service and other agencies with few or no foreign offices, the ATF was obliged to make the most of its participation in formal international gatherings to establish ties with foreign counterparts.

The principal law enforcement concerns of Immigration and Naturalization Service offices abroad were twofold: investigating and deterring efforts to smuggle illegal aliens into the United States and ensuring that aliens with criminal records did not enter the United States. Reasoning, like the DEA, "that it is easier and more cost efficient to intercept or prevent potential illegal aliens from entering the country before their actual arrival at our gates," INS decided in 1985 to increase the criminal investigative responsibilities of its overseas agents.[86] INS increasingly concerned itself not just with violations of the immigration laws but with any number of criminal activities in which the role of aliens had been conspicuous. Often, a violation of U.S. immigration laws, like tax violations, provided the relatively innocuous hook with which to indict criminals guilty of far more serious crimes. In one case, for instance, a senior member of the Japanese organized crime group Yakuza was convicted of false statements in connection with obtaining a visa and entry into the United States.[87] The INS's most extensive foreign interactions, however, involved Mexico and the nearly two-thousand-mile border separating the two countries (discussed in greater detail in the next chapter).

City and state police officials were typically the least involved in international law enforcement matters. During the 1980s, however, the growing number of joint investigations involving federal, state, and city law enforcement officials generated new opportunities for international interaction. Most relied on Interpol to handle the bulk of their international needs, but the fact that most criminal investigations in the United States were conducted by municipal police, combined with the fact that many criminal offenses still did not fall under federal jurisdiction, suggested that city and state police agencies throughout the United States became far more involved in transnational travel and communication than ever before. Not surprisingly, the city and state police forces with the greatest experience in international policing issues were those working near the borders with Mexico and Canada. Relations between police departments on either side of the U.S.-Canadian border tended to be close and professional. Relations along the Mexican border were more varied, ranging from close and long-standing personal relationships that cut through any red tape, to bitter antagonisms and suspicions. During the 1970s and 1980s, state and municipal police agencies near both borders took steps to regularize and formalize their cross-border relations, in part by creating specialized liaison units to handle cross-border matters. During the same time, but particularly after the mid-1980s, the federal law enforcement presence along the border increased substantially, motivated by the intensification of the war on drugs and by renewed attention to illegal migration from Mexico.[88]

Unlike other federal law enforcement agencies, the U.S. office of Interpol, known as the National Central Bureau (NCB), was not charged with the enforcement of any federal criminal laws. Its function was primarily one of facilitating communication between U.S. and foreign police agencies by providing both a central office through which international messages could be channeled and distributed. With some twenty thousand federal, state, and local police agencies in the United States, foreign police were often at a loss as to whom to contact in providing and seeking information and other assistance. The same was true of most police departments in the United States, many of which occasionally needed to communicate with foreign police but had little idea as to how to do so efficiently, if at all. As police departments became more aware of the accessibility of the Interpol system and the identity of the NCB, the process of internationalization began to penetrate the provincialism of many local police forces.

U.S. involvement in Interpol can be roughly divided into three phases. The first, from about 1950 to 1969, was more a case of noninvolvement. FBI Director Hoover generally shunned the international agency, preferred that U.S. police agencies rely on the LEGAT system to communicate internationally, and made small efforts to preclude other federal agencies from participating in Interpol. The second phase began in 1969, when the U.S. NCB, which had been officially created in 1962, was provided with an office and a staff of three. The scale of its operations throughout the 1970s remained limited, with the NCB handling an average of three hundred cases per year.[89] The third phase, beginning in 1979, was ushered in with the appointment of a dynamic Secret Service agent, Richard Stiener, as chief of the NCB. Stiener also embarked on an ambitious and successful campaign to increase dramatically the NCB's staff and budget, computerize its operations, involve the federal law enforcement agencies in its activities, publicize its existence and services to state police agencies, and enhance the NCB's role and status at Interpol headquarters. Between 1979 and 1990, the NCB's staff increased from six to 110, its budget from $125,000 to $6 million, and the number of law enforcement agencies represented at the NCB from one to sixteen. By 1990, most state police agencies were formally affiliated with the NCB and many had established their own Interpol liaison office. Between 1976 and 1986, the annual caseload of the NCB rose from about four thousand to 43,863 and the volume of message traffic from 14,365 to 101,859. These dramatic increases, we must stress, reflected a burgeoning of not just transnational criminal activity but also the growing capacity and desire of U.S. government agencies to handle international criminal law enforcement matters.

U.S. participation in Interpol contributed to the evolution of international policing in at least three ways. First, in providing a link between the police agencies of most governments that was relatively quick and efficient, it increased the capacity of city, state, and national law enforcement agencies to deal with the challenges posed by transnational crime. Interpol was primarily responsible for the increasing difficulty that fugitives faced in finding a haven where they could remain undetected. Interpol also offered an international professional association for policemen. By the 1980s, its annual meetings drew delegates from more than one hundred nations. Its regional conferences similarly played a role in bringing together police from nearby countries in a forum where they could exchange information and opinions and form personal relationships to cut through red tape and speed requests. Second, Interpol acted as a channel for the dissemination of new police methods and investigative techniques. Its publication, translated into half a dozen languages, was the only police magazine circulated around the world. Third, Interpol became an increasingly effective means for the U.S. government to internationalize its policing concerns. During the 1970s, the emphasis was on drug trafficking. In the 1980s, the U.S. government encouraged Interpol as an organization, and through Interpol other governments, to improve their international cooperation against terrorism and the financial aspects of drug trafficking. Until the early 1980s, Interpol resisted cooperating in terrorist cases, fearing that its reputation as a strictly apolitical organization would be undermined. But significant U.S. pressures, combined with the recognition that Interpol's failure to reform in this area would relegate it to the sidelines of a crucial domain of international law enforcement, led to a change in policy. As the United States had come to play a more dominant role in the previously Europe-centered organization (the head of the U.S. Secret Service was elected Interpol president in 1984), its ability to internationalize its own law enforcement concerns and approaches greatly expanded.

The Internationalization of Evidence Gathering

Obtaining evidence from abroad—in a form admissible in American judicial proceedings—had long been as essential to the success of criminal prosecutions as collecting intelligence and obtaining the offender. It was also the most dependent on legal formalities and afforded the least latitude for the sorts of informal measures and understandings on which police normally relied in their international dealings. The demands of American prosecutors for evidence located abroad grew dramatically beginning in the 1960s. The reasons were varied. Traditional transnational criminal activities such as drug trafficking, terrorism, tax evasion, and assorted frauds proliferated. Congress had both criminalized and asserted extraterritorial jurisdiction over an ever widening array of transnational activities and granted U.S. law enforcement agencies greater extraterritorial powers. The internationalization of the securities and commodities markets required the Securities and Exchange Commission and the Commodities Futures Trading Commission to expand the scope of their regulatory efforts overseas. And all of the federal law enforcement agencies had become far more aggressive in targeting, investigating, and prosecuting transnational activities.

U.S. law enforcement officials made great strides in the 1970s and 1980s in reducing the frictions that had impeded the exchange of evidence and in persuading foreign governments to relax their secrecy laws when criminal conduct was suspected. By 1990, the U.S. government had signed mutual legal assistance treaties (MLATs) with thirteen governments and was engaged in negotiations with many others; it had negotiated special narcotics-related exchange-of-information agreements with the governments of a number of Caribbean financial secrecy jurisdictions; it had expanded the number of tax conventions providing for exchange of information in tax evasion cases; it had amended its own laws to facilitate the collection and admissibility of evidence from abroad; it had persuaded foreign governments to change their laws in order to make evidence more available to U.S. officials investigating a variety of crimes, including tax and securities fraud; it had experimented with a number of more coercive, unilateral legal measures for obtaining evidence from abroad; and it had utilized international organizations such as Interpol and the United Nations drug control commissions, as well as summits of the G-7 governments, to urge foreign governments to adopt U.S. approaches to mutual legal assistance.[90]

These efforts can be seen as part and parcel of a global campaign, inspired originally by the United States but increasingly involving multinational initiatives, to better immobilize transnational criminals by obtaining the evidence required not just to indict and convict them in courts of law but also to freeze, seize, and forfeit their assets. As with other domains of international law enforcement, the broader story is one of trying both to transcend the basic obstacles created by notions of national sovereignty and to alleviate the frictions that arise when different law enforcement systems are obliged to interact; one in which the United States has made modest accommodations to foreign legal systems and foreign authorities much greater accommodations to U.S. demands; one in which cooperative efforts have mixed with more coercive inducements; and one involving not just bilateral treaties and other arrangements but also unilateral measures and multilateral undertakings. Many of the MLATs negotiated by U.S. officials starting in the 1970s are best understood in the context of the bilateral conflicts generated by U.S. efforts to obtain evidence unilaterally— efforts designed both to obtain evidence in individual investigations and prosecutions and to pressure foreign governments more generally to be more accommodating to U.S. law enforcement needs. Indeed, the principal incentive for many foreign governments to negotiate MLATs with the United States was the desire to curtail the resort by U.S. prosecutors, police agents, and courts to unilateral, extraterritorial means of collecting evidence from abroad.

Both the MLAT negotiations and many of the other initiatives intended to facilitate the collection of evidence from abroad can be understood as responses to the inadequacy of preexisting methods. The principal means of requesting evidence from foreign authorities had traditionally been by letters rogatory. These were written requests from a court in one state to a foreign court requesting the provision of evidence or some other form of assistance needed in a judicial proceeding. Law enforcement officials typically resorted to letters rogatory when Interpol and other international police channels were unable to produce the requested evidence, often because a court's authority was required to obtain the evidence.

Letters rogatory were relatively effective when dealing with foreign authorities familiar with both the letters rogatory process and U.S. evidentiary requirements. They proved ill-suited, however, to the increasingly complex and voluminous needs of modern international law enforcement efforts. MLATs were intended and designed to remedy many of the limitations of letters rogatory. MLATs obligated the requested country to provide evidence and other forms of assistance, and MLAT requests bypassed both U.S. courts and all diplomatic channels, thereby drastically shortening the time required to secure foreign assistance. MLATs also could establish a procedural framework for ensuring that the evidence obtained would be admissible in U.S. courts. Most important, MLATs (and the accompanying implementing legislation) could provide a powerful means of penetrating the financial secrecy laws that so often frustrated U.S. criminal investigators.[91]

U.S. law enforcement officials before World War II typically believed that their government could not sign any international legal assistance agreement given the extent of state jurisdiction over criminal procedure and the restraints imposed by the Sixth Amendment of the U.S. Constitution. This view faded in the postwar era with the internationalization of U.S. law enforcement responsibilities and the homogenization of state criminal procedures within the United States. Congressional legislation in 1948 and 1964 authorized an expansion of U.S. judicial assistance to foreign states.

When U.S. prosecutors and police looked abroad for evidence, they found their efforts seriously hampered by the inadequacies of foreign and U.S. laws as well as bureaucratic and nationalist resistance to the performance of U.S. judicial functions on foreign territory. Few foreign laws obliged their courts to employ their powers on behalf of foreign law enforcement authorities, much less to accommodate foreign judicial procedures. Foreign courts were prone to reject requests emanating from grand juries and various regulatory agencies that had no counterparts in their own countries. Some were reluctant to obtain any evidence for foreign criminal proceedings or to permit U.S. officials any leeway in collecting evidence. As in the United States, justice ministries abroad lacked any officials specifically charged with responding to letters rogatory. Even when foreign courts were willing to provide evidence, the chances were good that it would be provided in a form inadmissible in U.S. courts. Civil law judges typically did not take kindly to altering their customary procedures to accommodate U.S. constitutional and evidentiary needs such as the right of confrontation by defendants and the demand for verbatim transcripts of testimony. U.S. prosecutors had little choice but to rely on the goodwill and flexibility of foreign judges.

By the late 1960s, U.S. law enforcement officials were increasingly exasperated by the perceived widening gap between criminals' abilities to hide transactions and assets abroad and officials' abilities to detect and investigate what was going on. Organized crime, it was feared, was growing ever richer and more powerful, at least in part because of the protection afforded by foreign financial secrecy jurisdictions such as Switzerland. But

efforts by U.S. criminal investigators to obtain evidence from these jurisdictions were blocked time and time again by the refusal of foreign banks
and government officials to cooperate with U.S. criminal investigations.
During 1967–1968, agreement was reached among officials in the State,
Justice, and Treasury Departments and the Securities and Exchange Commission to seek an accord with the Swiss. The subsequent negotiations
lasted until 1973, and the treaty did not enter into force until 1977. The
U.S. objectives in the MLAT negotiations with the Swiss, and in most subsequent negotiations with other governments, were twofold. They wanted
the Swiss to be more forthcoming in providing evidence requested by
U.S. authorities, and they wanted to ensure that the evidence would be
provided in a form admissible in U.S. courts. These objectives would later
be supplemented by more ambitious objectives requiring the Swiss and
other negotiating partners not merely to accommodate U.S. evidentiary
demands but to adopt the assumptions and objectives of U.S. law enforcement officials as their own. But in the early 1970s, U.S. negotiators had no
choice but to set their sights on the more limited objectives. Indeed, even
they had only a hazy notion of where these first steps would lead.

The significance of the MLAT with Switzerland cannot be overemphasized. It was the first; it was tested in the courts; it paved the way for more
extensive forms of cooperation between the two countries; it provided a
useful model for subsequent MLAT negotiations; and it was utilized more
than all of the other MLATs combined. It was followed by treaties with the
Netherlands, Turkey, Italy, Colombia, Morocco, Canada, the Bahamas,
Thailand, Belgium, Mexico, Nigeria, and the Cayman Islands (represented
by Great Britain). The MLATs typically provided for all international requests to be supervised by a "central authority" in the requested country.
In the case of the United States, the Office of International Affairs in the
Criminal Division of the Justice Department, created in 1979 to oversee
most international law enforcement relations, was given the task of supervising the vast majority of requests for evidence in criminal cases. Most
MLATs encompassed similar types of assistance: locating persons, serving documents, producing records and documents, executing requests for
search and seizure, taking testimony, transferring persons for testimonial
purposes, and, particularly in the more recent treaties, immobilizing and
forfeiting assets. The MLATs committed the requested government to accord foreign requests much the same respect as they accord their own law

enforcement needs; they detailed the processes that must be followed so that the requests and responses conformed to the constitutional and evidentiary requirements of both states; and they typically provided for assistance in a wide array of criminal investigations and proceedings, including grand juries.[92]

In their efforts to persuade foreign governments to sign MLATs with the United States, U.S. officials applied both diplomatic pressures and an assortment of coercive legal mechanisms devised by U.S. prosecutors and approved by U.S. courts.[93] During the late 1970s, federal prosecutors began to subpoena foreign bank officials and attorneys and agents for foreign corporations who entered the United States. During the early 1980s, U.S. prosecutors also directed their subpoenas at U.S. branches of foreign banks and corporations for records stored in other countries. This technique, known as the "Bank of Nova Scotia subpoena" (after the first prominent target), proved more successful and controversial than any previous methods. In 1984, federal prosecutors gained additional powers when Congress approved legislation proposed by the Justice Department to improve its evidence-gathering capabilities. These included the powers to compel criminal defendants not to resist U.S. efforts to obtain documents located abroad and even to compel them to "consent" to third-party disclosure of documents protected by foreign secrecy laws. By the mid-1980s, this last technique, known as the "Ghidoni waiver," had become commonplace.

More often than not, the U.S. efforts succeeded both in obtaining the needed evidence and in pressuring foreign governments to negotiate more accommodating arrangements to handle such matters in the future. As in the U.S.-Swiss law enforcement relationship, cycles of conflict and cooperation followed one upon the other, with each new accommodation leading to new U.S. requests for even broader cooperation.

Viewed from the perspective of U.S. law enforcement officials, the evolution in international evidence-gathering capabilities in the 1970s and 1980s can be compared to an ever more powerful vacuum cleaner. The unilateral tactics devised during the early 1980s, such as the Bank of Nova Scotia subpoenas and the Ghidoni waivers, proved useful in obtaining evidence in specific cases and in inducing foreign governments to sign MLATs with the United States and otherwise improve their commitment and ability to provide assistance in criminal investigations. Changes in U.S. law by both the Congress and the federal courts facilitated the admissibility of evidence collected abroad. The creation of specialized offices in the Justice Department, State Department, and the Securities and Exchange Commission with expertise in international law enforcement matters provided a repository of information, assistance, and contacts of value to prosecutors throughout the country. Those offices also made possible a coherent foreign policy of evidence collection and transmission. The creation of comparable offices in foreign justice ministries provided U.S. officials with reliable transgovernmental partners who shared their objectives. All of these developments were part and parcel of the growth of international judicial assistance between the U.S. government and an expanding list of foreign governments. Increasingly, efforts to improve international cooperation in judicial assistance involved not just mutual accommodation but homogenization of legal systems.

International Asset Forfeiture and Anti–Money Laundering Initiatives

Throughout the 1980s, the most powerful engine driving advances in international law enforcement was the rising global concern over illicit drug trafficking. During the second half of the decade, U.S. influences began to be felt in the area of drug-related asset seizure and forfeiture. Governments throughout the world adopted legislation permitting the seizure and forfeiture of drug trafficker assets; regional organizations, notably in Europe, committed themselves to broader cooperation; and international organizations such as Interpol and the UN's drug control organs promoted model legislation and international cooperation. By far the most significant development was the negotiation of the 1988 United Nations Convention Against Illicit Traffic in Narcotic Drugs and Psychotropic Substances, which mandated extensive cooperation in all law enforcement tasks directed at international drug trafficking, including extradition, mutual legal assistance, and the seizure and forfeiture of assets. The UN Convention was widely seen as providing both added legitimacy and legal authority for many of the international law enforcement measures designed to investigate and prosecute drug trafficking.[94]

The heightened focus on money laundering was largely a function of the rising sensitivity among drug enforcement officials to the financial dimensions of drug trafficking. By the end of the 1980s, the notion that "going after the money" was the most effective way to immobilize drug traffickers had become the conventional wisdom among government investigators and legislators in the United States, Canada, and a number of other countries.[95] It was perceived as essential both to identifying and prosecuting the higher-level drug traffickers who rarely if ever came into contact with their illicit goods and to tracing, seizing, and forfeiting their assets. At the same time, the belief spread that those individuals who assisted drug traffickers in laundering the proceeds of their activities merited harsh criminal sanctions as well.

U.S. legislation directed at money laundering had begun with the enactment of the Bank Secrecy Act in 1970, although the law's requirements that banks report cash transactions of $10,000 or more and that individuals transporting $5,000 or more in cash across the border submit currency reports were not seriously enforced until the mid-1980s. In 1986, however, Congress specifically criminalized the act of laundering drug-related proceeds. The Kerry Amendment to the 1988 Anti–Drug Abuse Act substantially enhanced Washington's leverage in gaining international compliance with U.S. anti–money laundering objectives. As explained by Eric Helleiner, this move "empowered the U.S. government to cut foreigners off from access to the U.S. financial system, including their clearing systems, if their governments refused to reach specific anti–money laundering agreements with the U.S. Treasury. Foreigners had to take this threat seriously, especially since the U.S.-based clearing systems CHIPS (Clearing House Interbank Payment System) and Fedwire handle roughly 95 percent of all wire transfers sent and received in the world."[96] The Justice Department encouraged foreign governments to enact parallel legislation and to cooperate in U.S. investigations and prosecutions of drug-related money laundering by waiving bank secrecy laws in drug trafficking investigations.

In an indication of the growing importance of international cooperation in this area, the G-7 summits in 1988 and 1989 addressed the subjects of money laundering and asset seizure and forfeiture; a Financial Action Task Force created at the latter meeting included not just the G-7 governments of the United States, Japan, Britain, France, Canada, Italy, and West Germany but also the governments of Australia, Austria, Belgium, Luxembourg, the Netherlands, Spain, Sweden, and Switzerland.[97] In its first report in early 1990, the task force urged governments to ratify the UN Convention and to enact domestic legislation broadening the definition of money laundering and requiring financial institutions to screen and maintain records of customers and their transactions. By 1990, Britain, France, Spain, Switzerland, and Luxembourg had all criminalized money laundering; the European Community Commission and the Council of Europe's Pompidou Group had assumed active roles in promoting legislation and cooperation against money laundering; the Bank for International Settlements in Basel, Switzerland, had prepared a "code of conduct" for banks regarding suspicious transactions; and Interpol was actively promoting model legislation criminalizing money laundering. In a development of potentially great significance, the Council of Europe adopted a new Convention on Anti–Money Laundering and the Search, Seizure and Confiscation of Proceeds of Crime in November 1990 and invited the governments of Canada, Australia, the United States, and Eastern European nations to join. Prominent both at the forefront of these developments and behind the scenes in task force meetings and negotiations were U.S. officials.

The International Rendition of Fugitives

U.S. efforts to obtain custody of fugitives from abroad had always been hindered principally by consideration of the sovereignty, laws, and political reactions of foreign states. The evolution of U.S. extradition law and treaties was largely one of expanding the scope of rendition between the United States and foreign states. In each case of an extradition relationship between the U.S. government and a foreign government, a treaty was first required to establish the legal basis for fugitive rendition. Particularly significant in this evolutionary process was the gradual shift from the rather explicit and formalistic notions of reciprocity that characterized U.S. extradition treaty language and practice during the nineteenth century to a more substantive and instrumental notion of reciprocity by the middle of the twentieth century.

The two trends of ever increasing numbers of fugitives to extradite and ever more encompassing and accommodating extradition treaties did not, however, result in any substantial increase in extraditions until the 1970s. The single most important reason for the dramatic increase in the number of extraditions, as well as the even greater growth in the numbers of requests for evidence in criminal cases, was the creation of the Office of International Affairs (OIA) in the Justice Department in 1979. Established "for the purpose of centralizing and giving greater emphasis and visibility to [the Justice Department's] prosecutorial service functions in the international arena," OIA quickly emerged as a repository of information, experience, and advice on most international law enforcement matters.[98] Although a sister Office of Law Enforcement and Intelligence was created in the State Department's Legal Advisor's Office at about the same time, the attorneys in OIA assumed principal responsibility for processing fugitive rendition requests to and from the United States. They began to renegotiate dated U.S. extradition treaties; they provided assistance to federal prosecutors seeking the rendition of fugitives from abroad; they assumed an active role in supporting and representing foreign extradition requests to the United States; and they took over responsibility for processing all extradition requests from state prosecutors to foreign governments. Federal and state prosecutors no longer had to process their requests through unfamiliar, and often indifferent, State Department channels, and foreign governments no longer were obliged to hire local counsel in the United States to file and press their extradition requests. By the late 1980s, OIA's existence and capabilities were widely known among law enforcement officials within and without the United States—a fact that in and of itself generated ever increasing numbers of extradition requests.

OIA's successes were dependent on comparable institutional development abroad. The fact that similar specialized offices had already been created in many foreign justice ministries, and that others were soon to follow, provided OIA with the essential partners it required to conduct its transgovernmental affairs. Equally significant was the development during the 1980s of Interpol's international capabilities and the U.S. National Central Bureau of Interpol in the Justice Department. Even as formal extradition procedures continued to require the attentions of courts and prosecutors, the challenges of locating and arresting fugitives fell principally on the shoulders of police officials. Interpol's facilities, in particular its standardized system of notices, provided them with a rapid and fairly reliable system of keeping tabs on the movements of criminal suspects.[99]

The persistent enhancement of the U.S. government's capacity to extradite fugitives to and from foreign territories might have been expected to reduce its dependence on other means of international rendition. In fact, quite the opposite happened. Treaties took time to negotiate, and the number of officials in the Departments of State and Justice with the necessary expertise to undertake the process was small. The demand for fugitive rendition, by contrast, increased at a more rapid pace, particularly following World War II, and it accelerated dramatically with the internationalization of drug enforcement in the 1970s and 1980s. U.S. law enforcement agents, prosecutors, and the Justice Department responded by developing and employing an array of tactics to apprehend fugitives from foreign territories. One result was the regularization of what had become known as "irregular rendition."

Until well into the nineteenth century, Americans gave little thought to issues of international extradition. Criminals were more inclined to escape across state lines or into more remote areas of the country than to foreign lands.[100] The formal origins of U.S. extradition can best be dated to the 1840s, when the U.S. government signed its first full-fledged extradition treaty and Congress enacted its first federal extradition statute.[101] During the following decades, the U.S. government rapidly emerged as a world leader in the negotiation of bilateral extradition treaties. As extradition norms developed, as particular controversies required more formal and anticipatory resolutions, and as new governments replaced old, many treaties were either supplemented or replaced by entirely new treaties.

Treaty negotiations, which had ground to a virtual halt in the first few decades after World War II, picked up dramatically during the 1970s, motivated by both the general need to modernize the increasingly dated U.S. extradition treaties and the particular demands generated by the dramatic internationalization of U.S. drug enforcement efforts. The large number of bilateral extradition treaties negotiated by the U.S. government could be explained not just by its inability to extradite anyone in the absence of a treaty but also by its reluctance to join multilateral extradition conventions. This reluctance was due to the relative complexity of the U.S. legal system, with its common law traditions, federal distribution of jurisdiction, and highly intricate rules of evidence, none of which were particularly well suited to multilateral extradition arrangements with the majority of foreign states in which civil law traditions dominate. But much of the resistance could also be attributed to the tendency of multilateral arrangements to settle on the minimum common denominators of cooperation. Bilateral treaties, by contrast, afforded an opportunity to push each negotiating partner to include those provisions of greatest interest and advantage to the United States. The only exceptions to this aversion to multilateral extradition treaties—all of which date back no further than 1970—were the multilateral conventions directed at hijacking and other crimes involving aircraft, terrorism, crimes against diplomats, hostage taking, and illicit drug trafficking, each of which contained provisions regarding extradition.

The modern era of U.S. extradition treaty negotiations began in the early 1970s. U.S. negotiators sought to maximize the number of offenses for which a treaty partner would extradite; to narrow as much as possible the "political offense" exception, especially in negotiations with close allies; to accommodate the extraterritorial reach of U.S. and foreign criminal laws and jurisdictional notions; to persuade foreign governments to extradite their nationals or else ensure vicarious prosecution at the request of the U.S. government; to reconcile U.S. capital punishment laws with foreign governments' insistence that fugitives delivered by them not be executed; and, more generally, to clear up confusions and eliminate needless obstacles that had hobbled extradition relations under the older treaties.

An examination of the history of U.S. extradition treaties reveals both the trend toward ever increasing breadth and inclusiveness as well as the persistent need to eliminate and clarify ambiguities in the language of old treaties that had resulted in both U.S. and foreign courts and executive branch officials rejecting extradition requests. Beginning with the Jay Treaty's provision for the extradition of fugitives accused of murder and forgery, the list of extraditable offenses grew ever longer, until it was simply replaced during the 1980s by a fairly open-ended "dual criminality" provision authorizing extradition for any crime punishable in both countries by imprisonment for at least one year.

No extradition issue attracted as much attention and controversy as the political offense exception, a clause included in all U.S. extradition treaties as well as most other extradition treaties currently in force that circumscribes extradition in cases involving politically motivated crimes and prosecutions. In many respects, the "narrowing" of the political offense exception in U.S. law and policy during the 1980s represented less a rejection of the notion than a fairly explicit politicization of its application. Whereas it initially had been interpreted quite broadly by both the courts and the State Department to require denials of extradition requests even from governments with which the United States was on friendly terms, by the 1980s the State Department and other executive branch departments increasingly insisted that the political offense exception could not provide a defense against an extradition request from a government that was both friendly and democratic. They also appeared increasingly willing to act favorably on extradition requests from governments not known for the rectitude or due process of their judicial institutions.

The source of greatest frustration in U.S. efforts to prosecute foreign violators of its laws in U.S. courts was the refusal of most governments to extradite their own citizens. The legal traditions of most civil law countries as well as some common law countries regarded the nonextradition of their citizens as an important principle deeply ingrained in their legal traditions. Most European and Latin American governments traditionally refused to concede on the issue of extraditing their citizens, insisting that they would comply instead with U.S. requests to prosecute fugitives in their own courts. Among the few exceptions was the government of Colombia, which signed a new extradition treaty with the United States in 1979 (enacted in 1982) that provided for the extradition of nationals. This was neither the first nor the only Colombian extradition treaty to approve such exchanges, but it did represent something of an exception to Colombia's extradition traditions. What followed between 1984 and 1990 can be described as both a civil war and a nightmare. President Belisario Betancur activated the treaty in 1984 following the assassination of his justice minister, Rodrigo Lara Bonilla, by Colombia's increasingly powerful and brazen drug traffickers. The leading drug traffickers responded with an increasingly effective campaign of public relations, bribery, intimidation, and murder to shift public and official opinion against the treaty. Calling themselves "The Extraditables," they declared that their first priority was the removal of the extradition treaty with the United States, especially the provision permitting their own extradition. Most Colombians recognized that their own judicial system was incapable of bringing the traffickers to justice. Even so, many agreed in principle with the traffickers' criticism of the treaty. During the remainder of the 1980s, thousands of Colombians—including presidential candidates, cabinet ministers, and supreme court judges—were murdered, the Supreme Court vacillated between validating the treaty and undermining it, and Presidents Virgilio Barco and Cesar Gaviria went back and forth on implementing it.[102] The Extraditables finally achieved their objective in 1991, when Colombia adopted a new constitution that explicitly prohibited any future extraditions of its citizens.[103]

Continuity and Change in U.S. International Crime Control

From early in the nation's history to the last decade of the twentieth century, the core objectives of international crime control—deterring and apprehending criminals, seizing assets, and confiscating contraband—did not fundamentally change. The perennial concerns with controlling borders, suppressing smuggling, collecting revenues, and rendition of criminal fugitives remained constant even as the energies, personnel, resources, and international agreements devoted to these tasks multiplied. The most important change, however, was the proliferation of criminal laws requiring extraterritorial enforcement efforts. Late in the twentieth century, police and prosecutors no longer worried about fugitive slaves, illicit slavers, rum runners, and cross-border Apache raids. But unlike their counterparts from the nineteenth century, they had their hands full with illicit heroin and cocaine smugglers, securities law violators, high-tech smugglers, money launderers, and tax offenders. Thus, to describe the internationalization of U.S. law enforcement as simply a response to the internationalization of crime would be only partially true, given the substantial impact of U.S. legislation in defining as crimes, both substantively and jurisdictionally, activities that were not the business of U.S. law enforcers just a few decades earlier. Indeed, when we stretch our horizons backward to the early years of the American republic, we realize that most of what has engaged U.S. international law enforcement efforts in recent decades was then either inconceivable or legal. Eighteenth- and nineteenth-century Customs law enforcers would have recognized the efforts of contemporary Customs agents to collect the revenues, and of special agents to investigate transnational frauds and recover fugitives, and even of FBI and ATF agents to enforce the neutrality laws, but they would have regarded as quite novel the contemporary efforts to restrict the transnational movements of people, money, cannabis, and derivatives of the coca and opium plants.

In this regard, the dominant historical role of drug enforcement in propelling the internationalization of U.S. law enforcement cannot be overstressed. The war on drugs proclaimed by Nixon in 1969 and renewed on an even more ambitious scale in the 1980s provided the crucial impetus for a host of actions and agreements that otherwise would never have occurred. Drug enforcement provided the rationale to expand the overseas presence of not just the DEA but the FBI and Customs. By the early 1990s it accounted for roughly 70 percent of the fugitives sought by the U.S. Marshals Service. It led to the loosening of the Posse Comitatus Act to allow U.S. military forces to play a role in civilian law enforcement. It provided the impetus for the creation of paramilitary enforcement groups composed of U.S. military and police officials to target drug trafficking facilities in South America. It prompted the negotiation and renegotiation of dozens of extradition treaties as well as a number of MLATs. It led to a new role for the CIA and other intelligence agencies in criminal law enforcement matters. It helped stimulate the negotiation of a number of global drug enforcement conventions, including a 1988 UN Convention that dramatically increased the level of international law enforcement cooperation expected of governments. It exercised a profound influence on the nature of criminal investigation in dozens of countries. It compelled dozens of foreign governments to change their financial and corporate secrecy laws. It provided the central justification for the invasion of Panama. And it offered a powerful foot in the door with which to weaken domestic and foreign resistance to a range of other international criminal law enforcement endeavors. In short, were it not for the war on drugs, the internationalization of U.S. criminal law enforcement would have been dramatically less developed by the early 1990s. And, as we will see, the acceleration and broadening of international law enforcement efforts at the end of the twentieth and beginning of the twenty-first centuries, particularly in the realms of immigration control and counterterrorism, would very much build on and expand the global drug enforcement infrastructure created in earlier decades.

CHAPTER FOUR

❏ ❏ ❏

International Crime Control after the Cold War

Having explored the European and U.S. origins of international criminal law enforcement in the previous two chapters, we now turn to examine the acceleration and transformation of such policing in the immediate aftermath of the cold war. It is tempting, and not entirely inaccurate, to
view the intensified internationalization of crime control in the last decade
of the twentieth century as simply a reflection of the global proliferation
of transnational crime—the "dark side of globalization." Indeed, this view
increasingly came to dominate the policy discourse about crime and crime
control issues in the 1990s. However, much of the internationalization of
crime control was due to other factors. This included the post–cold war
political and bureaucratic scramble to find new security threats and missions; the promotion of regional economic integration projects in North
America and Europe, with spillover and feedback effects creating incentives and opportunities for greater cross-border law enforcement cooperation; and the unprecedented and unrivaled U.S. position of global power,
influence, and ambition.

From Cold War to Crime War:
The Fusion of U.S. Policing and Security

Where once anticommunism represented the principal moral imperative of
U.S. foreign policy, drug enforcement and other criminal justice objectives

emerged as the new moral imperatives in the last decade of the twentieth century. As transnational crime issues rose on the U.S. policy agenda and were redefined as security issues, foreign governments became increasingly wary of rousing U.S. ire by appearing to be insensitive to its criminal justice concerns. Much of the escalation of U.S. international crime control initiatives in the 1990s represented an extension of efforts already under way, but the end of the cold war meant that policing priorities and concerns could take center stage, no longer overshadowed by geopolitical rivalries and interstate military threats.[1]

Reflecting the new post–cold war mood in Washington, in 1994 the Center for Strategic and International Studies convened a conference of high-level law enforcement and intelligence officials, titled "Global Organized Crime: The New Evil Empire." The summary of the conference stated: "The dimensions of global organized crime present a greater international security challenge than anything Western democracies had to cope with during the cold war."[2] Articulating what was becoming an increasingly popular view in official policy circles, in 1995 Deputy U.S. Attorney General Jamie Gorelick told the Senate Intelligence Committee, "The end of the Cold War has changed the nature of the threats to our national security. No longer are national security risks exclusively or predominantly military in nature. Transnational phenomena such as terrorism, narcotics trafficking, alien smuggling, and the smuggling of nuclear material all have been recognized to have profound security implications for American policy." Gorelick concluded that "both conceptually and on the ground," there has been "a real shift in the paradigm of national security."[3] Formalizing this paradigm shift, in 1995 President Clinton issued Presidential Decision Directive 42, which officially defined transnational crime as a national security threat. The president told the United Nations that "the threat to our security is not in an enemy silo, but in the briefcase or the car bomb of a terrorist. Our enemies are also international criminals and drug traffickers who threaten the stability of new democracies and the future of our children."[4]

One indicator of the post–cold war blurring of the boundaries between U.S. law enforcement and security missions was that military equipment and technologies initially designed to deter military invaders were increasingly made available and adapted to deter transnational law evaders. For example, Airborne Warning and Control System surveillance planes began to monitor international drug flights; the North American Aerospace Defense Command, which was built to track incoming Soviet bombers and missiles, refocused some of its energies to tracking drug smugglers;[5] X-ray technology designed by the Department of Defense to detect Soviet missile warheads in trucks was adapted for use by U.S. Customs to find smuggled goods in cargo trucks;[6] researchers at Los Alamos National Laboratory, the birthplace of the atomic bomb, started developing sophisticated new technologies for drug control;[7] and the Pentagon's Defense Advanced Research Projects Agency began using its research on antisubmarine warfare to develop listening devices to detect drug smugglers.[8]

The use of cold war technologies for law enforcement missions provided a new growth area for defense contractors struggling to adjust to cuts in military spending,[9] and some within the military viewed this as an opportunity to preserve defense programs that had become hard to justify. In 1990, for example, "the Air Force wanted $242 million to start the central sector of the $2.3 billion Over-the-Horizon Backscatter radar network. Once a means of detecting nuclear cruise missiles fired from Soviet submarines in the Gulf of Mexico, Backscatter was now being sold as a way to spot drug couriers winging their way up from South America."[10]

In April 1994, Attorney General Janet Reno and Deputy Assistant Secretary of Defense John Deutch signed a memorandum on "operations other than war" in which they agreed to the development of "advanced technologies and systems" that can be used for both military and law enforcement operations. A Law Enforcement Technology Center was opened to apply war-fighting technology to crime fighting.[11] Experimental technologies previously off-limits to law enforcement were adapted for policing tasks such as border control. For instance, the CIA's Office of Technology began to work with the INS to use "face trace" technology, which allowed the Border Patrol to identify individuals by scanning their facial structures and matching them with outstanding warrants, and an electronic fingerprinting system (called IDENT), adapted from the Navy's Deployable Mass Population Identification and Tracking System, was set up at border stations and became the primary tool for keeping records of apprehended entrants. A Border Research and Technology Center was opened in San Diego in March 1995 to adapt military and intelligence technology to border law enforcement missions.[12]

The relationship between law enforcement and the intelligence communities also became more intimate. During the cold war, the division of responsibilities was clearer: law enforcement was thought of as largely a domestic matter, and intelligence was supposed to focus on external geopolitical rivalries. Of course, law enforcement and intelligence agents had long interacted and bumped into each other in the field, as happened increasingly in the early 1970s during the Nixon administration and in the 1980s during the Reagan years. And the rivalry and competition (often hidden from public view) between the FBI and the CIA over turf, resources, and status dated back to the end of World War II.[13] But in the changed security environment of the 1990s the relationship between intelligence and law enforcement became both more intense and more multidimensional. Stewart Baker, a former general counsel for the National Security Agency, observed, "As topics like international narcotics trafficking, terrorism, alien smuggling, and Russian organized crime rose in priority for the intelligence community, it became harder to distinguish between targets of law enforcement and those of national security."[14] In a July 1995 directive, President Clinton ordered the intelligence agencies to give priority to such "transnational threats" as organized crime, in addition to their traditional missions.[15] Reflecting the changing times, the March 1996 report of the Brown/Rudman Commission on the "Roles and Missions of the United States Intelligence Community" dedicated an entire chapter to combating organized crime.[16]

To improve coordination and cooperation between the law enforcement and intelligence communities, in 1994 the Department of Justice created the Executive Office for National Security within the Office of the Deputy Attorney General. Other new institutional mechanisms to facilitate more and better collaboration included the Intelligence–Law Enforcement Policy Board (cochaired by the deputy director of the CIA and the deputy attorney general, with membership on the board involving all of the law enforcement and intelligence agencies), the joint Intelligence–Law Enforcement Working Group, and the Special Task Force on Law Enforcement/Intelligence Overseas.[17] Key legal changes facilitated the growing overlap between police and intelligence work. The 1997 Intelligence Authorization Act amended the National Security Act to allow elements of the intelligence community, at the request of a law enforcement agency, to gather information about individuals in foreign countries who are not U.S. citizens.[18] This authorization extended to agencies such as the National

Security Agency (NSA), the National Reconnaissance Office, and the National Imagery and Mapping Agency. Critics expressed alarm that this change would, for the first time, give the NSA a law enforcement role.[19]

The intelligence community's earlier reluctance to engage in law enforcement–related activities, which it viewed as a distraction from its primary mission, was replaced by a growing recognition that international crime control could help sustain budgets, influence, and legitimacy. As part of the effort to reinvent itself after the cold war, the CIA embraced a more formal crime-fighting role, evident in the establishment of the DCI Crime and Counter-narcotics Center. DEA and FBI agents were assigned to work with the CIA at the Center. At the same time, CIA analysts were assigned to work out of the Department of Justice's Office of Intelligence Policy and Review. Creating a closer and more cooperative working relationship was a formidable challenge, however, given very different institutional cultures, distinct methods and mission objectives, and a long history of antagonism and mistrust. "The problem we face today," commented John Deutch, "is getting both these communities to work together and build on each other's strength and forget about the fact that this tussle goes back to the time of Allen Dulles and J. Edgar Hoover."[20]

Part of the problem was that the intelligence community had traditionally prioritized the accumulation of information and development of sources, whereas law enforcement prioritized using information to make busts and build cases. As one senior Justice Department official explained it, "The CIA is interested in maintaining sources, not in bringing thugs to trial."[21] Not only were these very different objectives, but they often clashed—sometimes embarrassingly so, as evident in numerous instances in which U.S. law enforcement targeted individuals who had made themselves useful to the CIA. For instance, Mexico's now defunct Federal Security Directorate, which had long enjoyed a close working relationship with the CIA, was implicated in the kidnapping, torture, and murder of a DEA agent, which was deeply damaging to U.S.-Mexico relations in the 1980s. More broadly, the agency had long shown a willingness to subvert drug enforcement in the name of anticommunism, from Southeast Asia in the 1960s and 1970s to Southwest Asia and Central America in the 1980s.[22] Thus, some observers no doubt found it rather ironic—and perhaps also saw a double meaning—when in 1990 the CIA announced that "narcotics is a new priority."[23]

Throughout the 1990s, the CIA took on an increasingly important role in law enforcement–related missions. It helped to arrest the terrorist Carlos the Jackal (who had been a fugitive for twenty years) in Sudan in 1994, aided in the dismantling of Colombia's Cali drug trafficking group, and helped track down and capture Ramzi Yousef, who had been charged as the leader of the 1993 World Trade Center bombing.[24] In some cases, the agency played an operational role on the ground. The most high-profile example was the 1992–1993 effort to track down and eliminate the Colombian drug trafficker Pablo Escobar. As described by journalist Mark Bowden: "There were so many American spy planes over the city [Medellin], at one point 17 at once, that the Air Force had to assign an AWAC, an airborne command and control center, to keep track of them."[25] This was part of a larger expansion of the CIA's involvement in antidrug activities in the region, which included providing analysis, training, equipment for surveillance and intelligence gathering, and development of undercover sources.[26]

These developments represented a partial rewriting of the CIA's initial job description. When the CIA was established by the National Security Act of 1947, it was forbidden from engaging in police work, including domestic surveillance.[27] However, as the agency was given more responsibilities related to transnational crime issues, sustaining this restriction became more difficult. A provision in the 1996 intelligence authorization bill gave the CIA the authority to collect evidence outside the country against foreigners suspected of breaking U.S. criminal laws.[28] This legal change brought with it the potential of opening a back door for using the CIA to police U.S. citizens. For instance, if evidence tying an American to a crime was uncovered during an investigation of a foreign suspect, it could then be utilized in a U.S. court against the U.S. citizen—even if the evidence was found through illegal means (such as abusive interrogations, break-ins without warrants, and unauthorized surveillance).[29] This shift provoked concern among a number of intelligence experts and those concerned with the protection of civil liberties. As retired Admiral Stansfield Turner, a former CIA director, noted, "The FBI agent's first reaction when given a job is, 'how do I do this within the law?' The CIA agent's first reaction when given a job is, 'how do I do this regardless of the law of the country in which I am operating?'"[30] Stewart Baker warned, "Combining domestic and foreign intelligence functions created the possibility that domestic law enforcement will be infected by the secrecy, deception, and ruthlessness that international espionage requires." At the same time, "if the distinction between intelligence and law enforcement grows too artificial, the judiciary could cripple intelligence surveillance by demanding that it conform to the same standards as law enforcement."[31]

Despite such warnings and concerns, the erosion of old distinctions between law enforcement and intelligence tasks continued to be promoted and rationalized in official policy debates as a necessary response to growing "transnational threats." Although law enforcement and intelligence work were far from becoming fully integrated, their growing interaction provided further evidence of the change in U.S. security definitions and priorities. Forcing intelligence and law enforcement agencies to work more closely together with overlapping responsibilities and missions predictably brought with it an intensification of old frictions and rivalries (particularly between the FBI and the CIA) over turf and resources.[32]

The growing fusion of law enforcement and security in the aftermath of the cold war was also evident in the deployment of U.S. military personnel in a policing mode. Although the Pentagon had long been reluctant to take on nontraditional tasks, the end of the cold war created both increased political pressure on the military and a greater willingness within the military to embrace new policing missions. Similar to the intelligence community, what had been regarded by the military establishment as an inappropriate and diversionary mission during the cold war years was now a newly important justification for budgets and resources. Some skeptics in the Pentagon viewed the military as too blunt an instrument for police tasks, but the shift in the political winds continued to push in that direction.

The country's escalating antidrug effort in the 1980s first opened the door for military involvement in domestic law enforcement. The military had been prohibited from engaging in domestic police activities ever since the Posse Comitatus Act of 1878. But the law was gradually loosened beginning in the early 1980s to permit greater military support for drug control operations. Despite much initial resistance within the military, by the end of the decade the Department of Defense had been designated as the lead agency for the detection and monitoring of aerial and maritime transit of illegal drugs destined for the United States. In 1989 the military was even authorized to make arrests of drug traffickers and fugitives on foreign territory—without the approval of the host country.[33]

Drug enforcement became the defining feature of post–cold war U.S. military relations with many of its southern neighbors. The U.S. Southern Command in Panama was transformed into a de facto forward base for drug interdiction. Its commander, General Maxwell Thurman, frankly observed that the drug war was "the only war we've got."[34] Drug control provided the official justification for the invasion of Panama and the indictment of Panamanian general Manuel Noriega on criminal charges.[35] With pressure, aid, and training from Washington, many Latin American drug-exporting countries deployed their militaries to the front lines of the drug war. By the end of the 1990s, antidrug programs represented more than 92 percent of U.S. military and police aid to the Western Hemisphere.[36] Colombia became the world's third-largest recipient of U.S. military assistance in 2000 when U.S. officials pushed through a $1.3 billion antidrug aid package, most of it slated for the Colombian military. By this time, around two hundred U.S. military advisors and one hundred DEA and intelligence agents were reportedly operating in Colombia.[37]

The growing overlap of U.S. military, intelligence, and law enforcement forces and resources in the escalating antidrug effort was strikingly illustrated by ambitious efforts in the 1990s to intercept drug smuggling aircraft in Andean airspace; the CIA, DEA, FBI, Coast Guard, and Department of Defense–related institutions, such as the Joint Interagency Task Force–South, DIA (Defense Intelligence Agency), the Office of Naval Intelligence, the National Mapping and Imagery Agency, and the NSA all joined in. Military personnel from the Andean countries were brought on U.S. drug surveillance aircraft, and the job of shooting down drug planes tasked to the local military.[38]

The militarization of the U.S.-led war on drugs also had an increasingly important—though often overlooked and underreported—privatized component, involving the selective outsourcing of drug enforcement tasks to private contractors (who often had military backgrounds).[39] Former U.S. ambassador to Colombia Myles Frechette explained the rationale to privatize: "Congress and the American people don't want any servicemen killed overseas. So it makes sense that if contractors want to risk their lives, they get the job."[40] Others challenged this trend. "Are we outsourcing in order to avoid public scrutiny, controversy, or embarrassment?" asked

Representative Jan Schakowsky (D–Illinois) in 2001. "Is it to hide body bags from the media and thus shield them from public opinion?"[41] Heated political debate arose when a Peruvian military plane shot down a civilian airplane carrying an American missionary family. The Peruvian air force had been supported by intelligence provided by a CIA-contracted U.S. company, Aviation Development Corporation. One veteran of anti-drug efforts in the Andes complained that "there wasn't one person aboard that [CIA-commissioned] plane sworn to uphold the Constitution of the United States. They were all . . . businessmen!"[42]

The Buildup of U.S. Border Controls

No place in the 1990s commanded more federal law enforcement attention than the U.S.-Mexico border.[43] Concerns about border enforcement were certainly not new, but the level of attention to immigration control was unprecedented. Immigration law enforcement along the border was transformed from a low-priority and politically marginalized activity into a high-intensity campaign. The sharp escalation of immigration controls in the 1990s was in some ways analogous to the surge in international drug enforcement efforts in the early 1970s. Both policing missions had existed on a small scale for decades, but were then truly transformed by the magnitude and demands of their sudden expansion. In contrast to the expansive cross-border reach of U.S. drug enforcement, however, intensified U.S. immigration controls focused almost exclusively on the border itself. Neither were they reinforced by anything comparable to the global drug prohibition regime. For most migrants, no crime was committed until the actual attempted entry without authorization. Mexican law enforcement authorities accordingly restricted their cooperation with U.S. authorities to apprehending professional migrant smugglers (rather than the migrants themselves), especially non-Mexican nationals.

Not since the early decades of the twentieth century, when the Border Patrol was formally established and the infrastructure of a border control apparatus was built, had patrolling the southwest border been so high on the U.S. law enforcement agenda. However, the new border crackdown was prompted more by domestic politics than a sudden influx of smuggled illegal migrants; after all, there had been large numbers of unauthorized entries for years (mostly Mexican nationals in search of employment) without provoking any significant increase in border enforcement. It was only when immigration was transformed into a highly charged electoral issue by political entrepreneurs in key states such as California that the federal government responded with a high-profile display of force on the border.

This show of force included doubling the size of the U.S. Border Patrol (the uniformed wing of the INS) between 1993 and 2000. The budget of the INS for border enforcement almost tripled between 1995 and 2001, reaching more than $2.5 billion by 2002. Once considered the neglected stepchild within the Department of Justice, the INS suddenly became the fastest-growing federal agency. By the end of the decade, the INS had more employees authorized to carry a gun than any other federal law enforcement force.[44] New personnel were matched by new border fencing, equipment, and surveillance technologies. Highly concentrated and highly visible border enforcement operations were launched at major border crossings, such as Operation Hold the Line in El Paso and Operation Gatekeeper south of San Diego.[45] Along the border south of San Diego, army reservists constructed a ten-foot-high steel wall made up of 180,000 metal sheets originally designed to create temporary landing fields during military operations. The fencing project was part of the larger convergence of immigration and drug enforcement: formally funded and rationalized as part of drug interdiction, in practice the new fence became a centerpiece of the U.S. immigration control strategy.

Continuing a trend that began in the 1980s, border drug interdiction operations also became more militarized. Joint Task Force Six, established in the fall of 1989 at Fort Bliss, Texas, was the chief military antidrug unit providing support to civilian law enforcement agencies. Although prohibited from making arrests, military personnel on the border were deployed for a wide variety of support activities, including reconnaissance and intelligence analysis, building and maintaining roads and fences, weapons and communications training, and operation of surveillance equipment. Special Forces training teams were sent to instruct law enforcement officers in topics such as marksmanship and interview and interrogation methods.[46] Soldiers from the army, Marine Corps, and National Guard conducted more than three thousand law enforcement–related missions along the U.S.-Mexico border in the 1990s.[47] In May 1997, a U.S. marine on a drug enforcement–related reconnaissance mission shot and killed a teenage goatherd near the border in Texas, provoking a local backlash and a suspension on the use of ground troops along the border.[48]

The border became more militarized on the Mexican side as well, as Mexican military forces were increasingly placed in charge of antidrug operations well beyond their traditional drug crop eradication duties. This was part of the broader U.S.-encouraged escalation of Mexican drug enforcement in the 1990s, in which the country's drug control budget tripled in size and came to dominate the criminal justice system. These initiatives had as much to do with Mexico's efforts to impress and appease the United States in the context of the passage of NAFTA and nurturing closer economic relations as it did with actually deterring the flow of drugs across the border. The growth of U.S.-Mexico antidrug cooperation helped to make drugs a less divisive and politicized issue in bilateral relations by the end of the decade—even as the flow of drugs did not noticeably diminish.[49]

In sharp contrast to dynamics along the U.S.-Mexico border, U.S.-Canada border enforcement remained low intensity, low profile, and low priority, notwithstanding substantial amounts of cross-border smuggling. Border control issues were largely kept out of the political spotlight, rarely taking center stage in bilateral relations. For Washington and Ottawa, this minimalist and low-visibility approach to border policing was mutually convenient and tolerated. The boom in legal commercial flows across the border overshadowed illegal flows such as the smuggling of drugs, migrants, arms, and vast quantities of untaxed cigarettes.[50] Canadian officials made great efforts to remain outside the orbit of U.S. border anxieties. Writing shortly before the terrorist attack on September 11, Demetrios Papademetriou and Deborah Meyers noted that "Canada has been largely insulated from America's often wild and unpredictable tilting at the windmills of illegal immigration, drug trafficking, and more recently, foreign terrorism—although not without a great deal of effort and skilled diplomacy."[51]

Policymakers on both sides of the border exercised mutual restraint to avoid politicizing illegal border crossings, while at the same time expanding and deepening cross-border law enforcement cooperation. Whereas U.S. politicians often chastised Mexico for being the primary transshipment point for cocaine entering the United States, Ottawa quietly accepted the fact that the United States was the primary transshipment point for cocaine entering Canada. Moreover, the United States was the clandestine source of most of the unregistered arms in Canada, which many Canadians viewed as a security problem but grudgingly accepted as the inevitable consequence of living next to a country with lax gun controls and the world's largest arms industry.[52] At the same time, Canada, especially British Columbia, had become a substantial exporter of high-potency marijuana to its southern neighbor.[53] A small but growing number of illegal migrants also entered the United States via Canada.

The contrast between the high-profile tightening of U.S.-Mexico border controls and the lack of attention to the U.S.-Canada border was dramatic. Stephen Flynn noted, "Before Sept. 11, half of the northern border's 126 official ports of entry were left unguarded at night. Typically, orange cones were simply put up in the center of the roadway to signal the border crossing was closed."[54] More U.S. Border Patrol agents were stationed in Brownsville, Texas, than along the entire U.S.-Canada border by the end of the 1990s. By 2001, there were only 334 U.S. agents assigned to police the four-thousand-mile-long northern border compared to nine thousand agents on the two-thousand-mile-long U.S.-Mexico border. This border situation was politically tolerable and manageable as long as most cargo and passengers were simply waved through with minimal scrutiny in a context of low-security concerns. Given the anemic border inspection infrastructure, Canadians reacted with alarm when a provision in the 1996 Illegal Immigration Reform and Immigrant Responsibility Act required documenting the entry and exit of all non-U.S. citizens at border crossings. The provision was originally intended to apply only to the U.S.-Mexico border but was extended to include the northern border. Canadian policymakers, border communities, and business lobbies successfully mobilized to block implementation of the new law, arguing that it would cause massive disruptions in cross-border trade and travel.

The northern border incident that drew the most political attention and concern was the Ahmed Ressam affair in December 1999. Ressam, an Algerian national who had been living in Canada for five years, was arrested after attempting to enter the state of Washington on a ferry from Victoria, British Columbia, with a trunk full of explosives. The political aftershocks from the Ressam affair marked the start of the new politicization of border control issues in bilateral relations. The episode prompted U.S. congressional hearings on northern border security and the first set of attacks in the U.S. media charging that Canada was soft on terrorism, particularly after it became known that Ressam had lived in Canada for a number of years as a refugee applicant.[55] This would prove to be a prelude to more intense media and political scrutiny after September 2001.

Beyond the Border: The Expanding Global Reach of U.S. Law Enforcement

The global reach of U.S. law enforcement also substantially expanded in the 1990s with the fall of the Iron Curtain and the end of the cold war. Law enforcement was now far less overshadowed by the security priorities and concerns that had dominated during the cold war. The former Soviet bloc states, which earlier had been the primary geographic target of the U.S. military, now represented a target of opportunity for U.S. law enforcement agencies to establish a presence in a previously inaccessible region.

In the aftermath of the cold war, international crime control priorities attained unprecedented status in Washington policy circles and diplomatic importance abroad. Agency budgets grew, interactions between U.S. and foreign law enforcement officials intensified, and new and more expansive bilateral and multilateral agreements were negotiated. The United States secured international police cooperation through a wide variety of mechanisms, including the provision of aid and technical assistance, diplomatic favor, threat of sanctions, and even the sharing of seized assets with foreign governments that assisted with the forfeiture of assets under U.S. law.

As the overseas footprint of U.S. law enforcement became more prominent, greater efforts were made to reduce fragmentation and encourage interagency coordination, evident in the proliferation of memorandums of understanding between Justice, State, and Treasury outlining procedures for the conduct of liaison officers and the sharing of information. International policing efforts were sometimes justified as simply an extension of U.S. domestic law enforcement: "All we are doing is following cases here in the United States to their origins abroad," explained then Deputy Attorney General Jamie Gorelick in 1996. "So we're performing a very traditional law enforcement function; it just takes us into foreign countries."[56] More than two thousand U.S. law enforcement personnel were operating abroad by the end of the 1990s.

The FBI was particularly ambitious in extending its overseas activities. Its legal attaché offices increased from fifteen in 1990 to forty-one in 2000,[57] including in Russia and other countries that had previously been largely inaccessible to U.S. law enforcement. As the FBI presence in these countries grew, so did its caseload. For instance, from July 1994 through July 1997, the cases filed from the FBI's new Legal Attaché Office in Moscow increased fifteen-fold, from 20 to 289.[58] In mid-1996, the FBI began a four-year plan to double the number of FBI agents serving in legal attaché offices in American embassies.[59] In testimony before Congress, FBI Director Louis Freeh described the legal attaché program as "the single most significant factor in the Bureau's ability to detect, deter, and investigate international crimes in which the United States or our citizens are victims."[60] According to Freeh, "We have the ability to work, literally, every place in the world." He described this as the "forward deployed part of the FBI, and it gives us a perimeter defense and an ability to work directly in liaison with our [foreign] colleagues on matters of grave importance."[61] For instance, after the terrorist bombings of U.S. embassies in Kenya and Tanzania, FBI agents were dispatched to East Africa to conduct more than one thousand interviews, with the investigation leading to Osama bin Laden's indictment in New York for plotting the bombings. Similarly, after seventeen sailors were killed by a terrorist attack on the USS *Cole* in October 2000, more than one hundred FBI agents, lab experts, and forensic specialists were dispatched to Yemen.[62]

The INS and other U.S. agencies, which traditionally had a very limited international reach, also began to push for a greater global profile. Borrowing from the logic and language long used by the United States to justify international antidrug operations, in June 1997 the INS announced a major expansion of its offices overseas to "go to the source" of the migrant smuggling problem. As part of Operation Global Reach, 150 INS personnel stationed at forty offices abroad focused on training foreign law enforcement and airline personnel to detect fraudulent documents, generate information for the prosecution of migrant smugglers, enhance cooperation with host countries, and strengthen local capacities to curb migrant smuggling.[63] The INS sponsored training sessions across the world, including in Austria, El Salvador, Germany, Great Britain, Mexico, Nicaragua, Panama, and Thailand. Thousands of foreign law enforcement personnel were trained through the Overseas Fraudulent Document Training Program.[64]

The State Department's Bureau for International Narcotics Matters, which had remained relatively small and marginalized in the years immediately after its creation in 1978, grew rapidly in both size and prestige during the 1990s. In 1995 it was reorganized and renamed the Bureau for International Narcotics and Law Enforcement Affairs, dubbed the "drugs-and-thugs" section to reflect its expanding mandate (including migrant smuggling, stolen vehicles, money laundering, and other forms of transnational crime). The Department's international narcotics control budget worldwide increased from $113 million in 1990 to $517 million in 1999, bolstering the influence and presence of the Narcotics Affairs Sections at U.S. embassies.[65] The State Department also promoted its global antidrug agenda through the annual *International Narcotics Control Strategy Report*, which was essentially a report card that graded countries in terms of their level of cooperation with U.S. antidrug objectives.[66] Although few countries were formally "decertified" (which brought with it sanctions such as aid cutoffs), this public evaluation mechanism was used as a political tool to draw media attention and shame drug-producing and transit countries into bolstering their antidrug programs. A similar type of State Department annual report card, involving a combination of shaming and threats of sanctions, was later created to rank and evaluate the compliance of foreign governments with U.S. criminalization and enforcement objectives in curbing the trafficking of women and children.[67]

Foreign law enforcement training and provision of technical assistance became an increasingly important component of U.S. international initiatives during the course of the decade. These programs not only helped to build up foreign law enforcement capacity in dealing with transnational crime but were an essential element in nurturing an international law enforcement community based on personal contacts among police agents. U.S. training for foreign police forces was not new, of course, with public safety and other training programs dating back to decades earlier as part of the broader cold war campaign against communism.[68] The DEA had also long provided specialized antidrug courses throughout the world. What was new in the post–cold war era was a greater emphasis on a much broader range of transnational crime issues (from financial crimes such as money laundering, to illegal migration and trafficking of women, to nuclear smuggling) and the involvement of an expanding number of U.S. federal agencies in training programs. Also novel was the location of much of the training, extending to areas of the world that had been largely beyond the reach of U.S. law enforcement during the cold war.

The centerpiece of this expansion in foreign training was the International Law Enforcement Academy that opened in Budapest in 1995 (modeled on the FBI Academy in Quantico, Virginia), with the FBI serving as the lead U.S. agency.[69] Eight-week classes were taught by U.S. and European law enforcement officials, with the first class graduating in June 1995.[70] President Clinton described the new academy as a model for a "network of centers all around the world to share the latest crime-fighting techniques and technology."[71] Part of the rationale for the Budapest location, FBI Director Freeh noted, was that it opened the possibility to "develop a network of police partners in countries where we do not have now those relationships."[72] Additional law enforcement training centers were subsequently established in Thailand and Botswana, and an International Law Enforcement Academy graduate school was created in Roswell, New Mexico, in 2001, for foreign law enforcement officials who had graduated from U.S. programs abroad. As in the past, the United States also continued to host a growing number of foreign law enforcement agents at specialized teaching centers, such as the FBI Academy at Quantico.

The accelerated pace of bilateral negotiations in the 1990s also eased the process of evidence gathering and extradition, further extending the extraterritorial reach of criminal law enforcement. This was reflected in a sharp increase in the number of U.S.-negotiated mutual legal assistance treaties and extradition agreements. Once past the initial hurdle of designing and negotiating the first set of MLATs in earlier years (discussed in the previous chapter), the process became less politicized as model frameworks were now available to be replicated and imitated in multiple MLAT negotiations with countries across the world. The number of MLATs in force jumped from four in 1989 to forty-eight by 2001. U.S. requests for mutual legal assistance grew substantially, and the number of incoming requests tripled during the 1990s, from 439 to 1,555. Thirty-three new extradition treaties also entered into force from 1990 through 2001.[73]

The long arm of U.S. international law enforcement extended not only further across territorial space but also into cyberspace, as policing the Internet became a realm of expanding jurisdictional claims and a growth area for both U.S. law enforcement agencies and international police cooperation. Cybercrime and cyberpolicing became new and rapidly growing areas of law enforcement competency, with specialized enforcement units with technical expertise created within the U.S. Secret Service, the FBI, and other agencies. The U.S. Customs Service set up a Cybersmuggling Center in the late 1990s, which was an outgrowth of its child pornography investigations from the 1980s. "If it is on the Net, we are there and looking at it," noted Glenn Nick, the assistant director of the new Cybersmuggling Center. "The web is like the biggest city on the planet. Wander around long enough and you're going to trip over something illegal."[74] The Cybersmuggling Center also helped to foster greater international law enforcement collaborations. For instance, Moscow authorities trained at the Center later took part in a U.S.-Russian investigation of an online operation involving the sale of child pornography videos that led to shutting down three child pornography distribution networks in early 2001.

The United States also played a leadership role at the multilateral level in motivating, designing, and implementing new cooperative agreements on a wide array of international criminal law enforcement issues, from tackling computer crimes to corruption to money laundering.[75] Much of this activity represented a broadening and further internationalization of Washington's law enforcement agenda, providing it with greater global legitimacy and making the criminal laws of other countries more closely conform to U.S. priorities and preferences. A striking illustration of this process was the negotiation of the 2000 UN Convention Against Transnational Organized Crime (the "Palermo Convention"), which, according to Jonathan Winer, a former senior State Department official responsible for promoting U.S. law enforcement interests abroad, "included three protocols that had been initiated by the U.S.—on trafficking in women, migrant smuggling, and illicit firearms, each of which promoted practices already adopted in the U.S. to commit other signatories to do the same on a global basis."[76] In explaining the Convention to a U.S. congressional committee, Samuel Witten, a legal advisor at the State Department, noted that the United States "can comply with the Convention's criminalization obligations without need for new legislation. The value of these Convention provisions for the United States is that they oblige other countries that have been slower to react legislatively to the threat of transnational organized crime to adopt new criminal laws in harmony with ours." For the United States, he said, "we will be able to use the Convention as a basis for new relationships with countries [with] which we lack bilateral mutual legal assistance treaties (MLATs), primarily in parts of Asia, Africa, and the Middle East."[77]

Much of the U.S. success in pushing its policing priorities through these sorts of cooperative mechanisms, Winer emphasized, was due to the fact that important details and common standards could be hammered out mostly by technocrats substantially insulated from domestic politics. Of particular importance, he noted, "this growing array of cooperative initiatives was designed to create a platform for law enforcement, customs, and judicial cooperation that would function irrespective of the particular predicate criminal activity to which such initiatives would be applied. Although some of them had arisen in response to a particular problem, such as international drug trafficking, tax evasion, or computer crime, in general, the initiatives were devised for general application, regardless of the nature of the problem they would address."[78]

For instance, in the area of cargo security, U.S. and European officials negotiated new global standards for shipping containers that were established at the World Customs Organization (WCO) in 2000. These standards, in turn, would facilitate law enforcement efforts targeting a broad range of cargo theft and smuggling practices. With the United States as its principal funder, the WCO became an increasingly important player in developing and standardizing international customs protocols. WCO meetings brought together heads of customs from across the world, representing what Brenda Chalfin has called a customs "brotherhood" at the global level that shares common outlooks and frameworks. She described these customs officials as "brokers of a global customs culture" and the WCO as an "administrative regime demonstrating surprising global convergence and coordination."[79]

Policing an Integrating Europe after the Cold War

The internationalization of policing in the 1990s was a far more institutionalized and multilateralized process on the European side of the Atlantic. The old system of police cooperation in Western Europe, substantially based on informal arrangements (such as TREVI, discussed in chapter 2) and often restricted to information exchange, was now being transformed into a more formalized system of police cooperation through the 1992

Maastricht Treaty's "Third Pillar" of Justice and Home Affairs.[80] Also, in contrast to the more globally ambitious post–cold war U.S. policing initiatives, Western European governments were primarily concerned with enhancing cross-border police cooperation in their immediate neighborhood and backyard. Similar to their U.S. counterparts, however, European officials rationalized the push to internationalize policing as a necessary reaction to the growth of transnational crime. Neil Walker has pointed out that this "reactive posture tends to mask the active choices that are being made," and that these choices have been informed by professional and bureaucratic interests, political opportunism in exploiting popular fears, and, most important, the larger polity-building agenda and debate within the European Union. Indeed, he suggests that the burst of initiatives in this policy area in the post–cold war era has been an important part of mobilizing and maintaining support for the European Union as an ongoing political project.[81]

The internationalization of European crime control in the aftermath of the cold war was a twofold process: on the one hand, a thickening of police cooperation and creation of cross-border policing institutions within the European Union (bringing with it new tensions, especially at the new frontiers of law enforcement collaboration), and, on the other hand, an outward extension of EU policing priorities and practices to immediate neighbors, especially to those countries hoping to join the EU. For applicant states, a precondition for joining the "inner club" of Europe was initiation into the police club. This would first require adopting "European standards" and much closer cooperation with EU member states on transnational crime-related issues.

The crumbling of the Soviet bloc in 1989 and the planned rapid integration of Europe during the 1990s promised new challenges and opportunities for international law enforcement. Western Europe's police were being obliged to work out the means of policing a multinational domain with fewer internal border controls on movement at the same time that external border controls were rapidly becoming more permeable. These developments generated a variety of proposals, all of which involved the intensification of the trends toward greater homogenization of criminal justice systems and regularization of police relations within Western Europe. Most police agencies insisted that the elimination of border controls would require more systematic and intrusive internal surveillance within each of the states. The Dutch and British governments, however, fiercely resisted pressures to require residents to carry identification papers, as was common elsewhere on the continent. Other proposals involved better controlling of external borders—or "hardening the outer shell," as some put it—not just vis-à-vis Eastern Europe but also in relation to non-European states that shared special relationships, such as former colonial ties; immigration policies became a subject of intense debate and pressure for mutual consultation and coordination.

There were reasons to be wary of the movement toward greater homogenization and centralization of criminal justice systems within Europe. Criminal laws and procedures often reflected the peculiar historical and cultural traditions of individual states; pressures for greater homogenization of these laws and procedures threatened to undermine these traditions, some of which involved restrictions on the state's police powers. The British and Dutch reluctance to conform with the internal identification document requirements of their neighbors was one example; others included the Belgian reluctance to legalize wiretapping; the Dutch preference for regulating rather than criminalizing retail cannabis sales and treating illicit drug abuse primarily as a public health issue rather than a criminal justice concern; the French resistance to strict controls on individual ownership of firearms; the French and Belgian reluctance to exchange information on transactions among commercial arms dealers; and the varying state traditions with respect to data protection, financial secrecy laws, and other areas of vice control. Different degrees of criminalization and police power were seen as both creating opportunities for criminals and complicating international law enforcement efforts; but there was an element to the promotion of greater homogenization that regarded it as a good in and of itself and diversity as a wrong inevitably in need of reform.

The principal check on both homogenization and centralization remained the persistent force of notions of national sovereignty. By and large, Europe's police were less enthusiastic than Europe's business community about the rapid push toward integration. The police recognized that their concerns, unlike those of the business community, were intimately connected, in both practice and symbol, to the sovereign powers of the state. Economic markets were being sufficiently internalized within Europe so that consumer markets and investment opportunities often transcended considerations of national sovereignty. By contrast, the police powers of the state—the right to arrest someone, to oblige him or her to answer questions, to tap telephones, and to search homes and personal effects—continued to have everything to do with national sovereignty. Few citizens of any country, even within Europe, were prepared to acknowledge the right of a foreign police official to arrest them, or even compel them to answer questions, in their own country, and few police officials were prepared to countenance police agents from abroad conducting unilateral operations in their own territory. Those areas that were least visible to public view (notably intelligence collection and analysis) had the greatest prospects of progressing further.

Nevertheless, European integration had given the police a powerful and overriding incentive and rationale to greatly increase the pace of their efforts at internationalization. By the early 1990s, European police conferences, study groups, and exchange programs were proliferating as never before. Police agencies were sending their officers to one another's training programs and designing special short courses for other European police; language training programs were being instituted; intensive consideration was being given to homogenization of communications systems, database systems, and national police computers; and plans were well under way to bolster direct communications with other EU police forces both through Interpol and by the appointment of European liaison officials not just at national headquarters but at city, state, and other subnational police agencies. All of these steps were of the sort that likely would have occurred in some form even without the pressures generated by formal integration; the principal impact of European integration and the dismantling of internal border controls was to give them an urgency that would not otherwise have existed.

Shifting Security Concerns and the Making of "Schengenland"

The new push for greater police cooperation also reflected a fundamental shift in perceived security threats. Concerns over cross-border law evasions rather than military invasions quickly emerged as the new security priority in Western Europe after the Berlin Wall came down and the Iron Curtain was lifted. Consequently, as Monica den Boer described it, "In a new

Europe where military activities are in the process of being dismantled, the police forces are moving into the confines of international security protection."[82] Didier Bigo observed that an "internal security field" was emerging in Western Europe that presupposed a single security continuum in which organized crime, terrorism, and illegal immigration were all placed together.[83] Mirroring developments in the United States, part of this shift included the encroachment of security services on areas traditionally thought of as primarily law enforcement matters, further blurring the traditional distinctions between high and low policing (discussed in chapter 2). The British, French, and German intelligence services, for example, shifted their attention to focus more on transnational crimes such as money laundering, drug smuggling, and the trafficking of nuclear material. Curbing human smuggling was later added to the agendas of some intelligence agencies. More cooperation and overlapping missions between the law enforcement and intelligence communities also brought greater interagency friction and competition between intelligence and law enforcement communities vying for turf, resources, and status.

Anxiety over perceived new security threats was greatly exacerbated by plans to dismantle internal border controls as part of the European integration project. The image of a border-free European Union, as envisioned by the Single European Act of 1986, was paralleled by anxiety-provoking images of a border-free Europe that could be exploited by transnational criminals and other "undesirables." Because it was widely assumed that the internal borders of Western Europe provided a deterrent against unlawful border crossings within Europe, it was also assumed that erasing those borders would encourage such crossings by criminals. This assumption was questionable, given how permeable the internal borders had already become before 1992. In the case of illegal drugs, for example, "contrary to what the general public often believes," noted Georges Estievenart of the European Commission's Monitoring Centre for Drugs and Drug Addiction, "the physical internal frontiers of the Community have long ceased to be the strategic spot where most drug hauls and arrests of traffickers take place."[84]

But even though the deterrent function of the internal border checks was more myth than reality, part of what worried European officials was that the formal opening of the borders among EU members would make them appear more open to illegal entry and fuel public apprehension and fear.[85] Entrepreneurial government officials, reinforced by media coverage, played to these concerns and pushed for compensatory measures to cope with the "internal security gap" that they argued would necessarily arise. As one team of European researchers noted, the elimination of border controls "has certainly been exploited by police and security services in order to gain a broader mandate, more resources and better equipment."[86] Penelope Turnbull and Wayne Sandholtz suggested that "there is little evidence that the elimination of border controls produced a surge in crime and illegal migration," though there were frequent public statements to that effect.[87] The dismantling of internal border controls provided the primary rationale for heightened cross-border police collaboration and tighter external border checks. EU members accelerated the harmonization of parts of their criminal justice systems, and policing cooperation became much more institutionalized. The aim of European police cooperation was to create a "security surplus" instead of a "security deficit." This meant establishing a "'cordon sanitaire' to keep out drug traffickers, terrorists and other criminals as well as unwanted immigrants. Greatly increased cooperation between police and judicial authorities, shared intelligence and stricter internal controls would offset the consequences of permitting these undesirables to circulate freely within Europe."[88]

EU policing initiatives increasingly involved a "pooling of sovereignty" and convergence toward more restrictive controls and more intensive monitoring of entries into a common EU space. The most important intergovernmental mechanism created for border control cooperation was the Schengen Agreement, implemented in 1995 and subsequently incorporated into the EU legal framework through the 1997 Treaty of Amsterdam (implemented in 1999).[89] Schengen members (initially just seven states but eventually extended to include all EU members except Britain and Ireland) agreed to eliminate internal border inspections and at the same time harmonize and tighten external border checks. This included the movement toward a common visa regime and an agreed asylum processing procedure, measures to enhance and facilitate criminal justice cooperation, and the creation of a shared computer information exchange system (the Schengen Information System) linking the databases of all Schengen countries containing the names of criminal aliens, rejected asylum applicants, and others deemed undesirable. A European space of free movement, "Schengen-land," thus became insulated by a hardened outer perimeter managed by a common set of rules and procedures (specified in the Schengen external frontier manual). Border control thus became an area of activity in which the EU began to take on state-like characteristics even while lacking all the formal trappings of a traditional territorial state.

Creating Schengenland required overcoming considerable historical mistrust, especially in regard to countries on the southern periphery such as Italy and Spain. There was some initial hesitation to allow Italy into Schengen, for instance, based on worries that the reach of the mafia would quickly spread north of the Alps with the dismantling of border controls, but this concern proved exaggerated. Technological developments were a crucial ingredient in making Schengen a reality. As Malcolm Anderson explains, "New technology made the policing of a common external border a practical possibility. Computer technology and data banks were sufficiently advanced to exchange in real time information on such matters as *personae non grata* in order to make control of a long and difficult frontier seem feasible."[90] This proved to be a precursor to a much greater reliance on border control technologies in later years, not just in Europe but across the globe.

Each Schengen member had its own incentives for embracing a more collective and coordinated border control effort. For Germany, the legacy of the country's authoritarian past and recent memories of the Berlin Wall made an aggressive unilateral reassertion of territorial controls less politically palatable than embedding German policing initiatives within a larger European policy on common external border controls (as outlined in the Schengen Accords). For Spain, in contrast, implementing Schengen standards provided a mechanism to reinforce the country's new identity as a legitimate member of Europe's inner circle. And for Italy, cracking down on smuggling across the Adriatic as part of its Schengen obligations helped to appease and pacify those EU members who often complained that the country was too corrupt and lax on border controls. For many countries, such as Belgium, the Netherlands, and Luxembourg, the Schengen Agreement meant drastically reduced border control duties, as they no longer had a land border to police. This would increasingly raise the delicate issue of burden sharing, as border control costs and responsibilities were progressively pushed outward to the external perimeter of the EU.[91]

Meanwhile, the dismantling of the old internal border checks between EU member states meant that a more dispersed, collaborative, and deterritorialized form of border control developed within the EU by the end of the decade. This included a new generation of bilateral agreements concluded by Germany with many of its neighbors that Peter Hobbing has described as a "quantum leap" in international police matters (involving such sensitive issues as hot pursuit and surveillance and undercover investigations across borders).[92] Michel Pinauldt, a French representative on the Central Group of Schengen, described the sharp contrast between the old and new border control practices:

> The security services were used to having fixed border posts that were properly set up with the necessary facilities to carry out border checks, they were used to covering a limited amount of terrain which they were very familiar with and practically overnight they had to change their working method finding that they no longer had fixed border posts to deal with but were rather on the move, moving much more into the hinterland to carry out checks. . . . [This] change in working method meant that our security services in France had to develop relationships of trust with the security services across the border in the other countries and gradually over a period of time through an exchange of information, through exchanges of officials, they have had to familiarize themselves with the way in which the other security services operate in order to ensure and feel comfortable with the fact that what they are giving up is being taken over properly and carried out properly by the security services in the other countries.[93]

The dismantling of internal border controls and greater reliance on cooperative policing mechanisms within the EU also necessarily produced new frictions between member states. As the EU collectively built a more expansive border control apparatus, the unevenness of the construction project became a source of political tension within the union. Of course, frictions over drug enforcement and other policing issues were not new. What was new was that these frictions were now playing out on a much wider EU stage (with the involvement of EU institutions) and taking place within the larger context of integration and elimination of internal border controls. France and Germany, for instance, often criticized the Netherlands as too lax on illegal drugs, and France occasionally threatened to reintroduce border checks in protest. Meanwhile, the British (who remained outside of the Schengen system) loudly complained that France was doing too little to stop unwanted refugees, mostly Afghanis and Kurds, who were attempting unauthorized entry into Britain via the Channel Tunnel. Britain subsequently added extra fencing, video surveillance cameras, and police to monitor the tunnel.[94]

British efforts to curb migrant smuggling across the channel included imposing heavier fines on carriers (car and truck drivers, airline and ferry companies) if they were caught—knowingly or unknowingly—carrying illegal passengers. This was part of a larger trend in which states increasingly turned to deputizing nonstate actors in their quest to enhance border controls. This included, for instance, relying more and more on airlines to scrutinize travel documents.[95] In 1994, most EU countries passed laws that expanded the obligations of carriers. This simply represented the rediscovery and popularization of an old policy instrument: the 1902 U.S. Passenger Act required steamship owners to return those passengers turned away at U.S. ports, and the 1944 Convention on International Civil Aviation outlined the responsibilities of airline carriers in checking passenger documents.[96] What was new in the 1990s was a much tougher application of these standards, an upsurge in their popularity as a law enforcement tool, and a transplanting of this policing instrument upward to the EU level.[97] The use of carrier sanctions facilitated both the extension of controls outward and the transfer of costs and responsibilities to third parties—pushing law enforcement "away from the border and outside the state."[98] Carriers faced powerful incentives to cooperate with law enforcement authorities: not only were they obligated to return passengers refused entry by border authorities, but they also faced heavy fines. Virginie Guiraudon has pointed out that "one consequence of carrier sanctions has been to criminalize the entry of asylum-seekers since they need either to acquire forged documents to board planes to later discard them or to seek entry through overland routes with the help of smugglers."[99]

Turning the EU's Eastern Neighbors into Buffer Zones

Eastern bloc states had developed their own multilateral law enforcement agreements during the cold war and were parties to many of the international law enforcement conventions.[100] Until well into the 1980s, however, law enforcement relations between Western Europe and the Eastern bloc had been infrequent and often hostile. Indeed, a large portion of criminal investigative tasks on either side of the political divide were devoted specifically to investigating criminal activity sponsored in one way or another by the other side: U.S. and Western European police agencies concerned themselves with law enforcement actions against terrorism, smuggling of high-technology goods, espionage, and the involvement of Bulgarian intelligence and commercial agencies with heroin trafficking. Eastern bloc police agencies, like the police agencies of the tsar and the Habsburgs, focused not just on counterespionage, but on maximizing their control over cross-border movements. There were exceptions, including periodic cooperation by criminal investigators against drug traffickers and other common criminals; fairly regular relations between police agencies in Austria and their colleagues in a few of the more receptive Soviet bloc states, notably Hungary; Romania's and Hungary's admissions into Interpol in 1973 and 1981, respectively; and occasional cooperation against hijackers and other international criminals. But by and large, the quantity and intensity of transnational law enforcement contacts between the two blocs paled in comparison to those within them.

As the cold war came to an end, however, the political obstacles to law enforcement cooperation diminished and the incentives grew. By 1990, most Eastern European countries had applied for membership in Interpol and all were pursuing closer contacts with police officials to the west.[101] The EU, in turn, wished to turn immediate eastern neighbors into law enforcement buffer zones to deter unauthorized entries and activities. A growing number of EU member states signed readmission agreements with their neighbors to the east in the 1990s as part of a larger effort to territorially exclude asylum seekers and other undesirable entrants. This practice began through bilateral accords but was later replicated at the EU-wide level. These agreements meant that it became virtually impossible for would-be asylum seekers to cross a land border into an EU member country without being turned back.

The prospect of incorporation into the EU assured Polish, Hungarian, and Czech cooperation in cracking down on the use of their territory as transit points for asylum seekers and migrant smugglers. This had an eastward ripple effect, as applicant states subsequently negotiated readmission agreements with their neighbors. Thus, many Eastern European countries shifted their border control priorities away from the draconian cold war–era measures to keep people from leaving and toward more collaborative measures to keep people from entering. Following EU guidelines, this involved a simultaneous dismantling and rebuilding of their border control systems. For these and other Eastern European accession states, admission into the EU required three simultaneous moves: a bolstering of their own law enforcement capabilities, greatly enhanced law enforcement cooperation with the EU, and a hardening of their borders with non-EU neighbors. Thus, the politics of EU enlargement was directly linked to the politics of police cooperation and tightening border controls. The EU was essentially able to thicken its border controls and partly externalize the burden of border enforcement by turning neighbors into gatekeepers.[102]

Law enforcement funding became an increasingly important component of EU aid to neighboring countries beginning in the mid-1990s. Substantial funds were made available through the Phare (Poland and Hungary Assistance for Economic Restructuring) Programme including for the training of border control personnel and upgrading equipment as well as the quality of passports and visas. In preparation for EU membership, candidate states were also expected to make major investments in police training, surveillance tools, and sophisticated data-gathering equipment. This process included the 1998 signing of a Pre-Accession Pact on Organized Crime with the applicant countries of Eastern Europe. The agreement called for greater sharing of law enforcement intelligence, training assistance, collaborative investigations, provision of equipment (such as vehicles, video cameras, and night vision goggles), and exchange of police officials.

Countries such as Poland, Hungary, and the Czech Republic pragmatically accepted their new policing duties, rushing to implement Schengen standards as part of the price of admission into the EU. This, in turn, caused border frictions with their neighbors to the east. The Czech government imposed new visa requirements for Romania, Bulgaria, and many former Soviet republics and even sent military troops to fortify its border defenses against illegal immigration.[103] Poland similarly imposed tighter entry restrictions, and new watchtowers were built and helicopters deployed to patrol the country's eastern borders. Maciej Kuczynski, the deputy director of the Polish Department of Migration and Refugee Affairs, candidly explained the situation: "If we want to integrate into the European Union, we have to show our goodwill in fighting illegal immigration."[104] In preparation for its entry into the EU in 2004, Poland agreed to further tighten controls along its eight-hundred-mile eastern border, including hiring thousands of additional border guards, building more border stations, purchasing new equipment, and implementing new laws against drug trafficking and unauthorized migration.[105]

An increasingly important dimension of the EU's interest and involvement in the western Balkans following the violent conflicts of the 1990s was to bolster border enforcement and international crime control efforts. The EU-sponsored CARDS Program (Community Assistance for Reconstruction, Development, and Stabilization) brought substantial aid to the western Balkans in the fields of police, justice, and frontier controls.[106] With prompting, training, funding, and technical assistance from the West, the Bosnian government created a State Border Service to better police its borders. Croatia, which aspired to EU membership, also reinforced patrols on its borders with Bosnia. The United States reinforced these efforts with technical assistance and training to implement EU standards.[107] Emphasizing the key U.S. role in developing local capacity to meet EU requirements, a senior Macedonian law enforcement official commented, "The road to Brussels goes through Washington."[108] To encourage and facilitate greater regionwide law enforcement collaboration, EU and U.S. officials helped to establish the Southeast European Cooperative Initiative, with the Bucharest-based SECI Center opening in early 2001 as a regional clearinghouse for information exchange related to transborder crime. Pointing to the proliferation of internationally sponsored crime control programs throughout the region, Susan Woodward has written that the underlying policy approach has "focused on criminalization, defining a set of activities as crimes, and on developing the operational and technical aspects of implementing state agreements on such criminalization."[109]

Building EU Law Enforcement Institutions

At the same time as the external borders of the EU were being hardened and extended outward by securing the law enforcement cooperation of neighboring states, the space within the borders of the European Union was becoming more domesticated through a greater homogenization of criminal justice norms and procedures and the regularization of law enforcement contacts and information exchange among member states. The 1992 Maastricht Treaty had initially brought policing into the supranational governance structure. At the start of the 1990s, policymaking in this area did not exist, yet during the decade it became "one of the most dynamic and expansionist areas of EU development."[110] Police cooperation within Western Europe became much more supranational in its aspirations with the 1997 Amsterdam Treaty, which outlined the creation of an Area of Freedom, Security, and Justice. By the end of the 1990s, this was the single busiest EU policy arena measured by the sheer number of new initiatives proposed and Council meetings taking place.[111]

The communitization of European policing was further accelerated by the Tampere Programme, adopted by the European Council in October 1999, which outlined a comprehensive program of building institutions in the field of police and justice cooperation and incorporating police and judicial cooperation more centrally and explicitly into EU foreign policy.[112] This included the establishment of a European Police College and European Police Chiefs Operational Task Force to share experience and best practices. Tampere involved an ambitious timetable with a "scoreboard" to help ensure that the agreements were adhered to. Pointing to the supranational aspirations of Tampere, Jörg Friedrichs has noted that in the presidency conclusions, the Area of Freedom, Security and Justice was even referred to as "our territory," implying the crafting of a new system of political authority with clearly demarcated boundaries.[113]

A centerpiece of the effort to establish supranational policing was the creation and evolution of Europol, headquartered in The Hague.[114] The new organization was set up to provide a central EU mechanism for greater cross-border cooperation and communication among police agencies. Germany was Europol's most enthusiastic early proponent, envisioning the eventual creation of a European equivalent of the FBI, with cross-border investigative powers and responsibilities.[115] Europol was headed by a German law enforcement official, Jürgen Storbeck, an articulate and highly visible advocate for the organization's expansion and cross-border cooperation more generally. But Europol's birth was slow and difficult, reflecting enduring problems of mistrust and national inhibitions about creating supranational policing institutions. Europol got its foot in the door of cross-border police cooperation in the early 1990s through the mission of drug control and related anti–money laundering activities. But after demonstrating its usefulness its mandate was broadened to include a much wider range of activities such as illegal migration, cross-border theft of vehicles, nuclear smuggling, human trafficking, counterfeiting of the euro, and terrorism. The Europol Convention was adopted in 1995, ratified in 1998, and became fully functional in 1999. A leading European criminologist has described the Europol Convention as a "silent revolution in the history of international police cooperation in Europe. Never before have so many forms of cross-border police cooperation been regulated in such detail by a convention."[116]

Overcoming initial political resistance, the Amsterdam Treaty gave Europol a number of important new policing tasks, including the authority to request that EU members carry out and coordinate investigations in specific cases, the power to create joint cross-border teams to assist in investigations, and the capacity to establish specific expertise that EU members could draw on to help with organized crime–related cases.[117] Each member state was also required to establish a Europol unit to encourage and facilitate law enforcement coordination and collaboration. The setting up of the Europol Computer System with a vast database also greatly facilitated the cross-border sharing of information on suspects and stolen goods. This added to other centralized databases, including the Schengen Information System (to track border crossers) and the Customs Information System (to tackle smuggling). Thus, a supranational organization that initially looked like little more than a regional-level variant of Interpol (prompting some grumbling about the apparent duplication) had by the end of the decade been transformed into a reflection of and a vehicle for much more intensive and extensive EU-wide police cooperation. Europol, which started out modestly in a service role as strictly an information clearinghouse, was increasingly taking on a more directive role.

Europol's supranational character, however, should not be overstated. On the one hand, the notion of a supranational police intelligence network struck many Europeans as reasonable. On the other hand, relatively few Europeans were willing as yet to accept the notion of granting arrest powers to a supranational European police agency. A significant impediment to the creation of a truly supranational police force was the persistent heterogeneity of criminal laws within Europe combined with a continued reluctance to concede sovereign jurisdiction in the domain of criminal justice. A European FBI presumed, to a significant extent, the existence of federal criminal statutes transcending the criminal codes of the member states—itself a notion that had already received considerable attention within Europe and that conforms with the broader concept of "un espace juridique Européen" (a European legal domain) articulated by French president Valery Giscard d'Estaing in 1977.

Nevertheless, from a broader historical perspective, the creation of Europol and other EU-wide criminal justice institutions in a mere decade represented a remarkable achievement. As Cyrille Fijnaut noted, "Before 1990, police co-operation in Europe was for the most part an informal, even a secret, affair that often remained limited to the exchange of information."[118] By the end of the decade, police cooperation had become much more institutionalized, formalized, and multilateralized. Thus, as discussed in the next chapter, when counterterrorism returned to the forefront of the European law enforcement agenda in the first decade of the twenty-first century, the playing field had substantially changed, making possible new forms of collaboration and cooperation that also brought new tensions and frictions. The new security context would also present an opportunity for policy entrepreneurs to push ahead with stalled initiatives that had met political resistance. At the same time, the more politicized nature of counterterrorism would, as in the past, test the limits of cooperation.

CHAPTER FIVE

□ □ □

International Crime Control after September 11

Despite the cliché that "everything changed" on September 11, 2001, the internationalization of policing in the aftermath of the terrorist bombings actually represents more of a rapid acceleration and deepening of preexisting trends than is generally recognized. This includes a further collapsing of distinctions between internal and external security, a repackaging of old missions as part of the new antiterrorism mission, and intensified securitization of cross-border trade, travel, and financial flows. The heightened stakes and more proactive nature of counterterrorism have also invited a further expansion of intelligence agencies into the realm of law enforcement. The terrorist attacks provided the catalyst, but the mobilization of an unprecedented global antiterrorism campaign has very much been shaped by and built on previous policies and an international policing infrastructure already in place. Moreover, rather than simply responding to a growing transnational terrorism threat, policy entrepreneurs have used the new security context to promote a much broader criminal law enforcement agenda at the regional and global levels. Sifting through the recent flurry of U.S.- and European-sponsored cross-border policing initiatives, in this chapter we differentiate among what is new, what is a continuation and extension of prior initiatives, and what reflects a partial return to policing practices and priorities of much earlier historical eras. We point to underlying patterns of continuity and change, stressing the importance of assessing the developments of recent years from the perspective of earlier decades and even centuries.

On both sides of the Atlantic, law enforcement strategists have been devising new ways to manage the growing tension between ambitious policing objectives and the imperatives of economic integration. This has spurred both the displacement of more police work onto the private sector and the development and deployment of more expansive surveillance, detection, and information technologies designed to deter and filter out criminalized transnational actors and activities without significantly impeding legitimate cross-border exchange. The basic dilemma of enforcing laws against undesirable transnational flows while at the same time facilitating and encouraging desirable flows is an old one, but the stakes have now sharply risen due to the potential for "catastrophic criminality" via the use of a smuggled nuclear device or other weapon of mass destruction by nonstate actors. Catastrophic security threats have traditionally been considered to be exclusively military matters—such as deterring invading armies or nuclear strikes—but are now also very much policing matters.

These policing trends and rising anxieties have brought law enforcement and national security institutions, strategies, and missions ever closer together. Some of these developments are novel, but a broader historical perspective reveals that current trends also represent a partial return to nineteenth-century policing dynamics, when "political policing" was high on state security agendas, security and law enforcement concerns were more intimately intertwined, and the deputizing of private actors to take on policing tasks was not uncommon. We have partly gone back to the future: now, as then, the politicized nature of counterterrorism has been a source of international friction, but as in the past, it may pave the way for a higher level of international police cooperation across a wide range of issue areas beyond counterterrorism than was previously imaginable. The historical pattern is therefore both cyclical and evolutionary, returning to some familiar early themes and patterns but also reaching new levels of cooperation in international crime control.

What may be emerging early in the twenty-first century is a new type of transatlantic security community, based more on policing alliances against nonstate actors than traditional security alliances against state-based military threats. This nascent law enforcement alliance, held together by an increasingly dense set of transgovernmental policing networks and international agreements, has been quietly built up and largely overlooked as media attention and political debate have focused on the highly charged transatlantic rift over the exercise of U.S. military power in Iraq and elsewhere. Whether and how much this rift ultimately undermines the transatlantic policing alliance remains to be seen, with much depending on the degree to which the counterterrorism issue can be depoliticized.

Expanding U.S. Policing Powers in a New Security Context

In the wake of the terrorist attacks on September 11, the U.S. Congress immediately moved to give the federal government expansive new domestic and international policing powers through the passage of the USA Patriot Act (Uniting and Strengthening America by Providing Appropriate Tools Required to Intercept and Obstruct Terrorism Act).[1] This sweeping law, hurriedly drafted and passed with overwhelming bipartisan support on October 26, 2001, created new crimes and tougher penalties for use against terrorists and provided officials with expanded authority to intercept communications, target computer-related crimes[2] and money laundering (through new regulations, criminal sanctions, and forfeiture), tighten border controls, and detain and deport suspects.[3] The Patriot Act accelerated the tearing down of the legal wall between intelligence and law enforcement—a wall that, as discussed in the previous chapter, was already semipermeable. This included giving the intelligence community more access to information gained during a criminal investigation, providing law enforcement with more intelligence capabilities, and loosening restrictions on surveillance through a revision of the Foreign Intelligence Surveillance Act.[4]

The law also gave authorities new tools that could be used for a range of law enforcement activities having little or nothing to do with counterterrorism, allowing law enforcement agencies to expand their policing powers more generally.[5] In the fall of 2002, the Justice Department acknowledged that it had utilized its new surveillance capabilities to investigate not only "terrorist conspirators" but also "kidnappers who communicated their demands via e-mail, a major drug distributor, identity thieves who obtained victims' bank account information and stole their money, a fugitive who fled on the eve of trial using a fake passport, and a four-time murderer."[6] The Patriot Act became an especially powerful tool against financial crimes, making it possible to confiscate millions of dollars from international bank accounts, in many instances with little or no link to terrorism. Even as Justice Department officials publicly described the new law as strictly a terrorism-fighting tool, internally they acknowledged that the law enabled carrying out a much larger crime-fighting agenda. "What the Justice Department has really done," noted one critic, "is to get things put into the law that have been on prosecutors' wish lists for years. They've used terrorism as a guise to expand law enforcement powers in areas that are totally unrelated to terrorism."[7] The number of counterterrorism investigations by the Department of Justice skyrocketed after September 11, but according to a January 2003 report by the General Accounting Office (the investigative arm of Congress), three-fourths of the convictions were erroneously categorized as "international terrorism" cases.[8]

Political scrutiny and pressure to reform the nation's counterterrorism apparatus was sustained in part through the high-profile report of the National Commission on Terrorist Attacks upon the United States (the "9/11 Commission Report"), helping to create the momentum for a greater centralization of the intelligence system through the National Intelligence Reform and Terrorism Prevention Act of 2004. One press account at the time described the push for intelligence reform as an "effort to integrate the military, covert actions, diplomacy, law enforcement, border security, and other aspects of national power into a seamless protective force."[9] The law also included new criminal penalties for various activities related to terrorism, from receiving military training from a terrorist group to providing material support to suspected terrorists. A little-noticed provision in the law gave the federal government expanded authority and tools to track overseas wire transfers. It authorized the Treasury Department to develop regulations requiring financial institutions to provide "certain cross-border electronic transmittals of funds" deemed necessary to curb money laundering and terrorist financing, potentially opening millions of international transactions to government scrutiny.[10] Other measures enhanced the Department of Justice's detention powers, authorized foreign governments to receive secret U.S. grand jury information in urgent terrorist cases, loosened the standards for FBI surveillance warrants, and eliminated some restrictions on interrogations.[11] Many of these measures had long been pushed by the White House and law enforcement agencies but staunchly opposed by defenders of civil liberties.

Bringing law enforcement and intelligence functions closer together predictably brought with it more bureaucratic frictions. Although these frictions could be traced back more than half a century, the growing involvement of the CIA in policing and the FBI in intelligence generated both more cooperation and more tension as they were forced to work more closely together. As the FBI's international duties and presence expanded, this became a greater source of competition with the CIA over turf and the recruitment of spies.[12] In an effort to boost its intelligence-reporting role, in December 2004 the FBI initiated discussions with the CIA to change the established ground rules regarding the conduct of domestic and international intelligence gathering.[13] This was part of the FBI's broader push to become more proactive rather than reactive and prioritize counterterrorism over more traditional law enforcement tasks.[14] In Afghanistan, for example, FBI agents reportedly accompanied soldiers on missions in order to interrogate prisoners, and in Pakistan, FBI and CIA agents apparently accompanied Pakistani security forces in the raid of an al Qaeda cell and capture of Abu Zubaydah.[15] In 2004, FBI Director Robert Mueller noted that the Bureau's counterterrorism force had more than doubled since 2001, partly by reassigning agents from more traditional crime-fighting tasks such as drug control.[16]

Washington also moved to selectively outsource detentions and interrogations, bypassing public scrutiny and normal legal requirements and procedures. Following the U.S. invasion of Afghanistan in late 2001, the U.S. naval base at Guantánamo Bay, Cuba, was quickly converted into a controversial detention center to house some six hundred al Qaeda and Taliban prisoners, to be held in legal limbo outside the jurisdiction of U.S. and foreign courts.[17] The United States also dramatically expanded a previously obscure program called "extraordinary rendition." This secretive program, sometimes involving covert abductions, facilitated the rendition of terrorist suspects from one country to another for interrogation and prosecution purposes. A classified directive signed by President George W. Bush shortly after September 11 authorized the CIA to secretly transfer suspects to foreign countries for interrogation (often on charter planes to avoid being noticed).[18] Critics contend that the implicit point of the rendition program was to take advantage of extreme interrogation methods practiced in countries such as Egypt, Jordan, Syria, and Morocco (which are known to torture suspects), representing a radical redefinition of interrogation parameters and standards with little public debate or accountability.[19]

Although typically operating outside the public eye, some of these renditions caught public attention and strained relations with close U.S. allies. For example, in one well-known incident, a Canadian citizen of Syrian origin was arrested in transit at New York's JFK Airport, where he was sent to Syria and allegedly tortured before being released after a lengthy detention. Apparently, Canadian authorities were not informed, and when reported in the Canadian press the incident sparked intense public debate. In another sensitive and controversial case, in June 2005 an Italian judge ordered the arrest of thirteen CIA agents suspected of carrying out the February 2003 kidnapping of Hasan Mustafa Osama Nasr outside of Italian law and his dispatch to Egypt, where he was allegedly tortured. Particularly embarrassing for the U.S. government was the case of Khaled el-Masri, a German citizen of Lebanese descent who was mistaken for an al Qaeda operative and abducted by U.S. agents on the Serbian-Macedonia border in 2003. He was held for five months in Macedonia and Afghanistan, where he was allegedly mistreated. In December 2005, he filed a lawsuit against the United States. The high-profile case became a source of strain in U.S.-German relations. Adding to the diplomatic tensions, in late 2005 there were mounting allegations of secret CIA-run prisons in Europe, which came to light in numerous media reports.

From the U.S.-Led War on Drugs to the War on Terror

The technical and legal instruments of international law enforcement developed through earlier antidrug and related anti–money laundering efforts were quickly adapted for the new antiterrorism campaign. For instance, the technocratic expertise and tools developed to trace money laundering and seize drug profits were redirected and extended to track and confiscate money allegedly intended to finance terrorist activities.[20] The traditional drug focus of anti–money laundering efforts was thus merged with a new and intensifying campaign against terrorist financing. The Bush administration's enthusiasm for international anti–money laundering efforts had actually waned immediately prior to September 11 but found new life and a new rationale in the wake of the attacks. The Patriot Act added new money laundering crimes related to terrorism and provided authorities with new and expanded powers to track such crimes and seize assets. The Financial Crimes Enforcement Network (FinCEN) of the U.S. Treasury Department, which was set up in 1990 to focus on drug-related money laundering, saw its mandate expanded by the Patriot Act to track "suspicious transactions" related to terrorist financing. Also, with FinCEN having helped dozens of countries across the globe establish financial intelligence units to combat money laundering in the 1990s, this newly developed local expertise could now be called on to combat terrorist financing. Information sharing in this area was further facilitated by the Egmont Group, a transnational enforcement network that the United States helped set up in the mid-1990s, linking a growing number of financial intelligence units across the globe.[21]

One consequence of this shift in priorities was a much greater targeting of *hawalas* and other informal value transfer mechanisms, which had long been used by diaspora communities for remittances and other cross-border financial transactions.[22] The potential diversion of funds from Islamic charities to finance terrorist activities also became a high-priority law enforcement target. But although the targets shifted, this was essentially an extension of the "follow-the-money" method to crime control that had become such a popular antidrug and anti–money laundering enforcement tool in earlier years.[23]

U.S. efforts to target and freeze terrorist assets were also greatly facilitated by creative new uses of the economic sanctions programs of the Office of Foreign Assets Control (OFAC), which had been built up in previous years.[24] U.S. unilateral actions in the immediate aftermath of September 11 led the way to broader multilateral agreements institutionalized and legitimized at the global level through UN Security Council Resolution 1373 in the fall of 2001. Much of the resolution focuses on tackling the funding of terrorist organizations and required signatories to criminalize support for terrorists, expedite the seizing of funds, and share operational information. The resolution also established a Counter Terrorism Committee (CTC) to oversee a monitoring system requiring member states to report on their implementation of the resolution. David Courtright noted, "Through the first four years of the Security Council's CTC program, the United States and Great Britain have remained firmly in control of its political direction."[25] Indeed, U.S. officials not only wrote much of the Security Council resolution but were the source of most of the intelligence determining who was on the UN's list of terrorist organizations. Thomas Biersteker argued that through this dominance of U.S. intelligence-gathering capacity, "the listing process is another example of US operational hegemony."[26]

But even as U.S.-led initiatives to deter money laundering and track terrorist financing represented greater state monitoring and criminalization of global financial flows, most of the actual policing was in practice privatized and subcontracted out: as a former senior State Department official put it, bankers were increasingly required to police suspicious transactions and relationships, becoming "deputy sheriffs for governments."[27] Private banks were required to carry out public policing tasks through a variety of reporting requirements, including reporting on and not doing business with individuals on lists of "banned persons" (with OFAC the most important source of such lists).[28] This deputization process was not new—it was developed through earlier anti–drug money laundering legislation and economic sanctions provisions—but was now redirected, deepened, and expanded to more intensively target terrorist financing.

Just as drug enforcement and related anti–money laundering initiatives had provided a foot in the door for U.S. law enforcement authorities in foreign countries in earlier years, so, too, did the counterterrorism mission after September 11, from Europe and the Middle East to Central Asia and the Pacific Basin.[29] For example, the number of foreign trainees in federally funded Anti-Terrorism Assistance Program courses increased from fewer than one thousand per year in the late 1990s to almost five thousand in 2002.[30] The heightened U.S. international law enforcement presence and influence was achieved not only through diplomatic arm-twisting but also through a certain degree of mutual interest, as a series of spectacular terrorist bombings across the globe—in Spain, Morocco, Egypt, Saudi Arabia, Indonesia, England and elsewhere—heightened the prioritization of counterterrorism. Resistance to U.S. pressures, demands, and presence thus softened, even as anti-American popular sentiment hardened. Of course, some of this cooperation was more apparent than real, representing a form of "paper compliance": going through the motions and filling out the required paperwork but involving only superficial or uneven implementation, due either to a lack of capacity or of will or a mixture of both. In some cases, part of the political motivation to sign on to the U.S.-led global antiterrorism campaign was to use it as a convenient legitimizing cover to suppress domestic political opposition and dissent.

Some U.S. law enforcement agencies that traditionally had little or nothing to do with counterterrorism scrambled to adjust and redefine their mission in the new security environment. This was strikingly evident in the case of drug control. The DEA, for instance, pushed to integrate the war on drugs with the war on terror through a renewed focus on "narcoterrorism," drawing greater attention to alleged links between drug trafficking and terrorist activities. A senior DEA official told a congressional committee in May 2003, "Prior to September 11th, 2001, the law enforcement community typically addressed drug trafficking and terrorist activities as separate issues. In the wake of the terrorist attacks in New York City, Washington, D.C., and Pennsylvania, these two criminal activities are virtually intertwined. For DEA, investigating the link between drugs and terrorism has taken on a renewed importance."[31] Similarly, the White House's Office of National Drug Control Policy (dubbed the "drug czar's office") sponsored a television advertising campaign in 2002 that highlighted the connection between drugs and terrorism. Terminology from the counterterrorism campaign became incorporated into the antidrug campaign: in 2003, the Southern Command's General James Hill kept referring to drugs as a "weapon of mass destruction."[32]

The repackaging of the war on drugs as part of the war on terrorism was especially critical in maintaining political support for growing levels of U.S. security assistance to Colombia, where the line between fighting drugs and fighting insurgents was becoming progressively blurred. In earlier years, U.S. officials were careful to emphasize that Washington was supporting Colombia's antidrug campaign rather than the antiguerrilla campaign, but the new emphasis on narcoterrorism made it less necessary for officials to publicly distance themselves from counterinsurgency. The term narcoterrorism was coined long before September 11 (dating back at least to the 1980s) but gained much wider currency and acceptance in the wake of the attacks, even though its clarity and analytical utility had been questioned. As part of an increase in international antiterrorism funding in March 2002, Congress authorized the Colombian military to use U.S. antidrug aid for a "unified campaign" to combat both drugs and insurgents, making it possible for the United States to fund a variety of non–drug-related military and law enforcement operations in Colombia. In late 2002, the Bush administration also overturned the executive order of the Clinton administration blocking the sharing of non–drug-related intelligence with Colombian security forces.[33]

The fusion of counternarcotics and counterterrorism had broader regional implications. As one observer commented, "For many in Washington, the war on drugs and the war on terror are virtually indistinguishable in Latin America."[34] In the immediate years after September 11, U.S. officials began to frame counterterrorism and counternarcotics efforts as part of a much larger security goal of imposing control over lawless zones. At a meeting with the region's defense ministers in November 2002, U.S. Secretary of Defense Donald Rumsfeld told his counterparts, "In this hemisphere, narco-terrorists, hostage takers and arms smugglers operate in ungoverned areas, using them as bases from which to destabilize democratic governments."[35] By this logic, frontier zones that had long been viewed as hubs of transnational criminality, such as the Darien Gap between Panama and Colombia and the triple border zone between Argentina, Paraguay, and Brazil, were now security priorities. Administration officials urged the regions' militaries to embrace a greater policing role to control these "ungoverned spaces." In March 2003, General James Hill described the shift in perceived security threats:

> Today, the threat to the countries of the region is not the military force of the adjacent neighbor or some invading foreign power. Today's foe is the terrorist, the narco-trafficker, the arms trafficker, the document forger, the international crime boss, and the money launderer. This threat is a weed that is planted, grown and nurtured in the fertile ground of ungoverned spaces such as coastlines, rivers and unpopulated border areas. This threat is watered and fertilized with money from drugs, illegal arms sales, and human trafficking. This threat respects neither geographical nor moral boundaries.[36]

In some places, the war on drugs not only merged with but became subordinated to the war on terrorism, just as the antidrug mission had long been subordinated to anticommunism during the cold war. This was most apparent in the case of Afghanistan, by far the world's largest opium producer. Even as U.S. officials publicly rationalized the bombing campaign in Afghanistan in the fall of 2001 as contributing to both the antidrug and antiterrorism efforts, drug control objectives quickly took a back seat once the Taliban regime was removed. Opium production skyrocketed in the years following the U.S.-led invasion.[37] In 2005, the Pentagon announced ambitious plans to reinvigorate the antidrug program in Afghanistan, including a direct U.S. military role in counterdrug operations.[38] Yet a large-scale and sustained crackdown on the illicit trade would likely threaten and meet strong resistance from the very military commanders and town leaders that the United States relied on for support in the counterterrorism campaign. Having drug control objectives supplanted by other security goals was an old and familiar story in Afghanistan (and elsewhere around the world),[39] where the CIA had conveniently turned a blind eye to drug smuggling by U.S.-backed anti-Soviet insurgents in the 1980s.[40]

Hardening, Internationalizing, and Digitizing U.S. Border Controls

In the years following the September 11 attacks, U.S. law enforcement strategists rushed to adapt the old border control infrastructure to the new focus on counterterrorism. It was an awkward and cumbersome retooling project, given the fundamental change in which targets were prioritized. This had enormous implications for the organization of border enforcement work, prompting three related shifts: much greater use of new surveillance and information technologies, an aggressive push to extend border controls outward (essentially de-bordering border controls), and more reliance on private sector collaboration in policing. All three shifts required much more intensive international cooperation, including the development and promotion of more standardized methods and procedures to track cross-border travel and cargo flows.

Efforts to reinvent and retool U.S. border controls in the aftermath of the terrorist attacks presented a formidable challenge to those agencies charged with the task of keeping out "undesirables." For instance, the INS border enforcement system was built to police large numbers of economically motivated, unauthorized migrant workers rather than to detect and deter a small number of determined individuals intending to commit politically motivated violent acts. Similarly, the U.S. Customs Service had traditionally focused primarily on intercepting and seizing drugs and other forms of contraband rather than keeping out weapons of mass destruction. These agencies were now suddenly expected to play a frontline role against terrorism. The new fear was that the same groups, methods, and routes long used to smuggle migrants and drugs into the country could now be used to smuggle in terrorists and weapons of mass destruction. Similarly, the same fraudulent document industry that had long provided identification cards for unauthorized migrants could also potentially provide these services to terrorists. Not only had border enforcement agencies been given a harder task that they were largely unprepared for, but they were now expected to be much more effective than in the past—indeed, the expectation was 100 percent deterrence (contrast this to the long tolerated modest levels of deterrence against drug trafficking and migrant smuggling). But while facing intense political pressure and scrutiny, they were also the recipients of substantial new funding. The fiscal year 2003 budget provided an increase of more than $2 billion for border security, including increasing the budget of the INS and the inspections budget of the Customs Service by about one-third.

In the wake of September 11, there was not only an infusion of more border law enforcement resources but also a consolidation and reorganization of multiple agencies under a new cabinet-level Department of Homeland Security (DHS). A once obscure term, "homeland security" suddenly became part of the everyday security discourse. The creation of the DHS, representing the largest reorganization of the federal government since the early years of the cold war, brought together portions of a number of existing border enforcement-related departments and agencies, including the Coast Guard, the INS, and the Customs Service. DHS began operating in 2003 with a budget of $37 billion and more than 170,000 employees. One can imagine that as this bureaucracy continues to grow, so, too, will its global engagement—practicing a form of homeland security abroad. Within the DHS, Customs and Border Protection established an Office of International Affairs responsible for all international activities and programs, including managing foreign training programs, overseeing the negotiation and implementation of agreements with foreign agencies, and conducting bilateral and multilateral relations with foreign agencies. As of early 2004, DHS had personnel in seventy-seven countries.[41]

The new security environment also opened more space to draw on military resources for homeland security tasks, including a further militarization of immigration law enforcement on the border. In the past, military units operating along the border were formally limited to assisting antidrug work: "It had to have a counterdrug nexus," noted a spokesperson for Joint Task Force North (which replaced Joint Task Force Six in September

2004). "Now our mission is a major supporter of homeland security." The new expanded mission is to support federal law enforcement agencies in the "interdiction of suspected transnational threats within and along the approaches to the United States," which can include targeting illegal immigration.[42] In September 2005, border officials in Arizona unveiled a new unmanned aerial surveillance system based on the satellite-controlled Predator-B spy drone used for military operations in the Middle East and elsewhere.[43] These developments were part of the larger securitization of immigration control issues in the post–September 11 era.[44] Reflecting the shifting priorities, federal prosecutions for immigration law violations more than doubled from 2001 to 2005, replacing drug law violations as the most frequently enforced federal crime.[45]

Balancing trade facilitation and border law enforcement also became much more complicated in the wake of the terrorist attacks.[46] On September 11, 2001, U.S. border inspectors were put on a level-one alert, defined as a "sustained, intensive, anti-terrorism operation." Cross-border traffic slowed to a trickle. This was not the first time the United States had put a sudden squeeze on the border; Operation Intercept more than three decades earlier had virtually shut down the border to pressure Mexico to do more against drug trafficking. What was different this time, however, was that the crackdown took place in the context of much greater economic interdependence and integration.[47] Also unlike the past, the new border crackdown targeted the U.S.-Canada border as well. In the days after the attacks, border waits for trucks hauling cargo across the U.S.-Canada border increased from about one or two minutes to ten to fifteen hours, causing chaos in one of the busiest trade relationships in the world.[48] Although all three NAFTA partners were beneficiaries of an interdependent regional economy, Mexico and Canada were far more dependent on trade with the United States than the other way around, and were therefore much more vulnerable to security-related border disruptions. This structural asymmetry powerfully conditioned cross-border law enforcement relations, giving Washington added policy leverage.

As discussed in the previous chapter, policing the U.S.-Canada border had been such a low priority for both countries that it had famously been dubbed "the longest undefended border in the world." After September 11, Canada found itself in the awkward and unfamiliar position of being perceived as a security concern. The anemic state of border controls became highly politicized and intensely scrutinized, giving Canada a heavy dose of the kind of negative attention in the U.S. media and in Washington policy debates that Mexico had long experienced. Indeed, the U.S.-Canada border became a political prop for those who blamed lax border controls for America's vulnerability to terrorism. Senator Byron Dorgan (D–North Dakota) held up a rubber cone at a congressional hearing on northern border security in late 2001 to show what meets those who arrive at some checkpoints after 10 P.M.: "This is America's security at our border crossings," he said. "America can't effectively combat terrorism if it doesn't control its borders."[49] Although the focus was the U.S.-Canada border and the concern was terrorism, the new border security discourse was not so different from the old drug and immigration control discourse that had long characterized U.S.-Mexico border relations.

After September 11, the U.S. Congress moved to triple the number of border agents on the northern border, and National Guard troops were also sent to help with patrols and inspections at ports of entry. The Coast Guard began to stop all boats crossing the Great Lakes and to escort gas and oil tankers. Along with new enforcement personnel came new surveillance equipment. New cameras with night-vision lenses were installed along parts of the border, and a satellite tracking system began to be used for detecting illegal entries. There were also early signs of militarizing border surveillance, with the United States planning on setting up five air and marine bases along the northern border.[50]

In the wake of the terrorist attacks, the Mexican and Canadian governments moved to signal that they were taking counterterrorism more seriously, partly to assure that their borders with the United States remain open to economic flows. Mexican officials detained hundreds of people of Middle Eastern origin, curbed the entry of citizens from a number of Central Asian and Middle Eastern countries, provided U.S. authorities with intelligence information on possible suspects based in Mexico, and targeted bank accounts of suspected terrorists. The Mexican government also announced the creation of a national immigration database and the establishment of new false document detectors at southern border checkpoints. In early 2002, it announced plans to set up new X-ray machines at its southern and northern border crossings. These various security measures essentially helped to thicken U.S. border controls, with Mexico serving as a de facto law enforcement buffer zone (paralleling in a less formal and institutionalized manner the EU's experience with its eastern neighbors).

Ottawa moved even more quickly to signal a greater commitment to counterterrorism, ordering a high state of alert at border crossings, enhancing the level of security at airports, adding new funding for detection technologies and personnel, initiating legislation to combat the financing of terrorism, and freezing the assets of known terrorist groups. Two thousand officers of the Royal Canadian Mounted Police were deployed to border patrol and counterterrorism tasks. Tougher immigration control measures included the introduction of a fraud-resistant resident card for new immigrants, increased detention capacity and deportation activity, greater security screening for refugee claimants, and a tightening of the visa regime, including adding a requirement that Saudi and Malaysian visitors obtain visas.[51] Like their Mexican counterparts, Canadian officials attempted to impress and appease Washington with new policing initiatives, while at the same time repeatedly emphasizing the importance of maintaining national sovereignty and policymaking autonomy and trying to avoid the impression that their policy changes reflected conforming to U.S. pressures and expectations.[52] Nevertheless, the incentives under conditions of asymmetrical interdependence and a new security context were clear: either take stronger measures to enhance border security or risk a unilateral U.S. hardening of the border. Canadians interpreted a post–September 11 warning by Secretary of State Colin Powell as a not-so-subtle threat: "Some nations need to be more vigilant against terrorism at their borders if they want their relationship with the U.S. to remain the same."[53]

Heightened concerns over border security, however, had to be reconciled with the enormous volume of legitimate crossings into the United States. The country's borders had to be filters more than simply barriers. Cross-border cargo trade alone had roughly doubled in the 1990s and was expected to double again in the decade ahead. In 2004, more than 427 million travelers, mostly noncitizens, were inspected at U.S. ports of entry; most arrived via the nation's land borders with Canada and Mexico. Finding a balance between facilitating the growing volume of legitimate border crossings and enforcing laws against unwanted crossings had long been the defining challenge of border control, but given the rising stakes, the balancing act became more difficult to sustain with the same old inspection methods and tools.

To create borders that performed as better security barriers and more efficient economic bridges, U.S. law enforcement strategists aggressively pushed for more intensive use of new technologies, greater private sector collusion in policing, and more expansive cross-border surveillance and law enforcement coordination. This was most clearly outlined in the "smart border" accord between Canada and the United States, signed in December 2001 and partly extended in a separate accord between Mexico and the United States in the spring of 2002. These agreements called for a more layered and risk management approach to monitoring cargo and travelers that by its very nature would necessitate far greater cross-border cooperation. In the case of travel, for instance, the agreements called for consultation on visa policies and greater screening of third-country nationals, common biometric identifiers, the development of preclearance procedures and provision of advanced passenger information, and the creation of compatible databases to foster cross-border information sharing.

U.S. officials applied this more high-tech and more internationalized approach to border enforcement not only regionally but also globally. As summarized by the White House in January 2002:

> The border of the future must integrate actions abroad to screen goods and people prior to their arrival in sovereign U.S. territory. . . . Agreements with our neighbors, major trading partners, and private industry will allow extensive pre-screening of low-risk traffic, thereby allowing limited assets to focus attention on high-risk traffic. The use of advanced technology to track the movement of cargo and the entry and exit of individuals is essential to the task of managing the movement of hundreds of millions of individuals, conveyances, and vehicles.[54]

The 9/11 Commission added an influential voice to the growing chorus calling for the internationalization of border controls: "The further away from our borders that screening [of travelers] occurs, the more security benefits we gain." The Commission argued that "the U.S. government cannot meet its own obligations to the American people to prevent the entry of terrorists without a major effort to collaborate with other governments. We should do more to exchange terrorist information with trusted allies, and raise U.S. and global border security standards for travel and border crossing over the medium and long term through extensive international cooperation." Pointing to the ability of terrorists to plot against American territory and interests from afar, the Commission concluded, "The American homeland is the planet."[55]

To more carefully track international travel, the United States began to aggressively push for more tamper-proof travel documents, greater sharing of passenger data, and more extensive preinspection of passengers. As a condition for access to U.S. territory, airlines were now required to electronically submit advance passenger manifests. Pushing to internationalize the U.S. border control agenda, the 2002 Enhanced Border Security and Visa Entry Reform Act mandated that foreign nationals' documents include machine-readable biometric data (such as digital fingerprints) to identify visitors.[56] In March 2004, the United States announced plans to send inspectors to foreign airports. Fifteen foreign airports were participating in preinspection as of spring 2005, and Congress mandated that this be expanded to at least twenty-five foreign airports.[57] Preinspection actually dates back to the 1990s, when the INS began using it on a limited basis as an immigration control tool, but it was reinvented and greatly expanded after September 11 as a counterterrorism tool. Although concerns over issues such as privacy, sovereignty, and funding had yet to be fully worked out, the strategic plan was clear. As described by Rey Koslowski, through the international standardization of documents and collection and sharing of biographical and biometric information, law enforcement authorities in source, transit, and destination countries would have at their disposal an enormous amount of digitized data that could then be "data-mined" to detect and investigate anomalies.[58]

Many of the technological innovations in surveillance and tracking of cross-border travelers, including the use of biometrics,[59] actually predated September 11, but were expanded and given much greater funding, legitimacy, and political support as homeland security concerns grew. More generally, as David Lyon pointed out, "Despite the media hype, responses to the attacks do not amount to an entirely new surveillance landscape. Rather, already existing surveillance systems are being reinforced and intensified."[60] The turn to a greater reliance on surveillance technologies, such as the introduction of automated face recognition systems at a growing number of airports, prompted growing concerns about invasions of privacy and an emerging "homeland security industrial complex."[61] It

also provoked charges that the political pressure to find a quick technological fix that minimized border disruptions had led to an embrace of
many wasteful and inefficient devices. "After 9/11, we had to show how
committed we were to spending hugely greater amounts of money than
ever before, as rapidly as possible," said Representative Christopher Cox
(R-California), chairman of the Homeland Security Committee. "That
brought us what we might expect, which is some expensive mistakes. This
has been the difficult learning curve of the new discipline known as homeland security." According to Randall J. Larsen, a retired Air Force colonel
and ex-government advisor on scientific issues, "Everyone was standing
in line with their silver bullets to make us more secure after Sept. 11." He
noted, "We bought a lot of stuff off the shelf that wasn't effective."[62]

The centerpiece of the high-tech U.S. approach to tracking cross-
border travel was US VISIT, the United States Visitor and Immigrant
Status Indicator Technology system, an ambitious new entry-exit screening system combining integrated databases and biometrics.[63] Launched in
2004, the new system required foreigners arriving in the United States
with visas to have their documents scanned and their fingerprints and
photos taken. US VISIT was then extended to include collecting biometric
data from visitors arriving from visa-waiver countries. As described by Accenture (the firm awarded the $10 billion contract to set up US VISIT),[64]
"The end vision for the US VISIT solution is built around the concept of
virtual border. The virtual border is designed to operate far beyond US
boundaries to help DHS assess the security risks of all US-bound travelers
and prevent potential threats from reaching US borders."[65] Those applying
for visas abroad would have digital fingerprints and photographs taken at
U.S. embassies and consulate offices, making it possible to compare this
biometric information with the biometrics collected through US VISIT
upon arrival at U.S. ports of entry.[66]

US VISIT is a prime example of a pre–September 11 idea that was later
touted as a "new" antiterrorism initiative. An entry-exit system had been
mandated by Congress in 1996 as an immigration control tool to crack
down on foreign visitors overstaying their visas, but its implementation
was repeatedly stalled in the face of organized opposition concerned about
potential travel delays. The initiative was revived and repackaged in the
aftermath of the terrorist attacks as a counterterrorism tool. US VISIT
was a more high-tech and more ambitious version of the earlier stalled ef-

fort, reflecting the heightened U.S. emphasis on technological solutions. It remains very much a work in progress. For example, DHS in early 2005 began to test the use of encrypted tags to track the entry and exit of border crossers as part of US VISIT. These electronic tags, called RFIDs (radio frequency identification), utilize tiny inexpensive microchips half the size of a grain of sand to transmit radio signals prompted by a signal from a specialized reader. U.S. border control officials expressed high hopes for such devices. Asa Hutchinson, the undersecretary for border and transportation security, explained: "Through the use of radio frequency technology, we see the potential to not only improve the security of our country, but also to make the most important infrastructure enhancements to the US land borders in more than 50 years."[67] RFIDs could eventually be embedded in all travel documents.

US VISIT-type systems are likely to be replicated across the globe in coming years. Koslowski has pointed out that as such systems proliferate, "at some point, the digitized biometrics of the vast majority of the world's international traveling public will be in the databases of the immigration and border control authorities of many countries." This, in turn, will generate new law enforcement challenges and concerns, as theft of digitized biometrics becomes both more attractive and more possible with the spread of such databases. And with database security beyond direct U.S. control, this will produce both new frictions and new calls for cooperation in database protection.[68]

While new surveillance technologies were being developed after September 11 to more effectively screen out undesirable border crossers, creating "smart borders" also involved identifying and facilitating "low-risk" frequent travelers. At some border crossings, additional special lanes were opened for those business commuters who underwent a security background check and paid a special border-crossing fee. Thousands of frequent travelers enrolled in the Secure Electronic Network for Travelers' Rapid Inspection system, which guaranteed a wait time of no more than fifteen minutes to enter the United States south of San Diego. Similarly, the Nexus program along the U.S.-Canada border allowed low-risk frequent travelers who had undergone background checks to quickly cross through designated ports of entry. Those enrolled in the Nexus program received a computerized photo identification card that could be electronically scanned at border crossings in dedicated lanes. A similar program, the Free and Secure Trade program, was being put in place to ease truck congestion at border ports of entry. Canada and the United States also launched a joint Nexus program for air travelers that included an evaluation of iris recognition biometric technology at the Ottawa and Montreal international airports. Another innovative air travel system available at some airports, called the Passenger Accelerated Service, allowed frequent travelers to insert an identity card and their hand into a scanning machine (using a hand geometry recognition system) to avoid long lines. The Patriot Act authorized setting up a computer database of "trusted travelers" allowed to use electronic identification cards to bypass regular security lines at airports.

The internationalization of border controls also involved developing more of a layered approach to cargo inspections at land, sea, and air ports of entry.[69] Not since the height of sea piracy in earlier centuries had there been such intense concern about the threat posed to cargo security by nonstate actors. Robert Bonner, the commissioner of customs and border protection, called ship containers "the potential Trojan horse of the 21st century" and declared that the sum of all fears is a "nuke-in-a-box."[70] Unlike earlier campaigns against sea piracy, however, the new policing strategy placed much greater weight on preventive measures.[71] This was best illustrated by the Container Security Initiative, launched in 2002 by the U.S. Customs Service, which created a preclearance system to facilitate the movement of cargo containers with documents submitted electronically twenty-four hours prior to arrival.[72] The initiative also deployed U.S. customs agents to work with local customs officials at foreign ports to identify and inspect high-risk cargo bound for the United States. The first phase of the initiative targeted twenty large ports in Europe and Asia and was extended in June 2003 to a number of smaller, strategically located ports. By mid-2005, thirty-seven of the world's biggest seaports had signed on to the Container Security Initiative, representing most of the cargo shipped to the United States. Ports enrolled in the program were required to set up scanning equipment to inspect the contents of cargo deemed high risk. The U.S. Department of Energy also began to put radiation detection equipment at major ports around the world. Foreign governments had strong incentives to cooperate with the inspections so that goods shipped from their ports would not face extra delays upon arrival at U.S. ports.[73]

Some of the costs of this emerging cargo screening and preclearance system were shifted to the private sector, as airlines, shipping companies, and travel agencies were essentially deputized, having to do more self-policing and electronically submit passenger and cargo manifests in advance. Carrier sanctions and denial of (or delayed) market access provided the stick, while preferential and speedier access provided the carrot to assure greater private sector cooperation and compliance. Thus, for instance, U.S. companies enrolled in the Customs-Trade Partnership Against Terrorism (requiring a background check and submission of a security profile outlining the various security measures the company was taking) could move through the fast lane. More than thirty-eight hundred companies—handling half of all goods entering the country—were signed up for the program as of September 2004. Truck drivers for companies certified by the program received a border-crossing card for expedited entry and had a transponder placed in their truck to transmit the manifest to customs agents prior to arrival at the port of entry.[74]

While border control, traditionally a unilateral activity of individual states focusing on borderline inspections, was in the process of being transformed into a more bilateral and multilateral activity requiring far more international coordination and standardization of procedures, it remained unclear how far such cooperation could go and be sustained. Pushing border controls outward would necessarily generate international resistance and friction given the added costs of new security measures and significant variation in data protection standards and sensitivity toward hosting foreign immigration and customs inspectors.[75] Koslowski has suggested that to fully develop the standards and fund the infrastructure for this type of internationalized border control system would likely require hegemonic leadership, provided either by the United States or some combination of the United States and the European Union. The rest of the world would feel intense pressure to adapt: "With increasingly globalized economies, those states that resist cooperating with the U.S. and the EU on border security may suffer significant economic costs from decreasing mobility of their nationals and exports," and countries in the developing world may end up in a position where they "will have choices forced upon them."[76]

Indeed, the United States provided much of the initiative and most of the models for the internationalization of maritime security after September 11. For example, the International Maritime Organization's International Shipping and Port Facility Security Code, adopted in 2002, substantially borrowed from and replicated the U.S. Maritime Transportation Security Act. The Code called for a uniform standard for assessing and limiting risks to ports and ships, with global compliance levels apparently reaching over 90 percent as of 2005. Similarly, the U.S. Container Security Initiative provided the initial model for the World Customs Organization's Framework of Standards to secure global trade (adopted by the WCO Council in June 2005), which U.S. officials were closely involved in formulating.[77] Peter Romaniuk has summarized the hegemonic U.S. role: "Since 9/11 US leadership in the area of maritime security—whether through international organizations, ad hoc cooperative mechanisms or the unilateral imposition of conditions on incoming ships and cargo—has lead to a 'race to the top' in regulatory standards and controls." He concluded that "US influence will ensure that this trend is maintained into the future."[78]

Another important U.S.-sponsored international maritime security campaign was the Proliferation Security Initiative (PSI), which began in May 2003 as a military and law enforcement interdiction effort on the high seas involving the search and detention of ships of "proliferation concern."[79] Justified by the administration as part of the effort to keep weapons of mass destruction out of the hands of nonstate actors, the U.S.-initiated maritime policing effort gained the support of more than sixty countries and also secured agreements with three countries where much of the world's shipping fleet is registered—Liberia, the Marshall Islands, and Panama—allowing authorities to search any suspected ship under those flags. Many governments remained wary of PSI, which often operated outside of public view,[80] charging that some of its provisions violate international maritime law.[81] U.S. officials, however, touted PSI as conforming to existing maritime norms, and the initiative gained greater international legitimacy through the UN secretary-general's endorsement and the UN Security Council's affirmation.[82]

The Return of Counterterrorism to Center Stage in European Policing

A number of European commentators have noted in recent years that counterterrorism has become an increasingly crowded policy arena claimed by a bewildering number of agencies and international forums jockeying for influence and position.[83] After September 11 and subsequent bombings in Madrid and London, terrorism made a dramatic comeback as the priority policing issue in Europe, restored to its more central status of a few decades earlier as well as a century earlier. This time, however, the policymaking playing field was much larger and more complex. As explained by Monica den Boer, the confusing hybrid policymaking process in the European Union, in which national and supranational approaches to policing coexisted, reflected both an enduring reluctance at the national level to share policing powers with EU institutions and an ambitious move to form a more federalized architecture for policing cooperation. Intergovernmental bargaining still remained the central feature of this policy field: states continued to be "the prime movers within a constellation of supranational institutions."[84]

As part of the flurry of legislative activity that emerged from the extraordinary European Council meeting of September 21, 2001, EU members agreed to tighten border controls, deepen and accelerate data sharing and mutual assistance between criminal justice systems, freeze terrorist assets and comply with UN Security Council Resolution 1373 on combating terrorism, insert antiterrorism clauses in agreements with third countries, increase cooperation with the United States and other external partners, empower Europol with a greater counterterrorism role, and form joint investigative teams to supplement the activities of Europol. They also agreed on a common definition of terrorism-related offenses and common penalties and a common EU list of terrorist organizations, and called for more communication and cooperation between intelligence and police services.[85]

A few months later, EU leaders substantially extended the EU's anti–money laundering directive (previously focused only on drug trafficking proceeds) to include terrorism and other serious crimes, and also broadened the reporting obligations to individuals beyond the banking industry. In early 2002, EU law enforcement officials outlined an accord requiring national courts to follow orders issued by other member states to freeze assets of terrorist and other criminal suspects. Later that year, EU leaders agreed to create a network of border control officials, launch joint training programs and set common equipment standards, centralize and pool funding of these new measures, and increase visa coordination (including establishing a common EU visa format with digital photographs and setting up a centralized EU visa database).[86]

As evident in these various EU initiatives, counterterrorism had important spillover effects, providing a catalyst for a much broader "Europeanisation of crime control policies."[87] Moreover, as den Boer notes, "There has been considerable spillover from counter-terrorism legislation to legislation in the immigration and asylum area. Legislation related to consular cooperation, visa policy and identity controls reveal that anti-terrorism efforts have also extended to immigration and border controls, which may be read as a consequence of the 'securitisation' of the migration discourse."[88] This very much mirrored developments on the U.S. side of the Atlantic.

Equally significant, many of the post–September 11 policy measures strengthened, sped up, and further institutionalized policing plans and activities that were already under way. Europol, for instance, had already extended its mandate to cover counterterrorism in 1999, and this was then extended further after the terrorist attacks. Prior to September 11, Europol had seven counterterrorism specialists, but by mid-October the number had grown to thirty-five.[89] September 11 also put passage of the European arrest warrant on the fast track. This novel legal tool, covering crimes punishable by three or more years of imprisonment, was viewed as a centerpiece of future criminal justice cooperation, replacing the traditional system of extradition. It was adopted after the terrorist attacks even though most of the thirty-two offenses it covered were unrelated to terrorism.[90] This turn to the principle of "mutual recognition" in criminal matters was a revolutionary development because it involved police agencies enforcing the judgments of foreign courts and may be a precursor to further initiatives in this direction.[91] At the same time, there were serious questions about the future of the European arrest warrant, as it remained unclear whether states were quite ready to cede so much sovereignty in this area.[92] One security analyst observed that the EU arrest warrant, "although proposed on the pretext of counterterrorism," seemed to be part of a broader agenda that included the expansion of "the EU's supranational legal jurisdiction."[93]

Another key example of spillover is that after the September 11 terrorist events, EU leaders were able to push ahead with plans to establish a "Eurojust" cross-border prosecution unit.[94] The idea of creating Eurojust dated back to the Tampere European Council meeting of mid-October 1999, but it was not formally agreed on by the Justice and Home Affairs Council until December 2001 (and became fully operational in early 2002).[95] The tasks of the Eurojust unit (composed of national lawyers, prosecutors, magistrates, judges, and other legal experts) included assisting investigations of cross-border crimes and enhancing coordination between judicial and legal authorities of member states. Eurojust was essentially the judicial counterpart to Europol, with a mandate covering the same range of cross-border crimes as well as additional crimes such as fraud and environmental crimes.[96] It was partly an outgrowth of the European Judicial Network, established in 1998 to create points of contact (within courts or prosecutors' offices) facilitating cross-border judicial cooperation and coordination among the fifteen member states of the European Union. Along with the European arrest warrant, the creation of Eurojust reflected the heightened importance of judicial cooperation in cross-border criminal justice matters. At the same time, the continued reluctance of member states to cede sovereignty in this area inhibited the establishment of a true European public prosecutor's office that could engage in investigations and prosecute cases in national courts. Some critics thus contended that Eurojust, as well as Europol, represented little more than "talk shops" with limited authority and funding, although proponents emphasized how new these institutions were and that "mere talk" was critical in fostering greater trust, communication, and coordination.[97] Viewing Europol and Eurojust from a longer-term perspective, Joanna Apap even suggested that they "may be an embryonic federal system for justice and law enforcement."[98]

The heightened concern over terrorism also created an opening to push for a much broader use of new surveillance technologies such as biometrics, especially in the realm of tracking the cross-border movement of people.[99] For example, Eurodac, an EU-wide electronic fingerprint system initially limited to tracking asylum seekers, was later extended to illegal immigrants. Jonathan Aus noted that "Eurodac is the first, but probably not the last application of biometric human identification technology within a supranational political entity."[100] The use of new technologies to enhance information exchange was strikingly evident in the development of the Schengen Information System II (expected to be operational by 2007). Once up and running, the new system will be able to store both digital images and biometric data and provide almost instantaneous responses to law enforcement requests for information by EU member states. The push to create this system was part of a much broader, EU-wide embrace of new information technologies for surveillance and policing after September 11, very much paralleling trends on the U.S. side of the Atlantic.[101]

As in the United States, the heightened prominence of counterterrorism in the post–September 11 era presented an enormous opportunity for EU criminal justice policy entrepreneurs to overcome resistance to a broad and ambitious agenda of deepening police cooperation and further elevate policing authority to the supranational level. This was even further accelerated in the wake of the Madrid bombings on March 11, 2004. According to Europe's leading civil rights monitoring organization, almost half of the fifty-seven proposals on the table at the EU Summit on March 25–26 in Brussels had little or no relation to combating terrorism.[102] EU leaders attempted to maintain the post–September 11 momentum through the so-called Hague Programme (adopted in November 2004 and approved in June 2005), an ambitious five-year plan with an emphasis on migration and terrorism that was a follow-up to the earlier Tampere Programme. This detailed wish list included the eventual creation of common EU visa offices, further integration of biometrics into documents, and the development of minimum standards for identification cards.[103]

Not unexpectedly, the implementation of new policing initiatives also provided a new source of cross-border friction and tension, already evident in early challenges to the implementation of the EU arrest warrant, which took effect in 2004.[104] This was part of a broader pattern in the evolution of international policing in which rising tides of cooperation opened up new frontiers for collaboration and conflict. These were the familiar growing pains of international police cooperation. What was new about the contemporary era was that the growing pains now were not just bilateral but were playing out within EU institutions and the broader context of integration and enlargement.

Among the most novel of the post–September 11 EU initiatives were proposals to "communitize" border management at the operational level. Although this faced considerable political resistance and practical obstacles, Malcolm Anderson observed that it is "firmly on the agenda and is likely to be implemented in some form."[105] The fact that this was even being contemplated reflected the remarkable maturation of EU police cooperation. A number of important initial steps were taken in this direction. In early May 2002, the European Commission produced a communication entitled "Towards Integrated Management of the External Borders of the

Member States of the EU." The core proposal includes the creation of an "external borders practitioners common unit" and the eventual creation of a European Corps of Border Guards.[106] That same month, EU countries carried out a fifteen-day trial operation in which guards from various member states took part in joint patrols in France, Italy, and Spain. At the end of the year, a ten-day joint patrol of the German-Polish border took place, involving police officers from Germany, Italy, and Greece operating together with equal public authority in checking vehicles, documents, and so on.[107] At the June 2002 European summit in Seville, Spain, European leaders laid the groundwork for a joint border police agency and EU task forces to combat smuggling.[108] As part of this plan, in early 2003 the EU launched Operation Ulysses, Europe's first collaborative maritime effort to interdict migrant smuggling vessels. The pilot project brought together patrol boats from Britain, France, Italy, Portugal, and Spain.[109]

In 2005, these efforts culminated in the establishment of a European Border Agency (EBA), headquartered in Warsaw with a staff of twenty-six (expected to grow to one hundred) and a Finnish colonel as director. Although the agency had no direct operational assignments (and thus was far from the initial proposals to create a European border guard force), its various activities—including coordinating operational cooperation among members, evaluating and approving proposals for joint operations, training and developing a core curriculum for border guards, and assisting with operational cooperation with third countries—promised to foster a much more cooperative and uniform approach to border management. In this regard, Peter Hobbing, the former head of the European Commission's Directorate General Justice and Home Affairs, has concluded:

With this wide spectrum of operations-related tasks, the Agency will doubtlessly be able to decisively contribute to the shaping of a Union model of operational cooperation. Further incentives such as financial subsidies and the offer of practical help through the EBA staff on the spot appear quite tempting and hard to resist in situations of need. One can assume that at mid-term, mutual trust between the EBA and national authorities will build up and requests for operational assistance will become more frequent. In the end, the difference between the EBA expert teams and rapid reaction forces.... may be hardly visible.[110]

Enthusiasm for joint authority over border controls was far from evenly shared, however. The EU's newest members to the east were particularly wary of the operational involvement of their western neighbors. Slovak Interior Minister Vladimir Palko denounced the "more radical ideas of pan-European border police forces," and Polish Interior Minister Ryszard Kalish stated, "Poland is opposed to the creation of a European border police force."[111] At the same time, these and other eastern EU member states called for a greater sharing of the substantial costs of policing the EU's eastern border, which countries such as Germany and France were opposed to without shared operational involvement. The sensitive issue of financial burden sharing and whether this would involve more collaborative border controls will no doubt remain a highly contentious issue, at least in the immediate term.

Thus, the post–September 11 developments in European criminal law enforcement cooperation should not be overstated or misunderstood as a harmonious process. Scratching just below the surface one could find deep contentiousness and age-old antagonisms. Particularly challenging was creating and maintaining a certain level of trust, made even more problematic as the EU enlarged in 2004 to include twenty-five member states and as the more politicized issue of counterterrorism became much more prominent.[112]

Nothing better illustrated both the importance and fragility of trust than the days following the terrorist bombings in London on July 7, 2005. In the immediate aftermath of the attacks, Scotland Yard invited law enforcement and intelligence officials from the United States and twenty-four European countries to meet to collectively help in finding the perpetrators. This impressive display of international teamwork was short-lived, however. A few days after the meeting, France's antiterrorism coordinator gave an interview in *Le Monde* in which he charged that the British had made Europe a greater target for terrorists through its support for the U.S.-led war in Iraq, and also asserted that the terrorists had used military-grade explosives (which turned out to be false). The interview and its aftermath had a poisonous effect on French-British relations, even provoking bitter speculation by the British that the French leaked false information on purpose.[113]

The Growth of Transatlantic Law Enforcement Cooperation

The European Union's law enforcement relations with the United States were also substantially deepened and transformed in the new security context. Whereas the EU's external policing relations during the previous decade focused mostly on its immediate neighbors to the east, after September 11 relations to the west were also greatly expanded. At the same time as the U.S.-led military invasion and occupation of Iraq were pushing the United States and Europe farther apart, much less noticed and appreciated was the flurry of transatlantic law enforcement initiatives that brought them closer together.[114] As Koslowski pointed out, "While the split between the U.S. and individual EU member states, such as France and Germany, over the Iraq war led some commentators to declare U.S.-European relations as being in crisis, France and Germany, among other EU member states, were busily signing agreements and exchanging information with U.S. border control authorities." Indeed, "the European Commission and the U.S. Department of Homeland Security (DHS) have been taking international cooperation into sensitive areas of state sovereignty dealing with border controls, including government surveillance, data collection and exchange that, prior to September 11, 2001, would have been unthinkable."[115] Greater law enforcement cooperation was secured not only through heavy-handed U.S. diplomatic pressure but also through a certain degree of mutual interest. The cross-border nature of al Qaeda–style terrorist networks provided the necessary transnational hook to prompt higher levels of transatlantic police cooperation than had been the case in the past. Although some major European powers, particularly France and Germany, were wary of the more unilateral and militarized U.S. approach to combating terrorism, the potential for catastrophic criminality (such as through the acquisition of a nuclear device or other weapon of mass destruction) provided a basis of mutual interest in cooperation.

Cooperation between the United States and EU members on counterterrorism issues was nothing new. For example, a series of summits initiated by the Clinton administration in the mid-1990s were attended by Germany, Italy, England, and France, leading to a number of actions such as the extradition of terrorists, the international criminalization of terrorist activities and the possession of biological weapons, and a broadening of the scope of forensic investigation related to terrorist incidents. But as Cyrille

Fijnaut noted, most of these actions were not incorporated into policy at the EU level but rather at the level of individual member states. Thus, what was distinct about the EU response to September 11 was that "for the first time, the European Union officially expressed its view as a Union on transatlantic cooperation in the fight against terrorism" and that "for the first time in its history something like a general antiterrorism policy was formulated."[116]

Washington used the September 11 and subsequent terrorist attacks elsewhere as a window of opportunity to promote a much broader and more ambitious transatlantic law enforcement agenda. The minutes of a closed-door meeting between U.S. and EU authorities were revealing: "The US delegation indicated that since the events of 11 September 2001, the whole system of visas, border controls, management of legal migration, etc. had come under close scrutiny and there was a consensus in the US on the need for an effective system across the board, not targeted specifically at terrorism, but taking the events of 11 September as the trigger for developing a new approach."[117] Thus, as one European commentator put it, "It is hard to avoid the impression that the transatlantic axis against terrorism has opened the EU-door to the USA far more widely than before." And this spilled over to other policing missions beyond counterterrorism: "Border controls, criminal justice cooperation, immigration and asylum policy have thus become elements inserted in a wider transatlantic security policy continuum."[118]

An open letter to the EU from President Bush in October 2001 outlined forty-seven separate requests for counterterrorism cooperation, and a cooperation agreement was signed in Copenhagen at the end of the following year. Washington signed a cooperation agreement with Europol in late 2001, which included providing U.S. authorities with access to its computer databases under EU guidelines. Europol and the FBI also exchanged liaison officers. September 11 provided the catalyst for the June 2003 treaty between the EU and the United States on extradition and legal assistance (the first such treaty signed by the EU with a third party), though the treaty had implications for cooperation well beyond counterterrorism. The treaty, which supplemented rather than replaced preexisting bilateral arrangements between the United States and individual EU members, provided for the creation of joint investigative teams, the utilization of video technology for taking testimony, and greater access to information on suspect bank accounts.[119] Both sides compromised on key points. The United States agreed to negotiate with the EU rather than with individual member states, and the EU agreed to U.S. demands to set up joint investigative teams and provide greater access to the financial records of suspects that had been protected by EU privacy laws.[120]

Even before September 11, the substantial transatlantic law enforcement infrastructure had included joint training through EU involvement in U.S. law enforcement academies and close collaboration in designing and pushing through various international initiatives against money laundering and computer-related crimes. But, as a former senior State Department official explained it, "The very strengths of these recent initiatives . . . —their technocratic design, their avoidance of the political, and their use to facilitate efficient sharing of information across political systems—made them politically vulnerable once they were applied to high-visibility political ends, such as fighting terrorists."[121]

The issue that provoked the most friction in transatlantic law enforcement relations in the immediate aftermath of September 11 was the heightened U.S. screening of U.S.-bound airline passengers and Washington's insistence on having access to passenger information prior to departure, which conflicted with the data protection laws of various EU member states. Eventually, the EU grudgingly relented (over the strenuous objections of privacy and civil liberties advocates), signing an agreement in May 2004 with Washington rather than risk making travel for Europeans more cumbersome and difficult. The U.S. insistence on prescreening was part of the larger effort discussed earlier to internationalize border controls and shift more gatekeeping responsibilities to the private sector (in this case, travel agencies and the airline industry). Similarly, EU member states and shippers agreed to cooperate with U.S. efforts to inspect cargo before U.S.-bound ships departed European ports. As part of the U.S. Container Security Initiative, Washington gained permission from Belgium, France, Germany, Italy, and the Netherlands to place U.S. Customs inspectors at key ports to review shipping manifests and certain U.S.-bound cargo. In late 2003, the United States and the European Union signed an agreement to create EU-wide standards for transatlantic freight.[122] U.S. officials continued to push their European counterparts for even more access to information. In May 2005, U.S. Secretary of Homeland Security Michael Chertoff announced that he would ask EU members to share more data on U.S.-bound cargo and air passengers. He said the United States wanted detailed information on passengers prior to U.S.-bound flights taking off, as well as additional details on who has access to ship containers, emphasizing that "the principal weapon we have in the war against terror is information."[123]

Beyond relying on a certain level of mutual interest, the U.S. strategy to secure greater law enforcement cooperation from European and other countries could best be described as coercive co-optation involving a mix of sticks and carrots. The stick was the threat of denial of market access and other privileges to countries and companies that failed to comply with U.S.-promoted standards and procedures, and the carrot was the offer of preferential access and other privileges to those who did comply. The United States was also able to influence the direction and priorities of EU law enforcement in more indirect and subtle ways, such as playing a lead role in setting the agenda of the G-8. The United States assumed the presidency of the group in 2004. Originally established to coordinate global economic policies, the G-8 (formerly the G-7, before Russia joined in 1997) was increasingly utilized as an effective mechanism to set common standards in international criminal law enforcement. G-8 recommendations were typically introduced at the EU-wide level through the group's EU members.[124] Critics saw this as a prime example of "policy laundering": the utilization of U.S.-dominated international forums that lacked transparency and democratic oversight as a vehicle to promote more invasive policy measures that would otherwise fail to be approved via traditional domestic political procedures.[125]

The full extent of U.S.-European counterterrorism cooperation and information sharing was difficult to assess, of course, given the highly secretive nature of this policy domain. A 2005 British press report noted that "EU governments have persistently tried to play down the extent of their cooperation with US agencies, for example between the FBI and Europol," and that leaked documents nevertheless "show that secret talks between senior American and European officials cover a wide range of sensitive issues, including extradition, the exchange of personal data, the funding of terrorist suspects, intelligence-gathering, and organized crime."[126] For example, although all references to the EU's discussions with the United States were removed from the public record of a meeting in Brussels in July 2004, the leaked document revealed that the deleted passages related to

U.S. demands for European assistance in tracking suspected terrorist funds and cooperation in "pro-active, intelligence-driven" investigations.[127]

While the United States and the European Union continued to collaborate more intensively (both publicly and privately), they also offered sharply contrasting models for the future of international criminal law enforcement cooperation. A former senior State Department official summed up these divergent paths:

> Those who believe the EU represents the future might describe the situation as follows: Driven by the need to integrate and to enlarge, the EU has created new integrated institutions capable of simultaneously serving the 25 member states of the EU and in subsidiary fashion, other invited guests, including the U.S., so long as the invited guests choose to abide by EU standards. These new institutions are developing growing capacities and over time will be the foundation of cross-border law enforcement and judicial cooperation, not only for the EU, but perhaps globally. An analysis that wishes to focus on U.S. power might see a very different universe. In this vision, the U.S., through its continuing market power in a global economy, and a global infrastructure for financial services, information systems, and transport, continues unilaterally to develop standards and approaches that may or may not fit the needs of other nations, but which are being adopted regardless, because no nation—not even a set of nations such as the 25 now within the EU—is able to disregard standards for cross-border activity set by the U.S. The EU can develop institutions as it may wish. But the U.S. itself is an institution, and where Goliath walks, others will follow.[128]

One can view these two paths as both competing and complementary. While reflecting distinct styles and approaches, both ultimately promote a further internationalization of policing. Transatlantic law enforcement relations in the coming years are thus likely to be characterized by continuing frictions amid growing cooperation. This is part of an old pattern. Whereas recent law enforcement tensions have been over data protection and privacy issues, a few decades ago the tensions were over the export of U.S. drug enforcement undercover methods to Europe, which met initial political resistance but were eventually incorporated into European policing practices.[129] Similarly, when the United States set up the Budapest-based International Law Enforcement Academy, the EU initially refused to have a relationship with it but eventually became a partner in the training programs.

Thus, although far from a harmonious process, a new type of trans-atlantic security community may be emerging early in the twenty-first century, based on more collaborative and high-tech screening and tracking of transnational flows of people, goods, money, and information. As part of this process, U.S. and European officials have been working together to develop common standards and procedures at the global level as part of the broader internationalization of crime control. (For instance, the EU and the U.S. have collaborated in establishing the International Ship and Port Facility Security Code at the International Maritime Organization and have jointly promoted initiatives in the area of container security and seals at the WCO and passenger name records and in-flight security at the International Civil Aviation Organization.) In sum, there has been growing U.S. and EU cooperation and convergence amid enduring political tension and regional variation.

CHAPTER SIX

❏ ❏ ❏

Past, Present, and Future Trajectories

While terrorists, drug traffickers, migrant smugglers, money launderers and other transnational law evaders provoke enormous attention and concern, far less noticed and even less understood is the growing global reach of law enforcers. In this book, we have examined the historical expansion and more recent dramatic acceleration and intensification of criminalization and crime control in international relations, from past campaigns against piracy and slavery to contemporary campaigns against drug trafficking and transnational terrorism. We have shown how and why states have criminalized particular cross-border activities and attempted to transcend the limitations imposed by national sovereignty on the task of deterring and apprehending transnational law evaders, seizing their assets, and confiscating contraband.

We have evaluated the rise and transformation of international crime control from three distinct angles. The first is from a global angle, focusing on the evolution and spread of prohibition norms across the world. The second is from a regional angle, focusing on Western Europe, the region of the world where cross-border law enforcement relations are the most intensive, advanced, and institutionalized. And the third is from the angle of a single country, the United States, and its emergence as a hegemonic policing power and leading global crusader against transnational crime. Taken together, these three angles account for much of what has been significant in the internationalization of crime control.

We have emphasized growing cooperation amid enduring conflict. On

the one hand, our story has been about a rising tide of international collaboration in policing transnational crime. The negotiation of bilateral and
multilateral law enforcement agreements; the creation of bilateral and multilateral law enforcement organizations, working groups, and conferences;
the inclusion of foreign police agents in training programs; the stationing
of liaison officers in foreign countries—all represent efforts to extend the
reach of law enforcement systems beyond borders, to achieve a greater
regularization of international law enforcement relations and homogenization of criminal law norms, and to minimize the frictions that result when
sovereign law enforcement systems interact. On the other hand, our story
has been about persistent international tension and conflict: the coercive
practices and contentious politics involved in defining crime and determining the procedures and tools to combat such crime.

We have stressed the dominant role of major Western powers and
Western-based transnational moral entrepreneurs in aggressively exporting
favored prohibition norms and in initiating and determining the content and
intensity of international crime control campaigns. Many of these campaigns
have been driven not just by the narrow political and economic interests
of powerful states but also by moral and emotional factors. Indeed, many
leading international crime control initiatives have not simply been about
enhancing control but about signaling moral resolve and collectively stig-
matizing particular cross-border activities. Thus, contrary to the conventional wisdom, the internationalization of crime control is far from simply
a natural, functional response to a growing global crime challenge. The
complexity and diversity of international crime control across time, place,
and issue area defy any single or simple explanation. Instead, they call for a
more analytically eclectic approach that selectively combines multiple perspectives.[1] In this concluding chapter, we bring together the central themes
in our story, assess popular arguments regarding the growing transnational
crime challenge to state power in an age of globalization, and evaluate what
past and present trajectories may tell us about the future.

The Primacy of Criminalization

The globalization of crime control, we have emphasized throughout this
book, cannot be explained entirely or even primarily in terms of the func-

tional need to respond to the globalization of crime. It is equally valid to turn this common explanation on its head. The underlying impetus of all international criminal law enforcement activities is the initial fact of criminalization by the state. New laws turn once legal cross-border activities into criminal activities, resulting in a sudden and sometimes dramatic overall increase in transnational crime. And new criminalizations often inspire and justify the creation of new international law enforcement capabilities, which in turn can invite additional laws and other initiatives. Thus, criminalization has been a powerful motor for state expansion—and based on current trends, we can expect it to be an even more important source of growth in the years ahead. The policing face of the state is becoming more and more prominently displayed, with its gaze increasingly extending beyond national borders.

As we contemplate the future of international criminal law enforcement and recollect its historical evolution, we do well to keep in mind the potential for today's laws to be repealed, for new criminal laws to emerge, and for policing priorities to shift. Although it may be easy for some to perceive the criminal law as essentially immutable, and to believe that what is regarded as criminal in one's own society has always been regarded as such both within and without, this is readily undermined by any historical or comparative examination.[2] One need only compare the "opium wars" of the mid-nineteenth century, in which the British deployed military force to maintain the legal trade in opium and reverse China's short-lived effort to criminalize it, to the "drug wars" of recent decades, in which the United States has used military force in the name of drug criminalization and even invaded Panama and arrested its leader, General Manuel Noriega, on drug trafficking charges (no doubt the most expensive drug bust in history). Thorsten Sellin long ago observed that the "crimes of yesteryear may be legal conduct today, while crimes in one contemporary state may be legal conduct in another."[3] It is important to recall, for instance, that the origins of international law enforcement in Europe were intimately connected with the efforts of European governments to surveil and apprehend military deserters, vagabonds, and political dissidents resident in other countries, and that many of the crimes for which they were sought are no longer regarded as criminal. Conversely, we do well to keep in mind that much of international criminal law enforcement in recent decades has been preoccupied with investigating and prosecuting activities that were not regarded as criminal a century ago. This is particularly true of transnational trafficking in cannabis, cocaine, heroin, and other drugs, as well as other corollary activities such as money laundering that were criminalized principally to aid drug law enforcement efforts. But it is also true of insider trading and other violations of securities and commodities laws, new sorts of tax law violations and export controls, environmental depredations, trafficking in cultural artifacts, animals, ivory, and other products of endangered species, intellectual property theft, and transnational migrations of peoples.

Homogenization and the Future of Global Prohibitions

It is difficult to understand the evolution of international law enforcement without recognizing the historical trend toward ever more homogeneous criminal law norms among countries. Criminal law norms around the world are far more similar today than they were at the beginning of the twentieth century, just as criminal law norms then were far more similar than they were at the start of the nineteenth century. But this trend toward greater homogeneity is inherently limited in global society. As long as the power to make and unmake criminal laws remains in the hands of states rather than supranational institutions, laws and their enforcement will always vary from one state to another depending on different and ever-changing moral notions and perceptions of foreign and domestic risks and threats.

The reasons for the current level of homogenization of criminal law norms across the world are many, but certainly the principal explanation is the global triumph of Western political power, with the result that Western criminal law norms have been imposed, imported, imitated, and/or adopted across much of the globe. Violent acquisitions on the high seas were redefined as acts of piracy and suppressed by the British Royal Navy and other naval forces. During the nineteenth century, Her Majesty's government focused its attentions on the global criminalization and abolition of the slave trade and the institution of slavery. During the twentieth century, the U.S. government promoted the globalization of a host of prohibitions. And during the first decade of the twenty-first century, Western powers have collaborated in internationalizing common rules and standards to more intensively police travel, cargo, and financial flows as part of a global antiterrorism campaign.

The capacity of a state to suppress transnational criminality depends greatly on the extent to which its criminal law norms conform with or vary from those of other states. The fact that one state views as legal that which another state views as criminal provides a substantial impediment to international crime control. During the mid-nineteenth century, for instance, the British government's efforts to eliminate the transatlantic slave trade were undermined by the persistent legality of slavery in Cuba, Brazil, and the United States. During the 1920s and early 1930s, U.S. efforts to curtail the illicit influx of alcoholic beverages were fatally handicapped by the fact that most foreign governments shared neither its zeal nor its taste for alcohol prohibition. The U.S.-sponsored global drug prohibition regime has long been hobbled not just by the dynamism of the illicit market and the ease of smuggling relatively compact, hardy, and profitable commodities but also by variations in local prohibition laws, enforcement capabilities, and enthusiasm for the laws themselves. In more recent years, efforts by U.S. law enforcement officials to investigate the extraterritorial dimensions of money laundering and securities law violations have been hindered by the uneven implementation of comparable criminal laws in foreign countries.

In the coming years, this pattern is likely to continue to repeat itself in other realms of international criminal law enforcement, perhaps most notably in the global policing of intellectual property theft, in which much of the developing world does not share the advanced industrialized world's enthusiasm for copyright and patent protection.[4] Securing international cooperation in this area is partly limited by charges of hypocrisy. Pat Choate points out that as a newly industrializing country in the nineteenth century, the United States engaged in the kinds of practices it is now asking developing countries to prohibit and crack down on. The U.S. Patent Act of 1793, for example, did not protect foreign inventors, meaning that an American could steal a foreign invention and legally develop it for commercial applications. Similarly, the U.S. Copyright Act of 1790 did not protect the copyright of foreign nationals. The United States was a hotbed of copyright piracy during the nineteenth century—just as China is today. Other industrializing countries, such as Germany and Japan, similarly engaged in intellectual property theft.[5] We can expect this historical pattern of theft-aided development to continue, but in a more contentious context of global efforts to criminalize violations of intellectual property rights.

As we have seen, the relatively few criminal law norms that evolve into global prohibition regimes typically have two features in common: they tend to mirror the criminal laws of countries that have dominated global society to date (i.e., European powers and the United States) and they target criminal activities that in one way or another transcend national borders. The transnational dimension of the proscribed activity provides both much of the incentive for states to devote efforts toward constructing a prohibition regime as well as the justification typically required to provoke and justify external intervention in the internal affairs of other states. Many global prohibition regimes are promoted not just by states but by transnational moral entrepreneurs who mobilize popular opinion and political support and lobby governments both within their host country and abroad.

Global prohibition regimes are more likely to involve moral and emotional considerations than are most other international regimes. Like many criminal laws, they seek not to regulate but to ban; the underlying assumption is that certain activities must be prohibited because they are evil. Transnational moral consensus regarding the evil of a particular activity is not, however, sufficient to ensure the creation of a global prohibition regime, much less its success in effectively suppressing a proscribed activity, even when it complements the political and economic interests of hegemonic and other states. If states are unable or unwilling to conform to the regime's mandate in practice and if deviant or dissident states and groups within individual states persistently refuse to conform to the regime's demands, they can significantly undermine the global prohibition regime, particularly if their capacity for involvement in the criminal activity is great. Examples include the disruptive impact of the Barbary pirates in the early decades of the nineteenth century, the U.S. and Brazilian slave markets in the middle of that century, the coca producers and cocaine refiners and exporters in South America during recent decades, and Japanese consumers of whale meat and ivory products in recent years.

The ultimate success of a global prohibition regime inevitably depends on the vulnerability of the targeted activity to enforcement efforts. Most difficult to suppress are those activities that require limited and readily available resources and no particular expertise to commit, those that are easily concealed, those that are unlikely to be reported to the authorities, and those for which consumer demand is substantial, resilient, and not readily substituted for by alternative activities or products. If the past is any guide to the future, we can expect that technological changes will continue to strongly influence the success or failure of prohibition regimes. Recall that piracy succumbed to enforcement efforts in good part because technological developments at sea strengthened the capacities of governments to project their naval forces wherever pirates sought refuge, and that recent technological developments now facilitate a limited resurgence of piracy. The regime directed at the suppression of currency counterfeiting has proven relatively successful to date because governments have managed to remain a technological step ahead of potential counterfeiters—but that, too, could change. The global drug prohibition regime will certainly undergo changes in future decades as both the technology of manufacturing synthetic psychoactive drugs and other stimuli and the technology of drug interdiction and drug testing evolve. And a new frontier of crime and crime control—cyberspace—is by its very nature defined by technological change, presenting distinct law enforcement and law evasion challenges and opportunities. The success of the antislavery regime, by contrast, was less a consequence of technological developments than of the peculiar vulnerability of slavery to changes in its legal status. As for efforts to eradicate prostitution, it is unlikely that any developments, technological or otherwise, will significantly improve the prospects of the prohibition regime directed at the suppression of what has been termed the "oldest profession."

But the failure of a global prohibition regime does not necessarily signal its future demise. Regardless of effectiveness, part of the appeal of a global prohibition regime is its symbolic allure and usefulness as a mechanism to express disapproval. Regime proponents seek not just to suppress undesirable activities but also to create and maintain moral boundaries between acceptable and unacceptable behavior in international society. This is particularly true of the global drug prohibition regime. Open defection from the regime is highly unlikely anytime soon. It would place the defecting country in the category of a pariah "narcostate," generate material repercussions in the form of sanctions and aid cutoffs, and deeply damage the country's moral standing in the international community. But moderate reforms are clearly under way, such that the 1988 antidrug convention

229

may one day be seen as the high point of criminalization in international drug control.[6] The inclusion of cannabis in the drug prohibition regime is increasingly in dispute as a growing number of countries follow in the footsteps of the Dutch by decriminalizing the plant and exploring ways to regulate its production and sale. The global ban on international commerce in coca teas, tonics, and other low-potency products of the coca plant has no basis in science or public health; Bolivia and Peru historically lacked the political will and power to challenge the United States on this point.[7] But the election in 2005 of a former head of the coca growers union, Evo Morales, as president of Bolivia has shifted the political equation. Most significant, the global AIDS pandemic is undermining U.S. efforts to enforce its zero tolerance view of global drug prohibition. Whereas until recently the United States could count on governments in Asia, Africa, and Scandinavia to bolster its claim that "harm reduction" principles and practices were inconsistent with international antidrug conventions, that is no longer the case. Latin America and much of Asia and Africa increasingly endorse the European Union's view that needle exchange and other harm reduction measures are essential to stem the spread of HIV/AIDS and that the antidrug conventions must be interpreted accordingly.[8] A new generation of transnational moral entrepreneurs has played an important role in these developments, grounding their advocacy in science, compassion, health, and human rights.[9]

Can and will a global terrorism prohibition regime emerge in years to come? This would seem particularly plausible given the high prioritization of terrorism concerns on the security agendas of the most powerful states in international society. Hijacking of airplanes already is the target of a successful global prohibition regime, and activities such as facilitating terrorist financing and providing weapons of mass destruction to groups labeled as terrorists are the targets of nascent regimes. International cooperation to secure global travel, trade, and financial channels from terrorist penetration is increasingly globalized and standardized. Yet creating and maintaining a comprehensive global prohibition regime against terrorism is an inherently elusive objective given the fundamental political differences over what constitutes terrorism. Thus, UN member states have collectively condemned terrorism in public pronouncements without actually agreeing on what exactly it is that they are condemning. The UN has traditionally shown great reluctance in prioritizing terrorism.[10] Even though this reluctance has eroded noticeably in the aftermath of September 11, the organization's embrace of counterterrorism remains ambivalent and may prove difficult to sustain.

Just as few people during the eighteenth century could have imagined the emergence of a global antislavery regime, and few in the nineteenth century could have envisioned a global ban on ivory, so, too, is it difficult to imagine any activities that are entirely legitimate today evolving into targets of global prohibitions. One worth contemplating is the international traffic in tobacco. The economic interests and cultural traditions underlying this traffic are almost as powerful as were those underlying the slave trade. Yet the consumption of tobacco is the single greatest cause of preventable deaths in dozens of countries; it is indisputably linked to the premature deaths of millions of people each year. Norms with respect to tobacco consumption, especially in public, have changed rapidly in the United States and some other countries in recent years. We can well imagine that some countries will choose to ban production and sale of tobacco and thereafter propagate their prohibitions to others, and that transnational moral entrepreneurs will proselytize and lobby for a global tobacco prohibition regime. Whether these efforts will follow in the footsteps of the stillborn alcohol prohibition regime promoted by the United States in the 1920s or be incorporated into the broader global drug prohibition regime is hard to say. Far preferable would be a global consensus in favor of regulation rather than prohibition, which is the thrust of the World Health Organization's Framework Convention on Tobacco Control.[11] Indeed, there is much to be said for the entire global drug prohibition regime evolving in the direction of the WHO's regulatory framework for tobacco.

Regularization and the Fate of International Police Cooperation

Even as the European Union, the Council of Europe, and the United States have sponsored and advocated multilateral efforts to make the criminal laws and criminal justice systems of states more alike, law enforcement officials have focused their efforts on regularizing their contacts, relationships, and exchanges across borders. In this respect at least, the proliferation of police liaisons and joint training programs in recent decades differs little from the international police efforts of their nineteenth-century forebears.

Then, as now, police have sought to cut through red tape, to avoid diplomatic imbroglios, and to obtain more and better assistance from foreign colleagues. Their cumulative progress has been substantial. No longer do police plead in vain, as they did just a few decades ago, to be allowed to communicate directly across borders instead of via foreign ministries and consulates. Transgovernmental enforcement networks are more expansive and intensive than ever before, encouraging and facilitating a thickening of cross-border policing relationships.

One significant outcome of the regularization of law enforcement relations across borders has been the emergence of an international law enforcement community, with its own distinct expertise, understandings, and subculture.[12] The common sentiment that a cop is a cop no matter whose badge is worn, and a criminal a criminal regardless of citizenship or where the crime was committed, serves as a form of transnational value system that can override both political differences and formal procedures. It provides the oil and glue of international law enforcement. This certainly helps to explain the current expansion and durability of U.S.-European law enforcement cooperation in a period otherwise defined by a highly contentious transatlantic diplomatic divide over the Bush administration's foreign policies in Iraq and elsewhere.

Transnational criminality of a political sort has provided the impetus for many of the most vigorous and unprecedented collaborations in the history of international crime control.[13] Until well into the nineteenth century, most international law enforcement initiatives focused on the surveillance and immobilization of political offenders. This preoccupation with political policing (or high policing) provided the impetus for most early extradition treaties, most transnational police interactions, and even the first multilateral efforts among governments to collaborate in the suppression of land-based crime. The desire of autocratic governments in Europe during the nineteenth century to surveil, harass, and apprehend political refugees and agitators beyond their borders inspired the first delegations of police attachés to foreign countries; anarchist assassinations of tsars, empresses, prime ministers, and presidents provided the sparks required to convene the first multilateral law enforcement conferences; and shared concern over transnational terrorism resulted in the creation of the first consultative body composed of interior ministers representing democratic states. In each case, the combination of sovereign jealousies and governmental complacence that had previously impeded effective international law enforcement efforts was overcome by fears, concerns, and outrage over politically motivated crimes. Those states most threatened were stirred to action, and those with little at stake were obliged to accommodate. This historical pattern has repeated itself most recently on an unprecedented and truly global scale in the aftermath of the terrorist attacks on September 11, 2001.

What most distinguishes the contemporary era is the relatively greater transnational nature and reach of some terrorist networks and the growing fear of catastrophic criminality involving the use of weapons of mass destruction by nonstate actors. As the technologies to create such weapons become more diffused, responsible governments have little choice but to coordinate their control and enforcement efforts ever more effectively. As with other types of transnational criminality, deviant or "outlaw states" and government agents represent a major part of the law enforcement challenge.[14]

Yet it is important to remember that the very political motivations for the crimes that so shocked states into action in past eras ultimately also imposed limits on their cooperation. Central to the success of multilateral law enforcement initiatives from the 1898 antianarchist conference to the creation of TREVI in the 1970s was the willingness of governments with quite disparate political perspectives and interests to acknowledge that certain types of violent political action could not be justified by either their motivation or their target. The same was true of the globally subscribed prohibition against piracy, the murder of diplomats, and the hijacking of airplanes. But the scope of such acknowledgment has always been limited by the persistence of differences of opinion among governments regarding the legal treatment of those individuals who engage in politically motivated violence. Even where many governments agree in principle, the strength of the consensus is often less than it appears.

We examine the past not only because it helps to explain why the present is the way it is but also because it suggests the possible way of the future. Based on past patterns, future international police cooperation will substantially depend on the degree to which law enforcement issues can be depoliticized. We do well to recall that only when governments in the twentieth century began to focus greater attention on the transnational dimensions of more "common" criminality did the possibility for more permanent and comprehensive agreements and institutions emerge.

The success and intensity of international law enforcement cooperation directed at counterfeiting, for example, can be explained not just by the powerful and mutual interests of governments, but also by the capacity of anticounterfeiting efforts to in some sense transcend politics. That same capacity also explains the unprecedented reach and intensity of international law enforcement efforts directed at illicit drug trafficking. Although the United States has provided the impetus for collaborative policing action, the criminalized activity itself is widely perceived as bereft of any legitimate political justification and offends the moral sensibilities of powerful nations. International drug enforcement efforts are thus readily perceived as transcending the parochial political interests of any one state—a perception that opens the door to relatively intensive forms of international police cooperation as well as relaxations of sovereign prerogatives that are a necessary precondition to such cooperation. The same dynamic has been evident in the case of international anti–money laundering measures, such as the evaluation mechanisms developed by the Financial Action Task Force. This initiative, although established and backed by the United States and other major powers, gained credibility "by the fact that the process was driven by neutral, technocratic analysis rather than politics, with decisions and recommended targets of sanctions taken largely by career civil service bureaucrats rather than by more politicized senior policymakers."[15]

Can counterterrorism efforts be similarly depoliticized? "While ideological sentiments on terrorism are very divided in the world of international diplomacy," Mathieu Deflem writes, "the target of terrorism at the level of police bureaucracy is defined in a language that can be shared among police institutions across the world. Indeed, indications are that police institutions have 'de-politicized' terrorism and stripped it of its (divisive) ideological justifications."[16] His perhaps overly optimistic conclusion is that "criminalization of terrorism—calling it a crime matter—enables police across the globe to rally around a common cause."[17] Malcolm Anderson, by contrast, believes that "effective and continuing cooperation in the field of counterterrorism is almost impossible to achieve because the basis of this cooperation must be agreement between governments on political rather than criminal law enforcement objectives."[18] The maturation of the international criminal law enforcement community provides support for Deflem's view, and Anderson's skepticism is well grounded in the realpolitik of power politics. We venture two predictions: that efforts to build a global counterterrorism regime will increasingly incorporate new prohibitions on specific tactics, analogous to hijacking, that even the most hostile of states agree must be deterred and delegitimized; and that political pressures to collaborate more closely on counterterrorism will provide the impetus and architecture for improved cooperation in other areas of crime control, such as curtailing cargo theft, tracking "conflict commodities," detecting suspect financial transactions, and policing the Internet. Just as the contemporary era of international crime control was powerfully shaped by U.S. insistence on international antidrug cooperation, so the emerging era of crime control will reflect the new emphasis on improving collaboration against terrorism. The result may well be far greater international police cooperation than was previously thought possible.[19]

Securitization and Desecuritization

The domains of counterterrorism, counterespionage, and other areas of international crime control (such as enforcement of export control laws) directed principally at transnational political threats to a regime's security straddle the often antagonistic worlds of criminal justice and national security. It is in this respect that the continuities between our account of contemporary international law enforcement efforts and those of the nineteenth century are most apparent. International law enforcement efforts directed at terrorism, espionage, and other security threats are most likely to involve informal unilateral and bilateral operations. Many of the normal legal constraints on police activities often do not apply; prosecutors are often kept in the dark; high-level political considerations often descend to interrupt routine cooperative relationships among law enforcement authorities or to authorize the sharing of highly sensitive intelligence; and formal multilateral relationships often prove to be less productive given the intense need for discretion and confidentiality with respect to sources and methods. Now, as in the past, terrorism is a crime in which intimate bilateral relationships between counterterrorism officials are key, and in which discreet unilateral activities, including state-sponsored assassinations and other "black bag" operations, play an important role.

The growing fusion of criminal justice and security concerns in recent decades also reflects the highly malleable nature of the concept of security.[20] A remarkably wide range of international policing issues have been securitized, desecuritized, and resecuritized over time. For instance, in the case of the United States, the contemporary securitization of many prominent criminal law enforcement issues represents a partial throwback to the early years of the nation's history, when security and law enforcement concerns overlapped at sea, where naval patrols sought to suppress piracy, and along U.S. borders until World War I, where posses, law enforcers, and military forces were often deployed. With the quieting of borders, the two sets of concerns were more or less disentangled. By World War II, the U.S. involvement in international law enforcement was far less reliant on navies and armies (not to mention posses and vigilante gangs, private police and bounty hunters) and, like that of many other countries, increasingly demilitarized and professionalized. During the decades following World War II, espionage and high-tech smuggling were virtually the only issues implicating both law enforcement and national security concerns.

But the desecuritization of U.S. law enforcement concerns was not irreversible. Changing markets and morals, and new laws and definitions of security, transformed international crime control in ways both new and familiar in the last decades of the twentieth century. During the 1980s, extraterritorial terrorism, traditionally a national security concern, was placed on the U.S. criminal law enforcement agenda by congressional statutes, and drug trafficking, traditionally a criminal justice matter, was formally elevated to the national security agenda by a national security directive. U.S. military and the intelligence agencies were directed to reorient their missions and priorities to devote greater attention to drug trafficking, money laundering, and other criminal activities. By the end of the twentieth century, this shift had progressed substantially, driven by the quest for new agendas and objectives to fill the vacuum left by the disintegration of the Soviet Union and the lifting of the Iron Curtain. The refusion of criminal justice and national security concerns in the post–cold war era was especially visible along the U.S.-Mexico border, where substantial efforts were under way to enhance the presence of federal law enforcement and even the military. The integration of security and border policing concerns was further accelerated and institutionalized through the creation of the Department of Homeland Security in the aftermath of the terrorist incidents on September 11, 2001. More broadly, security and law enforcement institutions are increasingly intertwined in the global counterterrorism campaign. As Peter Raven-Hansen has suggested, "Although federal antiterrorist law enforcement's self-transformation is well-advanced, the fusion of intelligence and military operations into law enforcement has barely begun. We are observing the early stages of a possible trend, not the end-points."[21]

These securitization trends have been equally evident in Western Europe, though in a less militarized and more multilateralized and institutionalized fashion. Old distinctions between high and low policing have become less and less meaningful. As one team of European police researchers has described it, at the EU level there has been a post–cold war ideological merging (with crime problems increasingly relabeled as security problems), an instrumental merging (as police agencies increasingly borrow instruments and tactics from the security and intelligence apparatus), and an institutional merging (with law enforcement and security institutions having increasingly overlapping missions).[22] These shifts began well before September 11, 2001, but have accelerated sharply. As articulated in the European Security Strategy (adopted in Brussels in December 2003), the cross-border dimensions of organized crime are now considered to be a leading security threat that can be tied to terrorism.[23]

Given the historical malleability of the concept of security, the day may come when international crimes such as those against the environment[24] are officially redefined as security issues while some other international crimes, such as drug trafficking, are desecuritized and redefined as public health rather than criminal justice concerns. It is also possible that the threat of global pandemics will lead to public health issues being redefined as priority security concerns.[25] The result may well be a new and uneasy integration of public health, security, and law enforcement missions and institutions.

The Europeanization of International Crime Control

It is in Europe where we have seen bilateral and multilateral dimensions of international policing and other aspects of international law enforcement proceed the furthest. The degree of convergence in crime control policies[26] and intensity of cross-border collaboration among criminal justice systems in Europe today would appear remarkable to all but the most optimistic of officials just a few decades ago. The reasons are multifold: nowhere else is such a large number of states grouped together in a territory so small; no-where else is the process of crossing national borders so unencumbered by either geographic or political impediments; nowhere else is the frequency and intensity of transnational interactions so great, or the interdependence of societies, economies, and states so complex and multidimensional; and nowhere else has the shared consciousness of belonging to a partly suprana-tional political community developed to such a high level. Police relations in Scandinavia and the Benelux countries increasingly resemble the quality of interstate police relations within the United States; those within an en-larging "Schengenland" are following suit. As Western Europe's neighbors have discovered, the politics of integration are intimately linked to the politics of embracing EU-wide policing standards.

To be sure, Europol cannot yet compare to the federal police agencies and multiagency strike forces that have proliferated in the United States, and the prospect of supranational police agencies with international ar-rest powers still seems chimerical. But the maturation of police relations in the European Union has certainly loosened the constraints of national sovereignty to a degree never before achieved and until recent decades un-imaginable. The result is that even as the police agencies of EU members have followed the hegemonic lead of the United States in certain areas, they have very much been at the forefront of cross-border efforts to reduce the frictions that impede international cooperation in criminal justice mat-ters.[27] The internationalization of policing by European states is far more intensive, even if not nearly as globally expansive, as U.S.-led international law enforcement efforts. Its development and influence today are felt much more at the regional than the global level, as evident in the EU's aggressive efforts to export "European standards" to the Balkans and elsewhere in its immediate periphery.

EU members recognize that their own claims to internal sovereignty depend increasingly on their capacity to control transnational interac-tions, and that this capacity in turn depends on the ability and willing-ness of other states to collaborate in control efforts. Conceding a right to hot pursuit to foreign police agents, revising municipal criminal laws and procedures to better accommodate foreign criminal justice systems, even acknowledging the legitimacy of supranational regulatory criminal jus-tice agencies—all represent concessions of the traditional prerogatives of "external" sovereignty vis-à-vis other states in return for greater gains in preserving "internal" sovereignty over one's territory in an interdependent world. Though still feeling much discomfort, EU members have accepted this sovereignty trade-off to an unprecedented and globally unrivaled degree. This has involved a partial "unbundling of territoriality," but it has been carried out in the name of the traditional objective of enhancing the policing of territorial access.[28]

Can this remarkable development not only be sustained but deepen and expand in the coming years and decades? These questions are part of a much larger ongoing debate regarding the future of the European integration project, with Euro-optimists pointing to the remarkable progress that has been made in a relatively short period of time and Euro-skeptics emphasizing the limits of greater integration, the enduring primacy of intergovernmental relations, and the perils of continued expansion (including a potential political backlash and even rollback of the integration process). Signs of fatigue include the French and Dutch rejections of the proposed EU Constitution in 2005 and a slowdown in the process of EU enlargement. It remains unclear whether this is merely a bump in the road or a major turning point.

Although obviously difficult to predict, it is not unimaginable that in a decade or two the EU will have some kind of common external border guard force, Europol will more closely resemble a European FBI, most EU member states will require their citizens to carry a uniform EU identity card with biometric identifiers, and the European arrest warrant will have survived its difficult birth and become an integral and even taken-for-granted part of European criminal justice cooperation. In this regard, the EU may behave more and more like a federalized territorial state, with many international crime control practices, in turn, treated as de facto domestic crime control matters. Although the European Union has been described as both "neo-Medieval" and a "post-Westphalian polity," in some policing realms such as border control it may in fact behave more and more like a traditional state, perhaps even coming to resemble interstate cooperation in criminal justice matters within the United States. This would, in effect, represent a quasi-federalization of international criminal law enforcement at the regional level.

The other big question, of course, is whether Europe's highly institutionalized and multilateralized level of cross-border police cooperation and homogenization of criminal justice systems can be exported and adopted elsewhere. In writing about the transformation of border controls in Europe, Malcolm Anderson cautions that although ideas of state sovereignty and territoriality have in the past been diffused from Europe to the rest of the globe, "it is far from inevitable that European precedents will have the same trajectory in the future."[29] Asia seems unlikely to follow Europe's lead. As Peter Katzenstein points out, "All governments perceive terrorism, illegal immigration, the smuggling of drugs and narcotics, and armed insurrection as increasingly important security threats. In sharp contrast to Europe, however, Asian governments remain largely uninterested in political solutions at the regional level."[30] Prospects are somewhat better in North America. The heated policy debates following the September 11 terrorist attacks included discussions of creating a "security perimeter" around the NAFTA partners, which would represent a substantial deepening—and indeed a "Europeanization"—of the North American integration project. But to truly "Schengenize" North American borders would require a level of formal institutionalization, multilateralism, and policy convergence that is difficult to imagine in the present political context. Based on current trends, the most likely scenario is not a full-scale "fortress North America" mirroring "fortress Europe," but a series of incremental, piecemeal initiatives, involving a mixture of enhanced cross-border police coordination and collaboration, partial and uneven policy convergence, and innovative new inspection methods and technologies. This may eventually develop into a less formal, less bureaucratized, quasi-continental security perimeter that selectively borrows from the European model.[31]

Thus, although it may be tempting to look at the direction of international law enforcement developments in Europe and assume that there, in time, will go the rest of the globe, the more modest conclusion that can and should be drawn is that the future of international law enforcement outside of Europe will consist of a wide variety of outcomes, almost all of which have already occurred within Europe. The impoverished regions of the world remain substantially underdeveloped in international law enforcement. This reflects the uneven state of law enforcement, particularly criminal investigation, in nations where military and paramilitary forces have played a more prominent role in police matters (often preoccupied with securing the state from internal threats and subversion). Perhaps most important, most states with relatively limited financial resources are prone to view much of international law enforcement as a luxury. Like the major

European states of earlier centuries, many poor countries are likely to react with relief to the flight of fugitives abroad; the expense of extradition, and of sending police agents abroad to conduct extraterritorial investigations, figure in their calculations in a way that they do not for more affluent states. At the same time, less developed countries are under increasing pressure to embrace the international law enforcement priorities and join the international policing campaigns of wealthier states. In this regard, EU relations with many of its eastern and southern neighbors share some of the characteristics of U.S. relations with many of its neighbors in the Americas. Policing matters promise to be an increasingly pivotal dimension of rich-poor relations in coming years.

The Americanization of International Crime Control

Among the features that differentiate U.S. international policing actions from those of European powers and most other states are the relatively higher number of endeavors in which U.S. officials act unilaterally and coercively. No other government behaves so aggressively in obtaining evidence from foreign jurisdictions, apprehending fugitives from abroad, indicting foreign officials in its own courts, and compelling foreign governments to change their criminal justice norms to conform to its own. Nor does any other government allocate comparable diplomatic energy and resources to carrying out its international criminal law enforcement priorities. The U.S. government is more willing than any other to intrude on the prerogatives of foreign sovereigns, to confront foreign political sensibilities, and to override foreign legal norms.

These aggressive activities have helped to convince foreign governments to modify their laws, set up law enforcement working groups and other cooperative arrangements with U.S. law enforcement officials, enter into extradition and mutual legal assistance treaty negotiations prompted by U.S. officials, and generally play a more active role in vicariously representing U.S. criminal justice interests. U.S. law enforcement agencies play an especially pivotal role in shaping a transnational police community and thickening intergovernmental law enforcement networks,[32] providing technical assistance and training for many foreign police officers, advocating for more intensive and systematic bilateral and multilateral cooperation, and prompting new initiatives in both criminal procedures and criminal legislation.

There are a number of reasons for the relative U.S. success in extending its law enforcement reach and priorities abroad. First, and most obvious, is U.S. hegemonic power. Foreign governments recognize that the cost of defying the United States may be substantial, especially if they represent relatively vulnerable and less developed countries. Foreign banks and corporations know that ignoring U.S. court orders for documents can lead to their exclusion from U.S. territory and markets. The second factor is the rapid rise of criminal justice officials, objectives, and concerns to the upper tier of U.S. foreign policy formulation and implementation, a phenomenon that can be substantially explained by the prominence of "law and order" issues in U.S. national politics since the late 1960s and the securitization of these issues in more recent years. The third factor is the ever present and seemingly ever more strident and pervasive sense of moralism associated with criminal justice efforts both domestically and internationally.[33]

Foreign governments have reacted to U.S. pressures, inducements, and examples in recent decades by creating new criminal laws targeting drug trafficking, money laundering and terrorist financing, insider trading, and organized crime and by reforming financial secrecy laws as well as their codes of criminal procedure to better conform to U.S. legal needs. Some foreign initiatives, moreover, are motivated by other governments' wishes to preempt U.S. criticism and unilateral action or win diplomatic favor from Washington. Foreign police have incorporated U.S. investigative techniques, and foreign courts and legislatures have followed up with the requisite legal authorizations. The internationalization of law enforcement is thus far from equal or reciprocal. For the most part, the United States provides the models and sets the priorities, and other governments do the accommodating. International agreements often require the adoption of new laws in foreign countries that reflect legislation already in place in the United States—evident, for instance, in the 1988 Vienna antidrug convention and the 2000 Palermo Convention on Transnational Organized Crime. At the same time, the U.S. government sometimes pushes other governments to adopt measures that it itself is unwilling to adopt, including providing aid and training to foreign militaries to direct and carry out frontline policing tasks that the U.S. military is prohibited from engaging in at home.

Thus, although the European Union plays an activist role in creating regional and international law enforcement institutions, it would not be too much of an exaggeration to say that much of the internationalization of crime control has in practice meant Americanization. The global reach of U.S. criminal law enforcement is likely to extend further in the immediate years ahead. Other countries' law enforcement systems may therefore increasingly reflect U.S. examples and norms, thereby enhancing the vicarious enforcement of U.S. laws, representing, in essence, a continued outsourcing of crime control. Although far more often overlooked than U.S. military power, in the realm of policing power the United States very much retains the title of global hegemon.

The exercise of U.S. hegemonic policing power can often be subtle, such as playing the lead role in setting the policing priorities of international institutions and providing much of the legal and technical expertise necessary to hammer out and implement bilateral and multilateral agreements. The charge that the United States has neglected and even subverted international institutions in favor of unilateralism in recent years has only limited validity in the realm of international law enforcement. When one digs beneath the surface of UN and many other multilateral crime control initiatives, one inevitably finds U.S. funds, personnel, model legislation, and diplomatic endeavors. Thus, far from taming and constraining U.S. power, in this policy realm international institutions extend, obscure, and legitimate it.

Both the United States and the weaker countries that it pressures on law enforcement issues have incentives to understate the power imbalance and coercive aspects of the relationship by framing the issue as conforming to international standards and obligations. For many states, it is politically more palatable to portray their behavior as meeting their international commitments rather than as caving in to U.S. demands. The appearance of consensus not only saves face for weaker states, but has the added advantage of projecting an image of being a good citizen in the international community, giving new meaning to the term "community policing." For the United States, exercising policing hegemony through international institutions enhances legitimacy, is easier and less costly than the raw exercise of power, and reduces reliance on brute force. This is a striking illustration of what Andrew Hurrell calls "coercive socialization."[34] It reaches its most institutionalized form in U.S.-sponsored global prohibition regimes, which, as Richard Friman argues, provide a mechanism for the United States to externalize many of the costs of law enforcement. He notes that even as U.S. influence over trade and monetary relations may be in decline, "the United States continues to dominate the structure and normative content of global prohibition regimes. To date, there is little indication that the United States is likely to reverse criminalization within existing national or global prohibition regimes or halt the proliferation of new prohibition regimes."[35]

The question is how long U.S. policing hegemony will last and who will emerge as the most likely challengers. In other words, at what point will we no longer be able to characterize the internationalization of crime control as Americanization? When will the fingerprints of U.S. negotiators fade in the creation of international agreements, and the footprints of U.S. law enforcement officials overseas become less pronounced? Will there be a counterprocess of de-Americanization? The EU may be a viable challenger in some international law enforcement arenas, especially if member states can strategically behave as a collective bloc. But for the most part, EU efforts are likely to complement more than challenge U.S. policing hegemony. At least in the short term, we can expect that the U.S.-European law enforcement relationship will continue to be based on a mixture of competition and collusion, reflecting an uneasy combination of political tension and regional divergence amid broader policy convergence and cooperation at the global level in policing transnational flows of people, goods, and money. As we have suggested, a new kind of transatlantic security community is arguably emerging through the expansion and institutionalization of these policing arrangements.[36]

Based on past historical patterns and trajectories, we can expect that as power centers shift, so too will international crime control priorities and practices. The diffusion of power away from the United States is likely to have important consequences for international crime control as policing preferences become more varied, priorities change, and coordination becomes more cumbersome. In this regard, the rise of China and other potential regional challengers in coming decades may erode the hegemony of U.S.-sponsored international crime control initiatives and approaches. For instance, China is likely to continue to place far greater emphasis on policing the Internet to enforce its strict censorship laws (aided by security tools, firewalls, and information provided by U.S. companies)[37] rather than enforcing intellectual property rights laws.[38] This, in turn, may become a growing source of international friction as China flexes its policing muscle and uses market access as a powerful leverage to pressure foreign governments and companies to cooperate in carrying out its own law enforcement agenda.

At the same time, U.S. influence may outlast its waning power in coming decades.[39] Some U.S.-backed international initiatives, such as the anti–money laundering monitoring efforts of the Financial Action Task Force, have generated their own momentum. Major international agreements that the United States played an instrumental role in creating have built on and reinforced each other and provided models for future agreements. For example, the Palermo Convention Against Transnational Organized Crime very much built on the Vienna Convention Against Illicit Traffic in Narcotic and Psychotropic Substances, and the more recent UN Convention Against Corruption, in turn, has built on the Palermo Convention (and is being ratified at a speed surpassing all others). If this pattern continues, we can expect future multilateral crime control agreements to at least partly borrow from these earlier models regardless of the level of U.S. sponsorship and influence.

State Power, Globalization, and Transnational Crime

Our examination of the historical and contemporary internationalization of crime control provides a corrective to the common perception—reinforced and perpetuated in media reports and policy debates—that states are somehow "losing control" in the face of ever growing transnational crime challenges in an era of globalization. There is certainly an enormous gap between stated policing goals and actual outcomes. More law enforcement can also simply prompt more sophisticated and geographically dispersed law evasion techniques; this, in turn, can make law enforcement more difficult and complicated, providing a rationale to further empower, fund, and expand the international reach of crime control efforts. Law enforcement pressure can perversely turn disorganized crime into more organized crime, as evident in the transformation of professional migrant smuggling in recent years. It can also exacerbate problems of corruption by creating incentives for criminals to spend more on bribes and payoffs. There are certainly built-in limits to how much states can deter certain criminalized transnational activities, especially if they wish to maintain open societies and keep their borders open to high volumes of legitimate cross-border exchange.[40]

But to then jump to the conclusion that states are losing control is highly misleading because it falsely implies that states were "in control" in the past. As we have seen, the limits of state controls and the challenges posed by transnational criminal activity are nothing new. Contrary to popular mythology about crime and globalization, there never was a golden age of state control.[41] Cross-border crime is as old as the creation of national borders and the imposition of state controls. Arguments that imply otherwise suffer from historical amnesia. Borders have always been far more permeable than the Westphalian ideal of the sovereign state would indicate.

Viewed from a broad historical perspective, state capacities to detect, deter, and detain transnational law evaders have, if anything, grown substantially. The number of safe havens for criminals across the globe has dramatically shrunk over time as the law enforcement reach of the state has expanded (consider, for example, the proliferation of extradition and mutual legal assistance treaties in recent decades). And it should be remembered that some key control tools, such as the universal adoption of the passport, arrived relatively late in the development of the modern state.[42] Moreover, one should not lose sight of the fact that it is the very existence of state controls that makes it necessary for smugglers and other criminalized transnational actors to try to devise such creative and elaborate means to evade and circumvent them. Transnational crimes such as drug trafficking and migrant smuggling are so enormously profitable precisely because states impose and enforce prohibitions. Transnational criminal organizations attempt to bully and buy off state officials, but in most cases this is primarily because they lack the capacity to bypass them. Corruption reflects state weakness, but also state power: most transnational criminals, after all, would prefer to evade state controls entirely rather than have to pay for state protection and nonenforcement of the law. Some governments "profit" from crime by informally taxing criminal earnings.[43] Some even offer "protection" to criminals, not only from agents of foreign governments but also, in the true style of mafiosi, from their own agents. This practice was as true of governments' treatment of pirates in the eighteenth century and slave traders in the nineteenth as it is true of drug smugglers and embargo busters today.

Regardless of effectiveness in combating transnational crime, it should also be emphasized that many international policing efforts and prohibition regimes have politically useful perceptual effects and symbolic uses that are too often taken for granted or overlooked. As one criminologist has put it in the case of drug control, "Drug police, like priests, are more important for what they symbolize and stand for than for what they do."[44] Thus, to judge the expansion of international prohibition regimes and policing practices strictly in terms of whether or not their stated instrumental goals are attained partly misses the point. Criminalizing and policing undesirable transnational activities is not only about apprehension and deterrence but also about employing the powers of the state to express moral resolve. This can have substantial payoffs for both political leaders and law enforcement practitioners by impressing and appeasing various domestic and international audiences.

It is commonly asserted that the forces of globalization are empowering nonstate transnational actors (both licit and illicit) and making borders and state controls increasingly antiquated, with the rapid spread of transnational criminal organizations viewed as a particularly extreme challenge to the state. For example, in the 1990s, Susan Strange boldly proclaimed transnational organized crime to be "perhaps *the* major threat to the world system,"[45] and more recently, Moises Naim has provocatively characterized the conflict between states and transnational crime as "the new wars of globalization," with states increasingly on the losing side.[46] There are elements of truth in these often sweeping claims. After all, illicit cross-border flows take advantage of the same transformations in global communication and transportation that facilitate licit flows. And some economic policies designed to encourage and facilitate the globalization of licit flows can unintentionally aid illicit flows.[47] The stakes are also certainly higher today given the potential for violent nonstate actors to gain access to nuclear material and other weapons of mass destruction through transnational smuggling channels. More generally, it is reasonable to conclude that transnational crime has grown as the amount of transnational activity in general has grown. But as an overall percentage of cross-border activity, it is probably no more (and possibly much less) today than in past eras. The dramatic liberalization of trade in recent decades has certainly reduced the incentives to engage in smuggling practices based on evading tariffs and export/import duties, which historically has been the basis of a significant proportion of global smuggling.

Moreover, many of the same transformations that facilitate the globalization of crime, including revolutions in transportation and communication, also greatly facilitate the globalization of crime control. Globalization therefore both challenges and empowers the state. For instance, even as new information technologies enable transnational criminal activities (and indeed create new categories of crimes such as cybersmuggling and cyberpiracy), these technological advances also greatly increase tracking and surveillance capacities and even create new forms of policing (such as cyberpolicing). Technology has dramatically lowered the costs and increased the intensity and frequency of transgovernmental law enforcement networks, allowing state actors to interact with their foreign counterparts more rapidly and frequently.[48]

New technologies will continue to enhance the ability of states to collaboratively police the cross-border movement of cargo, information, money, and people. In this regard, the emerging "virtual borders" touted by U.S. law enforcement strategists are essentially electronic borders.[49] As we have seen, the digitization of border enforcement has ranged from the use of more expansive and sophisticated databases for data mining and computer tracking systems to the development of more tamper-resistant travel documents and "smart" IDs with biometric identifiers (such as digital fingerprints and facial and retinal scans). Border controls are thus being reconfigured, redefined, and deterritorialized, even as the traditional objectives of apprehension, territorial exclusion, and control of the domestic realm endure. This is an old story, as technological innovations have long played a key role in the development of travel documents[50] and in enabling cross-border police investigations (such as the invention of photography and fingerprint systems).[51] At the same time, police agencies have long pointed to the crime-facilitating role of new technological developments as a rationale to further internationalize their policing efforts, and we can expect this to not only continue but to intensify in the future.[52] Cutting-edge technologies enabling future crimes such as DNA theft and illicit cloning may have equally significant policing applications, such as new types of DNA mapping and testing and other forms of identification (with profound implications for privacy protection).

Furthermore, leading private sector agents of globalization that are typically viewed (by both critics and proponents) as challenging and even circumventing the state, such as major financial institutions and multinational corporations, are being creatively enlisted and deputized by governments to help police transnational crime. Shipping companies and airlines are increasingly being compelled through both negative and positive inducements to more carefully track and screen cargo and passengers. The same is true for banks and other financial institutions in the monitoring and reporting of suspicious monetary transactions. And some communications companies have facilitated efforts by intelligence agencies (most notably the U.S. National Security Agency) to eavesdrop on and "data mine" international phone calls. These and other mechanisms make it possible to "monitor, surveil, or analyze data and behaviors beyond the reach or capacity of traditional state surveillance or monitoring power."[53] Although still very much in its infancy, one can see the makings of a global surveillance and monitoring system that increasingly relies on the private sector for tracking, documenting, reporting, and analyzing cross-border flows. This is not to deny the substantial limitations and shortcomings,[54] or that the privatization trend can be a double-edged sword that both subverts and bolsters state power.[55] Some aspects of privatization also raise serious concerns about transparency and accountability, concerns that some governments view as advantages and that indeed are part of the political motivation for subcontracting.[56]

In a few countries, most notably the United States, the multinational corporation even provides a vicarious means of extending the state's sovereign powers extraterritorially. Not just U.S. multinationals but foreign ones as well find that their affiliates and other contacts within the United States render all their operations outside the United States susceptible to court orders and sanctions imposed by U.S. courts as well as other requirements of U.S. laws. Foreign companies find themselves subject to U.S. antitrust laws and export control laws, and foreign banks can be ordered to hand over to U.S. criminal justice authorities financial documents stored in branches outside the United States, often in the face of financial secrecy laws and blocking statutes to the contrary. The capacity of the U.S. government to make the most of these options reflects not just the fact that almost all major multinational firms maintain affiliates and other contacts on U.S. soil but also the fact that those contacts are sufficiently important that these firms are willing to tolerate and accommodate U.S. extraterritorial assertions as a necessary cost of doing business.[57] The broader point, however, is that even as the proliferation of transnational interactions challenges the state's control of its territory, the same process also provides a rationale and opportunity for expanding its jurisdictional reach.

Our account of the internationalization of crime control thus suggests that the state is not, as some have alarmingly claimed, simply retreating and decaying in the face of ever more intensive transnational interactions. Quite the contrary, as Wolfram Hanrieder argued decades ago: "It is precisely the domestication of international politics which sustains (and demonstrates) the vitality of the nation-state. By extending domestic political processes and their corresponding attitudes into the international environment, the nation-state has eroded traditional aspects of international politics."[58] This domestication process is readily evident in the realm of international criminal law enforcement.

Lessons and Implications

The international orientation of policing priorities and international extension of policing practices have reached unprecedented levels. Though still far from forming a globetrotting international police force with sovereign authority, states now agree and collaborate on more cross-border policing matters than ever before. Substantially driven by the interests and moralizing impulses of major Western powers, a loosely institutionalized and coordinated international crime control system based on the homogenization of criminal law norms and regularization of law enforcement relations is emerging and promises to be an increasingly prominent dimension of global governance in the twenty-first century.

States have developed a broad range of collaborative tools to manage the challenges posed by transnational crime, but along with the advantages of international crime control we should recognize and confront the substantial downside. This includes growing problems of accountability and transparency (a widening "democratic deficit" as police functions become more internationalized and privatized), troubling civil liberties and human rights implications of the securitization of policing and the spread of more invasive laws and surveillance technologies in the wake of September

11,[59] the emergence of an international crime control industrial complex, and the rising costs for developing countries of complying with ever more stringent law enforcement expectations and demands of wealthy states. Many governments have also latched on to high-profile global policing campaigns not only to impress and appease various audiences but also to further other political agendas, including providing a thinly disguised cover and legitimizing instrument to suppress domestic dissent and tighten their grip on power.

Some leading international law enforcement efforts have generated enormous collateral damage. Take, for instance, the efforts to curb the smuggling of people and drugs. The tightening of U.S. and European immigration controls has prompted migrant smugglers to turn to more daring and dangerous border-crossing strategies, leading to hundreds of migrant deaths per year. The global antidrug campaign has been a driving force in forging cooperative links among criminal justice systems, but has also generated extraordinary levels of crime, violence, corruption, disease, and other ills. The U.S. approach to suppressing the trafficking of women and children has been far more focused on criminalizing the traffic than helping to protect the human rights of those being trafficked. Supply-side law enforcement initiatives abroad often endlessly chase the international symptoms rather than the source of the problem at home. Blaming and targeting international drug traffickers and migrant smugglers is politically easier than dealing honestly with the enormous consumer demand for psychoactive substances and cheap migrant labor. Criminalizing and targeting the supply side of these problems masks the fact that they are first and foremost public health and labor market regulation issues.[60]

More generally, criminalization and international crime control have too often substituted and distracted attention away from the need for more fundamental political, social, and economic reforms. Across much of the world, a punitive policing state increasingly overshadows and substitutes for a retreating welfare state, even as the social dislocations that result fuel further calls for more policing. It is perhaps no coincidence that the United States, the most enthusiastic promoter of criminalization at the global level, is also the world's leading incarcerator. With roughly 5 percent of the world's population, the United States claims roughly 25 percent of the world's incarcerated population.[61] Indeed, it incarcerates more people for drug law violations than Western Europe incarcerates for all offenses combined.[62] Unlike Great Britain's nineteenth-century campaign to prohibit slavery worldwide, which sought essentially to extend freedom by abolishing the legal institutions that permitted slavery, the U.S. antidrug campaign has resulted in millions of people being deprived of their freedom. There is surely something perverse about international crime control policy being so powerfully shaped by a nation that applies criminal sanctions to diverse activities with such striking alacrity. Most governments that look to the United States for leadership in international crime control matters would do well to examine the broader costs and consequences of U.S. criminal justice policies both within its borders and beyond.

We should also take care not to overstate the internationalization of crime control. The vast majority of policing remains largely insulated from foreign affairs. Attempts to further internationalize policing face considerable political resistance, provoke familiar turf battles and age-old concerns about infringements on national sovereignty, and are limited by enduring problems of mistrust. Moreover, cross-border law enforcement cooperation is too often treated as the end point rather than a means to an end.[63] Measuring the effectiveness of internationalization is frustratingly elusive, with the favored indicators easy to manipulate and often having more of a perceptual effect than substantive meaning. Conformity with international criminal law enforcement standards, ranging from the protection of endangered species to curbing money laundering and the trafficking of persons, often represents little more than "paper compliance," especially in less developed countries with anemic enforcement capacity. Major powers collaborate in devising and promoting standardized international rules and regulations to more carefully police cargo, travel, and financial flows, but actual implementation and capacity building remain at a relatively early stage of development.

We should be similarly wary of overstating how new and different the contemporary era is from past historical experience. Bold pronouncements regarding the emergence of a "postmodern state" and the "erosion and diminution of the state system" in the realm of cross-border policing seem exaggerated and premature.[64] Such proclamations of fundamental change may be intellectually fashionable, but we should recognize that there is a strong element of "back to the future" in current policing trends. Much of today's preoccupation with counterterrorism is in some respects a modern variant of what political policing meant in continental Europe more than a century ago. The growing privatization of policing can similarly be viewed as a modern-day variant on the reliance on posses, privateers, and private detective agencies such as the Pinkertons in earlier eras. And the contemporary process of securitization, in which military and intelligence agencies are increasingly utilized to confront acts defined as criminal (i.e., terrorism, drug trafficking, migrant smuggling), is in some ways a throwback to earlier centuries, when navies were deployed to eradicate piracy and the slave trade and troops were sent to crack down on border bandits and other transnational law evaders. In short, the contemporary period provokes a certain sense of déjà vu. The past may be prelude more than is typically recognized.

Finally, we should stress that, amid ever growing levels of global cooperation, international crime control will remain defined by persistent conflict and turbulent change. Continued heterogeneity is inevitable. No global sovereign claims universal policing authority. Criminal laws, procedures, and norms are constantly changing, at different rates, within different states, as a consequence of political, cultural, and technological transformations. Conflict is inevitable so as long as transnational moral entrepreneurs and the most powerful states seek to promote and impose their criminal norms on others. Just when it appears that a new level of common understanding and cooperation is reached and an unprecedented diminishing of frictions is achieved in international crime control, new criminalizations and criminal law enforcement initiatives emerge to generate new conflicts and tensions. Such is the dialectic of criminalization and crime control in international relations.

NOTES

□ □ □

Introduction

1. In congressional testimony, the international criminal law specialist Jack A. Blum pointed to this *Bonnie and Clyde* scene to describe the obstacles to policing cross-border crime. Cited in John Kerry, *The New War: The Web of Crime That Threatens America* (New York: Simon and Schuster, 1997), 172.

2. The institutions and processes of international crime control are typically extensions of those involved in domestic crime control, that is, police, prosecutors, and courts, and the rules that govern their action, combined with mechanisms designed to accommodate particular needs of international law enforcement. These include extradition and other bilateral and multilateral law enforcement treaties, international conventions, the criminal justice agencies of international organizations such as the United Nations, the international police organization known as Interpol, and a range of other collaborative law enforcement undertakings among those bound by regional and political links.

3. We define transnational crime as those activities involving the crossing of national borders and violation of at least one country's criminal laws. Most transnational crime is economically motivated and involves some form of smuggling. The most prominent exception, transnational terrorism, differs from other criminal activities in that it is politically motivated. We restrict our discussion to the policing of transnational crime and therefore do not include other domains of international policing such as the deployment of international peacekeepers.

4. Extraterritorial jurisdiction derives from the notion of personal law, which presupposes that individuals carry with them the laws of the place from which they came and should thus be tried by those laws rather than the laws of whatever land they may enter. The concept developed in Europe during the Middle Ages as a legal principle intended to assure the security of resident ambassadors and traders from abroad. See E. R. Adair, *The Extraterritoriality of Ambassadors in the Sixteenth and Seventeenth Centuries* (London: Longman, Green, 1929), 1–14. Virtually all

states assert some right to legislate, adjudicate, and enforce laws involving acts, actors, and things beyond their borders. Among the first, and clearest, articulations of the different bases of extraterritorial jurisdiction is the seminal *Harvard Research in International Law* draft published in 1935. See Research in International Law (Under the Auspices of the Faculty of Harvard Law School), "Part II, Jurisdiction with Respect to Crime," *American Journal of International Law*, Supp., 29 (1935): 439–651.

5. The historical trend reveals a sharp decline in interstate warfare, and most of the armed conflicts that remain take place within rather than between states. See John Mueller, *The Remnants of War* (Ithaca, NY: Cornell University Press, 2004).

6. The peace treaty between Ramses II of Egypt and the Hittite prince Hattusili (ca. 1280 B.C.), reportedly the oldest document in diplomatic history, included a provision authorizing the return of criminals who had fled to the other regime's territory. I. A. Shearer, *Extradition in International Law* (Dobbs Ferry, NY: Oceana Publications, 1971), 5, citing S. Langdon and A. H. Gardner, *Journal of Egyptian Archeology* 6 (1920): 179.

7. See the pioneering work of David H. Bayley, particularly *Patterns of Policing: An International Comparative Perspective* (New Brunswick, NJ: Rutgers University Press, 1985). Also see R. I. Mawby, ed., *Policing across the World: Issues for the Twenty-first Century* (London: UCL Press, 1999).

8. The starting point and end point of most theories of policing is the domestic realm. For general background, see Mike Maguire, Rod Morgan, and Robert Reiner, eds., *Oxford Handbook of Criminology*, 3rd ed. (Oxford: Oxford University Press, 2002); Richard V. Ericson and Kevin D. Haggerty, *Policing the Risk Society* (Toronto: University of Toronto Press, 1997); Tim Newburn, ed., *Handbook of Policing* (Devon, UK: Willan Publishers, 2003); Michael Tonry and Norval Morris, eds., *Modern Policing: Crime and Justice* (Chicago: University of Chicago Press, 1993).

9. See, for instance, Mathieu Deflem, *Policing World Society: Historical Foundations of International Police Cooperation* (Oxford: Oxford University Press, 2002); James Sheptycki, ed., *Issues in Transnational Policing* (New York: Routledge, 2000); William F. McDonald, ed., *Crime and Law Enforcement in the Global Village* (Cincinnati, OH: Anderson Publishing, 1997). Much of the writing in this area focuses on the criminal justice implications of European integration. Prominent early works include Malcolm Anderson et al., *Policing the European Union: Theory, Law, and Practice* (Oxford: Oxford University Press, 1996); Malcolm Anderson and Monica den Boer, eds., *Policing across National Boundaries* (London: Pinter, 1994).

10. This is readily evident by glancing through the table of contents of the leading journals in the field, such as *World Politics*, *International Security*, *International Organization*, and *International Studies Quarterly*.

11. Terrorism and counterterrorism had previously been an issue at the margins of the study of international relations and had received even less attention from criminologists and criminal justice specialists.

12. Transgovernmental relations are relations among subunits of different governments. See Joseph S. Nye and Robert O. Keohane, "Transnational Relations and World Politics: An Introduction," *International Organization* 25, no. 3 (summer 1971): 329–349; Anne-Marie Slaughter, *A New World Order* (Princeton, NJ: Princeton University Press, 2004); Kal Raustiala, "The Architecture of International Cooperation: Transgovernmental Networks and the Future of International Law," *Virginia Journal of International Law* 43, no. 1 (fall 2002): 1–92.

13. See the special issue of *International Organization* 54, no. 3, "Legalization in World Politics" (summer 2000), edited by Judith L. Goldstein, Miles Kahler, Robert O. Keohane, and Anne-Marie Slaughter.

14. For example, David Held et al., *Global Transformations: Politics, Economics, and Culture* (Stanford, CA: Stanford University Press, 1999), provides one of the most comprehensive accounts of globalization but excludes transnational crime and crime control issues. Partial exceptions to this neglect include James Mittelman, *The Globalization Syndrome* (Princeton, NJ: Princeton University Press, 2000); Susan Strange, *The Retreat of the State: The Diffusion of Power in the World Economy* (New York: Cambridge University Press, 1996). Also see H. Richard Friman and Peter Andreas, eds., *The Illicit Global Economy and State Power* (Lanham, MD: Rowman & Littlefield, 1999).

15. On the criminalization of financial flows as a form of reregulation, see Thomas J. Biersteker with Peter Romaniuk, "The Return of the State? Financial Re-regulation in the Pursuit of Security after September 11," in John Tirman, ed., *The Maze of Fear* (New York: New Press, 2004).

16. As described by James Mahoney, a narrative is "a useful tool for assessing causality in situations where temporal sequencing, particular events, and path dependence must be taken into account." "Nominal, Ordinal, and Narrative Appraisal in Macrocausal Analysis," *American Journal of Sociology* 104, no. 4 (1999): 1164.

17. On the explanatory advantages of "analytical eclecticism," see Peter J. Katzenstein and Nobuo Okawara, "Japan, Asian-Pacific Security, and the Case for Analytical Eclecticism," *International Security* 26, no. 3 (winter 2001): 153–185.

18. As Katzenstein and Okawara write, "The complex links between power, interest, and norms defy analytical capture by any one paradigm. They are made more intelligible by drawing selectively on different paradigms—that is, by analytical eclecticism, not parsimony." Ibid., 154.

19. For instance, promoting international crime control campaigns can substitute for carrying out more difficult and costly domestic policies. The U.S. experience offers many illustrations of international crime control serving domestic

agendas. The launching of the Nixon administration's global antidrug campaign in 1969, for example, was primarily an outward extension of a domestic initiative rather than simply a functional response to the growth of global drug trafficking. It was also used as a political tool to assert greater executive control over the federal bureaucracy. See especially Edward Jay Epstein, *Agency of Fear: Opiates and Political Power in America* (New York: G. P. Putnam's Sons, 1977).

20. The importance of bureaucratic competition is captured by the observation of a former senior U.S. official: "During my six years working on international law enforcement issues for the State Department under the Clinton Administration, the hodge-podge of Federal departments and agencies working on transborder drugs, thugs, and terrorist issues spent as much energy fighting one another as they did fighting the bad guys." Jonathan Winer, letter to the editor, *The National Interest* 68 (spring 2002): 148.

21. For example, initiatives in one policy sphere, such as promoting regional economic integration, can have feedback effects that stimulate cooperation in other policy realms, such as crime control. On policy feedback effects, see Paul Pierson, "When Effect Becomes Cause: Policy Feedback and Political Change," *World Politics* 45, no. 4 (July 1993): 595–628. On the relationship between economic integration and international policing, see Ethan A. Nadelmann, "Harmonization of Criminal Justice Systems," in Peter H. Smith, ed., *The Challenge of Integration: Europe and the Americas* (New Brunswick, NJ: Transaction Publishers, 1993).

22. The analogy falters, of course, when one considers both the absence of any supranational entity capable of playing a role comparable to the U.S. federal law enforcement system and the far more profound differences in language, culture, politics, and law among nations compared to the states of the United States.

23. This shares some of the characteristics of an "epistemic community." See Peter Haas, "Introduction: Epistemic Communities and International Policy Coordination," *International Organization* 46, no. 1 (1992): 1–35.

24. These are primarily rule-making and rule-enforcing networks. Rule-making networks develop common standards and procedures and hammer out bilateral and multilateral agreements on crime control–related issues. These are mostly composed of midlevel civil servants from various governmental agencies with legal and technical expertise. Enforcement networks are mostly concerned with practical day-to-day implementation issues, such as information gathering and sharing and technical assistance and training, and are based more on relations between law enforcement practitioners on the ground. On different types of transgovernmental networks, see Slaughter, *A New World Order*.

25. For insightful recent critiques of liberalism for discounting the importance of power, see Michael Barnett and Raymond Duvall, "Power in Global

Governance," and Andrew Hurrell, "Power, Institutions, and the Production of Inequality," both in Michael Barnett and Raymond Duvall, eds., *Power in Global Governance* (Cambridge, UK: Cambridge University Press, 2005). Hurrell notes that in liberal accounts of global governance, "power recedes so far into the background that we are left with a strikingly apolitical and far too cosy a view of institutions and of global governance—especially when viewed from the perspective of weaker states (indeed perhaps from anywhere outside the United States)" (49).

26. Realism is the theoretical tradition in international relations most associated with an emphasis on power, but the multiple forms and expressions of power cannot be captured by only one perspective. See Michael Barnett and Raymond Duvall, "Power in International Politics," *International Organization* 59, no. 1 (2005): 39–75.

27. Part of the process was more passive, as weaker states imitated and adapted the criminal laws and other norms of the more powerful states, or were absorbed or destroyed by them. See M. B. Hooker, *Legal Pluralism: An Introduction to Colonial and Neo-Colonial Laws* (Oxford: Clarendon Press, 1975); Aspirat Petschiri, *Eastern Importation of Western Criminal Law: Thailand as a Case Study* (Littleton, CO.: Fred B. Rothman, 1987).

28. The postwar American "empire," Samuel P. Huntington long ago pointed out, is "characterized not by acquisition of new territories but by their penetration." "Transnational Organizations in World Politics," *World Politics* 25, no. 3 (1973): 333–368.

29. Nye differentiates between "hard" and "soft" power: hard power is "command power that can be used to induce others to change their position"; soft power works in more subtle ways, such as setting agendas and developing practices that others wish to emulate: "It co-opts people rather than coerces them." However, our account suggests that such a sharp dichotomy is misleading, given that U.S. policing power often blends the two in the form of coercive co-optation. See Joseph S. Nye Jr., *The Paradox of American Power: Why the World's Only Superpower Can't Go It Alone* (New York: Oxford University Press, 2002), 9.

30. Our account confirms Raustiala's general observation that transgovernmental networks appear to "strengthen the power of the already powerful," that "the traditionally powerful states play leading roles in networks and it is the weak nations of the world that are adopting many of the regulatory policies of the more powerful," and that "the resulting convergence process often favors dominant economic actors such as the U.S." Raustiala, "The Architecture of International Cooperation," 24–25.

31. See, for example, Michael C. Desch, Jorge I. Domínguez, and Andres Serbin, eds., *From Pirates to Drug Lords: The Post–Cold War Caribbean Security Envi-*

ronment (Albany: State University of New York Press, 1998); Peter H. Smith, ed., *Drug Policy in the Americas* (Boulder, CO: Westview, 1992); John Bailey and Jorge Chabat, *Transnational Crime and Public Security: Challenges to Mexico and the United States* (La Jolla, CA: Center for United States–Mexican Studies, 2002).

32. In 2001 the United States blocked a legally binding international agreement that would have placed greater restrictions on the cross-border flow of small arms.

33. For summaries of international police cooperation across much of the developing world, see the relevant chapters in Daniel J. Koenig and Dilip K. Das, eds., *International Police Cooperation: A World Perspective* (Lanham, MD: Lexington Books, 2001). Although beyond the scope of our analysis, it should be noted that law enforcement relations between developing countries remain understudied and deserve much greater attention.

34. Most of these powerful states have been in the transatlantic region. An important exception beyond the focus of this book is Japan, where informal bilateralism (based on intensified contacts among police professionals in the Asian-Pacific region) has been the preferred approach to managing transnational crime issues. See Katzenstein and Okawara, "Japan, Asian-Pacific Security, and the Case for Analytical Eclecticism." On the evolution of Japanese security and law enforcement policies, see H. Richard Friman et al., "Immovable Object? Japan's Security Policy in East Asia," in Peter J. Katzenstein and Takashi Shiraishi, eds., *Beyond Japan: The Dynamics of East Asian Regionalism* (Ithaca, NY: Cornell University Press, 2006).

35. Note that human beings and human institutions have not been the only subjects of the criminal law. History abounds with cases in which animals, human corpses, and inanimate objects have been legally prosecuted, convicted, and punished for the commission of crimes. See E. P. Evans, *The Criminal Prosecution and Capital Punishment of Animals* (London: Faber & Faber, 1987); and with respect to human corpses, Johannes Nohl, *The Black Death: A Chronicle of the Plague*, trans. C. H. Clarke (New York: Harper & Brothers, 1925), 110.

36. Stephen D. Krasner, "Power, Politics, Institutions, and Transnational Relations," in Thomas Risse-Kappen, ed., *Bringing Transnational Relations Back In* (New York: Cambridge University Press, 1995), 268; Huntington, "Transnational Organizations in World Politics."

37. For an insightful early account, see Jorge I. Domínguez, "Smuggling," *Foreign Policy* 20 (fall 1975): 87–96, 161–164.

38. See Nikos Passas, "Globalization, Criminogenic Asymmetries, and Economic Crime," *European Journal of Law Reform* 1, no. 4 (1999): 399–423. The persistence of legal asymmetries significantly complicates international crime control. For instance, states may aid and abet violations of other states' legal controls. States that refuse to criminalize tax evasion, money laundering, or insider trading within their own borders often refuse to cooperate in other states' investigations

of these offenses; indeed, some actively invite citizens of other countries to engage in violations of their states' tax and securities laws by affording them the legal secrecy and technological resources required to commit such crimes discreetly and extraterritorially. Somewhat similarly, states may sponsor or engage in activities that their own laws criminalize. Many intelligence operations, for instance, violate not just the laws of the foreign states in which they are committed but often the laws of the sponsoring state.

39. Malcolm Anderson, *Policing the World: Interpol and the Politics of International Police Cooperation* (Oxford: Oxford University Press, 1989), 40.

40. See the discussions of criminalization in Clayton A. Hartjen, *Crime and Criminalization*, 2nd ed. (New York: Holt, Rinehart & Winston, 1978), 1–49.

41. For a recent account of the role of ethical arguments in international relations, see Neta C. Crawford, *Argument and Change in World Politics: Ethics, Decolonization, and Humanitarian Intervention* (Cambridge, UK: Cambridge University Press, 2002).

42. E. H. Carr, *The Twenty Years Crisis, 1919–1939*, rev. ed. (London: Perennial, 1964), 97. See especially chaps. 6–7.

43. On the symbolic role of laws and their enforcement, see David Garland, "Punishment and Culture: The Symbolic Dimension of Criminal Justice," *Studies in Law, Politics, and Society* 11 (1991): 191–222.

Chapter 1

1. Two of the best-known early accounts of international regimes are Stephen D. Krasner, ed., *International Regimes* (Ithaca, NY: Cornell University Press, 1983); and Robert O. Keohane, *After Hegemony: Cooperation and Discord in the World Political Economy* (Princeton, NJ: Princeton University Press, 1984). Also see Andreas Hasenclever, Peter Mayer, and Volker Rittberger, *Theories of International Regimes* (Cambridge, UK: Cambridge University Press, 1997).

2. For a useful review of the evolution and political importance of international norms, see Martha Finnemore and Kathryn Sikkink, "International Norm Dynamics and Political Change," *International Organization* 52, no. 4 (1998): 887–917.

3. The notion of "transnational moral entrepreneurs" involves a conjoining of Howard Becker's concept of "moral entrepreneurs" and Samuel Huntington's notion of "transnational organization." The former include those people who "operate with an absolute ethic" in seeking to create new rules to do away with a perceived great evil. Becker, *Outsiders: Studies in the Sociology of Deviance* (New York: Free Press, 1963), 147–163; Huntington, "Transnational Organizations in World Politics."

4. On the nature, origins, and strategies of transnational advocacy networks,

see Margaret E. Keck and Kathryn Sikkink, *Activists beyond Borders: Advocacy Networks in International Politics* (Ithaca, NY: Cornell University Press, 1998). See also Sanjeev Khagram, James V. Riker, and Kathryn Sikkink, eds., *Restructuring World Politics: Transnational Social Movements, Networks, and Norms* (Minneapolis: University of Minnesota Press, 2002).

5. This has been further reinforced and institutionalized through the 2000 UN Convention Against Transnational Organized Crime. As explained by one senior U.S. State Department official, "Few global criminal law enforcement conventions are so detailed and precise in setting out mechanisms for extraditing fugitives and assisting foreign criminal investigations and prosecutions. Many countries, particularly in the developing world, lack existing bilateral extradition or mutual legal assistance treaty relationships with one another, but now will be able to rely on this Convention to fill that legal gap for many serious crimes." Testimony of Samuel M. Witten, Deputy Legal Adviser, U.S. Department of State, "On the Inter-American Terrorism Convention," Hearing of the U.S. Senate Committee on Foreign Relations, *Law Enforcement Treaties,* 108th Congress, 2nd session, 17 June 2004, 14.

6. See Martin Wight, "Western Values in International Relations," in Herbert Butterfield and Martin Wight, eds., *Diplomatic Investigations: Essays in the Theory of International Politics* (London: George Allen and Unwin, 1966); Hedley Bull, "The Emergence of a Universal International Society," in Hedley Bull and Adam Watson, eds., *The Expansion of International Society* (Oxford: Oxford University Press, 1984), 117–126. For a recent extension to contemporary debates in international relations, see Barry Buzan, *From International to World Society? English School Theory and the Social Structure of Globalization* (Cambridge, UK: Cambridge University Press, 2004).

7. See Janice E. Thomson, "Sovereignty in Historical Perspective: The Evolution of State Control over Extraterritorial Violence," in James A. Caporaso, ed., *The Elusive State* (Newbury Park, CA: Sage, 1989), 227–254; Janice E. Thomson, *Mercenaries, Pirates and Sovereigns* (Princeton, NJ: Princeton University Press, 1994).

8. States that are willing and able to employ totalitarian measures, or whose laws are bolstered by strong social sanctions, are best able to suppress these types of criminal activities.

9. See, generally, Philip Gosse, *The History of Piracy* (New York: Longmans, Green, 1932).

10. For general background, see C. R. Pennell, ed., *Bandits at Sea: A Pirates Reader* (New York: New York University Press, 2001).

11. See the discussion in Fernand Braudel, *The Mediterranean and the Mediterranean World in the Age of Philip II*, vol. 2, trans. Sian Reynolds (New York: Harper Colophon Books, 1976), 865–891.

12. See, for example, David J. Starkey, E. S. Van Eyck Heslinga, and J. A. De Moor, eds., *Pirates and Privateers: New Perspectives on the War on Trade in the Eighteenth and Nineteenth Centuries* (Exeter, UK: University of Exeter Press, 1997).

13. Robert C. Ritchie, *Captain Kidd and the War against the Pirates* (Cambridge, MA: Harvard University Press, 1986), 11.

14. C. M. Senior, *A Nation of Pirates: English Piracy in Its Heyday* (New York: Crane, Russack, 1976), 149.

15. Ritchie, *Captain Kidd*, 152–154. On the rise and expansion of the British Empire in general, see Linda Colley, *Captives: The Story of Britain's Pursuit of Empire and How Its Soldiers and Civilians Were Held Captive by the Dream of Global Supremacy, 1600–1850* (New York: Pantheon, 2002).

16. Senior, *A Nation of Pirates*, 151.

17. Adam Watson, "European International Society and Its Expansion," in Bull and Watson, *The Expansion of International Society*, 13–32.

18. See, for instance, Nicholas Tarlin, *Piracy and Politics in the Malay World* (Melbourne, Australia: F.W. Cheshire, 1963).

19. Ralph T. Ward, *Pirates in History* (Baltimore, MD: York Press, 1974), 112–127; John B. Wolf, *The Barbary Coast* (New York: Norton, 1979), 299–321; Frank Lambert, *The Barbary Wars: American Independence in the Atlantic World* (New York: Hill & Wang, 2005).

20. Thomson, "Sovereignty in Historical Perspective," 248–249.

21. Ward, *Pirates in History*, 158.

22. Francis R. Stark, *The Abolition of Privateering and Declaration of Paris*, Ph.D. diss., Columbia University, 1897.

23. See, for instance, Jane Lucas de Grummon, *Renato Beluche: Smuggler, Privateer, and Patriot, 1780–1860* (Baton Rouge: Louisiana State University Press, 1983).

24. Thomson, "Sovereignty in Historical Perspective."

25. Sir Francis Piggott, *The Declaration of Paris, 1856* (London: University of London Press, 1919), 142–149.

26. "Privateer," in *The New Encyclopedia Britannica* (Chicago: Encyclopedia Britannica, 1991) 15th ed., 8: 713.

27. See Barry H. Dubner, *The Law of International Sea Piracy* (The Hague: Martinus Nijhoff, 1980).

28. Ward, *Pirates in History*, 158–159.

29. Ibid.

30. Jayant Abhyankar, "Maritime Fraud and Piracy," in Phil Williams and Dimitri Vlassis, eds., *Combating Transnational Crime: Concepts, Activities and Responses* (London: Frank Cass, 2001). Reflecting a renewed concern over piracy, in 1992 the International Maritime Bureau established a Piracy Reporting Center in Kuala Lumpur, an information center providing assistance against piracy. On the

limited law enforcement at sea in general, see William Langewiesche, *The Outlaw Sea: A World of Freedom, Chaos, and Crime* (New York: North Point Press, 2004).

31. Ship owners reported 445 attacks in 2003, 42 percent of which were located in the Strait of Malacca. Gal Luft and Anne Korin, "Terrorism Goes to Sea," *Foreign Affairs* (November/December 2004): 62.

32. See Peter Romaniuk, "Exporting Homeland Security: U.S. Power, Local Resistance, and Maritime Security in Southeast Asia," paper presented at the annual meeting of the American Political Science Association, Washington, DC, September 2005. See also the Web sites of these organizations: www.imo.org and www.wcoomd.org.

33. An April 10, 2004, *New York Times* editorial, "Piracy and Terrorism," noted that "Adm. Thomas Fargo, the commander of American forces in the Pacific, told a Congressional committee that the navy was considering armed patrols in the Strait of Malacca. American diplomats had to smooth ruffled feathers in Malaysia, whose government hadn't been consulted."

34. For general overviews, see Seymour Drescher, *From Slavery to Freedom: Comparative Studies in the Rise and Fall of Atlantic Slavery* (New York: New York University Press, 1999); Hugh Thomas, *The Slave Trade: The Story of the Atlantic Slave Trade, 1440–1870* (New York: Simon and Schuster, 1999); Suzanne Miers, *Slavery in the Twentieth Century: The Evolution of a Global Problem* (Lanham, MD: Altamira Press, 2003).

35. See Michael Craton, *Sinews of Empire: A Short History of British Slavery* (Garden City, NY: Anchor Books, 1974), for an analysis of the British role. The figure of 10 million is from Philip D. Curtin, *The Atlantic Slave Trade* (Madison: University of Wisconsin Press, 1969), 268.

36. See, generally, Suzanne Miers, *Britain and the Ending of the Slave Trade* (New York: Africana Publishing, 1975).

37. Craton, *Sinews of Empire*, 289, 378. See Christopher Lloyd, *The Navy and the Slave Trade: The Suppression of the African Slave Trade in the Nineteenth Century* (London: Longmans, Green, 1949); W. E. F. Ward, *The Royal Navy and the Slavers: The Suppression of the Atlantic Slave Trade* (London: Pantheon Books, 1970).

38. Miers, *Britain and the Ending of the Slave Trade*.

39. Harold Nicolson, *The Congress of Vienna: A Study in Allied Unity—1812–1822* (New York: Harcourt, Brace, 1946), 209–214.

40. See Eric E. Williams, *Capitalism and Slavery* (Chapel Hill: University of North Carolina Press, 1942); John Salter, "Adam Smith on Slavery," *History of Economic Ideas* 4, nos. 1–2 (1996): 225–251.

41. Thomas Clarkson, *Essay on the Impolicy of the African Slave Trade* (1788), excerpted in Michael Craton, James Walvin, and David Wright, eds., *Slavery, Abolition, and Emancipation: Black Slaves and the British Empire* (London: Longman Group, 1976), 248–253.

42. See Seymour Drescher, *Econocide: British Slavery in the Era of Abolition* (Pittsburgh, PA: University of Pittsburgh Press, 1977).

43. See Sir Reginald Coupland, *The British Anti-Slavery Movement*, 2nd ed. (London: Frank Cass, 1964); Howard Temperley, *British Antislavery: 1833–1870* (London: Longman, 1972); Edith Hurwitz, *Politics and the Public Conscience: Slave Emancipation and the Abolitionist Movement in Britain* (New York: Barnes & Noble Books, 1973); Miers, *Britain and the Ending of the Slave Trade*; Frank J. Klingberg, *The Anti-Slavery Movement in Britain: A Study in English Humanitarianism* (New Haven, CT: Yale University Press, 1926). Also see David Brion Davis, *Slavery and Human Progress* (New York: Oxford University Press, 1984), xviii, who argues that "the impetus behind British antislavery policies was mainly religious, though devout Victorians assumed that good economics was consistent with good religion." See also Alison Webster, "The Contribution of the Scottish Enlightenment to the Abandonment of the Institution of Slavery," *European Legacy* 8, no. 4 (2003): 481–489.

44. See especially Adam Hochschild, *Bury the Chains: Prophets and Rebels in the Fight to Free an Empire's Slaves* (Boston: Houghton Mifflin, 2005).

45. See Seymour Drescher, "Public Opinion and the Destruction of British Colonial Slavery," in James Walvin, ed., *Slavery and British Society—1776–1846* (Baton Rouge: Louisiana State University Press, 1982). On shifts in public opinion more generally, see J. R. Oldfield, *Popular Politics and British Anti-Slavery: The Mobilization of Public Opinion against the Slave Trade, 1787–1807* (Manchester, UK: Manchester University Press, 1995).

46. Coupland, *The British Anti-Slavery Movement*, 206–235. See also Daniel Liebowitz, *The Physician and the Slave Trade: John Kirk, the Livingstone Expeditions, and the Crusade against Slavery in East Africa* (New York: W.H. Freeman, 1999).

47. See C. Duncan Rice, *The Rise and Fall of Black Slavery* (Baton Rouge: Louisiana State University Press, 1975), 368.

48. See, generally, Miers, *Britain and the Ending of the Slave Trade*.

49. Ehud R. Toledano, *The Ottoman Slave Trade and Its Suppression: 1840–1890* (Princeton, NJ: Princeton University Press, 1982).

50. Lawrence C. Jennings, *French Reaction to British Slave Emancipation* (Baton Rogue: Louisiana State University Press, 1988), 144–167.

51. W. E. B. Du Bois, *The Suppression of the African Slave Trade to the United States of America, 1638–1870* (New York: Longmans, Green, 1896). On the diverse forms of slavery in the United States, see Ira Berlin, *Many Thousands Gone: First Two Centuries of Slavery in North America* (Cambridge, MA: Harvard University Press, 1998).

52. Miers, *Britain and the Ending of the Slave Trade*, 31; also see Temperley, *British Antislavery, 1833–1870*.

53. The efforts of the British and Foreign Anti-Slavery Society in France are

described in Jennings, *French Reaction to British Slave Emancipation*; those in the United States are described in Betty Fladeland, *Men and Brothers: Anglo-American Antislavery Cooperation* (Urbana: University of Illinois Press, 1972); and those in Brazil are briefly noted in Davis, *Slavery and Human Progress*, 291–298.

54. Davis, *Slavery and Human Progress*, 304.

55. On the role of transnational advocacy networks in this diffusion process, see Keck and Sikkink, *Activists beyond Borders*, 41–51.

56. See James Brewer Stewart, *Holy Warriors: The Abolitionists and American Slavery* (New York: Hill and Wang, 1976), 11–23.

57. See Fladeland, *Men and Brothers*.

58. Regarding France, see Edward Derbyshire Seeber, *Anti-Slavery Opinion in France During the Second Half of the Eighteenth Century* (Baltimore, MD: Johns Hopkins University Press, 1937); Shelby T. McCoy, *The Humanitarian Movement in Eighteenth-Century France* (Lexington: University of Kentucky Press, 1957), 82–128; Sue Peabody, *"There Are No Slaves in France": The Political Culture of Race and Slavery in the Ancien Régime* (New York: Oxford University Press, 1996). See, more generally, David Brion Davis, *The Problem of Slavery in Western Culture* (Ithaca, NY: Cornell University Press, 1966).

59. Davis, *Slavery and Human Progress*, 297.

60. Rebecca J. Scott, *Slave Emancipation in Cuba: The Transition to Free Labor, 1860–1899* (Princeton, NJ: Princeton University Press, 1985), 38; Robert Brent Toplin, *The Abolition of Slavery in Brazil* (New York: Atheneum, 1972), 41–42. On Britain's role in the transformation of the Cuban slave trade, see David Murray, *Odious Commerce: Britain, Spain and the Abolition of the Cuban Slave Trade* (Cambridge, UK: Cambridge University Press, 2002).

61. See Toplin, *The Abolition of Slavery in Brazil*, 42–43, 65; Arthur F. Corwin, *Spain and the Abolition of Slavery in Cuba: 1817–1886* (Austin: University of Texas Press, 1967).

62. Quoted in Davis, *Slavery and Human Progress*, 297.

63. Toledano, *The Ottoman Slave Trade and Its Suppression*, 272–278.

64. See Roger Sawyer, *Slavery in the Twentieth Century* (New York: Routledge & Kegan Paul, 1986); Orlando Patterson, *Slavery and Social Death: A Comparative Study* (Cambridge, MA: Harvard University Press, 1982); Michael L. Bush, *Servitude in Modern Times* (Cambridge, MA: Polity Press, 2000).

65. See Kevin Bales, *Disposable People: New Slavery in the Global Economy* (Berkeley: University of California Press, 1999), 14.

66. Crawford, *Argument and Change in World Politics*, 200, n. 160.

67. On the origins of the term, see Edward J. Bristow, *Prostitution and Prejudice: The Jewish Fight against White Slavery, 1870–1939* (New York: Schocken Books, 1982), 35–38; Vern Bullough and Bonnie Bullough, *Women and Prostitution: A Social History* (Buffalo, NY: Prometheus Books, 1987), 265.

68. Bullough and Bullough, *Women and Prostitution*, 263–264.

69. See Bristow, *Prostitution and Prejudice*, 36–37; Edward J. Bristow, *Vice and Vigilance* (Totowa, NJ: Rowman and Littlefield, 1977).

70. Bullough and Bullough, *Women and Prostitution*, 263.

71. See Helen Mathers, "The Evangelical Spirituality of a Victorian Feminist: Josephine Butler, 1828–1906," *Journal of Ecclesiastical History* 52 (2001): 282–312; Glen Petrie, *A Singular Iniquity: The Campaigns of Josephine Butler* (New York: Viking Press, 1971); Antoinette Burton, "States of Injury: Josephine Butler on Slavery, Citizenship, and the Boer War," *Social Politics* 5, no. 3 (1998): 338–361. Butler's travels to Italy are discussed in Mary Gibson, *Prostitution and the State in Italy: 1860–1915* (New Brunswick, NJ: Rutgers University Press, 1986), 41–48; on her travels to France, see Jill Harsin, *Policing Prostitution in Nineteenth Century Paris* (Princeton, NJ: Princeton University Press, 1985), 324–325.

72. See Paul McHugh, *Prostitution and Victorian Social Reform* (London: Croom Helm, 1980), 104–106.

73. The leading study of prostitution during the mid-nineteenth century, William Sanger's *History of Prostitution: Its Extent, Causes, and Effects throughout the World* (New York: Medical Publishing, 1897), "supported growing xenophobic attitudes [in the following decades] by underscoring that most prostitutes were recent immigrants." See Ruth Rosen, *The Lost Sisterhood: Prostitution in America 1900–1918* (Baltimore, MD: Johns Hopkins University Press, 1982), 10. Anti-Semites made much of the Jewish involvement in the white slave trade, depicting Jews as the principal organizers of the traffic. See Bristow, *Prostitution and Prejudice*. For a critical view on such charges against Jews, see Eli Faber, *Jews, Slaves and the Slave Trade: Setting the Record Straight* (New York: New York University Press, 2000).

74. Barbara Meil Hobson, *Uneasy Virtue: The Politics of Prostitution and the American Reform Tradition* (New York: Basic Books, 1987), 142. The new law, in turn, provided a crucial mechanism for expanding the federal government's policing power and capacity. See David J. Langum, *Crossing the Line: Legislating Morality and the Mann Act* (Chicago: University of Chicago Press, 1994); James Morone, *Hellfire Nation: The Politics of Sin in American History* (New Haven, CT: Yale University Press, 2003), 265–268.

75. See Charles Winnick and Paul M. Kinsie, *The Lively Commerce: Prostitution in the United States* (Chicago: Quadrangle Books, 1971), 269–280; Bristow, *Vice and Vigilance*, 175–199.

76. Gail Pheterson, ed., *A Vindication of the Rights of Whores* (Seattle, WA: Seal Press, 1989), 12.

77. Ibid.

78. Bristow, *Prostitution and Prejudice*, 320.

79. Susan J. Toepfer and Bryan S. Wells, "The Worldwide Market for Sex: A

Review of International and Regional Legal Prohibitions Regarding Trafficking in Women," *Michigan Journal of Gender and Law* 2 (1994): 92.

80. For overviews, see David Kyle and Rey Koslowski, eds., *Global Human Smuggling* (Baltimore, MD: Johns Hopkins University Press, 2001); Phil Williams, ed., *Illegal Immigration and Commercial Sex: The New Slave Trade* (London: Frank Cass, 1999); Siriporn Skrobanek, Nataya Boonpakdee, and Chutima Jantateero, *The Traffic in Women: Human Realities of the International Sex Trade* (London: Zed Books, 1997).

81. See Sally Stoecker and Louise Shelley, eds., *Human Traffic and Transnational Crime: Eurasian and American Perspectives* (Lanham, MD: Rowman & Littlefield, 2005). The trafficking of Eastern European women into the western Balkans has flourished in the aftermath of the violent ethnic conflicts of the 1990s, partly to service the large influx of international personnel in places such as Bosnia and Kosovo as part of the postwar reconstruction effort. See Sarah Mendelson, *Barracks and Brothels: Peacekeepers and Human Trafficking in the Balkans* (Washington, DC: Center for Strategic and International Studies, 2005).

82. Some Web sites, such as www.worldsexguide.com, explicitly facilitate sex tourism. On the mainstreaming of sexual representations through the Internet and satellite television and its impact on the sex industry, see Ian Taylor and Ruth Jamieson, "Sex Trafficking and the Mainstream of Market Culture," *Crime, Law and Social Change* 32, no. 3 (October 1999): 257–278.

83. See David Kyle and John Dale, "Agents of Human Smuggling Reconsidered," in Kyle and Koslowski, *Global Human Smuggling*; Vidyamali Samarasinghe, "Confronting Globalization in Anti-Trafficking Strategies in Asia," *Brown Journal of World Affairs* 10, no. 1 (summer/fall 2003): 98; Christina Arnold and Andrea Bertone, "Addressing the Sex Trade in Thailand: Some Lessons Learned from NGOs. Part I," *Gender Issues* 20, no. 1 (2002): 26–53.

84. See, for example, Jacqueline Berman, "(Un)popular Strangers and Crises (Un)bounded: Discourses of Sex Trafficking, the European Political Community and the Panicked State of the Modern State," *European Journal of International Relations* 9, no. 1 (2003): 37–86. For a similar critical perspective of the antitrafficking discourse, see Claudia Aradau, "The Perverse Politics of Four-Letter Words: Risk and Pity in the Securitization of Human Trafficking," *Millennium: Journal of International Studies* 33, no. 2 (2004): 251–277.

85. Mohamed Y. Mattar, "Monitoring the Status of Severe Forms of Trafficking in Foreign Countries: Sanctions Mandated under the U.S. Trafficking Victims Protection Act," *Brown Journal of World Affairs* 10, no. 1 (summer/fall 2003): 159–178.

86. See Kamala Kampadoo and Jo Doezema, eds., *Global Sex Workers: Rights, Resistance, and Redefinition* (New York: Routledge, 1998); Dina F. Haynes, "Used, Abused, Arrested and Deported: Extending Immigration Benefits to Protect the

Victims of Trafficking and to Secure the Prosecution of Traffickers," *Human Rights Quarterly* 26, no. 2 (2004): 221–272.

87. For a review of recent policy debates and splits within the women's movement on these issues, see Joyce Outshoorn, ed., *The Politics of Prostitution: Women's Movements, Democratic States, and the Globalization of Sex Commerce* (Cambridge, UK: Cambridge University Press, 2004).

88. Samarasinghe, "Confronting Globalization in Anti-Trafficking Strategies in Asia," 100.

89. Eileen Scully, "Pre–Cold War Traffic in Sexual Labor and Its Foes: Some Contemporary Lessons," in Kyle and Koslowski, *Global Human Smuggling*, 95.

90. In 2000, the U.S. Congress passed the Victims of Trafficking Protection Act, which was pushed by the combined lobbying of feminist groups and evangelical Christian organizations. The law requires the State Department to publish an annual report ranking countries in terms of their role in human trafficking and compliance with U.S.-specified standards of criminalization and enforcement, and combines shaming and threats of withholding aid and diplomatic favor. See Tara McKelvey, "Of Human Bondage," *American Prospect* 15, no. 11 (November 2004), 17–20.

91. As of October 2004, there were 147 signatories to the Convention and 117 signatories to the Protocol. The Convention also included the "Protocol against the Smuggling of Migrants by Land, Sea and Air" (which took effect in January 2004).

92. According to a senior U.S. State Department official, the Protocol was "originally proposed and drafted by the United States." Testimony of Samuel M. Witten, U.S. Senate Committee on Foreign Relations, 17 June 2004, 15.

93. On the contentiousness of the language adopted in the UN Trafficking Protocol, see Jo Doezema, "Who Gets to Choose? Coercion, Consent, and the UN Trafficking Protocol," *Gender and Development* 10, no. 1 (March 2002): 20–27.

94. See H. Richard Friman, "Globalization's Poster Child: Transnational Organized Crime and the Triumph of Liberalism?," paper presented at the 2005 annual convention of the International Studies Association, Honolulu, HI, 1–5 March 2005, 14.

95. Bullough and Bullough, *Women and Prostitution*, 301.

96. For a general historical review, see Nils Johan Ringdal, *Love for Sale: A World History of Prostitution* (New York: Grove Press, 2003).

97. See Andrew Weil, *The Natural Mind* (Boston: Houghton Mifflin, 1972), 17–38. A possible historical exception is the Eskimos, whose environment greatly limited their capacity to grow anything.

98. See, for example, David T. Courtwright, *Forces of Habit: Drugs and the Making of the Modern World* (Cambridge, MA: Harvard University Press, 2001).

99. For a historical overview of the making of international drug control agreements, see William B. McAllister, *Drug Diplomacy in the Twentieth Century: An International History* (New York: Routledge, 1999).

100. See John King Fairbank, *Trade and Diplomacy on the China Coast* (Cambridge, MA: Harvard University Press, 1953); P. W. Fay, *The Opium War, 1840–42* (Chapel Hill: University of North Carolina Press, 1975); Brian Inglis, *The Opium War* (London: Hodder and Stoughton, 1976). On the importance of opium to the British imperial economy, see Carl A. Trocki, *Opium, Empire and the Global Political Economy: A Study of the Asian Opium Trade* (London: Routledge, 1999).

101. Bruce D. Johnson, "Righteousness before Revenue: The Forgotten Moral Crusade against the Indo-Chinese Opium Trade," *Journal of Drug Issues* 5 (fall 1975): 304–326.

102. See Geoffrey Harding, *Opiate Addiction, Morality and Medicine* (London: Macmillan, 1988), 38–46.

103. See J. B. Brown, "Politics of the Poppy: The Society for the Suppression of the Opium Trade, 1874–1916," *Journal of Contemporary History* 8 (1973): 97–111. Also see Virginia Berridge, *Opium and the People: Opiate Use and Drug Control in Nineteenth and Early Twentieth Century England* (London: Free Association Books LTD, 1999), 173–194.

104. Berridge, *Opium and the People*, 198.

105. Arnold H. Taylor, *American Diplomacy and the Narcotics Traffic, 1900–1939: A Study in International Humanitarian Reform* (Durham, NC: Duke University Press, 1969), 29.

106. See McAllister, *Drug Diplomacy in the 20th Century*.

107. Berridge, *Opium and the People*, 135–149; H. Wayne Morgan, *Drugs in America: A Social History, 1800–1980* (Syracuse, NY: Syracuse University Press, 1980), 22–28; N. H. Jones, "A Critical Study of the Origins and Early Development of the Hypodermic Syringe," *Journal of the History of Medicine* 2 (1947): 201–249.

108. Dean Latimer and Jeff Goldberg, *Flowers in the Blood: The Story of Opium* (New York: Franklin Watts, 1981), 179–200.

109. See Paul Gootenberg, ed., *Cocaine: Global Histories* (New York: Routledge, 1999); Joseph Kennedy, *Coca Exotica: The Illustrated Story of Cocaine* (London: Associated University Presses, 1985).

110. See Richard Ashley, *Cocaine: Its History, Uses, and Effects* (New York: Warner Books, 1975), 50–68; Joel L. Phillips and Ronald D. Wynne, *Cocaine: The Mystique and the Reality* (New York: Avon Books, 1980), 27–70; Kennedy, *Coca Exotica*.

111. On changing views of cocaine in the United States, see Joseph F. Spillane, *Cocaine: From Medical Marvel to Modern Menace in the United States, 1884–1920* (Baltimore, MD: Johns Hopkins University Press, 2000).

112. See James Harvey Young, *The Toadstool Millionaires: A Social History of*

Patent Medicines in America before Federal Regulation (Princeton, NJ: Princeton University Press, 1961).

113. Berridge, *Opium and the People,* 113–70; Patricia G. Erickson et al., *The Steel Drug: Cocaine in Perspective* (Lexington, KY: Lexington Books, 1987), 11–19.

114. David F. Musto, *The American Disease: Origins of Narcotic Control* (New Haven, CT: Yale University Press, 1973).

115. Joseph R. Gusfield, *Symbolic Crusade: Status Politics and the American Temperance Movement* (Chicago: University of Illinois Press, 1963), 51–57.

116. David Courtwright, *Dark Paradise: Opiate Addiction in America before 1940* (Cambridge, MA: Harvard University Press, 1982), 35–61.

117. Edward M. Brecher and the Editors of *Consumer Reports, Licit and Illicit Drugs* (Boston: Little, Brown, 1972), 42–43.

118. Musto, *American Disease,* 6.

119. See Edward H. Williams, "The Drug Menace in the South," *Medical Record* 85 (1914); Phillips and Wynne, *Cocaine: The Mystique and the Reality,* 64–70; Morgan, *Drugs in America,* 92–93.

120. Jerome L. Himmelstein, *The Strange Career of Marijuana: Politics and Ideology of Drug Control in America* (Westport, CT: Greenwood Press, 1983); Musto, *American Disease,* 210–229.

121. Musto, *American Disease,* 31. Also see A. H. Taylor, *American Diplomacy and the Narcotics Traffic, 1900–1939,* 30.

122. Musto, *American Disease,* 66–67, 190–193.

123. Ibid., 190–193

124. John C. McWilliams, *The Protectors: Harry J. Anslinger and the Federal Bureau of Narcotics, 1930–1962* (Newark: University of Delaware Press, 1990).

125. See Kettil Bruun, Lynn Pan, and Ingemar Rexed, *The Gentleman's Club: International Control of Drugs and Alcohol* (Chicago: University of Chicago Press, 1975), 137–143; David R. Bewley-Taylor, *The United States and International Drug Control, 1909–1997* (London: Pinter, 1999), chaps. 3–4.

126. See Bruun et al., *The Gentleman's Club,* 113–131.

127. See ibid., 181–203. The scientific evidence regarding marijuana is discussed in the report of the U.S. Commission on Marihuana and Drug Abuse, *Marihuana: A Signal of Misunderstanding* (New York: Signet, 1972); Mitch Earlywine, *Understanding Marijuana: A New Look at the Scientific Evidence* (New York: Oxford University Press, 2002); Lynn Zimmer and John Morgan, *Marijuana Myths, Marijuana Facts: A Review of the Scientific Evidence* (New York: Lindesmith Center, 1997).

128. British Home Office, *Tackling Drug Misuse: A Summary of the Government's Strategy* (London: Home Office, 1988); Govert F. van de Wijngaart, "A Social History of Drug Use in the Netherlands: Policy Outcomes and Implications," *Journal of Drug Issues* 18 (summer 1988): 481–495.

129. Bruun et al., *The Gentleman's Club*, 165–180.

130. See Ian Tyrrell, "Women and Temperance in International Perspective: The World's WCTU, 1880s–1920s," in Susanna Barrows and Robin Room, eds., *Drinking: Behavior and Belief in Modern History* (Berkeley: University of California Press, 1991), 217–240.

131. For example, Iceland banned all wines and spirits from 1908 to 1934, Russia from 1914 to 1924, Norway from 1916 to 1927, and Finland from 1919 to 1932.

132. See Ernest Gordon, *The Anti-Alcohol Movement in Europe* (New York: Fleming H. Revell, 1913), as well as the reports of the annual proceedings of the International Congress Against Alcoholism.

133. Michael R. Aldrich and Robert W. Barker, "Historical Aspects of Cocaine Use and Abuse," in S. J. Mule, ed., *Cocaine: Chemical, Biological, Clinical, Social and Treatment Aspects* (Cleveland, OH: CRC Press, 1976), 1–12.

134. See, for instance, Vera Rubin and Lambros Comitas, *Ganja in Jamaica* (The Hague: Mouton, 1975), 20–35; James Fisher, "Cannabis in Nepal: An Overview," in Vera Rubin, ed., *Cannabis and Culture* (The Hague: Mouton, 1975), 247–255.

135. For a history of whaling regulation, see James E. Scarff, "The International Management of Whales, Dolphins, and Porpoises: An Interdisciplinary Assessment," *Ecology Law Quarterly* 6 (1977): 343–373.

136. Cited in R. Michael M'Gonigle, "The 'Economizing' of Ecology: Why Big, Rare Whales Still Die," *Ecology Law Quarterly* 9 (1980): 132. On the International Whaling Commission, see Michael Heazle, "The Politics of Uncertainty: The International Whaling Commission's Road to Management by Moratoria," *International Journal of Maritime History* 16, no. 2 (2004): 111–144.

137. See Robert McNally, *So Remorseless a Havoc* (Boston: Little, Brown, 1981), 3–69.

138. Scarff, "The International Management of Whales, Dolphins, and Porpoises," 384.

139. See the highly sympathetic account of Greenpeace in David Day, *The Whale War* (San Francisco: Sierra Club Books, 1987). For an overview of Greenpeace's antiwhaling activities, see http://whales.greenpeace.org.

140. Larson, "United States Whale Policy," 131–135.

141. Day, *Whale War*, 15–19.

142. Ibid.

143. Patricia Birnie, "The Role of Developing Countries in Nudging the International Whaling Commission from Regulating Whaling to Encouraging Nonconsumptive Uses of Whales," *Ecology Law Quarterly* 12 (1985): 966–967. During the 1960s, whale meat replaced baleen (whalebone) and oil as the primary consumptive use of baleen whales; the principal market is in Japan. The oil of the sperm whale, once valued as a fuel before petroleum became readily available

in the 1860s, is now used mainly as a high-grade machine lubricant. See Scarff, "The International Management of Whales, Dolphins, and Porpoises," 341–342. Whale oil is also converted into soaps and fatty acids, which are used in cosmetics and detergents.

144. Japan has expressed growing dissatisfaction with the restrictions imposed by the IWC and has threatened to withdraw. See Alex Kirby, "Japan Seeks Commercial Whaling OK," *BBC World Edition*, 19 July 2004. See, more generally, Amy L. Catalinac and Gerald Chan, "Japan, the West, and the Whaling Issue: Understanding the Japanese Side," *Japan Forum* 17, no. 1 (2005): 133–163.

145. For an overview of CITES and the difficulties of enforcement, see Rosalind Reeve, *Policing International Trade in Endangered Species: The CITES Treaty and Compliance* (London: Royal Institute of International Affairs, 2004). Also see Mara E. Zimmerman, "The Black Market for Wildlife: Combating Transnational Organized Crime in the Illegal Wildlife Trade," *Vanderbilt Journal of Transnational Law* 36 (November 2003): 1657–89, especially section 2, which summarizes the history and purpose of the Convention.

146. See, generally, Michael J. Glennon, "Has International Law Failed the Elephant?," *American Journal of International Law* 84 (January 1990): 1–43; R. T. Naylor, "The Underworld of Ivory," *Crime, Law, and Social Change* 42, nos. 4–5 (2004): 261–296.

147. See Ian Parker and Mohamed Amin, *Ivory Crisis* (London: Hogarth Press, 1983), 8.

148. Ibid.

149. For a defense of the conservationist policy, see Andrew J. Heimert, "How the Elephant Lost His Tusks," *Yale Law Journal* 106, no. 6 (April 1995): 1473–1506.

150. See Hisako Kiyono, *Japan's Trade in Ivory after the Tenth Conference of the Parties to CITES* (London: Traffic International, 2002).

151. A full listing is available at www.cites.org/eng/disc/species.shtml. Some 164 nations are signatories of the CITES treaty.

152. See Inga Saffron, *Caviar: The Strange History and Uncertain Future of the World's Most Coveted Delicacy* (New York: Broadway Books, 2002).

153. See Eric Hansen, *Orchid Fever: A Horticultural Tale of Love, Lust, and Lunacy* (New York: Pantheon Books, 2000). Those in the orchid business often describe it as an obsession. See, for example, Susan Orlean, *The Orchid Thief: A True Story of Beauty and Obsession* (New York: Ballantine, 2000).

154. Glennon, "Has International Law Failed the Elephant?," 208–209. Also see Carol Cunningham and Joel Berger, *Horn of Darkness: Rhinos on the Edge* (Oxford: Oxford University Press, 1997).

155. Money laundering is typically defined as the concealment of ill-gotten gains. On the stages of money laundering, see Jack Blum et al., *Financial Havens,*

Banking Secrecy and Money Laundering (Vienna: United Nations, 1998). R. T. Naylor notes, "Although the term 'money laundering' is relatively new, its practice is not; as long as there has been a need to hide a financial transfer, something like money laundering has occurred. It is a fair bet that the world's first genuine tax code, in Hammurabi's Babylonia, stimulated the imagination of those who sought to grant themselves a rebate." *Wages of Crime* (Ithaca, NY: Cornell University Press, 2002), 134.

156. Michael Levi, "Money Laundering and Its Regulation," *Annals of the American Academy of Political and Social Sciences* 582, no. 1 (2002), 181–194.

157. See the Web site of the FATF: http://www.fatf-gafi.org/.

158. See Sean D. Murphy, "Multilateral Listing of States as Money-Laundering Havens," *American Journal of International Law* 94, no. 4 (October 2000): 695.

159. Michael Levi, "Controlling the International Money Trail: What Lessons Have Been Learned?," paper presented at the seminar on Global Enforcement Regimes: Transnational Organized Crime, International Terrorism and Money Laundering, Transnational Institute, Amsterdam, 28–29 April 2005, 17.

160. Ibid., 12.

161. Eric Helleiner, "The Politics of Global Financial Reregulation: Lessons from the Fight against Money Laundering," Working Paper No. 15, Center for Economic Policy Analysis, Washington, DC, April 2000, 8.

162. Ibid.

163. Quoted in A. Courtney, "Washed and Brushed Up," *Banker* 146 (October 1996): 71–72, cited in R. T. Naylor, "Follow the Money Methods in Crime Control Policy," in Margaret E. Beare, ed., *Critical Reflections on Transnational Organized Crime, Money Laundering and Corruption* (Toronto: University of Toronto Press, 2003), 267.

164. For a particularly skeptical assessment, see Naylor, *Wages of Crime.* Effectiveness is notoriously difficult to measure given the difficulties of accurately estimating laundering activity.

165. The resolution also requires states to put in place antiterrorism measures related to immigration control, customs, and weapons trafficking, and calls for greater cooperation on law enforcement and extradition.

166. Mariano-Florentino Cuellar, "The Mismatch between State Power and State Capacity in Transnational Law Enforcement," *Berkeley Journal of International Law* 22, no. 15 (2004): 15–58.

167. This was even the featured theme in the 2002 James Bond movie, *Die Another Day.*

168. See Tracey Michelle Price, "The Kimberley Process: Conflict Diamonds, WTO Obligations, and the Universality Debate," *Minnesota Journal of Global Trade* 12, no. 1 (2003), 1–70.

169. Global Witness, *For a Few Dollars More: How Al Qaeda Moved into the*

Diamond Trade (London: Global Witness, 2003). See also the Web site of Global Witness: www.globalwitness.org.

170. See especially Jonathan M. Winer, "Tracking Conflict Commodities and Financing," in Karen Ballentine and Heiko Nitzschke, eds., *Profiting from Peace: Managing the Resource Dimensions of Civil War* (Boulder, CO: Lynne Rienner, 2005).

171. Kal Raustiala, "Compliance and Effectiveness in International Regulatory Cooperation," *Case Western Reserve Journal of International Law* 32, no. 3 (fall 2000): 387, 428.

172. Ibid., 430. Also see Kenneth C. Shadlen, Andrew Shrank, and Marcus J. Kurtz, "The Political Economy of Intellectual Property Protection: The Case of Software," *International Studies Quarterly* 49, no. 1 (March 2005): 45–71.

173. For a detailed recent account, see Andrew C. Mertha, *The Politics of Piracy: Intellectual Property in Contemporary China* (Ithaca, NY: Cornell University Press, 2005).

174. Mlada Bukovansky notes that there are powerful though often unstated moral connotations in the discourse surrounding an "emerging global anti-corruption regime." "Corruption Is Bad: Normative Dimensions of the Anti-Corruption Movement," Working Paper, Department of International Relations, Australian National University, Canberra, September 2002.

175. See Gemma Aiolfi and Mark Pieth, "How to Make a Convention Work: The Organization for Economic Co-Operation and Development Recommendation and Convention on Bribery as an Example of a New Horizon in International Law," in Cyrille Fijnaut and Leo Huberts, eds., *Corruption, Integrity and Law Enforcement* (The Hague: Kluwer International, 2002).

176. The twenty-nine OECD members, as well as Argentina, Brazil, Bulgaria, Chile, and the Czech Republic, signed on to the Convention, which went into force in 1999.

177. They conclude, "The OECD initiative has been one of the most important and unsung achievements of the Clinton administration foreign and trade policy." Patrick Glynn, Stephen Kobrin, and Moises Naim, "The Globalization of Corruption," in Kimberly Ann Elliott, ed., *Corruption and the Global Economy* (Washington, DC: Institute for International Economics, 1997), 20–21, 23.

178. See Ivan Krastev, *Shifting Obsessions: Three Essays on the Politics of Anticorruption* (Budapest: Central European University, 2004), 1.

179. See Hongying Wang and James N. Rosenau, "Transparency International and Corruption as an Issue of Global Governance," *Global Governance* 7, no. 1 (2001): 25–49. See also the Web site of Transparency International: www.transparency .org.

180. World Bank president James Wolfensohn opened the annual meetings of the World Bank and the IMF in 1996 by declaring the need to "deal with the

cancer of corruption." Similarly, IMF managing director Michael Camdessus issued a directive to all member states that they "must demonstrate that they have
no tolerance for corruption in any form." Quoted in Jennifer McCoy and Heather
Heckel, "The Emergence of a Global Anti-Corruption Norm," *International Politics* 38, no. 1 (March 2001): 76, 83.

181. Ibid., 83.

182. The details of the Convention are available at http://www.unodc.org/
unodc/en/crime_convention_corruption.html. As of December 2004, 110 countries had signed the Convention and fifteen had ratified it. The ratification of
thirty countries is necessary for the Convention to enter into force.

183. See Stephen Wrage and Alexandra Wrage, "Multinational Enterprises
as 'Moral Entrepreneurs' in a Global Prohibition Regime against Corruption,"
International Studies Perspectives 6, no. 3 (August 2005): 316–324.

184. John T. Noonan Jr., *Bribes* (New York: Macmillan, 1984), quoted in
Glynn, Kobrin, and Naim. "The Globalization of Corruption," 26.

185. For an insightful analysis, see Ivan Krastev, "The Strange (Re)Discovery
of Corruption," in Lord Dahrendorf et al., eds., *The Paradoxes of Unintended Consequences* (Budapest: Central European University Press, 2000).

186. Oran R. Young, "The Politics of International Regime Formation: Managing Resources and the Environment," *International Organization* 43 (summer
1989): 349–375; Stephen C. McCaffrey, "Crimes against the Environment," in
M. Cherif Bassiouni, ed., *International Criminal Law*, vol. 1 (Ardsley, NY: Transnational Publishers, 1986), 541–561.

187. Signed in 1989 and in force as of 1992, with 160 countries ratifying the
Convention.

188. Initiated in 1988 with twenty-seven signatories, and increasing to 188
signatories in 2004.

189. Jennifer Clapp, "The Illicit Trade in Hazardous Wastes and CFCs: International Responses to Environmental 'Bads,'" in Friman and Andreas, *The Illicit
Global Economy and State Power*, 101.

190. See P. N. Grabosky, "Crime in Cyberspace," in Williams and Vlassis,
Combating Transnational Crime.

191. Quoted in Preeti Vasishtha, "On the Trail of Cybersmugglers," *Government Computer News* 20, no. 9 (30 April 2001). Available at http://www.gcn.
com/vol 20_no9/news/4802-l.html.

192. "These summits generated a list of ten steps that needed to be carried
out by the participants, including modifying existing domestic regulations and
working toward international standards and cooperation." David L. Speer, "Redefining Borders: The Challenges of Cybercrime," *Crime, Law and Social Change*
34 (December 2000): 263.

193. According to a senior U.S. State Department official, the United States

played a "leading role" in the development of the Cybercrime Convention. See Testimony of Samuel M. Witten, U.S. Senate Committee on Foreign Relations, 17 June 2004, 9. For the text of the Convention, see http://conventions.coe.int/Treaty/en/Treaties/Html/185.htm.

194. Some critics are particularly concerned about the undermining of privacy protection on the Internet as governments collectively enhance their cyberspace surveillance and data interception powers. See Ryan M. F. Baron, "A Critique of the International Cybercrime Treaty," *CommLaw Conspectus: Journal of Communications Law and Policy* 10 (summer 2002): 263.

195. Marc D. Goodman and Susan W. Brenner, "The Emerging Consensus on Criminal Conduct in Cyberspace," *International Journal of Law and Technology* 10, no. 2 (2002): 139–223. Also see Ray August, "International Cyber-Jurisdiction: A Comparative Analysis," *American Business Law Journal* 39 (summer 2002): 531–573.

196. This stage of development is noted by Speer, "Redefining Borders."

197. For example, on April 22, 2004, "Operation Fastlink" involved law enforcement agencies from ten countries and the United States carrying out 120 searches across the globe to crack down on organizations involved in online piracy.

Chapter 2

1. See especially Deflem, *Policing World Society;* Hsi-Huey Liang, *The Rise of Modern Police and the European State System from Metternich to the Second World War* (Cambridge: Cambridge University Press, 1992), chap. 3.

2. On the distinction between "low" and "high" police, see J. P. Brodeur, "High Policing and Low Policing: Remarks about the Policing of Political Activities," *Social Problems* 30 (1983): 507–520.

3. See William J. Chambliss, "The Criminalization of Conduct," in H. Laurence Ross, ed., *Law and Deviance* (Beverly Hills, CA: Sage, 1981), 45–64.

4. See Bayley, *Patterns of Policing,* 189–211.

5. See, for instance, Martha Knisely Hugging, Mika Haritos-Fatouros, and Philip G. Zimbardo, *Violence Workers: Political Torturers and Murderers Reconstruct Brazilian Atrocities* (Berkeley: University of California Press, 2002).

6. See Paul Chevigny, *Cops and Rebels: A Study of Provocation* (New York: Pantheon Books, 1972), 223–276.

7. On the continued prominence of political policing during the past century as a check against communism in both democratic and authoritarian states, see Mark Mazower, ed., *The Policing of Politics in the Twentieth Century* (Providence, RI: Berghahn Books, 1997).

8. On the origins and evolution of policing, see Bayley, *Patterns of Policing,* 23–99.

9. See R. I. Mawby, "Models of Policing," in Newburn, *Handbook of Policing*; Liang, *The Rise of Modern Police*, 1–3.

10. See William G. Sinnigen, "The Roman Secret Service," *Classical Journal* 57 (November 1961): 65–72, which includes a fine discussion of the employment of plainclothes detectives, informants, undercover agents, and agents provocateurs; William G. Sinnigen, "Two Branches of the Late Roman Secret Service," *American Journal of Philology* 80 (1959): 238–254; Martin A. Kelly, "Western Civilization's First Detectives," *Police Studies* 10 (1987): 36–41. On Roman policing in the provinces, see R. W. Davies, "Police Work in Roman Times," *History Today* 18 (October 1968): 700–707. More generally, see Richard A. Bauman, *Crime and Punishment in Ancient Rome* (London: Routledge, 1996).

11. See David H. Bayley, "The Police and Political Development in Europe," in Charles Tilly, ed., *The Formation of National States in Western Europe* (Princeton, NJ: Princeton University Press, 1975).

12. Philip John Stead, *The Police of France* (New York: Macmillan, 1983), 17.

13. Alan Williams, *The Police of Paris, 1718–1789* (Baton Rouge: Louisiana State University Press, 1929), xvi.

14. Sir Leon Radzinowicz, *A History of English Criminal Law and Its Administration from 1750*, vol. 3 (London: Stevens and Sons, 1956), 470–472, 539–574.

15. Hsi-Huey Liang, "International Cooperation of Political Police in Europe, 1815–1914," *Mitteilungen des Osterreichischen Staatsarchivs* 33 (1980): 193–217.

16. Donald E. Emerson, *Metternich and the Political Police: Security and Subversion in the Hapsburg Monarchy (1815–1830)* (The Hague: Martinus Nijhoff, 1968), 52–54.

17. Clive Emsley, *Policing and Its Context: 1750–1870* (New York: Schocken Books, 1983): 101–102. For an insightful case study on informal police cooperation after 1848 with a focus on Hamburg, see Jens Jäger, "Die informelle Vernetzung politischer Polizei nach 1848" (The informal interconnectedness of political police after 1848), *Zeitschrift der Savigny-Stiftung für Rechtsgeschichte* 116 (1999): 266–313. On the Berliner Schutzmannschaft, see Wolfgang Knöbl, *Polizei und Herrschaft im Modernisierungsprozeß: Staatsbildung und innere Sicherheit in Preußen, England und Amerika 1700–1914* (Police and rule during the process of modernization: State creation and internal security in Prussia, England, and America 1700–1914) (Frankfurt: Campus, 1998), chap. 7.

18. Liang, "International Cooperation of Political Police in Europe, 1815–1914," 206.

19. Dieter Fricke, *Bismarcks Pratorianer: Die Berliner politische Polizei im Kampf gegen die deutsche Arbeiterbewegung, 1871–1898* (Bismarck's praetorians: The Berlin political police in the fight against the German worker movement, 1871–1898) (Berlin: Rutting & Loening, 1962), chap. 5. See also Werner Pöls, *Staat und Sozialdemokratie im Bismarckreich: Die Tätigkeit der politischen Polizei beim Polizei-*

präsidenten in Berlin in der Zeit des Sozialistengesetzes 1878–1890 (State and social democracy in Bismarck's Reich: Activities of the political police attached to the chief of the Berlin police headquarters in the time of the Socialist Act 1878–90) (Berlin: Walter de Gruyter, 1964), 200–221.

20. See Fricke, *Bismarcks Pratorianer*; Pöls, *Sozialdemokratie im Bismarkreich.*

21. See P. S. Squire, *The Third Department: The Establishment and Practices of the Political Police in the Russia of Nicholas I* (Cambridge, UK: Cambridge University Press, 1968); Sidney Monas, *The Third Section: Police and Society under Nicholas I* (Cambridge, MA: Harvard University Press, 1961). More generally, see Frederic S. Zuckerman, *The Tsarist Police Abroad: Policing Europe in a Modernising World* (New York: Palgrave Macmillan, 2003).

22. Squire, *The Third Department*, 207–210.

23. Ibid., 210–211.

24. James Joll, *The Anarchists* (Boston: Little, Brown, 1964), 88.

25. Squire, *The Third Department*, 212–215.

26. See Richard Jerome Johnson, *The Okhrana Abroad, 1885–1917: A Study in International Police Cooperation*, PhD diss., Columbia University, 1970; as well as the condensed version in Richard J. Johnson, "Zagranichnaia Agentura: The Tsarist Political Police in Europe," in George L. Mosse, ed., *Police Forces in History* (Beverly Hills, CA: Sage, 1975), 17–38, from which much of the following analysis is drawn. Also see Maurice LaPorte, *Histoire de L'Okhrana: La Police Secrete des Tsars, 1880–1917* (Paris: Payot, 1935), especially 187–211; for additional Russian-language references, see Edward Ellis Smith, *"The Okhrana"—The Russian Department of Police: A Bibliography* (Stanford, CA: Hoover Institution Bibliographical Series No. 33, 1967), 230–242. See also Ben B. Fischer, *Okhrana: The Paris Operations of the Russian Imperial Police* (Washington, DC: Center for the Study of Intelligence, 1997).

27. Robert C. Williams, *Culture in Exile: Russian Émigrés in Germany, 1881–1941* (Ithaca, NY: Cornell University Press, 1972), 21, 24, 45.

28. R. J. Johnson, "Zagranichnaia Agentura," 35–36.

29. See Alan Kimball, "The Harassment of Russian Revolutionaries Abroad: The London Trial of Vladimir Burtsev in 1898," *Oxford Slavonic Papers* 6 (1973): 48–65.

30. Liang, "International Cooperation of Political Police," 208.

31. Howard C. Payne, *The Police State of Louis Napoleon Bonaparte: 1851–1860* (Seattle: University of Washington Press, 1966), 155–160.

32. Howard C. Payne and Henry Grosshans, "The Exiled Revolutionaries and the French Political Police in the 1850s," *American Historical Review* 68 (1962–1963): 954–973.

33. Luc Keunings, "The Secret Police in Nineteenth-Century Brussels," *Intelligence and National Security* 4 (1989): 59–85, 71. See also Luc Keunings, "Or-

dre Public et Peur du Rouge au XIXeme Siècle: La Police, les Socialistes et les Anarchistes à Bruxelles (1886–1914)" (Public order and fear of the Reds in the nineteenth century: Police, socialists, and anarchists in Brussels, 1886–1914), *Belgisch Tijdschrift voor Nieuwste Geschiedenis* [Belgium] 25, nos. 3–4 (1994–1995): 329–396.

34. Payne, *The Police State of Louis Napoleon Bonaparte*, 158–159.

35. Keunings, "The Secret Police in Nineteenth-Century Brussels," 72.

36. Ibid.

37. Liang, "International Cooperation of Political Police," 209. On the history of policing in Britain, see Philip Rawlings, *Policing: A Short History* (Devon, UK: Willan Publishing, 2001); Clive Emsley, "The Birth and Development of the Police," in Newburn, *Handbook of Policing*.

38. Robert J. Goldstein, *Political Repression in 19th Century Europe* (Totowa, NJ: Barnes & Noble Books, 1983), 141.

39. See Ann G. Imlah, *Britain and Switzerland, 1845–1860* (London: Longmans, 1966), 40–88; Payne, *The Police State of Louis Napoleon Bonaparte*, 48, 156–158.

40. Fricke, *Bismarcks Pratorianer*, chap. 5.

41. Goldstein, *Political Repression in 19th Century Europe*, 265.

42. The following paragraphs draw heavily from the works of a British historian, Bernard Porter. See in particular *The Refugee Question in Mid-Victorian Politics* (New York: Cambridge University Press, 1979); *The Origins of the Vigilant State* (London: Weidenfeld & Nicolson, 1987); *Plots and Paranoia: A History of Political Espionage in Britain, 1790–1988* (London: Unwin Hyman, 1989).

43. The incident, and its broader political implications, are described in Harry William Rudman, *Italian Nationalism and English Letters* (New York: Columbia University Press, 1940), 58–79; and in F. B. Smith, "British Post Office Espionage, 1844," *Historical Studies* 14 (1970): 189–203.

44. James Walker, "The Secret Service under Charles II and James II," *Transactions of the Royal Historical Society*, 4th ser., 15 (1932): 211–235.

45. F. B. Smith, "British Post Office Espionage, 1844," 195.

46. Ibid., 160–162.

47. See Michael St. John Packe, *Orsini: The Story of a Conspirator* (Boston: Little, Brown, 1957).

48. See H. Hearder, "Napoleon III's Threat to Break Off Diplomatic Relations with England during the Crisis over the Orsini Attempt in 1858," *English Historical Review* 72 (1957): 474–481; Porter, *The Refugee Question in Mid-Victorian Politics*, especially chap. 6.

49. K. R. M. Short, *The Dynamite War: Irish-American Bombers in Victorian Britain* (Atlantic Highlands, NJ: Humanities Press, 1979), 17.

50. See Leon O'Broin, *Fenian Fever: An Anglo-American Dilemma* (London: Chatto & Windus, 1971); Porter, *Origins of the Vigilant State*, 26–51, 87–91.

51. Short, *The Dynamite War*, 179, 189, 191.

52. Rupert Allason, *The Branch: A History of the Metropolitan Police Special Branch 1883–1983* (London: Secker & Warburg, 1983), 8–9.

53. Short, *The Dynamite War*, 213.

54. Porter, *Origins of the Vigilant State*, 84–86.

55. See Bernard Porter, "The *Freiheit* Prosecutions, 1881–1882," *Historical Journal* 23 (1980): 833–856. See also A. D. Harvey, "Research Note: Johann Most in Prison—Three Unpublished Petitions," *Terrorism and Political Violence* 5, no. 4 (winter 1993): 336–345.

56. Porter, *Origins of the Vigilant State*, 41. Also see Rudolf Rocker, *Johann Most, das Leben eines Rebellen* (Johann Most, The Life of a Rebel) (Berlin: Verlag Syndikalist, F. Kater, 1924).

57. See Kimball, "The Harassment of Russian Revolutionaries Abroad."

58. Porter, *Plots and Paranoia*, 115–119.

59. Porter, *Origins of the Vigilant State*, 154, 181.

60. Ibid., 149–187.

61. The following section is substantially based on Richard Popplewell, "The Surveillance of Indian Revolutionaries in Great Britain and on the Continent, 1905–1914," *Intelligence and National Security* 3, no. 1 (1988): 56–76.

62. Porter, *Origins of the Vigilant State*, 164.

63. Ibid., 69, italics in original.

64. Ibid., 70.

65. The following discussion is based almost entirely on Richard Popplewell, "The Surveillance of Indian 'Seditionists' in North America, 1909–1915," in Christopher Andrew and Jeremy Noakes, eds., *Intelligence and International Relations: 1900–1945* (Exeter, UK: University of Exeter, Exeter Studies in History No. 15, 1987), 49–76.

66. The Ghadr Party is discussed in Emily C. Brown, *Har Dayal: Hindu Revolutionary and Rationalist* (Tucson: University of Arizona Press, 1975).

67. See ibid., 152–166.

68. See Samuel Edwards, *The Vidocq Dossier: The Story of the World's First Detective* (Boston: Houghton Mifflin, 1977), 32–96. See also James Morton, *The First Detective: The Life And Revolutionary Times of Eugene-François Vidocq, Criminal, Spy and Private Eye* (London: Ebury Press, 2005).

69. Jürgen Thorwald, *The Century of the Detective* (in German), trans. Richard Winston and Clara Winston (New York: Harcourt, Brace and World, 1965), 36–37; and see Gerald Howson, *Thief-Taker General* (London: Hutchison, 1970); Carl B. Klockers, "Jonathan Wild and the Modern Sting," in James A. Inciardi and Charles E. Faupel, eds., *History and Crime: Implications for Criminal Justice Policy* (Beverly Hills, CA: Sage, 1980), 225–260.

70. Radzinowicz, *A History of English Criminal Law*, 3: 54–58.

71. Ibid., 3: 38.

72. See Belton Cobb, *The First Detectives* (London: Faber and Faber, 1957). Also see Wilbur R. Miller, *Cops and Bobbies: Police Authority in New York and London, 1830–1870* (Chicago: University of Chicago Press, 1973), 34–35.

73. Thorwald, *The Century of the Detective*, 39.

74. See, for instance, Alan F. Hattersley, *The First South African Detectives* (Cape Town, South Africa: Howard Timmins, 1960).

75. Caroline Muir, "Glasgow: The Early Force," *Police Journal* 58 (January 1985): 65.

76. Nigel Cochrane, "The Coming of the 'G' Men: The Birth of the Public Detective Division, 1838–45," *Police Journal* 61 (January 1988): 47.

77. Thorwald, *The Century of the Detective*, 40–41.

78. See the account of the entire episode by one of the counterfeiters, George Bidwell, *Forging His Chains: The Autobiography of George Bidwell* (New York: Bidwell Publishing, 1889), 255–261.

79. Ibid., 250–255. Also see Richard Wilmer Rowan, *The Pinkertons: A Detective Dynasty* (Boston: Little, Brown, 1931), 277–289.

80. See Sir Basil Thompson, *The Story of Scotland Yard* (New York: Literary Guild, 1936), 174–178. Also see John Littlechild, *The Reminiscences of Chief-Inspector Littlechild*, 2nd ed. (London: Leadenhall Press, 1894), which contains numerous accounts of Scotland Yard's international interactions during the 1870s and 1880s.

81. Michael Fooner, *INTERPOL: The Inside Story of the International Crime-Fighting Organization* (Chicago: Henry Regnery, 1973), 10.

82. Michael Fooner, *INTERPOL: Issues in World Crime and International Criminal Justice* (New York: Plenum Press, 1989), 27.

83. I. A. Shearer, *Extradition in International Law* (Dobbs Ferry, NY: Oceana Publications, 1971), 7–10.

84. Ibid., 11–19.

85. Marc Ancel, "Some Reflections on the Value and Scope of Studies in Comparative Criminal Law," in Edward M. Wise and Gerhard O. W. Mueller, eds., *Studies in Comparative Criminal Law* (Springfield, IL: Charles C. Thomas, 1975), 3–10.

86. See generally Hermann Mannheim, ed., *Pioneers in Criminology* (Chicago: Quadrangle Books, 1960).

87. See Ancel, "Some Reflections on the Value and Scope of Studies in Comparative Criminal Law," 7; J. M. van Bemmelen, "William Adriaan Bonger," in Mannheim, *Pioneers in Criminology*, 354; M. Cherif Bassiouni, "A Century of Dedication to Criminal Justice and Human Rights: The International Association of Penal Law and the Institute of Higher Studies in Criminal Sciences," *De Paul Law Review* 38 (1989): 899–922.

88. Ancel, "Some Reflections on the Value and Scope of Studies in Comparative Criminal Law," 7–8.

89. Woodford McClellan, *Revolutionary Exiles: The Russians in the First International and the Paris Commune* (London: Frank Cass, 1979), 74–75, 136, 195–196.

90. Ralph Turner, "Hans Gross: The Model of the Detective," in Philip John Stead, ed., *Pioneers in Policing* (Montclair, NJ: Patterson Smith, 1977), 148–157.

91. See Samuel Henry Jeyes and Frederick Douglas How, *The Life of Sir Howard Vincent* (London: George Allen, 1912), 53–57.

92. See Elise K. Tipton, *The Japanese Police State: The Tokko in Interwar Japan* (Honolulu: University of Hawaii Press, 1990), 37–41; D. Eleanor Westney, "The Emulation of Western Organizations in Meiji Japan: The Case of the Paris Prefecture of Police and the Keishicho," *Journal of Japanese Studies* 8, no. 2 (1982): 307–342.

93. Thorwald, *The Century of the Detective*, 48; Henri Souchon, "Alphonse Bertillon: Criminalistics," in Stead, *Pioneers in Policing*, 121–147; Ilsen About, "Les Fondations d'un Système National d'Identification Policière en France 1893–1914: Anthropométrie, Signalements et Fichiers" (The foundations of the national system of police identification in France, 1893–1914: Anthropometry, descriptions, and files), *Genèses: Sciences Sociales et Histoire* (France) 54 (March 2004): 28–52. The anthropometric method of criminal investigation applied the systematic study of bodily measurements to police management of identification files.

94. See John Cronin, "The Fingerprinters: Identification as the Basic Police Science," in Stead, *Pioneers in Policing*, 159–177. More generally, see Simon A. Cole, *Suspect Identities: A History of Fingerprinting and Criminal Investigation* (Cambridge, MA: Harvard University Press, 2001).

95. Keunings, "The Secret Police in Nineteenth-Century Brussels," 74.

96. Liang, "International Cooperation of Political Police in Europe, 1815–1914," 199.

97. Ibid., 202.

98. See Richard Bach Jensen, "Daggers, Rifles, and Dynamite: Anarchist Terrorism in Nineteenth Century Europe," *Terrorism and Political Violence* 16, no. 1 (2004): 116–153.

99. Liang, "International Cooperation of Political Police in Europe, 1815–1914," 206; Porter, *Origins of the Vigilant State*, 40.

100. The discussion in this and the next two paragraphs is drawn largely from Richard Bach Jensen, "The International Anti-Anarchist Conference of 1898 and the Origins of Interpol," *Journal of Contemporary History* 16, no. 2 (April 1981): 323–347.

101. Ibid., 325–326.

102. Liang, "International Cooperation of Political Police in Europe, 1815–1914," 207.

103. Cited in Jensen, "The International Anti-Anarchist Conference of 1898 and the Origins of Interpol," 336.

104. Richard Bach Jensen has argued that an underlying reason for the U.S. reluctance to become involved in European antianarchist efforts during this period was its anemic national policing capacity. "The United States, International Policing and the War against Anarchist Terrorism, 1900–1914," *Terrorism and Political Violence* 13, no. 1 (spring 2001): 26.

105. Jensen, "The International Anti-Anarchist Conference of 1898 and the Origins of Interpol," 36.

106. Bristow, *Vice and Vigilance*, 171–172.

107. Paul Marabuto, *La Collaboration Policière Internationale* (Nice: Ecole Professionelle Don-Bosco, 1935), 134–135; Jensen, "The International Anti-Anarchist Conference," 346. See also Jens Jäger, "International Police Co-operation and the Associations for the Fight against White Slavery," *Paedagogica Historica* (Belgium) 38, nos. 2–3 (2002): 565–579.

108. Leonard S. Woolf, *International Government* (New York: Brentano's, 1916), 263.

109. The conclusions of the 1905 meeting of the International Criminological Association in Hamburg and the 1912 German police conference, both of which took up issues of international law enforcement, are reported in Friedrich Johannes Palitzsch, *Die Bekämpfung des internationalen Verbrechertums* [*The Combat against International Criminality*] (Hamburg: Meissner, 1926).

110. See Martha K. Huggins, "U.S.-Supported State Terror: A History of Police Training in Latin America," *Crime and Social Justice* 27–28 (1987): 149–171.

111. Raymond P. Fosdick, *European Police Systems* (New York: Century, 1915), 333–334.

112. Ibid., 334–335.

113. F. Larnaude and J.-A. Roux, *Premier Congres de Police Judiciaire Internationale (Monaco, Avril 1914)*: *Actes du Congres* (Paris: G. Godde, 1926).

114. Jean Nepote, "Interpol: The Development of International Policing," in Stead, *Pioneers in Policing*, 280–296.

115. Thorwald, *The Century of the Detective*, 89–90.

116. Anderson, *Policing the World*, 39.

117. See Nepote, "Interpol," 283–284.

118. See Frans Geysels, "Europe from the Inside," *Policing* 6 (1990): 338–354.

119. Ibid.

120. Anderson, *Policing the World*, 40.

121. See Vespasian V. Pella, "La Cooperation des Etats dans la Lutte Contre le Faux Monnayage." [Cooperation of States in the Struggle against Fake Currency] *Revue Générale de Droit International Public* 1, no. 34 (1927): 673–763.

122. Minutes of the International Police Congress, Vienna, 3–7 September

1923, extracted and translated into English in League of Nations, Financial Committee, Counterfeiting Currency, Doc. F, 296—Annex I, 2–3.

123. The case is briefly discussed in Arthur Nussbaum, *Money in the Law: National and International* (Brooklyn, NY: Foundation Press, 1950), 35–36.

124. See Ernestine Fitz-Maurice, "Convention for the Suppression of Counterfeiting Currency," *American Journal of International Law* 26 no. 3 (July 1932): 533–551.

125. Ibid., 534–535.

126. See ibid, 535–538, which contains a fine discussion of the negotiations.

127. The name Interpol came into common usage following the Second World War, when the organization's cable address was popularized in press conferences by the ICPC secretary-general. See Fooner, *INTERPOL: The Inside Story*, 27. The formal name of the organization was changed to the International Criminal Police Organization—Interpol in 1956.

128. On the origins of Interpol, see Anderson, *Policing the World*, 38–42; Deflem, *Policing World Society*, chap. 5. On Nazi control of the ICPC, see Mathieu Deflem, "The Logic of Nazification: The Case of the International Criminal Police Commission ('Interpol')," *International Journal of Comparative Sociology* 43, no. 1 (2002): 21–44. This is also discussed in Cyrille Fijnaut, "The International Criminal Police Commission and the Fight against Communism, 1923–1945," in Mazower, *The Policing of Politics in the Twentieth Century*, 114–123.

129. Harry Soderman, *Policeman's Lot* (New York: Funk & Wagnalls, 1956), 374–375.

130. Jean Belin, *My Work at the Sûreté*, trans. Eric Whelpton (London: George G. Harrap, 1950), 167.

131. Ernest K. Bramstedt, *Dictatorship and Political Police* (London: Kegan Paul, Trench, Trubner, 1945), 59–61. Also see Italo Giovanni Savella, *Mussolini's "Fouché": Arturo Bochini, the Fascist OVRA, and the Italian Police Tradition*, PhD diss., Rochester, NY: University of Rochester, 1996.

132. Huggins, "U.S.-Supported State Terror."

133. See Lennard D. Gerson, *The Secret Police in Lenin's Russia* (Philadelphia: Temple University Press, 1976), 231–237; George Leggett, *The Cheka: Lenin's Political Police* (Oxford: Clarendon Press, 1981). See also Louise I. Shelley, *Policing Soviet Society: The Evolution of State Control* (London: Routledge, 1996).

134. Belin, *My Work at the Sûreté*, 161.

135. See Vladeta Milićević, *A King Dies in Marseilles: The Crime and Its Background* (Bad Godesberg, Germany: Hohwacht, 1959), 78; Belin, *My Work at the Sureté*, 155–166.

136. Milićević, *A King Dies in Marseilles*, 12–16.

137. See Ved P. Nanda and M. Cherif Bassiouni, "The Crimes of Slavery and Slave Trade," in M. Cherif Bassiouni, ed., *International Criminal Law: Volume I. Crimes* (Ardsley, UK: Transnational Publishers, 1998), 325–342.

138. Hans-Heinrich Jescheck, "Development and Future Prospects," in Bassiouni, *International Criminal Law*, 83–107.

139. Cited in George E. Berkley, *The Democratic Policeman* (Boston: Beacon Press, 1969), 13.

140. Trevor Meldal-Johnsen and Vaughn Young, *The Interpol Connection: An Inquiry into the International Criminal Police Organization* (New York: Dial Press, 1979), 49–50.

141. Ibid., 55–73.

142. Ibid., 59.

143. See Cyrille Fijnaut, "Europeanisation or Americanisation of the Police in Europe?," in Netherlands Police Academy, ed., *Proceedings of the Second European Police Summer-Course* (Warnsveld, The Netherlands: Netherlands Police Academy, 1990), 20–21. On the Gestapo in general, see Frank Gutermuth and Arno Netzbandt, *Die Gestapo* (Berlin: Nicolaische Verlagsbuchhandlung, 2005).

144. See the far more thorough discussion in Anderson, *Policing the World*, 74–104.

145. See David P. Stewart, "Internationalizing the War on Drugs: The UN Convention against Illicit Traffic in Narcotic Drugs and Psychotropic Substances," *Denver Journal of International Law and Policy* 18 (1990): 387–404. For a more general overview, see McAllister, *Drug Diplomacy in the Twentieth Century*.

146. Ekkehart Müller-Rappard, "The European System," in M. Cherif Bassiouni, ed., *International Criminal Law, Volume II: Procedure* (Ardsley, UK: Transnational Publishers, 1998), 95–115. Also see Cyrille Fijnaut, "Transnational Organized Crime and Institutional Reform in the European Union: The Case of Judicial Cooperation," *Transnational Organized Crime* 4, nos. 3–4 (fall 1998): 281–282.

147. See the collection of essays and documents in Bassiouni, *International Criminal Law, Volume II: Procedure*.

148. A history of the BKA is provided by Wilhelm Dietl, *Die BKA-Story* (Munich: Droemer Knaur, 2000). For a critical assessment of German policing, see Norbert Pütter, *Der OK-Komplex: Organisierte Kriminalität und ihre Folgen für die Polizei in Deutschland* (The organized crime complex: Organized crime and its consequences for police in Germany) (Münster, Germany: Westfälisches Dampfboot, 1998).

149. K. Peterson, "International Police Cooperation in Scandinavia and in the EEC Countries," in *Report of the European Police Summer Course 1989* (Apeldoorn, The Netherlands: Netherlands Police Academy and Policy Study Centre, 1989), 21–32.

150. See Serge Brammertz, *Grenzüberschreitende polizeiliche Zusammenarbeit am Beispiel der Euregio Maas-Rhein* (Police cooperation across borders: The example of the Euregio Maas-Rhine) (Freiburg, Germany: Max-Planck-Institut für ausländisches und internationales Strafrecht, 1999).

151. Cyrille Fijnaut, "The Internationalization of Criminal Investigation in Western Europe," in Cyrille Fijnaut and R. H. Hermans, eds., *Police Cooperation in Europe* (Lochem, The Netherlands: Van den Brink, 1987), 40.

152. James Sheptycki, "Police Cooperation in the English Channel Region, 1968–1996," *European Journal of Crime, Criminal Law and Criminal Justice* 6, no. 3 (1998): 216–235.

153. Roger Birch, "Policing Europe in 1992," *Police Journal* 62 (July 1989): 203–210.

154. Paul Wilkinson, "European Police Cooperation," in John Roach and Jürgen Thomaneck, eds., *Police and Public Order in Europe* (Dover, UK: Croom Helm, 1985), 273–286.

155. Customs cooperation within the European Community was already highly advanced—indeed, outpacing cooperation in other realms of border management and involving the earliest adoption of shared computer databases. Peter Hobbing suggests that joint training and regular interaction at all levels helped to create an "EC-wide customs identity." "Management of External EU Borders: Enlargement and the European Border Guard Issue," paper presented at the Geneva Centre for the Democratic Control of Armed Forces, Geneva, Switzerland, March 2003, 9.

156. The following discussion is drawn from Fijnaut, "The Internationalization of Criminal Investigation in Western Europe," 37–42.

157. See Anderson, *Policing the World*, 127–147.

158. Italian terrorism is analyzed at greater length in Leonard Weinberg and William Lee Eubank, *The Rise and Fall of Italian Terrorism* (Boulder, CO.: Westview Press, 1987). German terrorism is discussed in Stefan Aust, *Der Baader Meinhof Komplex* (Munich: Goldmann, 1998); Klaus Pflieger, *Die Rote Armee Fraktion (RAF)* (Baden-Baden, Germany: Nomos, 2004).

159. See Ekkehart Müller-Rappard, "The European Response to International Terrorism," in M. Cherif Bassiouni, ed., *Legal Responses to International Terrorism: U.S. Procedural Aspects* (Boston: Martinus Nijhoff, 1988), 385–417.

160. On the obstacles to cooperation against terrorism in Europe, see Malcolm Anderson, "Counterterrorism as an Objective of European Police Cooperation," in Fernando Reinares, ed., *European Democracies against Terrorism: Governmental Policies and Intergovernmental Cooperation* (Aldershot, UK: Ashgate Publishing, 2000).

161. Fijnaut, "The Internationalization of Criminal Investigation in Western Europe," 40–42.

162. Peter J. Katzenstein, *A World of Regions: Asia and Europe in the American Imperium* (Ithaca, NY: Cornell University Press, 2005), 134–135.

163. Fijnaut, "The Internationalization of Criminal Investigation in Western Europe," 41.

164. On the importance of drug control in the TREVI agenda in the second

half of the 1980s, see Martin Elvins, *Anti-Drug Policies of the European Union* (Basingstoke, UK: Palgrave, 2003), 86.

165. Geysels, "Europe from the Inside," 348–351. The emergence and evolution of immigration control concerns on the European policy agenda is discussed in Ferrucio Pastore, "Visas, Borders, Immigration: Formation, Structure, and Current Evolution of the EU Entry Control System," in Neil Walker, ed., *Europe's Area of Freedom, Security and Justice* (Oxford: Oxford University Press, 2004).

166. Penelope Turnbull and Wayne Sandholtz, "Policing and Immigration: The Creation of New Policy Spaces," in Alec Stone Sweet, Wayne Sandholtz, and Neil Fligstein, eds., *The Institutionalization of Europe* (Oxford: Oxford University Press, 2001), 196.

167. See Ethan A. Nadelmann, "Unlaundering Dirty Money Abroad: U.S. Foreign Policy and Financial Secrecy Jurisdictions," *Inter-American Law Review* 18, no. 1 (fall 1986): 33–82.

168. Bruce Zagaris and Markus Bornheim, "International Cooperation against Money Laundering in the European Integration Context," *International Enforcement Law Reporter* 5 (December 1989): 441–448.

169. On the origins and evolution of Schengen, see Malcolm Anderson, "Genesis of Schengen, Historic Approach to the Initial Objectives and the Results Achieved," paper presented at the seminar "Schengen Re-visited," Présidence luxembourgeoise du Conseil de l'Union européenne, Luxembourg, 9–11 March 2005.

170. This would become a mounting concern in later years. See especially the Web site of Statewatch: www.statewatch.org.

171. Anderson et al., *Policing the European Union*, 58.

Chapter 3

1. See Raymond B. Fosdick, *American Police Systems* (New York: Century, 1921), for a discussion of the sorry state of American law enforcement in the early part of the century.

2. See Peter Andreas, *Border Games: Policing the U.S.-Mexico Divide* (Ithaca, NY: Cornell University Press, 2000); Peter Andreas and Thomas J. Biersteker, eds., *The Rebordering of North America: Integration and Exclusion in a New Security Context* (New York: Routledge, 2003).

3. See W. E. F. Ward, *The Royal Navy and the Slavers*, 149–161; Lloyd, *The Navy and the Slave Trade*, 176–183.

4. See Paul Finkelman, ed., *The African Slave Trade and American Courts* (New York: Garland, 1988).

5. "Dispatches of Spanish Officials Bearing on the Free Negro Settlement of Gracia Real De Santa Teresa de Mose, Florida," *Journal of Negro History* 9 (1924): 145.

6. Roman J. Zorn, "Criminal Extradition Menaces the Canadian Haven for Fugitive Slaves, 1841–1861," *Canadian Historical Review* 38 (1957): 285.

7. Arnett G. Lindsay, "Diplomatic Relations between the United States and Great Britain Bearing on the Return of Negro Slaves, 1783–1828," *Journal of Negro History* 5 (October 1920): 391–419; "Interesting Notes on Great Britain and Canada with Respect to the Negro," *Journal of Negro History* 13 (1928): 185–192.

8. See William Renwick Riddell, "The Slave in Canada," *Journal of Negro History* 5 (1920): 342–343; "Documents," *Journal of Negro History* 15 (1930): 115–116; Jason H. Silverman, *Unwelcome Guests* (Millwood, NY: Associated Family Press, 1985), 36.

9. See John Bassett Moore, *Treatise on Extradition* (1891; reprint, Buffalo, NY: William S. Hein, 1996), 95–97.

10. See Lester G. Bugbee, "Slavery in Early Texas," *Political Science Quarterly* 13, no. 3 (1898).

11. William H. Theobald, *Defrauding the Government* (New York: Myrtle, 1908), 353.

12. Garland Roark, *The Coin of Contraband* (Garden City, NY: Doubleday, 1964).

13. According to one account, "In 1879 the special agents force struggled to establish the true market value of fine kid gloves from France and proved that velvets imported from Germany were being systematically undervalued." Miriam Ottenberg, *The Federal Investigators* (Englewood Cliffs, NJ: Prentice-Hall, 1962), 291.

14. Chester A. Millspaugh, *Crime Control by the National Government* (Washington, DC: Brookings, 1938), 68.

15. See Carl E. Prince and Mollie Keller, *The U.S. Customs Service: A Bicentennial History* (Washington, DC: Government Printing Office, 1989), 171–194.

16. See J. Evetts Haley, *Jeff Milton: A Good Man with a Gun* (Norman: University of Oklahoma Press, 1948), 340–355.

17. Andreas, *Border Games*, 33. Also see the celebratory account by Mary Kidder Rak, *Border Patrol* (Boston: Houghton Mifflin, 1938).

18. See Elinore Denniston, *America's Silent Investigators* (New York: Dodd, Mead, 1964), 19–76.

19. Larry D. Ball, *The United States Marshals of New Mexico and Arizona Territories, 1846–1912* (Albuquerque: University of New Mexico Press, 1978), 4. Also see Rita W. Cooley, "The Office of United States Marshal," *Western Political Quarterly* 12, no. 1 (March 1959): 123–140.

20. See Michael Dorman, *The Secret Service Story* (New York: Delacorte Press, 1967), 4–7; David R. Johnson, *Illegal Tender: Counterfeiting and the Secret Service in Nineteenth-Century America* (Washington, DC: Smithsonian Books, 1995).

21. Thomas A. Reppetto, *The Blue Parade* (New York: Free Press, 1978), 31.

22. Don Wilkie, as told to Mark Lee Luther, *American Secret Service Agent* (New York: Frederick A. Stokes, 1934), 16–25.

23. Homer Cummings and Carl McFarland, *Federal Justice: Chapters in the History of Justice and the Federal Executive* (New York: Macmillan, 1937), 375–378.

24. On the origins of the FBI, see ibid., 375–380; Harry Allen Overstreet and Bonaro Overstreet, *The FBI in Our Open Society* (New York: Norton, 1969), chap. 2; Millspaugh, *Crime Control by the National Government*, 73–78; Athan Theoharis, *The FBI and American Democracy: A Brief Critical History* (Lawrence: University Press of Kansas, 2004).

25. Overstreet and Overstreet, 381.

26. See James Mackay, *Allan Pinkerton: The First Private Eye* (Hoboken, NJ: Wiley, 1997).

27. James D. Horan, "The Pinkerton Detective Agency," introductory essay in Allan Pinkerton, *Thirty Years a Detective* (1884; reprint, Montclair, NJ: Patterson Smith Publishing, 1975), vi.

28. See Frank Morn, *"The Eye That Never Sleeps": A History of the Pinkerton National Detective Agency* (Bloomington: Indiana University Press, 1982), 110–127. By the end of the twentieth century, the Pinkerton Corporation would have forty-seven thousand employees in more than 250 offices in North America, Latin America, Europe, and Asia. See Les Johnston, "Transnational Private Policing: The Impact of Global Commercial Security," in Sheptycki, *Issues in Transnational Policing*, 28.

29. Rowan, *The Pinkertons*, 281–289. The story is told from the perspective of one of the fugitives in George Bidwell, *Bidwell's Travels from Wall Street to London Prison* (Hartford, CT.: Bidwell Publishing, 1897).

30. Horan, "The Pinkerton Detective Agency," xviii.

31. Thorwald, *The Century of the Detective*, 91.

32. Louis R. Sadler, "The Historical Dynamics of Smuggling in the U.S.-Mexican Border Region, 1550–1998: Reflections on Markets, Cultures and Bureaucracies," in John Bailey and Roy Godson, eds., *Organized Crime and Democratic Governability: Mexico and the U.S.-Mexican Borderlands* (Pittsburgh, PA: University of Pittsburgh Press, 2000).

33. Robert D. Gregg, *The Influence of Border Troubles on Relations between the United States and Mexico: 1876–1910* (Baltimore, MD: Johns Hopkins University Press, 1937), 12–13.

34. Walter Prescott Webb, *The Texas Rangers: A Century of Frontier Defense* (Austin: University of Texas Press, 1935), 305–342. Also see Charles M. Robinson III, *The Men Who Wear the Star: The Story of the Texas Rangers* (New York: Random House, 2000); Robert M. Utley, *Lone Star Justice: The First Century of the Texas Rangers* (Oxford: Oxford University Press, 2002).

35. L. D. Ball, *The United States Marshals of New Mexico and Arizona Territories, 1846–1912*, 112–114.

36. Don M. Coerver and Linda B. Hall, *Texas and the Mexican Revolution: A Study in State and National Border Policy, 1910–1920* (San Antonio, TX: Trinity University Press, 1984), 24–27; Linda B. Hall and Don M. Coerver, *Revolution on the Border: The United States and Mexico, 1910–1920* (Albuquerque: University of New Mexico Press, 1988), 32–33.

37. See Frank E. Vandiver, *Black Jack: The Life and Times of John J. Pershing*, vol. 2 (College Station: Texas A&M University Press, 1977), 595–668; Clarence C. Clendenen, *Blood on the Border: The U.S. Army and the Mexican Irregulars* (New York: Macmillan, 1969), 248–284. For Mexican views during this period, see Joseph Stout Jr., *Border Conflict: Villistas, Carrancistas and the Punitive Expedition, 1915–1920* (Fort Worth: Texas Christian University Press, 1999). For an account of Villa's activities, see Friedrich Katz, *The Life and Times of Pancho Villa* (Stanford, CA: Stanford University Press, 1998).

38. Charles H. Harris III and Louis R. Sadler, "United States Government Archives and the Mexican Revolution," *New World: A Journal of Latin American Studies* 1 (1986): 108–116, reprinted in Charles H. Harris and Louis Sadler, *The Border and the Revolution: Clandestine Activities of the Mexican Revolution, 1910–1920* (Albuquerque: University of New Mexico Press, 2004), 133–141.

39. See, generally, Mark T. Gilderhus, *Diplomacy and Revolution: U.S.-Mexican Relations under Wilson and Carranza* (Tucson: University of Arizona Press, 1977).

40. Charles H. Harris III and Louis R. Sadler, "The 'Underside' of the Mexican Revolution: El Paso, 1912," *The Americas: A Quarterly Review of Inter-American Cultural History* 39 (July 1982): 69–83, reprinted in Harris and Sadler, *The Border and the Revolution*, 53–70.

41. Dorothy Pierson Kerig, *Luther T. Ellsworth, U.S. Consul on the Border During the Mexican Revolution* (El Paso: University of Texas at El Paso Press, 1975), 50.

42. Gerald Astor, *The New York Cops: An Informal History* (New York: Charles Scribner's Sons, 1971), 14.

43. Ibid., 65.

44. Thorwald, *Century of the Detective*, 95–98.

45. See Thomas Byrnes, *Rogue's Gallery* (1887; reprint, Secaucus, NJ: Castle, 1988).

46. See Reppetto, *The Blue Parade*; Gene E. Carte and Elaine H. Carte, *Police Reform in the United States: The Era of August Vollmer* (Berkeley: University of California Press, 1977).

47. Thorwald, *Century of the Detective*, 93.

48. International Association of Chiefs of Police, *Proceedings: 27th Convention*, Detroit, June 1920, 83.

49. Cole, *Suspect Identities*.

50. Morn, *"The Eye That Never Sleeps,"* 126.

51. International Association of Chiefs of Police, *Twelfth Annual Session*, Washington, DC, May 1905.

52. Ibid., 68–70.

53. Thorwald, *Century of the Detective*, 98–99.

54. International Association of Chiefs of Police, *Twelfth Annual Session*, 16–17.

55. Millspaugh, *Crime Control by the National Government*, 79–80.

56. Musto, *American Disease*, 211.

57. The Foreign Control Division is discussed briefly in Laurence F. Schmeckebier, *The Bureau of Prohibition: Its History, Activities and Organization* (Washington, DC: Brookings, 1929), 26–27, 156.

58. Douglas Clark Kinder, "Bureaucratic Cold Warrior: Harry J. Anslinger and Illicit Narcotics Traffic," *Pacific Historical Review* 50, no. 2 (May 1981): 172–173.

59. Bewley-Taylor, *The United States and International Drug Control, 1909–1997*, chaps. 3–4.

60. See Gernot Stenger, "The Development of American Export Control Legislation after World War II," *Wisconsin International Law Journal* 6, no. 1 (1987): 1–42.

61. Naylor, "Follow-the-Money Methods in Crime Control Policy."

62. For a fine historical overview, see Lawrence Freedman, *Crime and Punishment in American History* (New York: Basic Books, 1994).

63. See Bureau of Prisons, Dept. of Justice, *Proceedings of the Attorney General's Conference on Crime Held December 10–13, 1934 in Memorial Continental Hall, Washington, D.C.* (Washington, 1936); and the articles collected under the title "Extending Federal Powers over Crime," in *Law and Contemporary Problems* 1, no. 4 (October 1934): 399–508.

64. See Craig M. Bradley, "Racketeering and the Federalization of Crime," *American Criminal Law Review* 22 (1984): 213–266.

65. Epstein, *Agency of Fear.*

66. U.S. efforts to eliminate the government opium monopolies in Asia are discussed in Alfred R. Lindesmith, *The Addict and the Law* (Bloomington: Indiana University Press, 1965), 199–221.

67. Federal Bureau of Narcotics, U.S. Treasury Dept., *Traffic in Opium and Other Dangerous Drugs for the Year Ended December 31, 1945* (Washington, DC: Government Printing Office, 1946), 4.

68. The overseas exploits of the FBN agents are recounted in the autobiographies of two FBN agents: Charles Siragusa, as told to Robert Wiedrich, *The Trail of the Poppy* (Englewood Cliffs, NJ: Prentice-Hall, 1966); Sal Vizzini, with Oscar Fraley and Marshall Smith, *Vizzini: The Secret Lives of America's Most Successful Undercover Agent* (New York: Arbor House, 1972).

69. In 1954, the assistant secretary of the treasury in charge of enforcement

wrote that "to obtain and assure access to information from European police officials and an extra degree of collaboration and assistance by them to American Treasury agents carrying on Treasury business in Europe, it has been considered advisable to make certain payments to INTERPOL at a stipulated rate." Meldal-Johnsen and Young, *The Interpol Connection*, 100.

70. Quoted in ibid., 101–102.

71. The reshuffling of agencies during this period is discussed in David F. Musto and Pamela Korsmeyer, *The Quest for Drug Control: Politics and Federal Policy in a Period of Increasing Substance Abuse, 1963–1981* (New Haven, CT: Yale University Press, 2002).

72. For the number of agents for each year and the DEA's budget, see the DEA Web site: http://www.usdoj.gov/dea/agency/staffing.htm.

73. See Kenneth M. Murchison, "Prohibition and the Fourth Amendment: A New Look at Some Old Cases," *Journal of Criminal Law and Criminology* 73 (summer 1982): 471–532.

74. Jurg Gerber and Eric L. Jensen, eds., *Drug War American Style: The Internationalization of Failed Policy and Its Alternatives* (New York: Garland, 2001).

75. The FBI's activities in Latin America are discussed in Stanley E. Hilton, *Hitler's Secret War in South America, 1939–1945* (Baton Rouge: Louisiana State University Press, 1981), 196–229; Leslie B. Rout Jr. and John F. Bratzel, *The Shadow War: German Espionage and American Counterespionage in Latin America During World War II* (Frederick, MD: University Publications, 1986). A brief history of the FBI's role during this period can also be found on the FBI Web site: http://www.fbi.gov/libref/historic/history/worldwar.htm.

76. The Comprehensive Crime Control Act of 1984 included a new law that implements the International Convention Against the Taking of Hostages. The statute provides for U.S. federal jurisdiction over any hostage taking overseas in which the victim or the perpetrator is an American citizen, in which the United States is the target of the hostage taker's demands, or in which the offender is found within the United States. The Omnibus Diplomatic Security and Antiterrorism Act of 1986 broadened the extraterritorial jurisdiction of the United States over any terrorist act in which an American citizen was killed or seriously injured.

77. See U.S. House Committee on the Judiciary, *Extraterritorial Jurisdiction over Terrorist Acts Abroad: Hearings before the Subcommittee on Crime of the Committee on the Judiciary, House of Representatives, 101st Cong., 1st Sess.* (May–July 1989).

78. Peter T. Kilborn, "F.B.I. Chief: A U.S. Trial Far Off," *New York Times*, 13 October 1985, 26; "FBI Sends Agents to Italy to Monitor Case," *Boston Globe*, 13 October 1985, 28.

79. D. F. Martell, "FBI's Expanding Role in International Terrorism Investigations," *FBI Law Enforcement Bulletin* 56 (October 1987): 30.

80. Robert Pear, "F.B.I. Allowed to Investigate Crash That Killed Zia," *New York Times*, 25 June 1989, 13; U.S. House Committee on the Judiciary, *Extraterritorial Jurisdiction over Terrorist Acts Abroad.*

81. Steven Emerson and Brian Duffy, *The Fall of Pan Am 103: Inside the Lockerbie Investigation* (New York: G. P. Putnam's Sons, 1990).

82. The principal account of Customs' efforts to stem the flow of high technology and its turf struggles during this period is Linda Melvern, David Hebditch, and Nick Anning, *Techno-Bandits* (Boston: Houghton Mifflin, 1984).

83. See U.S. House of Representatives Committee on Appropriations, *Departments of Commerce, Justice, and State, the Judiciary, and Related Agencies Appropriations for 1990: Hearings before a Subcommittee*, 101st Cong., 1st sess., 1989, Part 2, 1814–1816.

84. Howard Safir, "International Court Security," *Pentacle* 7, no. 2 (summer 1987): 23–28.

85. For a critical insider account of the ATF, see William J. Vizzard, *In the Cross Fire: A Political History of the Bureau of Alcohol, Tobacco and Firearms* (Boulder, CO: Lynne Rienner, 1997).

86. See the periodical of the Immigration and Naturalization Service, *INS Reporter* (fall/winter 1985–1986): 13.

87. Ibid., 15.

88. On the escalation of federal border enforcement in the 1980s, see Timothy J. Dunn, *The Militarization of the U.S.-Mexico Border, 1978–1992* (Austin: University of Texas Press, 1995).

89. See U.S. General Accounting Office, *United States Participation in INTERPOL, the International Criminal Police Organization*, GAO/ID-76-77, Washington, DC, 27 December 1976; Diana Gulbinowicz, *The International Criminal Police Organization: A Case Study of Oversight of American Participation in an International Organization*, PhD diss., City University of New York, 1978.

90. See Nadelmann, "Unlaundering Dirty Money Abroad," 33.

91. On the advantages of MLATs from a senior practitioner perspective, see the speech of John E. Harris, Director, Office of International Affairs, Criminal Division, U.S. Department of Justice, "Mutual Legal Assistance Treaties: Necessity, Merits, and Problems Arising in the Negotiation Process," delivered at the Ministry of Justice of Japan, 10 February 2000, available at http://www.acpf.org/Activities/public%20lecture2000/lectureHarriss(E).html. He emphasizes that an MLAT is a "vessel for delivering transnational cooperation" and that it creates a "special relationship" between two states.

92. See Ethan A. Nadelmann, "Negotiations in Criminal Law Assistance Treaties," *American Journal of Comparative Law* 33 (1985): 467.

93. See Nadelmann, "Unlaundering Dirty Money Abroad."

94. For the text of the 1988 Convention, see http://www.unodc.org/pdf/convention_1988_en.pdf.

95. See W. C. Gilmore, *Dirty Money: The Evolution of Money Laundering Counter-Measures*, 2nd ed. (Strasbourg, France: Council of Europe, 1999); James Sheptycki, "Policing the Virtual Launderette: Money Laundering and Global Governance," in Sheptycki, *Issues in Transnational Policing*.

96. See Eric Helleiner, "State Power and the Regulation of Illicit Activity in Global Finance," in Friman and Andreas, *The Illicit Global Economy and State Power*, 72.

97. See FATF's Web site: www.fatf-gafi.org.

98. Michael Abbell and Bruno A. Ristau, *International Judicial Assistance*, vol. 4 (Washington, DC: International Law Institute, 1984), 16–17.

99. See Fooner, *INTERPOL: Issues in World Crime and International Criminal Justice*, 138–147.

100. Indeed, the request and delivery of criminal fugitives from one state to another was called "extradition" until the end of the nineteenth century, when John Bassett Moore's comprehensive and authoritative *A Treatise on Extradition and Interstate Rendition* (Boston: The Boston Book Company, 1891) drew a sharp distinction between international and intranational renditions. See John Bassett Moore, "The Difficulties of Extradition," *Publications of the American Academy of Political Science* 1, no. 4 (July 1911), reprinted in *The Collected Papers of John Bassett Moore*, vol. 2 (New Haven, CT: Yale University Press, 1944), 314–322, 320.

101. See Moore, *A Treatise on Extradition and Interstate Rendition*.

102. See Bruce Michael Bagley, "Dateline Drug Wars. Colombia: The Wrong Strategy," *Foreign Policy* 77 (winter 1989/90): 154–171.

103. Extradition would be reinstated in 1997 and become an increasingly popular policy instrument in the context of rapidly growing U.S. antidrug aid. See Juan Forero, "Surge in Extradition of Colombia Drug Suspects to U.S.," *New York Times*, 6 December 2004, A3.

Chapter 4

1. See Peter Andreas and Richard Price, "From War-Fighting to Crime-Fighting: Transforming the American National Security State," *International Studies Review* 3, no. 3 (fall 2001): 31–52.

2. Linnea P. Raine and Frank J. Cilluffo, eds., *Global Organized Crime: The New Evil Empire* (Washington, DC: Center for Strategic and International Studies, 1994), ix.

3. Testimony of Jamie Gorelick, Deputy Attorney General, Hearing of the U.S. Senate Select Committee on Intelligence, 104th Cong., 1st sess., 25 October 1995.

4. President Bill Clinton, Address at the United Nations Fiftieth Anniversary Charter Ceremony, San Francisco, 26 June 1995.

5. Eric Schmitt, "Colorado Bunker Built for Cold War Shifts Focus to Drug Battle," *New York Times*, 18 July 1993, 18.

6. "High-Tech Gadgets to Aid Law Enforcement Agencies: New Center to Help Develop Products," *Drug Policy Report* 1, no. 6 (July 1994); "DOD Studies X-ray Techniques for Examining Cargo Containers," *Drug Enforcement Report*, 23 May 1994; and Mark Fineman and Craig Pyes, "Cocaine Traffic," *Los Angeles Times*, 9 June 1996.

7. Douglas Jehl, "The Science of Fighting a Drug War," *Los Angeles Times*, 11 November 1989.

8. William Matthews, "'Toys' Dusted Off for War on Drugs," *Federal Times*, 16 April 1990.

9. Frank Greve, "Ailing Defense Contractors Urged to Arm the Drug War," *Miami Herald*, 15 July 1990.

10. David Morrison, "Police Action," *National Journal* 24, no. 5 (1 February 1992): 267–270.

11. "High-Tech Gadgets to Aid Law Enforcement Agencies."

12. Sandra Dibble, "Star Wars Arrives at the Border: High Tech Developed by the Military, CIA May Aid Enforcement," *San Diego Union-Tribune*, 18 March 1995.

13. See Mark Riebling, *Wedge: From Pearl Harbor to 9/11—How the Secret War between the FBI and CIA Has Endangered National Security* (New York: Touchstone Books, 2002).

14. Stewart A. Baker, "Should Spies Be Cops?" *Foreign Policy* 97 (winter 1994–1995): 36–52.

15. John Buntin, "Cops and Spies," *Government Executive*, April 1996, 40–48.

16. U.S. Special Commission on the Roles and Capabilities of the U.S. Intelligence Community, *Preparing for the 21st Century: An Appraisal of U.S. Intelligence*, 1 March 1996.

17. See testimony of Jamie Gorelick, Deputy Attorney General, Hearings of the Senate Select Committee on Intelligence, 25 October 1995. Also see U.S. House of Representatives Committee on Intelligence, *The Intelligence Community in the 21st Century*, Staff Study of the Permanent Select Committee on Intelligence, June 1996.

18. Bruce Zagaris has noted that "the new law constitutes a fundamental breach in the traditional separation of intelligence and law enforcement." "U.S. International Cooperation against Transnational Organized Crime," *Wayne Law Review* 44, no. 3 (fall 1998): 1414.

19. Richard A. Best Jr., *Intelligence and Law Enforcement: Countering Transnational*

Threats to the U.S., Congressional Research Service, Washington, DC, updated 3 December 2001, 17.

20. Quoted in Tim Weiner, "CIA's Most Important Mission: Itself," *New York Times Magazine*, 10 December 1995, 80.

21. Quoted in Martin Edwin Anderson, "Spy Agency Wars," *Washington Times*, 19 December 1994, A25.

22. See Alfred W. McCoy, *The Politics of Heroin: CIA Complicity in the Global Drug Trade*, rev. ed. (Chicago: Lawrence Hill Books, 2003).

23. Jeff Gerth, "CIA Shedding Its Reluctance to Aid in Fight against Drugs," *New York Times*, 25 March 1990, A1.

24. Weiner, "CIA's Most Important Mission: Itself," 62–104.

25. Quoted in Adam Isacson, "The U.S. Military and the War on Drugs," in Coletta A. Youngers and Eileen Rosen, eds., *Drugs and Democracy in Latin America: The Impact of U.S. Policy* (Boulder, CO: Lynne Rienner, 2005), 45.

26. Ibid., 42. He notes that the full extent of the CIA role is obscured by secrecy, including a classified budget.

27. When Congress authorized the creation of the CIA through the 1947 National Security Act, it stated, "The Agency shall have no police, subpoena, or law enforcement powers or internal security functions." Quoted in Peter Raven-Hansen, "Security's Conquest of Federal Law Enforcement," in Marcus G. Raskin and A. Carl LeVan, eds., *In Democracy's Shadow: The Secret World of National Security* (New York: Nation Books, 2005), 220.

28. Victoria Gotsch, "U.S. Permits Law Enforcement to Order Evidence Gathering from Intelligence Agencies," *International Enforcement Law Reporter* (December 1996): 1.

29. Warren Richey, "CIA to Take on Added Role: Catching Criminals Overseas," *Christian Science Monitor*, 27 September 1996.

30. Quoted in Benjamin Wittes, "Blurring the Line between Cops and Spies," *Legal Times*, 9 September 1996, 1.

31. Quoted in ibid., citing Baker, "Should Spies Be Cops?" 36–37. See also Nikos Passas and Richard B. Groskin, "International Undercover Operations," in G. Marx and C. Fijnaut, eds., *Undercover: Police Surveillance in Comparative Perspective* (Amsterdam: Kluwer, 1995); Jack Blum and Nikos Passas, "Controlling Cross-Border Undercover Operations," in S. Field and C. Pelser, eds., *Invading the Private: State Accountability and the New Policing in Europe* (Dartmouth, UK: Aldershot, 1998).

32. R. Jeffrey Smith, "Ground Rules for Disputed Territory," *Washington Post*, 26 October 1995, A29.

33. Michael Isikoff and Patrick E. Tyler, "U.S. Military Given Foreign Arrest Powers," *Washington Post*, 16 December 1989, A1.

34. Quoted in Isacson, "The U.S. Military and the War on Drugs," 28.

35. Buntin, "Cops and Spies."

36. For a detailed recent overview, see Isacson, "The U.S. Military and the War on Drugs."

37. See Cornelius Friesendorf, *Pushing Drugs: The Displacement of the Cocaine and Heroin Industry as a Side Effect of U.S. Foreign Policy*, PhD diss., University of Zurich, 2005, 150.

38. Ibid., 106–108.

39. For example, the State Department acknowledged that in 2002, it and the Pentagon had hired sixteen different companies to carry out $150.4 million in services. Eleven contractors died in Colombia between 1998 and 2003. See Isacson, "The U.S. Military and the War on Drugs," 43.

40. Quoted in Friesendorf, *Pushing Drugs*, 150.

41. Quoted in Isacson, "The U.S. Military and the War on Drugs," 44.

42. Quoted in Friesendorf, *Pushing Drugs*, 121.

43. For a more detailed account, see Andreas, *Border Games*.

44. "INS: Is Gatekeeper Working?," *Migration News* 7, no. 9 (September 2000); Belinda I. Reyes, Hans P. Johnson, and Richard Van Swearingen, *Holding the Line? The Effects of the Recent Border Buildup on Unauthorized Immigration* (San Francisco: Public Policy Institute of California, 2002), v.

45. See Joseph Nevins, *Operation Gatekeeper* (New York: Routledge, 2001).

46. Mike Glenn, "Laredo Patrol Welcomes Military, but Some Residents Say It's Too Much," *Houston Chronicle,* 3 September 2000, 1; Dale E. Brown, "Drugs on the Border: The Role of the Military," *Parameters* 21 (winter 1991–1992): 50–59.

47. John Flock, "Notes and Comments: The Legality of United States Military Operations along the United States–Mexico Border," *Southwestern Journal of Law and Trade of the Americas* vol. 5 (Fall 1998): 471. According to one military commander sent to help the Border Patrol near Laredo, Texas, air surveillance efforts were conducted as if on a combat mission: "When we go out and fly our missions, they are going to do a full battle drill." He noted, "We do everything but weapons engagement." Quoted in Glenn, "Laredo Patrol Welcomes Military, but Some Residents Say It's Too Much," 1.

48. For a detailed account of this incident, see Timothy J. Dunn, "Waging a War on Immigrants at the U.S.-Mexico Border," in Peter B. Kraska, ed., *Militarizing the American Criminal Justice System: The Changing Roles of the American Armed Forces and the Police* (Boston: Northeastern University Press, 2001).

49. On the politics of U.S.-Mexico border drug enforcement in the context of NAFTA, see Peter Andreas, "Building Bridges and Barricades: Trade Facilitation and Drug Enforcement on the U.S.-Mexico Border," in Bailey and Chabat, *Transnational Crime and Public Security.*

50. In 1994, the Canadian government calculated that one-third of all cigarette

cartons bought in Canada had been smuggled in (in contrast to only 1 out of 176 cartons in 1985). Virtually all of these contraband cigarettes had been exported to the United States from Canada and then smuggled back into the country to evade taxes—with Canadian cigarette manufacturers apparently well aware that the seemingly booming U.S. market for their product was fictional. See Margaret E. Beare, "Organized Corporate Criminality: Corporate Complicity in Tobacco Smuggling," in Beare, *Critical Reflections on Transnational Organized Crime, Money Laundering and Corruption*.

51. Demetrios Papademetriou and Deborah Waller Meyers, "Introduction: Overview, Context, and a Vision for the Future," in Demetrios Papademetriou and Deborah Waller Meyers, *Caught in the Middle: Border Communities in an Era of Globalization* (Washington, DC: Carnegie Endowment for International Peace, 2001), 36.

52. One undercover Canadian investigation in 1994 found that most of the guns purchased on the black market were smuggled into Canada from the United States. Mark Clayton, "To Curb Violence, Canada Tries to Block Guns from US," *Christian Science Monitor*, 14 March 1995, 1.

53. A 2003 cover story in *Forbes* called marijuana "Canada's most valuable agricultural product—bigger than wheat, cattle, or timber." Quentin Hardy, "Inside Dope," *Forbes* 172, no. 10 (November 2003): 146–154. Canadian officials calculated in 2003 that $4 billion to $7 billion worth of Canadian marijuana is sold in the United States annually. DeNeen L. Brown, "Canada May Allow Small Amounts of Marijuana," *Washington Post*, 28 May 2003, A1.

54. Stephen Flynn, *America the Vulnerable* (New York: HarperCollins, 2004), 187.

55. The *Washington Times* quoted unnamed U.S. officials on its front page claiming that "Canada's soft laws on political asylum opened a back door" for Ressam. In the *Los Angeles Times*, commentator Edward Luttwak charged that in Canada, "security controls are famously lax because politically correct Canadians do not differentiate between 76-year old Madame Dupont coming to visit her grandchildren and bearded young men from Islamic countries." Quoted in Andrew Phillips, "Border Crackdown," *Macleans* 10 January 2002, 22.

56. Quoted in Buntin, "Cops and Spies," 41. Available at http://www.govexec.com/archdoc/0496s5.htm.

57. Department of Justice, Office of the Inspector General, *Federal Bureau of Investigation Legal Attaché Program*, Report No. 04-18, Washington, DC, March 2004, available at http://www.usdoj.gov/oig/audit/FBI/0418/exec.htm.

58. See White House, *International Crime Control Strategy*, Washington, DC, June 1998, available at http://www.fas.org/irp/offdocs/iccs/iccstoc.html.

59. R. Jeffrey Smith and Thomas W. Lippman, "FBI Plans to Expand Overseas," *Washington Post*, 20 August 1996, A1.

60. Statement of Louis J. Freeh, Director, Federal Bureau of Investigation, before the Senate Appropriations Committee, Subcommittee on Foreign Operations, 20 March 1997.

61. Quoted in David A. Vise, "New Global Role Puts FBI in Unsavory Company," *Washington Post*, 29 October 2000, A1.

62. Ibid.

63. Between 1997 and 2001, the INS trained more than forty-five thousand host country officials and airline staff and intercepted seventy-four thousand fraudulently documented migrants trying to use these countries as an entry point to the United States. See U.S. Department of Justice, "INS Fact Sheet: INS 'Global Reach' Initiative Counters Rise in International Migrant Smuggling," 27 June 2001.

64. Otwin Marenin, "United States International Policing Activities: An Overview," in Koenig and Das, *International Police Cooperation*, 306.

65. Isacson, "The U.S. Military in the War on Drugs," 26. An important component of the State Department's growth in this area involved expanded funding for counternarcotics training. For instance, in 1999, the State Department funded 696 antidrug law enforcement courses in more than ninety-five countries, costing more than $30 million. Rachel Neild, "U.S. Police Assistance and Drug Control Policies," in Youngers and Rosin, *Drugs and Democracy in Latin America*, 70. It also provided funding for the U.S. Coast Guard to train more than three hundred foreign law enforcement officials in maritime law enforcement in 2001 (ibid., 81).

66. Reports for various years are available at www.state.gov/p/inl/rls/nrcrpt.

67. Reports for various years are available at www.state.gov/g/tip/rls/tiprpt.

68. In the case of Latin America, for example, see Martha Huggins, *Political Policing: The United States and Latin America* (Durham, NC: Duke University Press, 1998).

69. See Leslie E. King and Judson M. Ray, "Developing Transnational Law Enforcement Cooperation: The FBI Training Initiatives," *Journal of Contemporary Criminal Justice* 16, no. 4 (2000): 386–408.

70. Ordway P. Burden, "Law Enforcement Agencies Working Overseas," *CJ International* 11, no. 6 (November–December 1995): 17.

71. Quoted in Marenin, "United States International Police Activities: An Overview," 307.

72. Quoted in David Johnston, "Strength Is Seen in U.S. Export: Law Enforcement," *New York Times*, 17 April 1995, A1.

73. Department of Justice, Office of Inspector General, Evaluation and Inspections Division, *Review of the Office of International Affairs' Role in the International Extradition of Fugitives*, Report No. 1-2002-008, Washington, DC, March 2002, available at http://www.usdoj.gov/oig/reports/OBD/e0208/extradition.pdf.

74. Quoted in "Surfing with U.S. Customs," *CNN Online*, 20 October 1999.

75. Eric Helleiner noted, "Analysts of the recent international money laundering initiatives are unanimous in describing them as U.S.-led initiatives and the U.S. role has been crucial to their success." "State Power and the Regulation of Illicit Activity in Global Finance," 60.

76. Jonathan M. Winer, "Cops across Borders: The Evolution of Transatlantic Law Enforcement and Judicial Cooperation," paper presented at the Council on Foreign Relations, "Roundtable on Old Rules, New Threats," 1 September 2004, 6. For the text of the Convention and its Protocols, see www.unodc.org/palermo/convmain.html.

77. Testimony of Samuel M. Witten, Deputy Legal Adviser, U.S. Department of State, "On the Inter-American Terrorism Convention," Hearing of the U.S. Senate Committee on Foreign Relations, *Law Enforcement Treaties*, 108th Congress, 2nd sess., 17 June 2004, 13–14.

78. Winer, "Cops across Borders," 2.

79. See Brenda Chalfin, "The Traffic in Sovereignty: Customs Regimes as Global Governance," application for Woodrow Wilson Center Fellowship, October 2004, 1.

80. The distinction between old and new systems of police cooperation in Europe is emphasized by Anderson et al., *Policing the European Union*, 84.

81. Neil Walker, "In Search of the Area of Freedom, Security and Justice: A Constitutional Odyssey," in Walker, *Europe's Area of Freedom, Security and Justice*, 13.

82. Monica den Boer, "Moving between Bogus and Bona Fide: The Policing of Inclusion and Exclusion in Europe," in Robert Miles and Dietrich Thränhardt, eds., *Migration and European Integration: The Dynamics of Inclusion and Exclusion* (London: Pinter, 1995), 107.

83. Didier Bigo, "The European Internal Security Field: Stakes and Rivalries in a Newly Developing Area of Police Intervention," in Anderson and den Boer, *Policing across National Borders*, 165.

84. Georges Estievenart, "The European Community and the Global Drug Phenomenon: Current Situation and Outlook," in Georges Estievenart et al., ed., *Policies and Strategies to Combat Drugs in Europe* (Norwell, MA: Kluwer Academic, 1995), 58–59.

85. Turnbull and Sandholtz, "Policing and Immigration," 211–212.

86. Anderson et al., *Policing the European Union*, 61.

87. Turnbull and Sandholtz, "Policing and Immigration," 211.

88. House of Lords Select Committee on the European Communities, quoted in Eugene McLaughlin, "The Democratic Deficit: European Union and the Accountability of the British Police," *British Journal of Criminology* 32, no. 4 (1992): 481.

89. The Amsterdam Treaty outlined the creation of an Area of Freedom, Secu-

rity, and Justice. As part of the monitoring and implementation structure created by the Amsterdam Treaty, the Directorate-General on Justice and Home Affairs set up and maintained a scorecard to keep track of how each member state was implementing the agreed changes in their criminal justice systems. For the text of the Amsterdam Treaty, see www.eurotreaties.com/amsterdamtext.html. On the Schengen Agreement, see http://europa.eu.int/scadplus/leg/en/lvb/l33020 .htm.

90. Anderson, "Genesis of Schengen," 8.

91. See Peter Hobbing, "Integrated Border Management at the EU Level," CEPS Working Document, No. 227/August 2005 (Brussels: Centre for European Policy Studies), available at http://www.ceps.be/default.php.

92. Ibid., 16.

93. House of Lords, 1999, Question 48, Minutes of Evidence, 2 December 1998, quoted in William Walters, "Mapping Schengenland: Denaturalizing the Border," *Environment and Planning D: Society and Space* 20, no. 5 (2002): 573.

94. Jenny MacKenzie, "Britain Toughens Immigration Stance," *Christian Science Monitor*, 16 August 2002, 7.

95. In the U.S. case, see especially Janet Gilboy, "Implications of 'Third Party' Involvement in Enforcement: The INS, Illegal Travelers, and International Airlines," *Law and Society Review* 31, no. 3 (1997): 505–529.

96. See Gallya Lahav and Virginie Guiraudon, "Comparative Perspectives on Border Control: Away from the Border and Outside the State," in Peter Andreas and Timothy Snyder, eds., *The Wall around the West: State Borders and Immigration Controls in North America and Europe* (Lanham, MD: Rowman & Littlefield, 2000). They also note that the role of air carriers in immigration control was first secured at the Paris Conference in 1919, "which in effect placed airspace, the domain through which airlines must travel, under sovereign control. By virtue of owning airspace, airlines became subject to national restrictions, and dependent on state actors for market operation" (63).

97. Virginie Guiraudon, "Enlisting Third Parties in Border Control: A Comparative Study of Its Causes and Consequences," paper presented at the Geneva Centre for Democratic Control of Armed Forces, Geneva, Switzerland, 13–15 March 2003, 4.

98. Lahav and Guiraudon, "Comparative Perspectives on Border Control."

99. Guiraudon, "Enlisting Third Parties in Border Control," 6.

100. See Lech Gardocki, "The Socialist System," in M. Cherif Bassiouni, ed., *International Criminal Law, Volume II: Procedure* (Ardsley, UK: Transnational Publishers, 1986), 133–149.

101. Frank Gregory, "Unprecedented Partnerships in Crime Control: Law Enforcement Issues and Linkages between Eastern and Western Europe Since 1989," in Anderson and den Boer, *Policing across National Boundaries*.

102. See Milada Anna Vachudova, "Eastern Europe as Gatekeeper: The Immigration and Asylum Policies of an Enlarging European Union," in Andreas and Snyder, *The Wall around the West*.

103. "Immigration in Eastern Europe," *Migration News* 6, no. 2 (February 1999).

104. Quoted in Dean E. Murphy, "Poland Becomes Journey's End for Migrants," *Los Angeles Times*, 27 December 1997, 11.

105. Ian Black, "Poland to Reinforce New EU Border," *Guardian*, 31 July 2002, 12; "EU and Poland Clinch Deal on Border Controls," Agence France-Presse, 30 July 2002; Marcin Grajewski, "EU Agrees to Polish Plan to Strengthen Eastern Border," Reuters, 24 July 2002.

106. See http://europa.eu.int/comm/enlargement/cards/index_en.htm.

107. See Statement of Bruce C. Swartz, Deputy Assistant Attorney General, Criminal Division, Hearing of the U.S. Senate Committee on Foreign Relations, Subcommittee on European Affairs, *Combating Transnational Crime and Corruption in Europe*, 108th Cong., 1st sess., 30 October 2003. He noted that the Criminal Division engaged in activities such as the development of organized crime task forces and assistance in legislative drafting, and that "Division employees often provide assistance and training in conjunction with law enforcement officials from Western Europe." Available at http://foreign.senate.gov/testimony/2003 SwartzTestimony031030.pdf.

108. Comment by senior Macedonian law enforcement official at the Conference on Trafficking in Women in the Balkans, Ford Institute, University of Pittsburgh, 13–14 May 2005.

109. Susan L. Woodward, "Enhancing Cooperation against Transborder Crime in Southeast Europe: Is There an Emerging Epistemic Community?," *Journal of Southeast European and Black Sea Studies* 4, no. 2 (May 2004): 227.

110. Jörg Monar, "The Problems of Balance in EU Justice and Home Affairs and the Impact of 11 September," in Malcolm Anderson and Joanna Apap, eds., *Police and Justice Cooperation and the New European Borders* (The Hague: Kluwer Law International, 2002), 165.

111. Neil Walker, "The Pattern of Transnational Policing," in Newburn, *Handbook of Policing*, 121.

112. See the text of the presidency conclusions at www.europarl.eu.int/summits/ tam_en.htm.

113. Jörg Friedrichs, "When Push Comes to Shove: The Territorial Monopoly of Force and the Travails of Neomedieval Europe," paper presented at the Conference of Europeanists, Chicago, 11–13 March 2004, 22.

114. For a general review, see John Occhipinti, *The Politics of EU Police Cooperation: Toward a European FBI?* (Boulder, CO: Lynne Rienner, 2003); Michael Santiago, *Europol and Police Cooperation in Europe* (Lewiston, ME: Edwin Mellen Press,

2000). See Europol's Web site: www.europol.eu.int. For critical perspectives on Europol and other European initiatives in the field of justice and home affairs, see the database of Statewatch: http://database.statewatch.org/search.asp.

115. More generally, Germany was the leading champion of the internationalization of policing in Europe, with Chancellor Helmut Kohl a particularly effective and vocal policy entrepreneur. See Turnbull and Sandholtz, "Policing and Immigration," 215.

116. Fijnaut, "Transnational Organized Crime and Institutional Reform in the European Union," 288.

117. N. Walker, "The Pattern of Transnational Policing," 121.

118. Cyrille Fijnaut, "Police Co-operation and the Area of Freedom, Security, and Justice," in Walker, *Europe's Area of Freedom, Security and Justice*, 253.

Chapter 5

1. The text of the Act is available at http://thomas.loc.gov/cgi-bin/query/z?c107:H.R.3162.ENR.

2. David Lyon has pointed out that "foreign hackers can be prosecuted by the USA under the Patriot Act when computers in the USA or abroad are attacked. Because such a large volume of global internet traffic flows through the USA (80 percent of Asian, African, and South American access points, for example), it can be criminalized under US law." *Surveillance after September 11* (Malden, MA: Polity Press, 2003), 123.

3. For a summary, see Charles Doyle, *The USA Patriot Act: A Sketch*, Congressional Research Service, Washington, DC, 18 April 2002.

4. Some prominent voices have expressed growing concerns over the possibility of the United States becoming an "intelligence state." See Philip B. Heymann, *Terrorism, Freedom, and Security: Winning without War* (Cambridge, MA: MIT Press, 2003).

5. Eric Lichtblau, "U.S. Uses Terror Law to Pursue Crimes from Drugs to Swindling," *New York Times*, 28 September 2003, 1A.

6. Quoted in Vanessa Blum, "Guarding against Mission Creep: Critics Fear Routine DOJ Use of Terror Laws," *Legal Times*, 25 November 2002, 1.

7. Quoted in Lichtblau, "U.S. Uses Terror Law to Pursue Crimes from Drugs to Swindling," 1A.

8. Ibid.

9. Peter Grier and Faye Bowers, "What Spy Reforms Mean," *Christian Science Monitor*, 8 December 2004, 1.

10. Eric Lichtblau, "U.S. Seeks Access to Bank Records to Deter Terror," *New York Times*, 10 April 2005, 1A.

11. Dan Eggen, "Measure Expands Police Powers; Intelligence Bill Includes

Disputed Anti-Terror Moves," *Washington Post*, 10 December 2004, A1; Douglas Jehl and David Johnston, "White House Fought New Curbs on Interrogations, Officials Say," *New York Times*, 13 January 2005, A1.

12. David Johnston and Douglas Jehl, "FBI's Recruiting of Spies Causes New Rift with CIA," *New York Times*, 11 February 2005, A19.

13. Richard B. Schmitt and Greg Miller, "FBI in Talks to Extend Reach," *Los Angeles Times*, 28 January 2005, A1.

14. See U.S. Senate Appropriations Committee, *Commerce-Justice-State Subcommittee Hearing on the Transformation of the Federal Bureau of Investigation*, 108th Cong., 2nd sess., 23 March 2004.

15. Ronald J. Sievert, "War on Terrorism or Global Law Enforcement Operation?," *Notre Dame Law Review* 78, no. 2 (2003): 309, 317.

16. "America's Uneasy Mandate for Domestic Intelligence," *Congressional Quarterly Weekly*, 24 April 2004.

17. For a critique of this practice from the perspective of international human rights law, see Alfred de Zayas, "Human Rights and Indefinite Detention," *International Review of the Red Cross* 87, no. 857 (March 2005): 15–38.

18. The agency apparently used planes owned by an array of shell companies to move suspects around the world. See Scott Shane, Stephen Grey, and Margot Williams, "CIA Expanding Terror Battle under Guise of Charter Flights," *New York Times*, 31 May 2005, 1A.

19. See, for example, Jane Mayer, "Outsourcing Torture," *New Yorker* 81, no. 1 (15 February 2005): 106–123.

20. For a more detailed discussion, see Bruce Zagaris et al., "Selected Symposium Remarks, 'Financial Aspects of the War on Terror,' The Merging of Counter-Terrorism and Anti-Money Laundering," *Law and Policy in International Business* 34 (Fall 2002): 1–108.

21. See the organization's Web site: http://www.egmont.org.

22. See especially Nikos Passas, "Law Enforcement Challenges in Hawala Operations and Criminal Abuse," *Journal of Money Laundering Control* 8, no. 2 (2002): 112–129.

23. For a critical account, see R. T. Naylor, "Wash-Out: A Critique of Follow-the-Money Methods in Crime Control Policy," *Crime, Law, and Social Change* 32 (1999): 1–57.

24. "The OFAC sanctions named hundreds of organizations, entities and individuals as subject to sanctions, and threatened other countries with having the assets of their financial institutions and businesses subject to sanctions in a secondary freezing if they did business with any of the named organizations, entities or individuals." Jonathan Winer, "Cops across Borders," 7.

25. David Cortright, "A Critical Evaluation of the UN Counter-Terrorism Program: Accomplishments and Challenges," paper presented at the seminar on

Global Enforcement Regimes: Transnational Organized Crime, International Terrorism and Money Laundering, Transnational Institute, Amsterdam, 28–29 April 2005, 4.

26. See Thomas J. Biersteker, "Counter-Terrorism Measures Undertaken under UN Security Council Auspices," in Alyson J. K. Bailes and Isabel Frommelt, eds., *Business and Security: Public-Private Sector Relationships in a New Security Environment* (Oxford: Oxford University Press, 2004), 68.

27. Jonathan M. Winer, "Building Global Jurisdiction, Systems and Capacity to Build Global Security: Or Even a Superpower Needs Friends," paper presented at the "Roundtable on Old Rules, New Threats," Council on Foreign Relations, Washington, DC, 6 March 2003, 2.

28. See Michael Levi and Bill Gilmore, "Terrorist Finance, Money Laundering and the Rise and Rise of Mutual Evaluation: A New Paradigm of Crime Control?," in "The Financing of Terrorism," special issue, *European Journal of Law Reform* 4, no. 2 (2002): 337–364.

29. This included dispatching investigators from U.S. municipal police forces. In 2002, New York Police Commissioner Raymond W. Kelly (who had previously headed the U.S. Customs Service) decided to send his own detectives to police departments in foreign cities—much to the chagrin of the FBI, which would prefer to be the source of foreign law enforcement information collection. As of May 2005, the New York Police Department's overseas liaison program had representatives in seven cities from Tel Aviv to Singapore. "The program tries to ensure that the New York question gets asked in any counterterrorism investigation," said David Cohen, the department's deputy commissioner for intelligence (and a former CIA officer for thirty-five years). Department investigators arrived in Madrid within hours of the terrorist railway bombing in March 2004—even before the FBI's own experts had arrived. Judith Miller, "A New York Detective's Tricky Beat in Israel," *New York Times*, 15 May 2005, 26.

30. See U.S. Department of State, "The Anti-Terrorism Assistance Program: Report to Congress for Fiscal Year 2002," February 2003.

31. Federal Documents Clearing House, FDCH Political Transcripts, "U.S. Senator Orrin Hatch (R-UT) Holds Hearing on International Drug Trafficking and Terrorism," 20 May 2003.

32. Quoted in Isacson, "The U.S. Military in the War on Drugs," 48.

33. Ibid. Also see Washington Office on Latin America, "Blurring the Lines: Trends in U.S. Military Programs with Latin America," Washington, DC, September 2004, available at http://ciponline.org/facts.

34. Isacson, "The U.S. Military in the War on Drugs," 50.

35. Quoted in ibid., 49.

36. Quoted in Washington Office on Latin America, "Blurring the Lines: Trends in U.S. Military Programs."

37. United Nations reports on opium production in Afghanistan can be accessed at www.unodc.org/afg/en/reports_surveys.html.

38. Thom Shanker, "Pentagon Sees Antidrug Effort in Afghanistan," *New York Times*, 25 March 2005, 1A.

39. See A. W. McCoy, *The Politics of Heroin*, especially chap. 9.

40. Tim Golden, "A War on Terror Meets a War on Drugs," *New York Times*, 25 November 2001, sec. 4, 4.

41. See Cresencio Arcos, "The Role of the Department of Homeland Security Overseas," Heritage Lectures, No. 840, The Heritage Foundation, 7 June 2004, available at http://www.heritage.org/Research/HomelandDefense/hl840.cfm.

42. Quoted in Bill Hess, "Military's Use on the Border Expands," *Sierra Vista Herald*, Sierra Vista, Arizona, 21 April 2005. While a greater militarization of border control was partly inhibited by the large-scale deployment of military forces to Iraq and elsewhere, some aspects of border policing provided training in desert warfare. For example, an Alaska-based Stryker unit (designed to roll out quickly on eight-wheeled armored vehicles using surveillance and reconnaissance to generate information) on its way to Iraq spent sixty days in the New Mexico desert working alongside the Border Patrol and reportedly was responsible for the Border Patrol's apprehension of twenty-five hundred illegal immigrants. See ibid.

43. Michael Marizco, "Most Advanced Attempt to Take Control of Area," *Arizona Daily Star* (Tucson), 30 September 2005.

44. See H. Richard Friman, "Breaching the Firewall: Terror, Crime and Securitizing Immigration," paper presented at the annual convention of the International Studies Association, Portland, OR, 26 February–1 March 2003.

45. Eric Lichtblau, "Prosecutions in Immigration Doubled in Last Four Years," *New York Times*, 29 September 2005.

46. See Andreas and Biersteker, *The Rebordering of North America*.

47. For example, U.S.-Mexico trade more than tripled between 1993 and 2000, from $81 billion to $247 billion (making Mexico the second largest trading partner of the United States). By the end of the 1990s, nearly 300 million people, 90 million cars, and 4 million trucks and railcars were entering the United States from Mexico every year.

48. In 2001, the U.S. and Canada were conducting about $1.3 billion worth of two-way trade a day, most of it shipped by truck across the border.

49. Quoted in Bart Jansen, "Bills Aim to Shore Up the Northern Border," *Portland Press Herald* (Maine), 4 October 2001, 1A.

50. The first base opened in August 2004 in Bellingham, WA. Commenting on the new bases, Gary Bracken, communications director for the U.S. Office of Air and Marine Operations, explained, "We're working with partners in the U.S. and Canada to curb illegal activity all along the border." Quoted in Catherine Solyom, "Undefended Border Defenseless No More: Five Bases Planned to Curb

Illegal Activity between Canada and the United States," *The Gazette* (Montreal), 27 August 2004, A3.

51. The most substantial immediate changes in Canadian law after the terrorist attacks have been the 2001 Anti-Terrorism Act and the 2002 Public Safety Act, which have given new surveillance and enforcement powers to police and security agencies.

52. For example, Canadian Immigration Minister Elinor Caplan insisted that U.S.-Canada policy discussions were about information sharing (such as visa screening, preclearance of flights abroad, and sharing passenger information prior to flight arrivals), not policy convergence: "Let there not be any misunderstanding. Canadian laws will be made right here in the Canadian parliament." Quoted in Howard Adelman, "Governance, Immigration Policy, and Security: Canada and the United States Post-9/11," in Tirman, *The Maze of Fear*, 111.

53. Quoted in Greg Weston, "Fix Leaky Borders: U.S," *Toronto Sun*, 20 September 2001, 7.

54. The White House, Office of the Press Secretary, "Border Security: Smart Borders for the 21st Century," press release, 25 January 2002, available at http://www.whitehouse.gov/news/releases/2002/01/20020125.html.

55. *The 9-11 Commission Report: Final Report of the National Commission on Terrorist Attacks upon the United States* (New York: Norton, 2004), 389, 390, 362.

56. The International Civil Aviation Organization established standards for biometric identifiers in May 2003, determining that face recognition is the most universal interoperable biometric for machine-readable documents. Ibid., 13.

57. Lisa M. Seghetti, Jennifer E. Lake, and William H. Robinson, "Border and Transportation Security: Selected Programs and Policies," Congressional Research Service, Washington, DC, 29 March 2005, 7.

58. Rey Koslowski, "Possible Steps toward an International Regime for Mobility and Security," *Global Migration Perspectives* 8 (October 2004): 15. On data mining, see Oscar H. Gandy, "Data Mining and Surveillance in the Post-9/11 Environment," in Kirstie Ball and Frank Webster, eds., *The Intensification of Surveillance* (London: Pluto Press, 2003). High-tech firms with data-mining software were among the first to respond to the Bush administration's public appeal for help in identifying suspected terrorists. See David Wood, Eli Konvitz, and Kirstie Ball, "The Constant State of Emergency? Surveillance after 9/11," in Ball and Webster, *The Intensification of Surveillance*, 138.

59. In 2000, MIT's *Technology Review* called biometrics one of the "top ten emerging technologies that will change the world." Quoted in Jonathan P. Aus, "Supranational Governance in an 'Area of Freedom, Security and Justice': Eurodac and the Politics of Biometric Control," Sussex European Institute Working Paper, Brighton, UK, December 2003, 18.

60. Lyon, *Surveillance after September 11*, 15.

61. Citing market researchers at Homeland Security Corp., *BusinessWeek* reported in 2004, "The homeland defense industry, a $4 billion market in 2000, is expected to balloon to more than $170 billion in 2006." Eric Wahlgren, "Terror May Be Your Portfolio's Security," *BusinessWeek Online* 16 August 2004, available at http://www.businessweek.com/bwdaily/dnflash/aug2004/nf20040816_9987_db014.htm.

62. Quoted in Eric Lipton, "U.S. to Spend Billions More to Alter Security Systems," *New York Times*, 8 May 2005, A1.

63. For a detailed evaluation, see Rey Koslowski, *Real Challenges for Virtual Borders: The Implementation of US-VISIT* (Washington, DC: Migration Policy Institute, June 2005).

64. According to one business press report, "Accenture wowed government officials with a demo that included biometric devices that scanned fingerprints and wireless tags that tracked immigrants' whereabouts." "Accenture Hits the Daily Double," *BusinessWeek Online*, 12 July 2004, available at http://www.businessweek.com/magazine/content/04_28/b3891113_mz063.htm.

65. Accenture Digital Forum, "US DHS Awards Accenture-Led Smart Border Alliance the Contract to Develop and Implement US VISIT Program at Air, Land and Sea Ports of Entry," press release, 1 June 2004, 1, available at http://www.accenture.com/xd/xd.asp?it=enweb&xd=_dyn\dynamicpressrelease_730.xml.

66. Rey Koslowski, "Intersections of Information Technology and Human Mobility: Globalization vs. Homeland Security," position paper presented at the ESRC/SSRC Money and Migration after Globalization Colloquium, St. Hughes College, University of Oxford, 25–28 March 2004, 19.

67. Quoted in Jo Best, "US to Slap Tourists with RFID," *Silicon.com*, 26 January 2005, available at http://management.silicon.com/government/0,39024677,39127374,00.htm.

68. Koslowski, *Real Challenges for Virtual Borders*, 52.

69. See Stephen E. Flynn, "The False Conundrum: Continental Integration versus Homeland Security," in Andreas and Biersteker, *The Rebordering of North America*, 110–127; Robert C. Bonner, U.S. Commissioner of Customs, "Pushing Borders Outwards: Rethinking Customs Enforcement," speech presented at the Center for Strategic and International Studies, Washington, DC, 17 January 2002.

70. Quoted in Eric Lipton, "Loophole Seen in U.S. Efforts to Secure Overseas Ports," *New York Times,* 25 May 2005, A6.

71. See Jessica Romero, "Prevention of Maritime Terrorism: The Container Security Initiative," *Chicago Journal of International Law* 4, no. 2 (fall 2003): 597 606.

72. The initiative was an outgrowth of U.S.-Canadian efforts to more carefully screen maritime cargo arriving in Canada and transshipped to the United

States (as well as cargo arriving in the United States and transshipped to Canada). See ibid.

73. Philip Shenon, "U.S. Widens Checks at Foreign Ports," *New York Times*, 12 June 2003, 1A; Lipton, "Loopholes Seen in U.S. Effort."

74. Nicholas Stein, "America's 21st Century Borders," *Fortune* 150, no. 5 (6 September 2004): 114–120. Transponders utilized Global Positioning Satellite (GPS) technology. GPS technology could be used not only to track trucks but also cargo containers, passenger vehicles, cell phones, humans, and even pets embedded with personal microchips.

75. On international cooperation on border controls, see especially Rey Koslowski, "International Cooperation to Create Smart Borders," paper presented at the conference on North American Integration: Migration, Trade and Security, Institute for Research on Public Policy, Ottawa, 1–2 April 2004; Koslowski, "Possible Steps toward an International Regime for Mobility and Security."

76. Koslowski, "Possible Steps toward an International Regime for Mobility and Security," 21.

77. See Romaniuk, "Exporting Homeland Security," 18–19.

78. Peter Romaniuk, "Progress in Maritime Security," unpublished paper, Department of Political Science, Brown University, Providence, RI, 18 February 2005, 7.

79. For a review, see Andrew C. Winner, "The Proliferation Security Initiative: The New Face of Interdiction," *Washington Quarterly* 28, no. 2 (2005): 129–143.

80. In May 2005, a senior U.S. official claimed that there had been many "quiet successes" in the interdiction campaign, though the only publicly disclosed case was the interception of a freighter in the Mediterranean carrying nuclear components to Libya in October 2003. David E. Sanger, "Rice to Discuss Antiproliferation Program," *Washington Post*, 31 May 2005, 3A.

81. Romaniuk, "Progress in Maritime Security," 5.

82. Romaniuk, "Exporting Homeland Security."

83. See especially Monica den Boer, "9-11 and the Europeanisation of Anti-Terrorism Policy: A Critical Assessment," Policy Paper No. 6, Groupement D'Etudes de Recherches, Paris, September 2003.

84. Ibid., 26.

85. EU initiatives following the September 11 attacks are summarized in Kristin Archick, *Europe and Counterterrorism: Strengthening Police and Judicial Cooperation*, Congressional Research Service, Washington, DC, 23 July 2002. Also see Niall Burgess and David Spence, "The European Union: New Threats and the Problem of Coherence," in Bailes and Frommelt, *Business and Security*.

86. See Archick, *Europe and Counterterrorism*, appendix A.

87. den Boer, "9-11 and the Europeanisation of Anti-Terrorism Policy," 1.

88. Ibid., 15.

89. Ibid., 16.

90. Walker, "The Patterns of Transnational Policing," 129.

91. See Joanna Apap and Sergio Carrera, "The European Arrest Warrant: A Good Testing Ground for Mutual Recognition in the Enlarged EU?," commentary, Centre for European Policy Studies, Policy Brief No. 46, 29 September 2005, available at http://www.ceps.be/Article.php?article_id=295&.

92. Ibid., 5.

93. Jonathan Stevenson, "How Europe and the United States Defend Themselves," *Foreign Affairs* 82, no. 2 (March/April 2003): 83.

94. Monar, "The Problem of Balance in EU Justice and Home Affairs and the Impact of 11 September."

95. See Eurojust's Web site: www.eurojust.eu.int.

96. For a more detailed discussion, see Christine Van Den WynGaert, "Eurojust and the European Public Prosecutor in the *Corpus Juris* Model: Water and Fire?," in Walker, *Europe's Area of Freedom, Security and Justice*; M. Coninsx, "Eurojust and EU Judicial Cooperation in the Fight against Terrorism," in C. Fijnaut, J. Wouters, and F. Naert, eds., *Legal Instruments in the Fight against International Terrorism: A Transatlantic Dialogue* (Leiden, The Netherlands: Martinus Nijhoff, 2004).

97. These perspectives are summarized in Kristin Archick, "Europe and Counterterrorism: Strengthening Police and Judicial Cooperation," Congressional Research Service, Washington, DC, 23 July 2002, 10.

98. Joanna Apap, "Problems and Solutions for New Member States in Implementing the JHA Acquis," Working Document No. 212, Centre for European Policy Studies, Brussels, October 2004, 14.

99. For a discussion of the various databases for immigration control, see Pastore, "Visas, Borders, Immigration," 117–119.

100. Aus, "Supranational Governance in an 'Area of Freedom, Security and Justice,'" 4.

101. See especially Michael Levi and David S. Wall, "Technologies, Security, and Privacy in the Post-9/11 European Information Society," *Journal of Law and Society* 31, no. 2 (June 2004): 194–220.

102. See "Statewatch 'Scoreboard' on Post-Madrid Counter-Terrorism Plans," available at http://www.statewatch.org.

103. See special issue on implementing the Hague Programme, *Statewatch European Monitor* 5, no. 1 (January–July 2005).

104. In July 2005, Germany's highest court refused a Spanish judge's request to extradite a citizen suspected of assisting al Qaeda, ruling that the law creating

the EU arrest warrant was void—despite the fact that it had been ratified by the German Parliament the previous November. Richard Bernstein, "German High Court Overrules Spanish Judge's Order for the Extradition of al Qaeda Suspect," *New York Times*, 19 July 2005, A11.

105. Malcolm Anderson, "The Transformation of Border Controls: What Is Different about Europe?," in Joanna Apap, ed., *Justice and Home Affairs in the EU* (Cheltenham, UK: Edward Elgar, 2004), 294.

106. "Fortress Europe—Stage 2: EU Border Police Proposed," http://www .statewatch.org/news/2002/may/05border.htm.

107. See Hobbing, "Management of External EU Borders," 20.

108. Sebastian Rotella, "EU Adopts Strategy to Stem Flow: Illegal Immigrants," *DAWN* (Karachi, Pakistan), 24 June 2002.

109. Paulo Prada, "Spain Moves on Immigrant Beachhead," *Boston Globe*, 23 February 2003, A13.

110. Hobbing, "Integrated Border Management at the EU Level."

111. Quoted in ibid., 8.

112. On trust in cross-border law enforcement relations in Europe, see especially Malcolm Anderson and Joanna Apap, eds., *New European Border and Security Cooperation: Promoting Trust in an Enlarging European Union* (Brussels: Center for European Policy Studies, 2002).

113. Elaine Sciolino, "Politics Intrudes in Bombing Inquiry, Deepening the French-British Rift," *New York Times*, 17 July 2005, A10.

114. For a review of some of these initiatives, see Testimony of U.S. Deputy Assistant Attorney General Bruce C. Swartz before the Joint Hearing of the Subcommittee on Europe and the Subcommittee on International Terrorism, Non-Proliferation, and Human Rights, House Committee on International Relations, *U.S.-European Cooperation on Counterterrorism: Achievements and Challenges*, 108th Cong., 2nd sess., 14 September 2004.

115. Koslowski, "Possible Steps toward an International Regime for Mobility and Security," 13.

116. Cyrille Fijnaut, "The Attacks on 11 September 2001, and the Immediate Response of the European Union and the United States," in Fijnaut et al., *Legal Instruments in the Fight against International Terrorism*, 22–24.

117. Council of the European Union, "Outcome of Proceedings of the Strategic Committee on Immigration, Frontiers and Asylum Meeting with the United States Dated 26 October 2001," doc. 13803/01 ASIM 21 USA 24, Brussels, 12 November 2001, quoted in Guiraudon, "Enlisting Third Parties in Border Control," 13.

118. Monica den Boer, "Transnational Law Enforcement: Crossing the Borders of Statehood," paper presented at SGIR-ECPR Conference on Constructing World Orders, The Hague, 11 September 2004, 20.

119. Bruce Zagaris, "US-EU Extradition and Mutual Assistance Agreements

Are an Important Milestone," *International Law Enforcement Reporter* 19, no. 11 (November 2003).

120. Winer, "Cops across Borders," 7.

121. Ibid., 2.

122. Intellibridge Global Intelligence Solutions, "EU, United States Announce Agreement to Facilitate Cooperation on Container Security," *Homeland Security Monitor*, 19 November 2003.

123. Quoted in Eric Lipton, "More European Data Sought by Security Chief," *New York Times*, 20 May 2005, A21.

124. Critics contend that this process includes increasingly intrusive and controversial G-8–proposed counterterrorism measures, such as "special investigative techniques" and use of "intelligence information" in courts, which threaten to intrude into and politicize other domains of EU law enforcement. See especially Tony Bunyan, "The Exceptional and Draconian Become the Norm," paper presented at the TNI Crime and Globalization Seminar, "Global Enforcement Regimes: Transnational Organized Crime, International Terrorism and Money Laundering," Amsterdam, 28–29 April 2005, available at http://www.tni.org/.

125. See especially www.policylaundering.org/PolicyLaunderingIntro.html.

126. Richard Norton-Taylor, "Documents Reveal Hidden EU Cooperation with US," *Guardian* (London), 1 September 2005, 1.

127. Ibid.

128. Winer, "Cops across Borders," 7.

129. See Ethan Nadelmann, "U.S. Police Activities in Europe," in Cyrille Fijnaut, ed., *The Internationalization of Police Co-operation in Western Europe* (Deventer: The Netherlands: Kluwer Law and Taxation Publishers, 1993).

Chapter 6

1. See Rudra Sil and Peter J. Katzenstein, "What Is Analytic Eclecticism and Why Do We Need It? A Pragmatic Perspective on Problems and Mechanisms in the Study of World Politics," paper presented at the annual meeting of the American Political Science Association, Washington, DC, September 2005.

2. Chambliss, "The Criminalization of Conduct," 45.

3. Thorsten Sellin, *Culture Conflict and Crime* (New York: Social Science Research Council, 1938), 22.

4. On China, see Mertha, *The Politics of Piracy.*

5. Pat Choate, *Hot Property: The Stealing of Ideas in an Age of Globalization* (New York: Knopf, 2005).

6. See the special issue of *International Journal of Drug Policy* 14, no. 2 (April 2003); David R. Bewley-Taylor, "Harm Reduction and the Global Drug Control Regime: Contemporary Problems and Future Prospects," *Drug and Alcohol Re-*

view 23, no. 4 (December 2004): 23, 483–489. Also see Martin Jelsma and Pien Metaal, "Cracks in the Vienna Consensus: The UN Drug Control Debate," *Drug War Monitor*, Washington Office on Latin America, January 2004.

7. See Transnational Institute, Debate Paper No. 10, April 2004; Transnational Institute, Drug Policy Briefing No. 5, April 2003, available at http://www.tni.org.

8. See Transnational Institute, Drug Policy Briefing No. 13, April 2005, available at http://www.tni.org.

9. See, for example, http://www.drugpolicy.org; Ethan Nadelmann, "Challenging the Global Prohibition Regime," *The International Journal of Drug Policy* 9, no. 2 (April 1998): 85–93. Available at http://www.drugtext.org/library/articles/98921.htm.

10. See Edward Luck, "Another Reluctant Belligerent: The United Nations and the War on Terrorism," in Richard Price and Mark W. Zacher, eds., *The United Nations and Global Security* (New York: Palgrave, 2004).

11. For more information, see http://www.who.int/features/2003/08/en.

12. Criminologists have long pointed to the importance of police subcultures but have rarely extended this to the international realm. An exception is James Sheptycki, "The Global Cops Cometh: Reflections on Transnationalization, Knowledge Work and Police Subculture," *British Journal of Sociology* 49, no. 1 (March 1998): 57–74.

13. All international law enforcement endeavors are, in a sense, political, but the degree of politicization varies dramatically. At one extreme are counterespionage, counterterrorism, and export control activities. All these implicate traditional notions of national security, invite the involvement of the intelligence and military agencies, and provide substantial latitude for explicitly political and discretionary interventions into routine criminal justice processes. At the other extreme are extradition and other international law enforcement efforts directed at apprehending common murderers, rapists, and thieves; these are handled primarily by criminal justice personnel with minimal political input by foreign ministry and diplomatic officials. In the middle are a variety of activities that range from unilateral state efforts to enforce states' own tax, customs, and immigration laws to multilateral efforts to deter and investigate drug trafficking and other activities criminalized through international conventions.

14. See, for example, Charles D. Ferguson and William C. Potter, *The Four Faces of Nuclear Terrorism* (New York: Routledge, 2005).

15. Winer, "Tracking Conflict Commodities and Financing," 77.

16. Mathieu Deflem, "Law Enforcement 9-11: Questioning the Policing of International Terrorism," *Pro Bono* 9, no. 1 (Fall 2002): 8.

17. Deflem, *Policing World Society*, 230.

18. Anderson, "Counterterrorism as an Objective of European Police Cooperation," 227.

19. As Mathieu Deflem reminds us, international cooperation in crime control at the turn of the nineteenth century was "facilitated by prior practices of cooperation that had been initiated for political reasons." Mathieu Deflem, "Wild Beasts without Nationality?, The Uncertain Origins of INTERPOL, 1898, 1910," in Philip Reichel, ed., *Handbook of Transnational Crime and Justice* (Thousand Oaks, CA: Sage), 276.

20. On the process of securitization, see Barry Buzan, Ole Waever, and Jaap de Wilde, *Security: A New Framework for Analysis* (Boulder, CO: Lynne Rienner, 1997).

21. See Raven-Hansen, "Security's Conquest of Federal Law Enforcement," 227.

22. Anderson et al., *Policing the European Union*, 165.

23. This document is available on the European Union Web site: http://www.eu.int.

24. Environmental issues have already become partly securitized. See Daniel H. Deudney and Christopher A. Mathew, eds., *Contested Grounds: Security and Conflict in the New Environmental Politics* (Albany: State University of New York Press, 1999).

25. See the collection of articles on "The Next Pandemic?" in the July/August 2005 issue of *Foreign Affairs* 84, no. 4.

26. For example, Cyrille Fijnaut and Letizia Paoli write that the "internationalisation of policy on organized crime well explains why changes that have taken place on several fronts in individual countries are so similar." "Comparative Synthesis of Part III," in Cyrille Fijnaut and Letizia Paoli, eds., *Organized Crime in Europe: Concepts, Patterns and Control Policies in the European Union and Beyond* (Dordrecht, The Netherlands: Springer, Kluwer 2005), 1037.

27. This has been greatly facilitated by the development of personal contacts and professional relationships between representatives of national police agencies. See especially Didier Bigo, "Liaison Officers in Europe: New Officers in the European Security Field," in Sheptycki, *Issues in Transnational Policing*.

28. On "unbundling territoriality," see John Gerard Ruggie, "Territoriality and Beyond: Problematizing Modernity in International Relations," *International Organization* 47, no. 4 (1993): 139–174.

29. Malcolm Anderson, "The Transformation of Border Controls: A European Precedent?," in Andreas and Snyder, *The Wall around the West*, 26.

30. Katzenstein, *A World of Regions*, 136–137.

31. This vision is articulated in a May 2005 Council on Foreign Relations–sponsored Independent Task Force Report, "Building a North American Community," which includes proposals for creating a common security perimeter by 2010, introducing a biometrics-based "North American border pass," and the development of a unified border action plan and expanded border customs facilities. The report is available at http://www.cfr.org/publication.html?id=8102.

32. Anne-Marie Slaughter has noted that although we might expect the EU to "support the creation of global government networks," it is actually "the United States that has led the way in supporting these networks at the global level." Slaughter's general point very much applies to the realm of policing. *A New World Order*, 265.

33. For a historical account of the powerful moralizing impulses in U.S. politics, see Morone, *Hellfire Nation*. Although not Morone's focus, the "politics of sin" that he identifies as a catalyst for state expansion at the domestic level also extends to the international realm through U.S.-promoted crime control campaigns.

34. Hurrell, "Power, Institutions, and the Production of Inequality," 53. Also see G. John Ikenberry and Charles Kupchan, "Socialization and Hegemonic Power," *International Organization* 44, no. 3 (1990): 283–315.

35. Friman, "Globalization's Poster Child," 18.

36. On security communities, see Emanuel Adler and Michael Barnett, eds., *Security Communities* (Cambridge, UK: Cambridge University Press, 1998).

37. Tina Rosenberg, "Building the Great Firewall of China, with Foreign Help," editorial, *New York Times*, 18 September 2005, sec. 4, 11.

38. In September 2005, for example, the Chinese government stepped up its policing of online information by imposing much tighter controls on the scope of content allowed on Web sites. Joseph Kahn, "China Tightens Its Restrictions for News Media on the Internet," *New York Times*, 26 September 2005, A9.

39. There is certainly much historical precedence for this. Consider, for example, the continued legacy of colonialism.

40. More generally, as Herbert L. Packer long ago argued, there are inherent limits to what criminal sanctions can accomplish. *The Limits of the Criminal Sanction* (Stanford, CA: Stanford University Press, 1968).

41. Janice E. Thomson and Stephen D. Krasner, "Global Transactions and the Consolidation of Sovereignty," in Ernst-Otto Czempiel and James N. Rosenau, eds., *Global Changes and Theoretical Challenges: Approaches to World Politics for the 1990s* (Lexington, KY: Lexington Books, 1989), 198.

42. John Torpey, *The Invention of the Passport: Surveillance, Citizenship, and the State* (New York: Cambridge University Press, 2000); Mark Salter, *Rights of Passage: The Passport in International Relations* (Boulder, CO: Lynne Rienner, 2003).

43. See, for example, Hans Van der Veen, "Taxing the Drug Trade: Coercive Exploitation and the Financing of Rule," *Crime, Law, and Social Change* 40, no. 4 (December 2003): 349–390.

44. Peter K. Manning, *The Narc's Game* (Cambridge, MA: MIT Press, 1980), 253.

45. Strange, *The Retreat of the State*, 121. For a thoughtful critique, see H. Richard Friman, "Caught in the Madness? State Power and Transnational Organized Crime in the Work of Susan Strange," *Alternatives* 28, no. 4 (2003): 473–489.

46. Moises Naim, *Illicit: How Smugglers, Traffickers and Copycats Are Hijacking the Global Economy* (New York: Doubleday, 2005); Moises Naim, "The Five Wars of Globalization," *Foreign Policy* (January/February 2003): 29–37.

47. See Peter Andreas, "Transnational Crime and Economic Globalization," in Mats Berdal and Monica Serrano, eds., *Transnational Organized Crime and International Security* (Boulder, CO: Lynne Rienner, 2002).

48. On the role of technology in enhancing transgovernmental networks, see Raustiala, "The Architecture of International Cooperation," 21–22.

49. On the turn to new information technologies in state control efforts, see Flynn, "The False Conundrum"; Rey Koslowski, "International Migration and Border Control in the Information Age," unpublished paper, Rutgers University, Newark, NJ, 12 April 2002.

50. See Jane Kaplan and John Torpey, eds., *Documenting Individual Identity: State Practices in the Modern World* (Princeton, NJ: Princeton University Press, 2001).

51. For a fascinating historical account, see Cole, *Suspect Identities.*

52. See especially Mathieu Deflem, "Technology and the Internationalization of Policing: A Comparative Historical Perspective," *Justice Quarterly* 19, no. 3 (September 2002): 453–475.

53. K. A. Taipale, "Transnational Intelligence and Surveillance: Security Envelopes, Trusted Systems, and the Panoptic Global Security State," draft paper prepared for the conference "Beyond Terror: A New Security Agenda," Watson Institute for International Studies, Brown University, Providence, RI, 3–4 June 2005, 4.

54. In the case of cargo tracking, see Stephen E. Flynn, "Addressing the Shortcomings of the Customs-Trade Partnership against Terrorism (C-TPAT) and the Container Security Initiative," testimony before the hearing of the Permanent Sub-Committee on Investigations, Committee on Homeland Security and Governmental Affairs, U.S. Senate, 26 May 2005.

55. A particularly extreme illustration of this is the practice of subcontracting customs work to multinational security firms. In Ghana, a Swiss-based corporation, COTECNA, has essentially become the country's customs service. The company is involved in customs work in fourteen countries in Africa and Latin America, and its Japanese partner carries out similar functions in many Asian countries. Brenda Chalfin argues that "the multinationalization of Customs operations simultaneously compromises and shores up state power." She concludes, "This is a situation where the state is abrogating its exclusive territorial control—to a foreign body, no less—in order to strengthen its capacity to regulate and oversee that territory." "Working the Border in Ghana: Technologies of Sovereignty and Its Others," Occasional Papers No. 16, School of Social Science, Institute for Advanced Study, Princeton, NJ, November 2003, 3–5.

56. On the growth of private policing, see Johnston, "Transnational Private Policing."

57. See Michael Schroeder and Silvia Ascarelli, "Global Cop—New Role for the SEC: Policing Companies beyond U.S. Borders," *Wall Street Journal*, 30 July 2004, 1A. The authors note that the Securities and Exchange Commission is gaining a reputation as "the cop on the beat for the world's securities markets."

58. Wolfram F. Hanrieder, "Dissolving International Politics: Reflections on the Nation-State," *American Political Science Review* 72, no. 4 (1978): 1276–1287.

59. Some observers have provocatively pointed to the possible emergence of a globalized variant of Jeremy Bentham's panopticon, a design for prisons and other institutions that makes it possible to watch the inhabitants without their knowing if or when they are being watched. See Kirstie Ball and Frank Webster, "The Intensification of Surveillance," in Ball and Webster, *The Intensification of Surveillance*.

60. In the case of Mexican migration to the United States, see Douglas Massey, *Beyond Smoke and Mirrors: Mexican Immigration in an Era of Economic Integration* (New York: Russell Sage, 2003).

61. See Marc Mauer, *Comparative International Rates of Incarceration: An Examination of Causes and Trends* (Washington, DC: Sentencing Project, 2003), available at http://www.sentencingproject.org/pdfs/pub9036.pdf; Roy Walmsley, "Global Incarceration and Prison Trends," *Forum on Crime and Society* 3, nos. 1–2 (December 2003): 65–78, available at http://www.unodc.org/pdf/crime/forum/forum3_Art3.pdf.

62. See Roy Walmsley, *World Prison Population List: Research Findings No. 88* (London: Home Office Research, Development and Statistics Directorate, 1999); Vincent Schiraldi, , *Poor Prescription: The Costs of Imprisoning Drug Offenders in the United States*, (San Francisco: Center on Juvenile and Criminal Justice, 2002).

63. For a critique, see M. R. Chatterton, "Reflections on International Police Cooperation: Putting Police Cooperation in Its Place—An Organizational Perspective," in Koenig and Das, *International Police Cooperation*.

64. See James Sheptycki, "Transnational Policing and the Makings of a Postmodern State," *British Journal of Criminology* 35, no. 4 (autumn 1995): 616.

INDEX

□ □ □